E^{The}NTICEMENT
of RELIGION

The ENTICEMENT of RELIGION

KEES W. BOLLE

University of Notre Dame Press
Notre Dame, Indiana

Manufactured in the United States of America

The author and publisher are grateful to Menard Press
and to Princeton University Press for permissions in quoting
the poems of Osip Mandelstam.

Library of Congress Cataloging-in-Publication Data
Bolle, Kees W.
    The enticement of religion / Kees W. Bolle.
      p.   cm.
    Includes bibliographical references and index.
    ISBN 0-268-02764-1 (cloth : alk. paper)
    ISBN 0-268-02765-X (pbk. : alk. paper)
    1. Religion.   I. Title.
BL48 .B585   2002
200 — dc21
                                2002012295

dedicated to

JACQUES MAQUET

Faithful Friend and Wise Counselor

CONTENTS

Preface   xi

PART ONE. THE FACTS OF RELIGION

Chapter One.   Introduction   3
The Question of Beginnings   3
Two Sides   7
The Perspective of the History of Religions   13
The Name "History of Religions"   15
A Bridge Between the Two Sides   17

Chapter Two.   The History of Religions   20
Object and Task of the History of Religions   20
What Is Religion?   22
Religious Symbolization   23
The Right Use of Words: Religion, (Religious) Symbolism   27
The Right Use of Words: Tradition   28
The Right Use of Words: Faith   37
The Right Use of Words: Worldview, Supernatural, Ideology   38
The Right Use of Words: The Problem of Feelings   41

Chapter Three.   The Ordinariness of Religion   46
Religion Is Everywhere   46
Three Modes of Religious Expression   48
Mythical Elements in Modern Industrial Society   60
Religion and Our Personal Wishes   63
Social and Ethical Impact   65
Political Impact   69
Religious Symbolism and Science   74

Chapter Four.   Myth and Poetry   81
   Myth and Poetry?   81
   Emily Dickinson   85
   Variations in Culture   92

Chapter Five.   Beginning to Understand Religions   100
   "The Religions of the World"   100
   Knowledge   101
   Prophetic or Historical Religions   103
   Another Type: Natural Religions   105
   The Major Difficulty with Typologies   106
   Empiricism and Common Sense   107
   Truth   117

PART TWO. HISTORICAL SURVEY OF WESTERN
INTELLECTUAL APPROACHES TO RELIGION

Chapter Six.   From the Classics to the Renaissance   125
   Why an Intellectual History?   125
   "Our" Classical World Within the World   127
   Greeks and Romans and Their Influence   132
   The World of the Bible   138
   Early Christianity   141
   The Middle Ages and the Renaissance   144
   Learning and Discussions Between Religions   149

Chapter Seven.   Toward Modernity   154
   "The Birth of Reason"   154
   Philosophers   157
   Empiricism   163
   The Wider Movement Toward Modernity   168
   The Enlightenment   171
   David Hume   179
   Reason in Two Exceptional Figures: Vico and Hamann   182
   Eighteenth-Century Historians of Religions   189

Chapter Eight.   The Romantic Movement   193
   Johann Gottfried Herder   195
   Friedrich Schleiermacher   199

Contents   ix

Friedrich Wilhelm Joseph Schelling   202
William Blake, Herman Melville, and Søren Kierkegaard   206
New Religious Data   212
Romantics Who Studied the New Data: Benjamin Constant,   216
Joseph von Görres, Friedrich Creuzer, Karl Otfried Müller,
and Friedrich Max Müller

Chapter Nine.   The Nineteenth Century   228
Economic Thinkers   229
Theologians and Missionaries   232
Social Studies   238
Philosophers and Anthropologists   242

Chapter Ten.   The Painful Birth of Society: The Twentieth Century 249
Joseph Conrad, Friedrich Nietzsche, and Charles Péguy   251
Great Modern Thinkers: Wilhelm Dilthey, Edmund Husserl   260
Ludwig Joseph Johann Wittgenstein and Karl Jaspers   266
"Reductionisms." More Philosophy. The Search for Certainty   271
Many Ways of Study   275
Twentieth-Century Historians of Religions   279
Twentieth-Century Historians of Religions (Continued)   283
The History of Religions in the United States   288

Chapter Eleven.   Farewell to Too Much of a System   297
Conclusions and More Questions   297
Orientations Today in the United States   302
Farewell to Too Much of a System   309

Index   315

One of the most famous books on religion to appear in the West was published at the end of the eighteenth century. Its title proclaimed that it was addressed to the "educated despisers" of religion. We too are familiar with more or less cultured despisers of religion. Moreover, we now are surrounded by people producing books to right the situation. And I find myself in their midst.

I have tried in this introductory work to present those things that are most obvious about religion in general and about the specific religions of the world. Such a presentation is the first requirement of any serious inquiry; we should be able to recognize what we want to focus on. With the subject of religion and religions, obvious things often go unnoticed, obscured by the clamor of opinions as to what religion means, what its causes and purposes are, or whether there are any causes or purposes to it.

Someone who commented on the manuscript of my book was taken aback by its lack of dense technical terms; he seemed to consider the book's lightness a defect. I think he fell victim to one of the great blunders in *education* that causes the rise of generations upon generations of "*educated* despisers of religion*." Soon after I began writing, a good friend sent me a copy of an old piece by Russell Baker on the difference between "serious" and "solemn." I've quoted from it in the first chapter. No doubt, the "stuff" of which religion is made is serious. But is it solemn? Scholars struggle about what it means; their analyses and mental gymnastics can easily become solemnities, and usually do. Yet countless religious materials show how people are liberated — in fact, *saved* — from the dreary mental prisons they build for themselves.

I hasten to add that I have taken to heart many attempts by thinkers, scholars, and artists to articulate religious meanings. Without their help, even the most appropriately lighthearted attempt at interpreting religions would be doomed to failure. In the second half of this book I have tried to show that some endeavors at explanation address themselves more successfully and justly than others to what really and obviously matters in the symbols, myths, rituals, in the documents, and the empirical evidence we have of the world's religions.

I did not try to invent new theories, or to borrow ones invented or set afloat by others for whom religion is often a thing on the fringes of human existence. I avoided terms that have grown meaningless—*discourse,* for example. I do not talk about metaphor or "the other" as if they presented a key to religious documents. The old-fashioned thing about the following pages is the claim that religious creations mean something and have all by themselves everything needed to present *sponte sua* what they mean, without the help of extraneous fashions. I hope that this introductory book may take away some of the undue solemnity and many of the needless fears that now cloud the subject of religion.

Most sections in the present work end with a bibliography. I have done my best to select books that are readable and relevant to the questions discussed. If the work is used as a "textbook," instructors should of course feel free to offer other suggestions.

I owe much to very many undergraduate students at UCLA. More than any group I could single out, they taught me the difference between seriousness and solemnity. I owe a debt of gratitude to colleagues, especially the philosopher Bill Peck; also to students, staff, and other friends I made at Reed College; as well as to Mr. Jerome A. DeGraaff, Social Science Librarian of Portland State University's library, who provided many an essential detail. The concrete suggestions and textual references my wife, Sara, gave me account for some of the most illustrative passages taken from the ancient texts of her expertise and from modern novels. I take a personal and special delight in thanking Marcel Sempere for the cartoons he drew for my book. My delight is indeed special, as this artist, in fact a relative, shares the –shall we say spontaneous, or automatic?— disdain for religion that has become characteristic of academic intellectuals.

In this place I want to insert a personal word of apology to Marcel for *not* including his cartoons, and publicly confess that *I* am to blame for the omission. I like his cartoons immensely, but I am also a teacher who has become thoroughly aware of the widespread, uncritical, and irrational disdain for religious matters. In spite of the fact that such irrational disdain rests on sheer ignorance, or rather, because of it, it does not need the reinforcement of a hasty glance at a comic picture. I certainly do plan to use the cartoons in lectures, for the human voice is still more powerful than the printed word, and even my own aging vocal chords can show people how uninformed, hasty in our judgment, and fundamentally wrong we can be in our observations and inferences.

Concerning translations from non-English-language sources, it should be noted that translations are mine if no translator is mentioned by name.

As always, I am deeply indebted to Ellen T. Kaplan, who has corrected, improved, and not infrequently salvaged my writings for close to forty years. Once again, she went through my pages and straightened out many an unevenness. I thank the director, Barbara Hanrahan, and the staff of the University of Notre Dame Press for the care given to the production of this book, and in particular the manuscript editor, Margo Shearman, for her relentless precision. Whatever faults remain are wholly mine.

K. W. B.
Biddeford, Maine
January 13, 2002

PART ONE

THE FACTS
OF RELIGION

Introduction

THE QUESTION OF BEGINNINGS

An introduction to the history of religions fills a need, and not merely for people who want to become specialists in the subject of "Religion." The need that exists is considerably broader and more urgent. Among those whom we know as "educated," there is an *ignorance* about religious matters that we would hardly tolerate with respect to basic mathematics, physics, or ordinary facts of society or politics. The lack of comprehension in the area of religious facts is painful among most majors in our colleges — whatever their field in the humanities, the social studies, or the sciences. Not infrequently, it is breathtaking even among specialists with advanced academic degrees.

The introduction to any intellectual discipline, to any branch of knowl-edge (*scientia,* science, learning, scholarship), is a serious matter. Compared with other fields of study, the study of religion — even the modern study of religions — is old, and in many places well established. Just the same, providing a proper introduction is essential in order to show the founda-tion on which we build the edifice of our study.

An introduction may trigger a silly enthusiasm, preserve an already existing prejudice, or cause a bias to arise. Biases, silly prejudices, and en-thusiasms characterize our age of the large crowd. It should be obvious that neither momentary enthusiasms nor prejudices can make a good beginning for any study. Introductions that are serious must concern *methodology,* which means the systematic attempt to show the ways to approach the object of a discipline of study, and *epistemology*, the theory of what it means to know. Epistemology can be called "the knowledge of knowledge," and it deals with the most basic questions of any intellectual inquiry.

Most people think of an introductory book as the first one that may be read in a subject. To some extent this thought is correct. You are likely to read a first book on plane geometry before you turn to the complex calculations of astronomy. Everyone who has entered the world of physics, as a rule, has first become acquainted with mathematics. One's interest may have begun through the elementary arithmetic of picking up blocks and counting them. Whatever that beginning, it is likely to have had its influence on a developing mind and the formulation of questions to be asked.

In some fields, such as history and philology (the basic text-oriented field for all study of literature), *introduction* is a distinct intellectual activity.[1] For centuries, people in these fields realized that so much was uncertain, the difficulty of avoiding basic, elementary mistakes so great, that first principles needed lasting attention.

Each and every school has some students who think they are too bright to need introductory courses. In fact, the world at large has many such people, and all of them make the acquisition of understanding very difficult for themselves. In the history of religions, I think, we suffer even more from such self-overestimation than elsewhere. We are very likely to have some private opinions about religion, and these may come easily to us—but their sum total cannot begin to take the place of a proper introduction.

Personally, I might have been an astronomer rather than a historian of religions if my math teacher had introduced calculus to me in a somewhat different way. He might have told my class that Isaac Newton was drawn to the problem of infinite series because he was intrigued by the infinity of God. He might have told my fellow pupils and me that Leibniz, the other founder of calculus, was fascinated by notions of infinite numbers for a similar reason. Instead of being struck by the human inquiry into relations and proportions, I was turned off by the "gimmicks" of applied formulas and ready-made tables. Many years later, I discovered that I needed math and astronomy in order to understand certain religious symbolisms. I now know that my math teacher was not very good; he missed the wonderment toward his own discipline that is necessary to guide beginners. He taught as if his science were a bag of tricks, hermetically sealed from any contact with other inquiries. But no intellectual pursuit is isolated. Of course, my math teacher's way is not how we should make our first steps.

For the history of religions, it is of epistemological importance to realize that wrong beginnings can establish biases that take a long time to overcome. One of the most prevalent biases among seemingly educated people is the feeling that real knowledge exists only in what is referred to as "the sciences." The other fields of study, equally loosely referred to as "the humanities," supposedly have nothing like it. Much of such blatant nonsense begins with a wrongheaded "introduction." Unintentionally and unfortunately, our system of compulsory education, barely a century and a half old, though producing the widespread ability to read, was among the stimuli toward such superficiality. Mere information came to be mistaken for knowledge. Display of knowledge — otherwise known as taking exams — deteriorates into mere regurgitation of facts that one has not properly understood. This trivializing of mental inquiry pervades our culture — only think of certain television shows — and jeopardizes genuine knowledge.

A real beginning is and remains a quest. It is the quest that begins in astonishment that something can be known at all, that knowledge may indeed be possible. How can I know? How is it that there is something rather than nothing? Such meditations are irrepressible questions that remain introductory and preserve their introductory value no matter how far we advance. An introduction is a basic inquiry that continues throughout the length and breadth of the study we engage in.

One more comment should be made. Great teachers have always been bold enough to ask questions so basic, so elementary, as to convey the impression that they were involved in playing games. Yet this playfulness goes hand in hand with their great learning. For the seriousness of a scholarly activity is also an intense joy.

Karl Barth, who is generally regarded as the most important Christian theologian of the twentieth century, had a special fondness for the music of Mozart, and many of his fellow theologians insistently questioned what they saw as this discrepancy. Was Barth, who had written so much about such weighty topics as revelation, church, the destiny of man, really doing theology as it should be done, considering this peculiar love for Mozart's operas? One day Karl Barth decided to answer. "I have sometimes been asked," he said, whether, if I were to have proceeded on the basis of my theology, I should not have discovered quite different masters in music. I must insist . . . : no, it is Mozart and no one else. I confess that thanks to the invention of the phonograph, which can never be praised enough, I have for years and years begun each day with Mozart, and only then (aside from the daily newspapers) turned to my Dogmatics. I even have to confess that if I ever get to heaven, I would first of all seek out Mozart and only then inquire after Augustine, St. Thomas, Luther, Calvin, and Schleiermacher.[2]

Barth's questioners were solemn and chose to suspect Barth of frivolity. Barth was a very serious inquirer, and hence he had a sense of play. In studying religious phenomena, we shall have other occasions to return to this distinction.

For the *New York Times* of April 30, 1978, the critical (and humorous!) columnist Russell Baker made the same distinction between "solemn" and "serious" in a most direct, unmistakable manner:

Here is a letter of friendly advice. "Be serious," it says. What it means, of course, is, "Be solemn." The distinction between being serious and being solemn seems to be vanishing among Americans, just as surely as the distinction between "now" and "presently" and the distinction between liberty and making a mess.

Being solemn is easy. Being serious is hard. You probably have to be born serious, or at least go through a very interesting childhood. Children almost always begin by being serious, which is what makes them so entertaining when compared to adults as a class.

Adults, on the whole, are solemn. The transition from seriousness to solemnity occurs in adolescence, a period in which Nature, for reasons of her own, plunges people into foolish frivolity. During this period the organism struggles to regain dignity by recovering childhood's genius for seriousness. It is usually a hopeless cause.

As a result, you have to settle for solemnity. Being solemn has almost nothing to do with being serious, but on the other hand, you can't go on being adolescent forever, unless you are in the performing arts, and anyhow most people can't tell the difference. In fact, though Americans talk a great deal about the virtue of being serious, they generally prefer people who are solemn over people who are serious.

In politics, the rare candidate who is serious, like Adlai Stevenson, is easily overwhelmed by one who is solemn, like General Eisenhower. This is probably because it is hard for most people to recognize seriousness, which is rare, especially in politics, but comfortable to endorse solemnity, which is commonplace as jogging. . . .

Literature
For basic questions concerning logic and epistemology, see Willard Van Orman Quine, *From a Logical Point of View* (New York: Harper, 1963). A very useful essay on the nature and history of epistemology is Richard I. Aaron, "Epistemology," *The Encyclopaedia Britannica, Macropaedia,* 15th ed. (Chicago: Benton, 1974), vol. 6. A classic introduction to the history of religions (somewhat outdated, yet still valuable) is Morris Jastrow, *The Study of Religion,* first published in 1901 and republished with an introduction by William A. Clebsch and Charles H. Long (Chico, Calif.: Scholars Press, 1981). More recent introductions: Eric J. Sharpe, *Comparative Religion: A History,* 2nd ed. (La Salle, Ill.: Open Court, 1990); William E. Paden, *Religious Worlds: The Comparative Study of Religion* (Boston: Beacon, 1988); Mircea Eliade, *The Sacred and the Profane: The Nature of Religion* (New York: Harcourt, 1959); Jan de Vries, *Perspectives in the History of Religions* (Berkeley–Los Angeles: University of California Press, 1977).

Two Sides

Few people can become acquainted with a field or topic of study without some anxiety. Nor should it be otherwise. Our concerns may arise from the sheer multitude of fields of study and promising approaches to be found when looking, for instance, at bookstore shelves or going through a university catalog. Is there rhyme or reason to the compilation of things? The catalog of a modern university is a pile of things whose only order is alphabetical. It presents little or nothing to lay out a sensible program of action. For instance, if you are interested in psychology, you will look up the Department of "Psychology" under the letter P. However, you may find references to "psychology" also under listings in sociology, anthropology, some literature departments, and elsewhere. Likewise, the place of religion is not easy to locate; in large modern state schools, indeed, the matter is extremely confused. There may or may not be a department with the name. There will be a sprinkling of courses dealing with religion under the headings of psychology, sociology, anthropology, art, every literature, ancient or modern, history, and certainly under philosophy. What, then, should our focus be, and how should we proportion our attention?

The assortment of departmental course listings is not clarified by the few large but fairly arbitrary designations of "divisions": humanities, social studies (often called "social sciences"), and natural sciences. One may also find instead of, or in addition to, this assortment a whole list of colleges, again in alphabetical order: agriculture, architecture, arts, business, earth sciences, and so on. There may also be "schools" of medicine, law, theater arts, music, dance, design, engineering, and so forth.

The confusion we meet today is the result of a process of specialization that began in earnest in the nineteenth century, and accelerated in the twentieth, especially after the Second World War. We have ended up with educational institutions that look very much like business corporations, each one with a number of power groups within itself, fighting over the budget. Questions about education, curricula, and sensible ways to conduct inquiries were pushed to the background.

Yet one need not despair in the face of this initial confusion about the multitude of offerings. It is useful to realize that the order we would like is not presented to us on a platter. The multitude of subjects, fields, and approaches can be looked upon as a very large treasure awaiting us. However, the most important conclusion, which we cannot fail to draw, is that we have to resort to our own devices. The ability of computers to sort out matters is not of great help here: there is no substitute for our own search for a sense of direction. *We* have to make sensible, intellectually defensible choices.[3]

It is encouraging to acknowledge that the confusion we find ourselves in is not new in all respects. Long before modern universities and colleges came about, the world of people and of nature already perturbed human wits. And even in ancient days, human minds searched for and found principles and guidelines for intellectual inquiry. Indeed there is a basic orientation for inquiry that has been discovered and rediscovered through the ages in the midst of chaos and confusion.

I think we might express it for ourselves as follows. We must do two things: compile information, and find the right questions to ask. In the procedure of a serious inquiry, we should see these two activities as dis-

tinct sides. Each one remains distinct while neither can ever cease to inter-
act with the other. Many have tried to adhere to just one side, but never
with great success. We should never lose sight of the fact that the two activities need each other and at the same time are in some way at odds with
each other.

The monumental Indian thinker Śankara (seventh or eighth century
A. D.) wrote a small book for the benefit of pupils on their quest for spiritual knowledge. He begins by discussing what qualifies the good student,
and he emphasizes that a good student should be interested in the distinction between what is transitory and what is enduring. It is obvious for ourselves that what is transitory, ephemeral, sums up the manifoldness of
facts we observe and think about—and which are a major source of our
confusion. What is enduring is more difficult to describe. But it has everything to do with the coherence and goal of knowledge we hope to reach.

Heraclitus (sixth century B. C.) is one of the early Greek thinkers by
whom we have no complete works but only fragments—that is, quotations of him by later philosophers. Quite a few of his often quoted statements that have impressed people ever since reveal the same distinction
between the ephemeral and the enduring, the multitude of things and the
correct questioning. Two in particular are eloquent and point directly to
the complementary components of human mental operations:

> Men who love wisdom should acquaint themselves with a great many
> particulars.

> Much learning does not teach understanding.[4]

"A great many particulars" amounts to what we call "the facts" we wish
to examine, whether in physics, history, or religions. But the "wisdom" we
seek concerns our quest for a unity of understanding.

Heraclitus's assertion that much learning does not teach understanding
hits the mark at once. We learn, we tabulate, we memorize, but we do not
understand unless we begin to realize that our progress toward serious
knowledge is in fact identical with a conscious confrontation between the
two sides of mental activity.

As a rule, people who like to use their minds do prefer to be called
"inquirers" rather than "collectors." To be truly inquisitive seems more
dignified than "merely" to gather and arrange data. Therefore it will be

THE LION-MAKERS

In a certain town were four Brahmans who lived in friendship. Three of them had reached the far shore of all scholarship, but lacked sense. The other found scholarship distasteful; he had nothing but sense.

One day they met for consultation. "What is the use of our attainments," said they, "if one does not travel, win the favor of kings, and acquire money? Whatever we do, let us all travel."

But when they had gone a little way, the eldest of them said: "One of us, the fourth, is a dullard, having nothing but sense. Now nobody gains the favorable attention of kings by simple sense without scholarship. Therefore we will not share our earnings with him. Let him turn back and go home."

Then the second said: "My intelligent friend, you lack scholarship. Please go home." But the third said: "No, no. This is no way to behave. For we have played together since we were little boys. Come along, my noble friend. You shall have a share of the money we earn."

With this agreement they continued their journey, and in the forest they found the bones of a dead lion. Thereupon one of them said: "A good opportunity to test the ripeness of our scholarship. Here lies some kind of creature, dead. Let us bring it to life by means of the scholarship we have honestly won."

Then the first said: "I know how to assemble the skeleton." The second said: "I can supply skin, flesh, and blood." The third said: "I can give it life."

So the first assembled the skeleton, the second provided skin, flesh, and blood. But while the third was intent on giving the breath of life, the man of sense advised against it, remarking: "This is a lion. If you bring him to life, he will kill every one of us."

"You simpleton!" said the other. "It is not I who will reduce scholarship to a nullity." "In that case," came the reply, "wait a moment, while I climb this convenient tree."

When this had been done, the lion was brought to life, rose up, and killed all three. But the man of sense, after the lion had gone elsewhere, climbed down and went home.[6]

beneficial to listen to one more ancient voice. It is that of Confucius, the great teacher of China (around 500 B.C.), who said, "To learn without thinking is stultifying, to think without learning is dangerous."[5]

This insight into the necessity of two sides in our inquiries is so obvious, once we notice it, that we find it everywhere. In recent times it is discussed in the work of the anthropologist Claude Lévi-Strauss. In his book *The Savage Mind,* Lévi-Strauss gives a fascinating account of what he calls "the science of the concrete," which he finds in tribal societies throughout the world. [7] Lévi-Strauss discovered that peoples who until not long ago would have been called "primitives" exhibit an amazing power of observation of natural phenomena. In addition, he shows, they classify what they observe in accordance with precise principles. (He speaks of "the logic of totemic classifications.") The type of distinction we are making seems to be a universal feature of the process of knowing.

This feature of the contrasting unity of the many things observed and the search for understanding is also embedded in the languages of the Western tradition. In English, we would not equate factual knowledge with real understanding. The word *science* has its origin in the Latin *scientia,* which is sheer learning and hence would never be identified with *sapientia,* wisdom. [8] Our tradition is permeated with reminders.

In the study of religions we have to come to terms with a great many religious facts in world history and in many civilizations. The object of study for historians of religions consists in those given facts. Those facts are our data. *Data* is the plural of the Latin word *datum,* which means something given. The data of religion are our object, in the same way the data of nature are the object for the natural scientist. Our review of the principal facts of religions in the first half of this book will not be only a list of data but at the same time, at every point, a brief consideration of the question of whether our way of viewing this or that datum is justified. In other words, at every step of our study, the data require theory, and the theory should relate to the data. The statement by Heraclitus about "wisdom" does not necessarily imply the immediate availability of a universal vision in which we see everything in perfect lucidity. What relates the two sides to each other is *the requirement that we work in both directions.*

We might visualize a scheme in which a vertical line distinguishes the order of thought in which we develop our theories from the given facts:

Data | The Order of Thought

The dividing line may serve to remind us that there is no easy, self-evident passage from one side to the other. We realize that the choice of facts (i.e., the data) somehow originates in the order of thought — but how this happens is unclear. The relationship that does exist is where the fascination in the process of knowing begins.

We might also place a question at the head of each column we have visualized. In our scheme, on the left we ask: What is there to study? To the right the question is: How should I think?

| What Is There to Study? | How Should I Think? |
| Data | The Order of Thought |

We need to make use of different kinds of disciplines in order to do justice to the two different questions. Only descriptive disciplines can answer "What is there to study?" But the question that begins with "How should" asks for a standard, a norm that must be observed. Here only the disciplines that are called "normative," "systematic," or "philosophical" can yield an answer. These disciplines are the traditional ones in a department of philosophy: the philosophy that through the ages has been considered "the highest," known as *metaphysics,* asks what we should consider true (or even "the truth"); *ethics* is concerned with human behavior, and investigates what should be thought of as good; *aesthetics* raises the question of what is normative for "the beautiful." All three assume the practice of logic, basic to all reasoning, as it deals directly with the proper order of thought and argument. It is the science of valid thought. Valid arguing is of immediate importance for one more normative discipline, firmly rooted in Western academic tradition (but missing in American state schools): this is theology, or more precisely, dogmatic theology. It is the discipline that is of course inseparable from the Western Christian tradition. The question at its center is: Given the revelation (or the guidance) of God, how should I think?

Many people today tend to regard the normative disciplines as an area for personal preferences. This is a dreadful mistake, for normative or philosophical disciplines are not covers for our whims, private feelings, or desires, but training grounds for positions we should be able to defend in public. It is unacceptable in any chosen field of study to turn against norms that are valid in logic and observation.

False modesty makes many a studious person imagine that philosophical questions are too profound for him or her. In a discussion a college student once said to me, "But I am only in design!" This reference to her major finished for her the relevance of the entire problem of thinking in an orderly manner.

In fact, no area of inquiry, no matter how modest its practitioner, can flourish without thought. Students in design need descriptive and normative fields, just like anyone else. Among the descriptive fields, they could count mathematics, especially geometry, and art history. Certainly anatomy would also make sense for someone specializing in design. And as to the normative side of the "scheme," aesthetics, the science of beauty, should not be omitted. One who makes art his or her study should be able to articulate why something is beautiful.

Someone else came to see me after his graduation with a degree in chemistry. This was at the height of the cold war, and it had become clear to this student that the primary area of employment open to him was in the concoction of poisons. He was aware that it is never too late to change one's orientation or one's course of life—although his suggestion that studying the history of religions would be devoid of such problems of conscience revealed the depth of his ignorance. The same student would have saved himself a lot of nervous energy if he had realized during his study of chemistry that some inquiry into the field of ethics might have shed a lot of light. Not merely with respect to philosophical ideas concerning the basis of the natural world, but also in the area of moral questions, a chemist would be well served by a study of such problems.

Literature
Philip Wheelwright, *Heraclitus* (New York: Atheneum, 1964); Claude Lévi-Strauss, *The Savage Mind* (Chicago: University of Chicago Press, 1966), chap. 1 and 2: "The Science of the Concrete" and "The Logic of Totemic 74"); Karl Barth, *Evangelical Theology* (Grand Rapids, Mich.: Eerdmans, 1963), "Commentary" and chap. 1, "The Place of Theology," pp. 3–59.

THE PERSPECTIVE OF THE HISTORY OF RELIGIONS

What we have discussed so far about the visualization of a "scheme" is in principle the same for all study. When we fill in the array of details the differences appear, and we are able to see the coherence of a particular field of study in its relationship to other fields of human knowledge. So it is for the history of religions:

What Is There? (= Data: What Is Given) *Relevant Descriptive Fields:*	How Should I Think? Order of Thought *Relevant Normative Fields:*
Prehistory	Philosophy
Archaeology	
	Metaphysics
Linguistics	
	Ethics
Philology	
	Aesthetics
History	
	[Theology]
Art History	
Sociology	
Anthropology	
Psychology etc.	

The list on the left should be obvious in its relevance to religio-historical studies. In particular, prehistory, archaeology, philology, and the fieldwork reports of anthropologists (or ethnologists) provide us with primary documents concerning religions. Documents are called "primary" when they are religious phenomena (e.g., an authoritative text, a holy image) or immediate witnesses to the religious phenomena. (By contrast, anything written about religious facts by outsiders and later writers is merely "secondary," as is the present book.) The list of disciplines that give us data could be lengthened. For historians of religions with a special interest in temples, architecture might appear on the list. For others who deal with calendar systems (which are always related to religious traditions), some knowledge of astronomy is called for.

With respect to the normative (sometimes called systematic) disciplines, philosophy is always required, for insofar as all religious data in some manner make a claim to truth, the investigator should be familiar with philosophical views. As religions affect behavior, questions of ethics cannot be avoided. As religious traditions generally develop their own criteria of beauty, aesthetics is needed to aid us in reasoning coherently about what may be called "beautiful." The significance of theology to the study of religions has been debated for some time, and is problematic enough to suggest that it be placed in brackets here.[9] For the moment, let me merely say that acquiring a just view of religious facts involves a growing awareness of the way in which we ourselves are conditioned by our civilization. No doubt many readers of this book have been affected by Christianity directly or indirectly. It is obviously important that we be as aware as possible of the influences of Christianity on our judgment when we try to understand religious phenomena inside or outside Christendom.

In the list of "descriptive fields," history has a very special place. The meaning of religious facts is a topic that can easily be understood as in need of philosophical considerations. What should be at least as obvious, but is hardly ever spelled out, is that without the study of history, human expressions, hence also religious expressions, cannot be understood. The notion of "meaning" itself is by nature historical. Words are not labels of ingredients in a laboratory; they are not timeless; they change in what they refer to, or their "overtones" vary in the course of time. What their expression means can be traced not only by looking at a static frame of reference, but also and especially by studying their changes through time. This brings out one of the main reasons why we call our discipline the "history of religions."

Literature
Raffaele Pettazzoni, *Essays on the History of Religions* (Leiden: Brill, 1954), chap. 19, "History and Phenomenology in the Science of Religion," pp. 215–19; Angelo Brelich, "Prolégomènes à une histoire des religions," in Henri-Charles Puech, ed., *Histoire des religions,* "Encyclopédie de la Pléiade" (Paris: Gallimard, 1970), vol. 1, pp. 1–59.

THE NAME "HISTORY OF RELIGIONS"

The "history of religions" has become the preferred name for our discipline. In the nineteenth century, and during part of the twentieth, some people used the term "comparative religion." (The French often spoke of *l'étude comparée des religions,* the Germans of *Vergleichende Religionswissenschaft.*) The roots of those once fashionable names are not unrelated to a time in which the "hard" sciences came to flourish: chemistry, physics, biology. The notion of history lost some of its appeal, and the notion of evolution gained popularity. Human cultures and religions, so it seemed to many, could be viewed as "objectively," as schematically and timelessly, as matter, energy, and animal species. The problem with this view is that neither cultures nor religions change uniformly. One cannot speak of the changes, for instance, in the image of God and gods, in terms that constitute a "law." Except perhaps for the flimsiest resemblance in the eyes of an uninformed, casual observer, there is no comparison possible between the proceedings of the historian of religions and, say, the chemist. What the student of religions has to deal with is the rather unpredictable "creative" way of changing through time that we call "history."

If we take history seriously, the term *comparative* is an unnecessary tautological adjective for describing our field. All study of history is by nature comparative. One cannot make sense of the history of a city—for instance, Calcutta—if one has no knowledge of other cities. Likewise, a historical study of the Russian Revolution could scarcely be conducted by someone who had never heard of the French Revolution. Comparison is to be taken for granted in all history, including the history of religions.[10]

The name *history* for our discipline is, then, worth underlining, because people who turn to the study of religions are inevitably interested in questions of truth. However, dealing with history means tempering any premature obsession with the settling of truth claims. And let us not delude ourselves that an unseemly rush toward truth claims belongs only to the uneducated or to people whose politics we frown upon. Too exclusive a concentration on what we might call "the right side of the scheme" can be quite characteristic of philosophers and theologians. Historical discoveries and renewals in history escape them because of their "systematic" hurry. It is a danger that concerns all our studies.

It is but natural that in each religious tradition people have the urge to find the "pure" forms to be adhered to. It is in fact the question of truth that urges them on. No historian can ignore such concerns for purity. We have to recognize, nevertheless, that an original, *pure* form of Christianity, or Islam, or any other religion we can study, never existed in time. One scholar wrote in 1924: "Every religion has its prehistory, and where there does not seem to be one, it is merely due to our ignorance, or to our insufficient research. In this respect each religion is a 'syncretism.'"[11] ("Syncretism" means a growing together, or intermingling of elements from different origins.)

Literature
Hannah Arendt, "The Concept of History," in *Between Past and Future* (New York: Penguin, 1968), pp. 41–90; Marc Bloch, *The Historian's Craft*, trans. Joseph R. Strayer (New York: Vintage, 1953).

A Bridge Between the Two Sides

Whatever your own field of concentration, your own field is always in the center!

Descriptive Fields   Your Field   Normative Fields

At first glance it might seem unusual that each and every discipline should cross the barrier. Yet the inquisitive mind solves this riddle easily. Within the configuration of the scheme we are visualizing, the image of a center crowded with disciplines is illuminating. It means that there is a place where we cannot avoid bumping into each other and coming to terms with each other. It is the place where what is and what should be thought touch. In this arena, serious clashes may occur, and real agreements can be reached. If the term *discourse* takes on its full meaning, this is where it occurs.

This central arena is not a mere image. Real inquiry occurs only in real discussion, in the midst of the multitude of inquiries. It is false modesty when we hide behind our specialization, suggesting that we have our own facts at our fingertips and cannot be held responsible for questions from elsewhere. A classicist who says, "I can't tell you anything about Shakespeare because I am a classicist," is not a good classicist. He ignores the question "What makes for good literature?" His or her own field of choice, if practiced properly, cannot tolerate any glossing over of that question. This hypothetical classicist has equivalents in every discipline.

The Frenchman Charles Péguy is known as a writer of long essays. Often he wrote as if carrying on discussions with himself. In one place he interrupts himself and suddenly begins to speak of the importance of his own principal interest, philosophy:

Philosophy is the most beautiful of all vocations. One always should believe that the vocation one holds is the most beautiful of all vocations. And it is, first of all, a vocation. It is necessary to say that Philosophy is the most beautiful of vocations in a time when, more than all disciplines, and before all disciplines, it is exposed to ridicule, to mortal blows, . . . to the worst demagoguery, to subjugation.[12]

Without getting involved in the circumstances that prompted these words by Péguy, it is in order to realize that an involvement, a passion for the field to which one dedicates oneself, is not something to be hidden under any real or pretended timidity. One can rightfully say that our chosen study is always under attack, and we are the ones to defend it.

The pride in one's own field that one is entitled to is by no means only a matter of personal taste, although it goes without saying that one should like what one has chosen to do. The justified pride is rather related to the thesis that each discipline that is truly a discipline knows of itself that it begins on a basis that is worthy of recognition in some manner as the basis for all intellectual inquiry. This does not mean that in the following pages I am going to present thoughts that can be substituted for an elementary textbook in mathematics, physics, or economics. But it does mean that the manner of thinking that underlies my field can be recognized across the entire human intellectual spectrum as acceptable.

For all who deal with the history of religions, our field is in the center. It crosses the barrier between the descriptive and the normative disciplines. It must try to do so, as all other specialties should, in a responsible and consistent way. And here, to indicate the very heart of the history of religions as a discipline, we add the term *hermeneutics;* it is the technical term for the activity of fair and consistent interpretation. For in that activity of interpreting the religious documents toward which we are responsible, everything we do converges.

Descriptive Disciplines   Normative Disciplines

|

History of Religions:
Hermeneutics

Literature

José Ortega y Gasset, *Some Lessons in Metaphysics* (New York: Norton, 1969), lesson 1, pp. 13–27; Charles Péguy, "A nos amis, à nos abonnés," *Oeuvres en*

prose 1909–1914 (Paris: Bibliothèque de la Pléiade, Gallimard, 1961), p. 13;
Charles Péguy, *Men and Saints, Prose and Poetry,* trans. Anne and Julian Green
(New York: Pantheon, 1944), see especially "The Humanities," pp. 23–52.

Notes

1. In German, the term *Einleitungswissenschaft* is used for this special intellectual activity.

2. Karl Barth, *Wolfgang Amadeus Mozart,* trans. Clarence K. Pott, foreword
by John Updike (Grand Rapids, Mich.: Eerdmans, 1986), pp. 15–16.

3. College students know or remember that dignitaries known as "coun-
selors" are of little assistance; as a rule, they too know little more than what the
catalog tells them.

4. Philip Wheelwright, *Heraclitus* (New York: Atheneum, 1964), p. 19.

5. A. C. Graham, *Disputers of the Tao, Philosophical Argument in Ancient
China* (La Salle, Ill.: Open Court, 1991), p. 10.

6. Arthur W. Ryder, trans., *The Panchatantra* (Chicago: University of Chicago Press, 1956).

7. Claude Lévi-Strauss, *La pensée sauvage* (Paris: Plon, 1962); English trans.,
The Savage Mind (London: Weidenfeld and Nicolson; Chicago: University of
Chicago Press, 1966).

8. For the use of *sapientia* and *scientia,* see Cicero, *De finibus* III, 48, and
V, 48.7.

9. I am by no means discounting the significance of theology! The legitimate question the Christian theologian raises is "Given the revelation of God,
how should we think?"

10. The adjective *comparative* is suspect among many. Wrongly so. Though of
special importance in the study of history, it qualifies a great many disciplines.
See E. W. Müller, "Plädoyer für die komparativen Geisteswissenschaften,"
Paideuma 39 (1993), pp. 7–23. Although the author abstains from any reference
to the essential comparative function in all processes of knowing, he points to a
number of disciplines that by nature rely on comparison.

11. Joachim Wach, *Religionswissenschaft, Prolegomena zu ihrer wissenschaft-
stheoretischen Grundlegung* (Leipzig: Hinrichs, 1924), p. 86.

12. Charles Péguy, "A nos amis, à nos abonnés," *Oeuvres en prose 1909–1914*
(Paris: Bibliothèque de la Pléiade, Gallimard, 1961), p. 13.

The History of Religions

OBJECT AND TASK OF THE HISTORY OF RELIGIONS

Religious Facts. The object of the history of religions consists in religious facts; these are the facts that show by their very appearance their religious nature. They are not necessarily written documents. It is important, as we have seen, to draw on archaeology and prehistory among the descriptive fields that provide us with materials. We know of foundations of temples that are without inscription. We know from even earlier periods that people erected stones, and assembled rocks and boulders. Some of these prehistoric monuments served as gravesites, in all likelihood for important elders, or were memorials or sacred sites. In spite of the difficulty in interpreting signs unaccompanied by words, such items are recognizable as religious documents.

The data for the historian of religions, his or her primary documents, are the expressions of religion. We recognize them as a botanist recognizes trees, or a geologist rocks. So far, at any rate, there is no mystery involved.

Religion and Religions. The word *religion* nevertheless is one of the most puzzling of terms. It leads us to questions that are truly perplexing. But let us begin by dispelling some unnecessary ones. The Latin *religio*, from which our word comes, was originally used in a different way. It could be used in the plural, *religiones*, and could occasionally refer to what we today would call "superstitions," for instance in Cicero. The etymology

20

of our *religion,* however, is not as significant as the changes that took place in the *idea* of religion over the course of time.

In the time span of human life on earth, our very notion of *religion* and its synonyms in various languages is relatively recent. Ancient Iran was the cradle of several religious creations, and there too, for the first time, we find a term referring to our "religions," the cumulative traditions, each of which is recognizable in its distinctiveness.[1]

In the previous pages, I have used the term *religion* in the singular and in the plural. This practice has something to do with the fact that in order to be good inquirers, we have to be industrious gatherers of facts at the same time. Our mind posits the idea of "religion," and yet we observe a multitude of "religions." On this level of discussion, there is nothing extraordinary or ambiguous about our saying "religion" and "religions." By analogy, in botany, for example, we have to speak of many plants and of plant life. The same plurality and singularity occur.

There is, however, a special feature to the simultaneous plural and singular use of *religion* which may serve as a first indication of the distinctive nature of our discipline. For in our discipline it is of great importance to realize that the difference between this singular and this plural is not merely a grammatical feature or a matter of counting. Rather, we are employing two necessary perspectives, and both are demanded by our object of study.

To be sure, there is a multitude of religions: there are local tribal traditions, the innumerable religions of prehistory, Hinduism, Buddhism, Judaism, Christianity, Islam, and so on. There is, however, also a certain uniformity in the way in which all these different traditions express themselves. When we hear Javanese music, or African music, or the music of Bach, we notice very different means of expression, in rhythm, or the presence or absence of chords, or the significance given to melody, yet we have no problem saying "music." Similarly, we recognize the singular *religion* in the plurality of religions.

Let us note that this recognition has nothing to do with anything like "faith" or "God" or any sort of "doctrine." There is no Hindu "creed"; no Hindu ever found it necessary to sum up what a Hindu should "believe." Buddhists know about gods, but neither God nor gods are significant in their religion. And yet, both Hindus and Buddhists make pilgrimages, and go through ceremonies that in some manner resemble what Christians would call sacraments. The sum total of such things everywhere is more than enough to allow us to use the singular *religion.*

Among the primary documents of each religion we find evidence of an awareness of this distinctiveness of customs and at the same time of this certain sameness or unity in humanity. On the first page of the Bible, we are told of the creation of Adam. Adam is the first human being. The Hebrew word *Adam* means man or human being. "And God made man, according to the image of God he made him, male and female he made them" (Genesis 1:27). What one cannot fail to observe is that *human beings* are created, and not a particular group that is singled out as "first." This is even more striking when we consider that shortly thereafter in the biblical story people become divided into groups, and that the heart of the biblical story concerns the history of the Israelites, whose God has a name different from the gods of others. In other words, it is as if the "ambiguity" of the particular together with the universal is embedded in the tradition. An attentive reading of the biblical texts confirms that the *structure* of the religion of Israel points to this. (A "structure," although also merely a "concept," is what in our interpretive efforts we arrive at as what makes the religion what it is.)

Among many other examples, we might think of the friezes of Balinese temples depicting various figures; one, for example, includes the clear representation of a Dutchman, with beer mug and tobacco pipe. The image as a whole is a portrayal of the "entire world," for the Dutch, who colonized Indonesia, once they were there, needed to be included as part of the "all reality." Balinese Hinduism did not engage in any more exclusiveness than the first page of the creation story of Genesis. Balinese religion, which is a special and complex form of Hinduism, was not disturbed by the discovery of human beings from the outside, the Dutch.

Literature
William E. Paden, *Religious Worlds* (Boston: Beacon, 1988); Eric J. Sharpe, *Comparative Religion, A History* (La Salle, Ill.: Open Court, 1991); G. van der Leeuw, *Religion in Essence and Manifestation* (New York: Harper, 1963); W. Warde Fowler, "The Latin History of the Word *Religio*," in Whitfield Foy, ed., *The Religious Quest. A Reader* (London: Routledge, 1988), pp. 330–36.

WHAT IS RELIGION?

The term *history* owes its meaning to the Greek Herodotus (fifth century B.C.), who was called "the father of History" by the Roman thinker and statesman Cicero (106–43 B.C.).[2] *Historia*, history, means basically inquiry or research; it is the inquiry into human documents, all that is made and remembered, recorded and narrated by people. And of course, religious documents are among those human documents. Hence, in the study of the history of religions we are speaking of an intellectual, academically disciplined manner of investigating the thing we call religion, or religions.

We know of no human civilization without religion. The innumerable facts that we recognize as "religious" occur everywhere. It would seem that we have no option but to see religious facts as integral to human beings. We are following standard scientific procedures when we say that as historians of religions we concentrate on human beings as religious beings. After all, biologists study human beings as biological beings, sociologists study them as social beings. Neither a biologist nor a sociologist could say, "This person here is more biological, or more social, than that one there." Exactly like that, the historian of religions regards all humans as religious in structure.

Then what is this religious nature that is so general? It is, in short, the human characteristic of symbolizing in a very particular way.

Literature
G. van der Leeuw, *Religion in Essence and Manifestation;* Raffaele Pettazzoni, *Essays on the History of Religions* (Leiden: Brill, 1954); Adolf Portmann, "Biology and the Phenomenon of the Spiritual," *Eranos* (1946) in Joseph Campbell, ed., *Spirit and Nature* (New York: Pantheon, 1954).

RELIGIOUS SYMBOLIZATION

Universally, people make use of symbols. They create these symbols — although an individual cannot sit down and decide to make one up. A symbol is not an individual, and certainly not a whimsical, thing. Only think of some well-known examples, such as the Christian cross, the Hindu syllable ŌM, the Qur'an (the immediate, present Word of God in Islam). When we speak of basic religious symbols, we do not merely mean "signs." On signs, functioning also in any civilization, we have simple public agreement, as with traffic signals and stop signs. Logicians and mathematicians use the term *symbol* for things that really are signs. The algebraic $(a + b)^2 = a^2 + 2ab + b^2$ is a way of expressing what a certain equation always is, no matter what the values are for a and b. Here we are dealing only with a brief way of expressing provable generalizations. Religious symbols are not like that.

The fundamental symbols that typify religion can be said to be more deeply embedded in human existence than any "mere signs"; they have a special priority. This is not a veiled distinction, for the fact that all of us can tell religious matters from other matters is located precisely in the symbolism involved.

Religious symbols are part of a reality that our common, more "mechanical" academic jargon has difficulty with. Unlike mere signs, they do not represent anything to which our rational reflection can immediately assign a place. In that respect, they resemble the images in dreams.[3] The givenness of such symbols has spawned a vast number of scholarly and philosophical writings. Nevertheless, it remains difficult for some people filled with the certainties and abstractions of a modern high school education (filled with those certainties even if they have moved on to college and beyond) to imagine that religious symbolism is part of common human experience. As if instinctively, they ask, Isn't all knowledge "rational" and "conscious"?

The problem goes further. In spite of some seeming resemblance to dream imagery, religious symbolization is not un-conscious. Although it does take us into the unmapped territory of human imaginative functions, at the same time it is part of the most ordinary reality. The symbolization that occupies the historian of religions is not utilitarian (after the manner of traffic signs), nor is it a matter of conceptual equations or abstract identifications (as in mathematics). Yet it is always concrete and precise.

Only examples can help us grasp the nature of religious symbols. We have already mentioned the Christian cross, the sacred syllable ŌM in Hinduism, and the holy book of Islam; some of us may look upon those examples, no matter how important to others, as distant items of information, devoid of anything immediate and concrete. Yet illuminating examples that can speak to our imagination are not hard to find. They are close at hand.

Consider the experience of a young man in Chicago, whose words I read not long ago in my newspaper. In prison, he was approached by certain people—people whom the learned and "secular" often look down upon as "evangelicals" or "fundamentalists," and who go to the streets and jails and approach youths who belong to gangs. This young man tells the reporter that as a member of a gang, he knew what a "vow" was: in the gang you swear to give your life for one another. But then, in jail, he finds that none of his brothers makes haste even to visit him. And now, for the first time, he hears of something that we can quite properly call "the central Christian symbolism." He hears that someone died for him and has set him free. In other words, he hears the language that some of us might refer to as "mere Christian parlance," of Jesus Christ's death on the cross. The young man, however, is struck by more than mere words. This is indeed an instance of truly functioning, live religious symbolism. It is inseparable from what human beings experience quite consciously. In this particular instance, a person's inner core is illuminated, someone's life no longer isolated. The boy's experience of what he hears connects him to something greater, indeed, absolute, outside of him.

In fact, the world of symbolization that we cannot call by any other name but "religious" surrounds all of us, whether we live in the foxholes of the inner cities or in more pleasant academic environs where perhaps one likes to imagine that one is lucky enough not to need to be consoled by "illusions." How often have you discussed the death penalty? Or the question of abortion? Invariably, the parties for or against are convinced of their views, yet rest their case on grounds that do not seem to lend themselves to clear articulation. For all the sides involved, the issue of life and its control, of the preservation and the cutting off of life, is rooted in certainties of a symbolism that is structurally religious. And few know how to articulate that in our age.

Symbol comes from a Greek verb, *sumballein,* meaning "throwing together" or "getting together." Two parts that are separate from each other nevertheless fit and compose a whole. (Though it is used in several senses in classical Greek, such as "sign," "contract," "agreement," one original use of the term *sumbolon,* symbol, comes from a suggestive custom. In the ancient world, symbols functioned as proofs of identity between people. When a young man left on a journey, his father would give him his part of a stone that, years earlier, the father and a friend had broken in half. This half would fit with its counterpart, in the possession of the father's friend. And now, the *sumbolon,* this token of a human tie and hospitality, served as proof of the relationship and guaranteed a roof over the son's head.)

A religious symbol ties two or more entities together that in practical use do not go together, and empirically and rationally may seem to have nothing in common. All thought that is based on such relationships is called "symbolism."

A symbolism that is more widespread than any other is related to the moon. The moon has fascinated people, more than the sun, from the earliest ages of mankind. Its waxing, waning, and disappearance were obviously felt to be significant. The multitude and universal occurrence of lunar myths point to their antiquity—no doubt predating our earliest historical records by far.[4] What makes the image of the moon symbolic is its place as a knot connecting different things.

The moon is at once, and most understandably, related to human experience of time, life, birth, death, revival. The calendar system is primarily built on lunar cycles, and thus the symbol takes us into the realm that our modern habits would reserve for "science." In addition, the menstrual cycle of women is placed in the same symbolic lunar complex. The religious imagination does not seem bothered by the heterogeneity of elements that are related in the symbol. Even the most "primitive" human being must have been aware that there was nothing resembling a precise, causal, or useful correlation between the periods of women and the phases of the moon. And yet, from the most ancient records on, major goddesses, who wield power over life and death, are associated with the moon.

Is there an order to the human capacity for symbolizing? Yes, there is, even if from a modern intellectual perspective it seems "irrational" and hence dubious. Cultural anthropologists, historians of religions, and art historians have all dealt with an order they sensed (though struggling to express it) in all these matters that has faded from our sight much more recently than most people today realize. One great art historian with an open eye for religious phenomena said, "Symbolism is a language and a precise form of thought . . ."[5]

The historian of religions Mircea Eliade (1907–86) gave some of his most important lessons in informal meetings with his students. On one such occasion, at his home, he meditated aloud. One can take away from a human being almost everything he has—his limbs, hearing, eyesight, and so on—and still he remains a human being; but if you take away his ability to symbolize, then what remains is not a man.

It is worth pointing out that our study of people as symbol-makers, and hence religious beings, by no means denies the worthiness of other disciplines. It goes without saying that a technologist or historian of science will pay attention to man as a toolmaker (*homo faber*); an economist will naturally concentrate on humans as beings who are involved in the market and in profit-making. And even if an anthropologist insists on focusing on man as a rational being, holding that this is the only meaning of "*homo sapiens,*" it is surely something that can be done. Certainly, no one would dare contradict the thesis of Aristotle that man is a social being. However, all these "types" of human beings do not cease to be religious. As historians of religions, we know of saints, ascetics, legendary and other, really existing characters who do not care for profit-making, and may want to desert the marketplaces. There are also completely sane people who question the course of man the toolmaker which led us to the pollution of the air, the water, and the earth. What all have in common is that peculiar human imagination that creates and receives symbols.

Literature

Susanne Langer, *Philosophy in a New Key: A Study in the Symbolism of Reason, Rite, and Art* (1942; Cambridge: Harvard University Press, 1974), is the most stimulating work to have brought the subject of symbolizing to the fore. The most extensive one-volume work on religious symbols remains Mircea Eliade, *Patterns in Comparative Religion* (London & New York: Sheed and Ward, 1958). See also Count Goblet d' Alviella, *The Migration of Symbols* (1894; New York: University Books, 1956). A bundle of essays by Jonathan Z. Smith, *Imagining Religion: From Babylon to Jonestown* (Chicago: University of Chicago Press, 1982), elaborates on the relation between religious symbolism and the imagination (thereby making the imagination of the historian of religions a central issue). See also James Shreeve, *The Neandertal Enigma. Solving the Mystery of Modern Human Origins* (New York: William Morrow, 1995).

THE RIGHT USE OF WORDS: RELIGION, (RELIGIOUS) SYMBOLISM

Now we should make our statements about "religion" and "symbolism" a bit more precise. I want to begin by focusing on the need for the use of appropriate terms.

First, there is our use of the term *religious symbolism* itself. If what I have said in the previous pages is clear, *religious symbolism* may be tautological. What makes people religious is the fact that they symbolize. *Religion* and *symbolizing* are identical. Hence, we are entitled to use the two terms interchangeably. "All people are religious by nature" is the same as "All people symbolize."

This statement, which is quite correct, can be hard to grasp in the presence of a hazy but resilient bias that holds that some people are "very religious," some people are "not very religious," and so forth—as if "being religious" were a quality of which one could have either more or less. Let us reflect again, however, that in popular parlance it would also seem as if the social nature of people were a matter of degree, differing from one person to another, even though, as a sociologist would point out, the actual fact is that all people are social beings by nature. Being engendered by a father and born from a mother has made us that way. How else did we learn to speak? In exactly that manner, we are by nature symbol-creating and symbol-receiving beings. (Of course, we should not confuse our identically religious nature with the particulars of and differences between various religious traditions, and with the difference between great mystics and most of the rest of us. Nor would we confuse our identically social nature as human beings with our endowments in "sociability." The biologist, of course, is aware of expressions such as "Senator X is a very lively speaker!" It is obvious that life is not studied scientifically on the level of such common observations.)

We have not yet discussed the one aspect of symbolism that is most important for the subject of religion, but is also controversial. It is the question of *what the symbol refers to*. In the case of the ties between old friends and their families no dispute is likely to arise. But, one may ask, what does the symbolism of death and life or of menstrual cycles *really* refer to?

Here, I think, is the reason why the expression *religious symbolism* is not as tautologous as it seemed. Religious symbols, many historians of religions (including Mircea Eliade) argue, are typified by the fact that they have a *transcendent referent*. The moon of our example may seem "known" to us—indeed we are familiar with space travel that allows men to land on the moon. However, for all ancient traditions, the moon was literally *transcendent*, "going beyond" the world in which we perceive and think. And precisely that element of transcendency of which the very idea seems to have receded for most of us is most striking in the religious symbolization human beings engage in. In what follows, we shall have many occasions to return to this issue. Let me say for the moment that it is premature to dismiss "religious symbolism" as "antiquated science," which has been surpassed by us. In our modern, advanced world, as I hope to indicate, we have merely fallen into the habit of glossing over the *religious* symbolism in which we ourselves are involved.

THE RIGHT USE OF WORDS: TRADITION

The word *tradition* is valuable. Hinduism, Taoism, Christianity, and so on are religious traditions. We should be aware, however, of the sense in which we use the term. Very often, the word *traditional* seems to imply "something of the past," if not a "relic." This connotation would make it seem, for example, as if Hinduism were traditional by virtue of its acceptance of the Vedas, its three-thousand-year-old sacred scriptures. There is often a suggestion that a custom is observed "because it is tradition," as if it were something quaint and no longer relevant.

In most cases these references and endeavors at explanation miss the mark. If we speak of tradition in Hinduism or the religion of ancient Rome in the serious study of religion, what we must realize is that "tradition" is not an unchanging thing, written or otherwise, but an *activity*. The Latin *traditio* refers first of all to *tradere,* "to hand down," "to pass on" from one generation to another. This is an *act*. And even without a great deal of knowledge we can understand that tradition in this primary meaning is not something unchanging and static but, on the contrary, something constantly in flux.

In the following examples, it is of the greatest importance for our understanding to ban from our minds the misapprehension of "unchanging" and "static" in the life of religious traditions. I will simply present events and texts with little or no comment. They all have their crux in something that *happens* or *changes*. It is irrelevant for the moment that all of them may seem far away in the past or distant from our present existence.

By way of introduction, imagine for a moment that right now a Presbyterian minister in Chicago has found himself in conversation with a colleague, also a Presbyterian, from, let us say, eighteenth-century New England. What would these two talk about? The eighteenth-century clergyman, in all likelihood, would know the writings of John Calvin very well, in French, and probably also in Latin. He would not be likely to find his friend of our century well versed on that score. If our present-day minister were to tell him about his readings in pastoral psychology, the eighteenth-century man would be greatly puzzled. And he would be baffled when told about women colleagues in the church.

The changeability attested in the course of a mere two centuries has its parallels in all religious traditions. In the three thousand years of Hinduism, changes occurred that led from elaborate ritual forms of religion to forms of yoga and devotion that no one could have predicted or imagined on the basis of the oldest, most venerable texts. Not only did many more texts appear in the course of time, but, most strikingly, the very activity of passing on the teachings involved new listening to and new interpreting of old texts. The lack of attention to the *life* in any religious tradition can make us oblivious to forms of change that stare us in the face. One such form of change is the infinite variety of ways in which *critique* is built into the tradition.

The Israelite prophet Amos lived in the eighth century B.C. In a powerful narration in the biblical Book of Amos, the prophet announces the judgment of God. Of course, everyone in the tradition knew about God's power to judge. However, the words of Amos provide a new perspective: Amos enumerates all the peoples surrounding Israel on whom the judgment of God will come down, and in his enumeration he comes geographically closer and closer to Israel and Judah—the very lands "guaranteed" by God. "For crime after crime of ———— I will grant them no reprieve" is the phrase that is repeated in the beginning pages. And of course, no one would feel particularly shaken by condemnation of relatively distant lands or enemies: Damascus, Gaza, Tyre, Ammon, Moab. But then, the same words begin the climax of the judgment:

> For crime after crime of Judah
> I will grant them no reprieve,
>
> .   .   .   .
>
> Therefore will I send fire upon Judah,
> fire that shall consume the palaces of Jerusalem.
>
> .   .   .   .
>
> For crime after crime of Israel
> I will grant them no reprieve,
> because they sell the innocent for silver
> and the destitute for a pair of shoes,
> They grind the heads of the poor into the earth
> and thrust the humble out of their way.
> Father and son resort to the same girl,
> to the profanation of my holy name.
>
> .   .   .   .
>
> Listen, I groan under the burden of you,
> as a wagon creaks under a full load.
> Flight shall not save the swift,
> the strong man shall not rally his strength.
> The warrior shall not save himself,
> the archer shall not stand his ground;
> the swift of foot shall not be saved,
> nor the horseman escape;

on that day the bravest of warriors
shall be stripped of his arms and run away.
This is the very word of the Lord.
                    (Amos 2:4–16)[6]

What we have in a case like this is hardly the consolidation of an unmoving "block" of tradition. It is rather a shockingly new discomfort. (Amos's activity was the opposite of something I remember from my own boyhood in the Netherlands. In 1940, shortly before Germany invaded, bombed, and occupied the country, a pious old aunt of mine said, "Surely, the Lord will save Holland.") The critique within a tradition can break through forcefully, changing the understanding of a people's religious heritage.

In the Midrashim, rabbinical "expositions" of biblical texts, we find interpretations in the form of discussions that students of literature might call "imaginative." And indeed, they are—but their imagination shares in the symbolizing power of the Scriptures they interpret. It is not a matter of mere literary ornamentation. The following example is an answer to the question of where the light came from. The light in question is the light that according to the first page of the Bible was created in the beginning—while the sun and the moon and the other heavenly bodies, according to the same account, came about only on the fourth day. Obviously, something unlike modern astronomy is at issue. The question is worth asking, and it does receive an answer:

> Once Rabbi Shimon ben Yehozedek addressed Rabbi Shmuel ben Nachman and said, "I hear that thou art a Baal Aggadah [a master of narrative interpretation, distinguished from legal interpretation]; canst thou therefore tell me whence the light was created?" "We learn," he replied in a whisper, "that God wrapped Himself with light as with a garment, and He has caused the splendor thereof to shine from one end of the world to the other." The other said, "Why whisperest thou, I wonder, since Scripture says so plainly (Psalm 104.2) 'Who covereth Himself with light as with a garment'?" The reply was, "I heard it in a whisper, and in a whisper I have told it to thee."[7]

We see a new, transformed, more "inner" and "devout" understanding of an authoritative text than earlier tradition had known. It is not at all difficult to move from this renewal in the Jewish tradition to what the

Danish theologian Søren Kierkegaard (1813–55) did within his Christian tradition. In his work too, a new, "inner" understanding is quite visible.

Kierkegaard moreover nurtured an ironic genius that was a remarkable tool for reinterpretive change in Christianity. He wrote not only many books but also letters to the editors of newspapers, as a rule under a pseudonym. (In that way he occasionally reviewed his own books!) In one of his little essays, where he pokes fun at the smug, self-congratulatory Christianity of his time and place, he explains at length, as if glorifying the achievements of his time, how Denmark has become thoroughly penetrated by, indeed soaked in, Christianity. If the Lord came back and looked around, the Lord would be amazed at the strides his movement had made, and revise his own gloomy forecasts. "Yea," Kierkegaard says,

> I venture to go a step further—it inspires me with enthusiasm, for this you must remember is a eulogy upon the human race—I venture to maintain that on the average, the Jews who dwell among us are to a certain degree Christians, Christians like all the others—to that degree we are all Christians, in that degree the New Testament is no longer truth.
>
>   . . . I venture . . . to go a step further, without expressing, however, any definite opinions, seeing that in this respect I lack precise information, and hence submit to persons well informed, the specialists, the question whether among the domestic animals, the nobler ones, the horse, the dog, the cow, there might not be visible some Christian token. That is not unlikely. Just think what it means to live in a Christian state, a Christian nation, where everything is Christian, and we are all Christians, where, however a man twists and turns, he sees nothing but Christianity and Christendom, the truth and witnesses to the truth—it is not unlikely that this may have an influence upon the nobler domestic animals, and thereby turn upon that which, according to the judgment of both the veterinary and the priest, is the most important thing, namely, the progeny. Jacob's cunning device is well known, how in order to get speckled lambs he laid speckled rods in the watering troughs, so that the ewes saw nothing but speckles and therefore gave birth to speckled lambs. It is not unlikely—although I do not presume to have any definite opinion, as I am not a specialist, and therefore would rather submit the question to a committee composed, for example, of veterinaries and priests—it is not unlikely that it will end with domestic animals in "Christendom" bringing into the world a Christian progeny.
>
>   I am almost dizzy at the thought . . .

Thou Saviour of the world, Thou didst anxiously exclaim, "When I come again, shall I find faith on the earth?" and didst bow Thy head in death; Thou surely didst not have the least idea that in such a measure Thine expectations would be surpassed . . .[8]

The irony Kierkegaard pours on the self-satisfaction of his age's churches and the widespread uncritical certainty of the ongoing improvement of the world is hard to miss. Though different from what we read in Amos, a new, very critical and transforming element is generated.

Buddhism has its own long history with its own transformative occurrences. In all instances, the achievement of total liberation (enlightenment, *nirvāṇa*) is the final goal. To gain such liberation, many hindrances must be overcome. And in one of the later movements in Buddhism, known in Japan as Zen Buddhism, entertaining and illuminating anecdotes have been recorded on this score. The following is understandable at once — without any prior knowledge of complex texts on meditation and philosophy:

Nan-in, a Japanese master during the Meiji era (1868 – 1912), received a university professor who came to inquire about Zen.

Nan-in served tea. He poured his visitor's cup full, and then kept on pouring.

The professor watched the overflow until he no longer could restrain himself. "It is overfull. No more will go in!"

"Like this cup," Nan-in said, "you are full of your own opinions and speculations. How can I show you Zen unless you first empty your cup?"[9]

Also from Zen Buddhism comes the following story. As in the previous case, its instructive power crosses all barriers. Even if Buddhist Enlightenment is a mystery to the reader, the barriers to be crossed are perfectly clear.

Tanzan and Ekido were once traveling together down a muddy road. A heavy rain was still falling.

Coming around a bend, they met a lovely girl in a silk kimono and sash, unable to cross the intersection.

"Come on, girl," said Tanzan at once. Lifting her in his arms, he carried her over the mud.

Ekido did not speak again until that night when they reached a lodging temple. Then he could no longer restrain himself. "We monks don't go near females," he told Tanzan, "especially not young and lovely ones. It is dangerous. Why did you do that?"

"I left the girl there," said Tanzan. "Are you still carrying her?"[10]

In all these illustrations we see changes that actually occur in some manner all the time. Each generation, after all, takes what it receives from parents, educators, previous history, and "makes something of it." It makes it into its own, appropriates it. And of course, variations are the rule of the game, no matter how much we may come to resemble our parents in seemingly unchanged, external features.

Are there clear examples of the same appropriating and transforming process in our contemporary world? Very many indeed, and the only difficulty is making a choice. To me two seem quite illustrative for our topic, religion. The first one takes up an old story, but the author is a man of our time, and as a modern listener I forget that the story is old; it addresses itself to the world we know.

Belcampo is a Dutch writer who only a few decades ago published an unlikely collection of short stories about saints. One tale is about Saint Basil, a great man of the early church in Caesarea, capital of Cappadocia. In that city lived an evil man, who, Belcampo tells us, was in the insurance business. He deceives his clients, makes abundant use of the small print in contracts, and rakes in profit. The evil man's wife is not at all pleased with her husband's doings, and one countermove she indulges in is a secret love affair. No one, neither her husband nor her children, finds out about the liaison. Then suddenly, both her husband and her lover die. Worrying about her sinful life, she consults the bishop, Basil, who is thought to be able to exert some influence on God's judgments. The woman writes down all her misdeeds on a piece of paper. Belcampo tells us she took the piece of paper from the pile her husband used for his business contracts. Bishop Basil is old, and his eyesight poor. And the woman decides to write down every sinful trifle she can remember, such as once having dropped a plate on purpose, and replying curtly to her children. Only at the end, little space being left, in very small letters does she write about her adultery. She begs Basil for forgiveness and hands him the paper. A week later, in spite of his poor eyes, he recognizes her at once, her list of sins in his hand, and says, "I did my best for you." The paper is clean, all her writing wiped off— except, however, for the very small letters. The bishop apologizes: he could not decipher those tiniest letters. And besides, for whatever is left to be done, it will be best for her to see a holy hermit, Effren by name, who has better eyes and is more meritorious as well.

The woman goes on her journey, three days into the desert, to meet Effren. The holy man Effren listens to the woman's story and recalls that many years earlier, he had visited Caesarea and felt irritated by the pomp surrounding Bishop Basil, ornate in the procession with thousands of participants at a great Christian festival. However, at that very occasion, Basil had suddenly stopped his chariot, sought out Effren in the multitude, and whispered into his ear, "Stroking the back of your Cyprian cat just once, you certainly reap greater joy than I do with all this hocuspocus here. See to it that you get back to your desert in a hurry." This event set Effren thinking, and he concluded that in the end it was best for everybody to get holy in his own way.

Effren, the holy hermit, tells the woman that Basil, if he had really wanted to know what she wrote, surely would have ordered a deacon to read the small letters to him. Hence, he must have known that the pilgrimage through the desert would be enough penitence for her sins. The thing to do now was travel back, another three days through the desert, and visit Basil again.

The woman goes back to Caesarea, only to find herself in the midst of the funeral procession taking Basil to his grave. She cries out that Basil is nothing but a cheat for sneaking out at this moment. "You are no saint, but a hypocrite!" she says. "You are carrying all my sins! If I am damned, my damnation will fall on your head!" She forces herself through the crowd to the flower-covered casket and places her paper on it. At once, however, the cane of one of the funeral servants flicks the paper off the wreaths. Even angrier, the woman grabs it, ready to roll it in a wad and throw it back onto the casket. But then she notices that something has happened. The small letters have disappeared and the sheet is clean.[11]

"All right," someone says, "but this is Christian stuff." For I have taught the history of religions long enough to know that in any audience, someone says just that. For such a person, let me quote Günther Grass's poem on an egg. Yes, an egg. The egg is among the most ancient symbols of mankind, probably even more ancient than the moon, if that is conceivable. For the egg was there at the time when people had not yet learned to hunt big game, when they fed themselves by hunting tiny creatures that they could grab by hand or hit with a stone, and for the rest, they gathered what was there, such as berries, roots, and of course, eggs. Eggs never ceased to fascinate people, and fairy tales and other folk literature are full of them. The goose that laid golden eggs is known to all. And in ancient Indian literature, the golden egg of Brahman contains in itself the whole of the universe that is about to be born. Here is a bona fide "pagan" symbol, with no Christian taints to speak of. And lo and behold, we have a midtwentieth-century writer who produced one of the most glorious midtwentieth-century novels, *The Tin Drum* (also devoid of any detectable Christian taints, and arguably the best piece of literature to come out of the experience of the Second World War), and in an unguarded moment, he writes a poem about an egg. It is still the primordial egg, containing everything—and yet, there is a twist, as much as in Amos's view of existing in the tradition guarded by God. And peculiarly, as in the case of Amos, in the end we have glimpses of horror and uncertainty rather than peace and certainty.

In Grass's poem, we are all living in this egg. It is the place in which we are living our "normal" life; it is the world in which we are encased, cooped up, without any certainty as to how long, or why. We talk, we chatter with each other about how long we'll be here in this place, where we have covered the inside of the shell with "dirty drawings and the Christian names of our enemies." We are being hatched. That we know, he writes. But obviously, our ignorance in this confinement is depressing. It seems that our habitual chattering raises doubts even as to the certainty that we are really being hatched. Could it be that there is no end, no purpose to any of this?

And what if we are not being hatched?
. . . .
If our horizon is only that
of our scribbles and always will be?[12]

The Spanish thinker José Ortega y Gasset has had a great deal to say about the nature of "tradition" in all human life, and in 1959 he wrote:

"To read" begins by signifying the project of understanding a text fully. Now this is impossible. It is only possible with a great effort to extract a more or less important portion of what the text has tried to say, communicate, make known; but there will always remain an "illegible" residue. It is, on the other hand, probable that, while we are making this effort, we may read, at the same time, into the text; that is, we may

understand things which the author has not "meant" to say, and, nevertheless, he has "said" them; he has presented them to us involuntarily—
even more, against his professed purpose . . .

    1. Every utterance is deficient—it says less than it wishes to say.

    2. Every utterance is exuberant—it conveys more than it plans.[13]

In our most common habits of "taking in" what is presented to us in writing (and, by extension, through other means as well), we participate in the
transforming process of tradition.

THE RIGHT USE OF WORDS: FAITH

Faith is frequently used as a synonym of *religion*. It is best to avoid that
usage. Although it is fairly old, it remains misleading. We should make an
effort to use the term *religions* in its obvious sense of "cumulative traditions." As to *faith*, that word has a special religious meaning that is restricted to only a few religions, of which the obvious examples are Christianity and Islam. The term is used also in Judaism, yet in the structure of
Judaism, no prominent place is assigned to a confession of "faith" but
cultic observances are much closer to the center of the tradition; the Giving of the Law is not merely affirmed but celebrated. In the liturgy of the
Christian church, on the other hand, the congregation stands up and
pronounces its creed aloud. It is an act performed vis-à-vis the world, for
whose sake, according to Christian tradition, God was revealed in Jesus
Christ. In the study of religions, we of course cannot ignore such crucial
details. Hence the common, journalistic habit of referring to "the faiths of
the world" has no place in our inquiries—except as a curious misunder-
standing in the history of ideas. Many Muslims died for their faith. Martin
Luther (1483–1546), leader of the German Reformation, with greater
emphasis than any, proclaimed the salvation of man "by faith alone." No
verbal expressions of that sort would have made any sense in Hinduism,
Buddhism, Taoism, or any other religious tradition. (Though intense inner
certainty of course can occur anywhere.)

    The intellectual history that led to the equation of "religion" and "faith"
is complex and should not detain us too much at this point. Suffice it
to say that one contributing factor within Christianity, the major tradition
of the West, was the increased and central importance of the sermon as
instruction, understood as communication of knowledge. Inevitably this

gave a certain cast to the notion of "faith"; it came to be seen as *information* of some sort. Another significant factor was the special secularization process that has typified the Western world: an objection to and rejection of dogma. This process was permeated with the assumption that freedom of human reason was the wave of the future. A new, dependable, scientific knowledge was set in opposition to the presumably misguided (religious) knowledge of the past. In reaction to this "scientific" rejection of religion, religious belief itself became more objectified in a kind of competition with the factualness of "science." The mistaken use of *religion* and *faith* as synonyms has been further vulgarized by popular psychology. Popular psychology, as practiced by all the media, associates "religions" with groups of people who supposedly are held together only by a set of ideas, which are considered to be their "faith" or their "beliefs."

With respect to the spiritual quests of human beings, these convictions embedded in "the ways of the West" might actually be described as expressions of ignorance and uncritical assumptions! As for Christianity—and the history of Christianity is the principal condition under which the typically Western secularization processes were formed—this religion has had its great thinkers who rather precisely formulated rubrics of "knowledge." We are deeply influenced by their distinction of three forms: *opinio, scientia,* and *fides. Opinio,* opinion, is something I know or think, but have no way to convince anyone else of. *Scientia,* learning or science, is something I know and have public, generally available means to communicate to others. *Fides,* faith, may also in principle be available to all, but God is the one who provides it.

In Hinduism and Buddhism, virtually all thinkers have always made clear that the purpose of philosophy is not knowledge, not the perfect clarification of science, but *mokṣa, nirvāṇa,* liberation, freedom, enlightenment. Erudition, science, obviously does not help very much in that direction. If we want to understand anything of the religions of the world, we had better pay attention to what they say.

THE RIGHT USE OF WORDS: WORLDVIEW, SUPERNATURAL, IDEOLOGY

These are the final terms toward which I would like to advocate caution. It is often said that religions present one "worldview" or another—as if that were the principal object of a religion. But our concern over a "worldview" is by no means as profound as we think. The notion "worldview" rarely loses the connotation of a more or less rational idea in which our view of the universe centers.[14]

In the texts of the Bible, which were not written in one fell swoop but reflect great changes over more than a millennium, we see very different worldviews—yet none of those differences seemed to keep anyone awake at night. They did not interfere with anything of religious significance. Variants in the story of the birth of the world occur at the very beginning of the Bible in Genesis 1 and 2. God is said to create the four segments of the world successively: the light, the sky (or in older translations, "the firmament"), the seas, and the land (Genesis 1:1–2:4a) and, in accordance with these parts, their creatures (celestial bodies, birds, fish, animals, and people). The second story (Genesis 2:4b–25) presents first the creation of man, then the plants, the animals, and finally woman. One might speculate that something was left out of the second story, but as we have it, it seems to assume the existence of "heaven and earth" (Genesis 2:4b) as something self-evident. In the first account God creates by means of the word, while the second depicts God's creation of living beings out of the substances that were already in existence. One could go on listing variants between these two stories and in other books in the Bible, including the Psalms, the Book of Job, and Isaiah. Moreover, for more than a century, scholars have increased our knowledge of the entire region of the ancient Near East; we now know that a number of views of the world were held in common and embroidered upon. Historically, the biblical texts are part of a very large heritage in which various views of the world are reflected in the course of time. The New Testament is of course of a much later date than the Old Testament, is written in Greek, and reflects other views of the world. Most striking is the theme that the world was created by means of God's *Logos,* Word—a notion that in late Antiquity gained ground in many circles as the central principle of all there is. (This central principle approaches a philosophical idea and does not allow a simplistic equation with God's creative, spoken word in Genesis 1.)

The most important thing to realize in our present context is that none of such differences in "worldview" played a significant role in the religious discussions that were carried on. Religiously, the notion of salvation—such as *nirvana* in Buddhism—was consistently of much more significance than any details concerning "worldviews."

The undue use of *worldview* to refer to what a religion is about reached a climax in Western scholarly discussions around 1900, hence at a time when the West was optimistic about its abilities and when confidence in what our scientific knowledge could achieve had few detractors. It became almost customary to group all preclassical and distant nations together as people whose religious customs were basically a matter of erroneous views ("magic"), to be understood as a primitive form of science. Those early religions were supposedly made up of prescientific worldviews, in contrast to our own correct, advanced sciences.

In whatever confusion still surfaces in modern discussions on the subject, we have to think once again of the many factors influencing the rise of an interest in the power of human reason and the rise of modern science—which will occupy us in greater detail in the second half of this book. Suffice it to say that the supposed persecution of early modern discoverers by the church on account of an ecclesiastical objection to the idea of the earth turning around the sun has been blown out of proportion by modern school education. The supposed "war" between religion and science too will occupy us again. Many a modern Indian astronomer peers through his modern telescope, observes lunar or solar eclipses, then descends into the holy river Ganges for his ablutions, and he is not disturbed by any contradiction. Nikita Khrushchev, while premier of the Soviet Union (1958–1964), is reported to have asked the first Russian astronauts upon their return from outer space whether they had seen any signs of God. Krushchev's particular mismatching of religion and a "scientific" outlook is symptomatic of a self-satisfied ignorance that reaches well beyond the former Soviet Union. One must learn to think carefully and choose words correctly in order to raise a significant question about religion.

Supernatural is another word that is not helpful in discussing religion. It has been used, of course, and sometimes properly to refer to matters that could not be grouped among "natural" phenomena. Our common cultural orientation, however, has come to regard "nature" as the wide realm that our reason can analyze and explain. To call something "supernatural" does not say more than that it goes beyond the realm of our reason. The dreams and experiences of North American Indian medicine men are not in the area of what our reason normally deals with. Saying that, however, adds nothing to our understanding. That which our reason normally deals with is essentially what we are *conditioned* to regard as open to our investigation. The word *supernatural* easily comes to imply "not real" or "illusory." It has shades of the improper sense of *faith* or *beliefs,* suggesting a list of irrational ideas held by a community to which the speaker does not belong. Not even by implication can we label groups of human beings in that way if we intend to follow a proper method in the inquiry into religious phenomena. In all traditions the distinction between sane and insane is made. The question of anyone's religious orientation has little to do with that, for human beings symbolize, as we know, and their sanity as human beings would be questionable only if they did not.

The term *ideology* is sometimes found in discussions about religion and religions. This term—though rather recent in our vocabulary, first occurring in the eighteenth century—has had interesting shifts in meaning. Initially referring to what the word itself suggests, "the science of ideas," it soon came to refer to any "ideal or abstract theorizing."[15] This is what Karl Marx picked up. He, virtually all his followers, and many others as well, who held that only material, especially economic, reality is what matters, gave it a certain derogatory meaning. The term came to mean primarily "a questionable set of ideas." It ended up referring to any more or less coherent set of ideas governing social and political action. This means that somehow an ideology functions as a convenient label or cover-up for group interests. And predictably, it is always people outside the group who refer to the group's "ideology." In whichever sense the term is used, when it is used to indicate what governs a religious tradition, the label *ideology* is premature. It obviously ignores any notion of "salvation" as worthy of investigation. (In my opinion we would do well to remember G. van der Leeuw's wisdom that in some way each and every religion is a religion of salvation.) The idea that "religious symbolizing" might constitute a distinct source of creativity is dismissed when one identifies a religion as "an ideology." I suggest we shun the term until and unless we specifically need it for what religious documents tell us.

THE RIGHT USE OF WORDS: THE PROBLEM OF FEELINGS

> The principal fruit of prayer is not warmth and sweetness,
> but fear of God and contrition.
>   —Theophan the Recluse (1815–94)[16]

It is not possible to avoid saying something about the fashion of psychologizing. In my view, what has done a great deal of damage to the understanding of religious phenomena and many other ordinary human things is the vocabulary generally known as "psychobabble." This is an unintended but immediate spin-off of psychology, a discipline that has generated a number of problems over the past decades.

In modern institutions of higher education, nothing has done more harm than popular psychologizing. It has taken the place left empty by diminished interest in serious inquiries into epistemology, the question of what it really means to know. Declining interest in the study of history and philosophy, and properly prepared study of language and literature, the general lack of interest in the history of science among scientists — all of these problems together created a hole that demanded to be filled. Even though some serious scholars addressed themselves to the problem, people experienced a vacuum, and many college students perceived that vacuum as an individual emptiness. It was not so much a definable problem as a felt lack of something. Popular psychology was not so much applied on purpose by anyone in particular as it flowed into the hole by force of gravity. But had it been possible to introduce psychobabble intentionally as an anti-intellectual weapon, it could not have been more effective in bringing about the general decline in serious discussion. It seems to have spearheaded a movement of intellectual decay.

The result of this development stares us in the face when we open magazines, read books, watch television. We have families that are dysfunctional, we no longer have friendship but bonding, we have the activity known as "parenting," we have plenty of "role models," and we have prison inmates who speak about "peer pressure" that made them transgress the law. All over the place, we have vague and sloppy language that substitutes for plain speech, and we are bombarded with statistics that appear to suggest something or other but have no meaningful knowledge to convey. We get so used to this way of communicating that we begin to imagine that the world we "made up" in this manner is real. A critical question is raised, and the questioner is asked if he "has a problem" with something. It is not easy to focus on and analyze a real problem in this atmosphere. We have allowed this fog to roll over us. It blankets us with a soft psycho-diagnosing of all our questionings and relieves us of responsibility. And yet we need nothing so much as a mature conscience and a full-grown sense of responsibility.

The characteristic feature of psychobabble is the presumption that anything anyone feels is worthy of attention simply by virtue of the fact that he or she feels it. That is simply untrue. This rise of cheap psychologizing betrays a lack of academic rigor. What we are dealing with is an attitude that poisons or at least perverts the study of human beings. In the study of religion and religions especially, it damages serious inquiry. We can under-

stand how it came about historically. In the first place, our Western, industrial world has produced a loss of community- and family-tied traditions
to the point where the lone individual has very little in the way of an
unapologetic alliance to a religious heritage by which to orient himself or
herself. In the United States, the history of pietism and individual conversion, experience engrained in American church history, is also a weighty
factor in the process. Finally, the introduction of European psychoanalytic
theories since the end of the Second World War amounted to a tidal wave
of explanations—some quite serious, many less so—in literature, in art,
and in the clinic.[17]

Intellectually, it should be clear that no single discipline, including psychology itself as a discipline of inquiry, can take the place of ontology or
metaphysics. For some particulars in this matter, we shall have to wait for
the second part of this book. For the moment, it will be enough to say that
no question arising in the study of religion and religions can be answered
by a statement beginning with the words "I feel . . . ," and we should be
suspicious about treatises on religion that avoid the term *religion* itself.

We owe a valuable collection of Hawaiian religious documents to His
Hawaiian Majesty, King David Kalakaua, who lived from 1836 to 1890—
the worst period of disruption of traditional Hawaiian life under the onslaught of missionizing and culture-bringing invaders. A new edition of this
work was brought out in 1972.[18] It was adorned with a new preface. One
blushes reading that preface. A word that is strikingly missing in it is *religion*. The writer of the preface is a man of our age with its ever-present
background music of soft psychologizing. He does not speak of "religion"
but of the "ways and beliefs" of Hawaii.[19] These words sound better; they are
individual feel-good matters, matters personally chosen. The writer shows
he is educated by stating vacuously: "We now know that the dignity of a
people rests largely in respect for their culture and the activities in which
that culture is expressed."[20]

The soft psychologizing we have become habituated to makes us forget
that religion is not merely the assembly of customs in which each individual preserves his self-esteem. It is the ground on which people live, and
on which men and women can be forced to sell themselves or die when the
steamroller of a different, militant religiosity cannot be turned back. The
rape of Hawaii and its traditions needs far more than mere eyewash from a
student who claims an interest in religion and religion's role in human
lives. Subjects such as these need honesty; they demand it and do not ask
to be covered by soft and vacuous terms that may be more pleasing to us.

Next to remembering that religion is a matter of salvation—and that implies death and life, despair and renewal—we had better keep in mind that behind such peaceable and more fashionable expressions as the "dignity" of people and human "respect for culture" unspeakable miseries and horrors are hiding. They include the miseries and horrors our great Western civilizations have brought about in many regions of the world, especially in regions whose inhabitants were first called "savages" or "primitives." Designating their splendid characteristics today with our own new and softer terms that seem more pleasant to us will not set things right. It is sentimental hogwash. Our object of study is too important for us to indulge in uncritical and cheap shortcuts.

NOTES

1. The notion of "religion" is thoroughly discussed by Professor Wilfred Cantwell Smith in *The Meaning and End of Religion* (New York: Macmillan, 1962). Of special significance is the contrast he formulates between the "cumulative traditions" (his term) and the transcendent reality in which each religion finds itself. See especially Chapter 6, "The Cumulative Tradition" (pp. 154–69).

2. Cicero, *De legibus* I, 5; *De oratore* II, 55.

3. See Susanne K. Langer, *Symbolism in a New Key,* 3rd ed. (Cambridge: Harvard University Press, 1974), pp. 37–38.

4. R. Pettazzoni, ed., *Miti e leggende,* 4 vols. (1948–63; reprint, New York: Arno Press, 1978), vol. 1, part 1 (Africa), selections 3, 6, 44, part 2 (Australia), selections 17, 29; vol. 3 (North America), selections 25, 88, 228; and many more. Joseph Campbell, ed., *Man and Time. Papers from the Eranos Yearbooks* (New York: Pantheon, 1957), *passim.* Marija Gimbutas, *The Gods and Goddesses of Old Europe* (Berkeley: University of California Press, 1974), pp. 91, 152, 169–71. See also Stith Thompson, *Motif-Index of Folk-Literature,* 6 vols., rev. and enlarged ed. (Bloomington: Indiana University Press, n.d.); see for precise references to "Moon" pp. 518–19 of the index vol. (vol. 6).

5. Ananda K. Coomaraswamy, "The Nature of Buddhist Art," in Roger Lipsey, ed., *Coomaraswamy,* vol. 1, *Selected Papers* (Princeton: Princeton University Press, 1977), p. 174.

6. The New English Bible translation.

7. *Bereshith Rabbah,* chap. 3, trans. by M. H. Harris, in *Hebraic Literature* (New York: Tudor Publishing, 1939), pp. 242–43.

8. Walter Lowrie, ed. and trans., Søren Kierkegaard, *Attack upon "Christendom,"* 1854–1855 (Princeton: Princeton University Press, 1968), pp. 105–6.

9. Paul Reps, ed., *Zen Flesh, Zen Bones: A Collection of Zen and Pre-Zen Writings* (Garden City, N.Y.: Doubleday, 1961), p. 5.

10. Ibid., p. 18.

11. For the text of the story, see Belcampo, *Rozen op de rails* (Amsterdam: Querido, 1979), pp. 31–40.

12. From Günter Grass, *In the Egg and Other Poems*, trans. Michael Hamburger and Christopher Middleton (New York: Harvest, 1977), pp. 36–39.

13. José Ortega y Gasset, "The Difficulty of Reading," *Diogenes* 28 (Winter 1959), pp. 1–2.

14. It is interesting that the term *worldview* was not listed in standard English dictionaries until recently.

15. Compare the more elaborate entry "Ideology" in the *Oxford Universal Dictionary*.

16. Timothy Ware, ed., *The Art of Prayer. An Orthodox Anthology* (London and Boston: Faber and Faber, 1966), p. 131.

17. A detailed book on problems of psychology and religious experience is W.W. Meister, *Psychoanalysis and Religious Experience* (New Haven: Yale University Press, 1984).

18. His Hawaiian Majesty Kalakaua, *The Legends and Myths of Hawaii. The Fables and Folk-Lore of a Strange People,* with an introduction to the new edition by Terence Barrow (Rutland, Vt.: Charles Tuttle, 1972).

19. In Kalakaua, p. 5.

20. In Kalakaua, p. 3.

The Ordinariness
of Religion

RELIGION IS EVERYWHERE

Only religions, in the plural, are particular; they provide us with evidence. Granted that we always recognize religion by its symbolization, and do not mistake it for anything else, *religion,* in the singular, remains an abstraction—one that we can use only if we keep in mind that we rely on the evidence that the *many* religions provide.

We can say that no human traditions have ever been found that are devoid of religion. We know of prehistoric burial sites, and whoever says "burial sites" cannot help but realize this means "religion." The alternative of attributing to our prehistoric forebears a sense of hygiene that led them to the custom of burying the dead is unreasonable, considering the very recent discovery of bacteria and communicable diseases. Moreover, the collective evidence of *enormous* efforts and very special markers could not possibly be explained in terms of our present-day tidiness. In many instances, heavy boulders were transported to form a proper room for the dead. Often we find that ochre was used; ochre is a reddish substance that can be made from natural material—iron oxide, which occurs naturally in some places in the earth—but could not have created itself. When ochre has been used on the east side of a grave, one does not need to speculate in order to make an association with the direction of sunrise, and to say "religious symbolism" even if no words have come down to us to answer all the questions we

46

would like to raise. We move from prehistory into history with the Egyptians (who made strides in such matters as medical surgery—for which we are at once ready with our modern eulogies). Here our written documents begin, as they do in ancient Mesopotamia, and they multiply our data concerning religion and religions. Beyond that, every schoolchild knows of ancient Egypt's amazing architecture, the most famous of burial monuments: the pyramids. Clearly, even though most details and changes are obscure to us, the religious symbolism of prehistory lived on in the attention paid to questions of life and death.

One particular instance in prehistory that is illustrative for us with respect to the permanence and universality of religion concerns a gravesite in the environs of what prehistorians call "Peking man" (*Homo pekinensis*). Some 475,000 years ago, people—to be precise, hominids of the species Homo erectus—lived in what we know as China. Their fossil remains were found (the first in 1927) in a cave at Chou-k'ou-tien near Peking (Beijing). One interesting grave shows the burial site of three people, a man, and two women, one on each side of him. These contents of the grave are interesting in themselves. Paleo-anthropological analysis has suggested that the three individuals are prototypes (or mixtures) of different "racial types" in Asia and perhaps also of European man. Whether they lived in the area before the origin of the other "races" and gave rise to them, or were the result of intermarriage of already existing groups, their remains witness to a unity of human existence. Ochre was applied to the burial site toward the east. What does that mean in detail? We wish we knew—but we need have absolutely no problem in saying, "Religion!"[1]

Since antiquity, thinkers and travelers have speculated about the origin of religion, and they have shown a certain eagerness to discover people without it but have had no convincing success. There is no convincing evidence of people who lack religion. Herodotus spoke of the Pelasgians as original inhabitants of Greece who received religion from the Egyptians. Early in the nineteenth century, romantics played with the idea that the origin of all religion lay in India. They liked to imagine that missionary-like emissaries had brought religion to the early inhabitants of Greece, who, supposedly, had not known religion. Not too long ago, an attempt to establish evidence of a prereligious human state arose with the discovery of a certain tribe in the Philippines. Supposedly, this tribe was untouched by outsiders, had a natural gentility, and was not in need of "religion."[2] Each presentation of evidence, however, turned out to be a misinterpretation or a hoax.

THREE MODES OF RELIGIOUS EXPRESSION

We owe the best articulation of an obvious yet very significant fact to the French sociologist Émile Durkheim (1858–1917). He observed that generally, all things are classified into two categories commonly designated by two terms "which are translated well enough by the words profane and sacred."[3] We have already stated that what any religious symbolization refers to is a "transcendent referent." Of course, neither the word *transcendent* nor the word *sacred* should tempt us to imagine that all traditions speak about metaphysics or theology. Indeed, the notion of "sacredness" and "the holy" has a heaviness that may not even be applicable to some traditions.

When we speak of religion in the singular, and hence in a more abstract way than any particular religion would express itself, we obviously speak about the universal human habit of symbolic expression. Within this general symbolizing we can distinguish three distinct forms of expression. In the large compilation of evidence we have throughout history, religion is recognizable by its expression in *places,* in *acts,* and in *words.* In varying proportions, these three modes show themselves in every religious tradition we know of. As a rule an emphasis on one of the three modes is evident in each tradition and enables us to get closer to the heart of the tradition. It is not that we arrive at the "essence" of religion by distinguishing these three modes of expression; but it helps our understanding, it helps us not to overindulge in abstract theorizing, and it helps us to see the first clear differences in the world's religions.

The obvious and simple distinction of three modes of expression has nothing to do with the many ready-made notions that are offered as typifying religions: "God" or "faith" or "doctrine" or any other certainty that by its nature is locked into a particular historical tradition and is not universally characteristic of religion. Those who have never asked a serious question concerning religions are accustomed to calling a religion "monotheistic" or "polytheistic" and imagining that those labels tell us something important. Such concepts seem to "settle" the argument as to the nature of a religion, and they are freely used by many well-educated persons as if they actually meant something.[4] All such characterizations are of little or no significance with respect to what religions actually say and to what really orients people in any religion. What religions say and what their practitioners experience, however, does lend itself to the scheme of the same three general modes of symbolization. It will become increasingly clear that the obvious distinction of these three expressions is of extra-ordinary importance in preventing us from jumping to premature judg-ments about our materials. Let us begin with a brief description of each.[5]

Places.   Symbolisms of place abound. Many temples, and all temples in ancient Egypt, are referred to as "the navel of the world." It is an eloquent way of pointing to the place of birth, of origin—the nuclear origin of all reality. Such places are sacred, unlike other (profane) places.

In a time when most men still wore hats, every traditional Catholic used to lift, or at least tip, his hat when passing a church. Why? Each church in the tradition of Roman Catholicism is the dwelling place of the Lord. Jesus Christ's body—in the form of the sacred host distributed in the celebration of Holy Communion (the Eucharist)—is present at or near the altar. Hence, God himself is there. Even the most ardent Protes-tant was never expected to lift his hat passing his church. And why not? Because in good Protestant tradition, since the Reformation movement of Luther, Calvin, and Zwingli, the bread and the wine, being the body and blood of Jesus Christ, are not sacred in their continuous presence; only the living presence of the congregation celebrating in community with the Lord is truly sacred. The Episcopal Church, the American arm of the worldwide Anglican Church, is clearly part of the Protestant tradition in this by seeing to it that after the Communion celebration every bit of the elements left over is consumed. They cannot be preserved. At the next celebration, the act of consecration must be performed anew. In the real sense of the word, the church is not the "House of the Lord" in between the celebrations.

Each Hindu temple is a sacred place, for it is the palace of the residing god or goddess.[6] The priests bathe, dress, and feed the deity and render all the services needed, beginning with the morning bath of the image. Each temple, whether of Viṣṇu, Śiva, the Great Goddess (Devī), or any "minor" god or goddess ("minor" must be placed in quotes, for no divinity is really ever minor), is even more typically a sacred place than any church in Christianity. A Hindu temple is not by its nature or design a gathering place of a congregation. Devotees come to "have darśan," which means to "have a view" or see the divine presence, and to pay their respect and pre-sent a gift.

"Do Hindus really believe that God is present there in the image of Viṣṇu?" Questions like that often come up in our midst. And non-Hindus expect a yes or no answer. Neither one is forthcoming. In the first place, "believing" that all of God is physically present is something unimaginable for a serious Hindu. (Keep in mind also that no Christian chewing and swallowing the host and the wine at the Eucharist is asked to taste flesh and blood.) Hinduism, especially in its treatises on Hindu art, has developed subtle reasonings on the subject that we call "symbolism." Thus, Viṣṇu is transcendent and yet forms a totality with his icon.

Islam has its most sacred site at the Kaʻbah, the "cube," a stone that stands in the center of the Grand Mosque of Mecca. This stone was sacred long before the establishment of Islam, and no Muslim claims that he worships it; but the stone marks the sanctuary consecrated to God. Every Muslim tries if possible to go on a pilgrimage (the hajj) to Mecca at least once in his life, and this particular place is the climactic destination of the pilgrimage.[7] It is the center of God's power as well as of prayer, radiating in all directions over the entire earth.

Christianity is of course familiar with pilgrimages, and Christians know what a sacred place is — even if in many cases their church is sacred only part of the time. Do such matters show any similarity to ways in which the self-styled "secular" among us see the world *we* call "reality"? Before we deny it, we would do well to consider a place in Washington, D. C. I am thinking of the steps of the Supreme Court building. It is the place where a great demonstration led by Martin Luther King, Jr., converged, and where he addressed the thousands gathered. At many other occasions too, great numbers of people have felt themselves drawn to the same place, as if by magic.

Literature
Diana L. Eck, *Banaras, City of Light* (Princeton: Princeton University Press, 1982); Mircea Eliade, *The Sacred and the Profane* (New York: Harcourt, 1959; many reprints), chap. 1, "Sacred Space and Making the World Sacred," pp. 19–65.

Rituals.   Those who were surprised at the objective difference we have just discussed between Catholic and Protestant churches will perhaps be even more surprised by religious expressions in actions. Yet things that are *done* can express what is central in a religion.

The religious tradition in early India that we call by the names Vedism and Brahmanism is probably the most typical example of a religion that is mainly ritual. Lasting sacred places had no role, or no role of significance. Instead, ritual sacrificial ceremonies were central. A man who was quali-

fied (and important or wealthy enough) to perform a great religious ceremony could proceed to do so. His actions themselves amounted to a participation in what was handed down as "sacredness." This Brahmanic sacrificer could be a local chieftain. He could not be a bachelor; only a married
man was entitled to become a *yajamāna* (a sacrificer), and his wife had an
important role to play. He would need to request the approval of a royal
ruler for the use of a piece of land on which to perform the sacrificial ceremonies, raising the request ceremonially and receiving the prescribed, cere-
monial answer. At the beginning of the ritual, the *yajamāna* would be initiated, for the transaction with gods required him first to be purified, and
transformed from an ordinary "profane" human being into a divine one.
(Conversely, at the end of the sacrifice—days, weeks, or months later,
depending on the type of ceremony—he would be handed back with
equal ritual to his ordinary state.) At the sacrifices proper, the gods were
invited and took the seats prepared for them. The fire was the mediator-
god (Agni), who conducted the sacrificial offering to the world of the gods.
If the particular rite called for the gift of the sacrificial drink called *soma,*
the priestly chants referred to Vayu, the god of the "middle-region," the air,
the "first drinker of the *soma*." As the gift made its way toward heaven,
Indra, the king of the gods, was invoked as recipient. All in all, the "sacred"
was not so much something located somewhere in a thing or place, as it
was an experience within what was done.

The Aztec of ancient Mexico present the prime example of massive
human sacrificial procedures. Theirs was a "state cult," yet a cult so bloody,
so breathtaking for all who merely watched the events, as to touch even
modern people who learn about it. When we read the descriptions of
hearts being ripped out of bodies, we are baffled. Even those who merely
watched these procedures were in some sense participating. "According to
Aztec religious theory, blood had to be spilled to make the cosmos continue to exist," one scholar writes.[8] Yet the application of a "theory" here
raises more questions than it answers. Are we asked to think that priests
were trained to do what they did in order to make sure the sun would rise
or the rainy season happen on time? Were they utilitarians? All we can see
is that here acts were undeniably the central vehicle of the "dark hole" of
religion that since Durkheim we call "sacredness."

With the writings of Plato, we may feel more comfortable. Not only did
Plato write well (much better than most of his professorial interpreters),
but he is always reflective, and hence far removed from sacrificial blood-
thirstiness. And yet, in some significant passages, Plato explains certain

ideas and acts with reference to sacrifice. The subject of love is discussed at length in the *Symposium* and the *Phaedo*. As in other dialogues, in the *Symposium* Socrates is the most important speaker. And close to the end of the discussion, he recounts what many years earlier he learned from a woman, Diotima by name. As to love, Socrates says, "in this subject she was skilled."[9] Love is of course a god, Eros (or also a goddess, Aphrodite), as we know from Greek mythology — and Diotima teaches Socrates that this great deity of beautiful things "was neither beautiful nor good." But, she goes on, "do not therefore suppose he must be ugly and bad, but something betwixt the two." Greeks know that all deities are perfectly good and beautiful, but this particular deity is characterized by a lack; something is missing. Hence, Love, Diotima explains, is neither a mortal nor an immortal. He is something "between a mortal and an immortal."

"And what is that, Diotima?"

"A great spirit, Socrates: for the whole of the spiritual is between the divine and mortal."

"Possessing what power?" I [Socrates] asked.

"Interpreting and transporting human things to the gods and divine things to men; entreaties and sacrifices from below, and ordinances and requitals from above: being midway between, it makes each to supplement the other, so that the whole is combined in one. Through it are conveyed all divination and priestcraft concerning sacrifice and ritual and incantations."

The illustrative use of sacrifice, of what is going on between people and gods, is no mere embellishment. The significance of active human involvement is the obvious point, and it may help us to understand one mode of "the religious" that appears remote to many of us.

Perhaps a principal reason why the idea of "the sacred in the form of ritual activity" is so difficult to conceive is the fact that our life is one of reading and watching screens. It is not a life of action but of words and concepts. We are able to say that the Supreme Court building in Washington, D. C., functions for us as a "sacred place." But we are at a loss when it comes to finding an example of truly significant action. This does not mean we have suddenly become the exception to the rule that all people are constitutionally religious beings; but for us the most viable channel of "the sacred" is elsewhere.

Literature
G. van der Leeuw, *Religion in Essence and Manifestation* (New York: Harper, 1963), vol. 1, pp. 339–92.

Words.   Collections of myths and studies of myth have multiplied for decades. This fact alone may tell us that the subject of myths is closer to us than sacred places and sacred actions. Let me begin by discussing the term *myth* itself. It is a Greek term, *muthos,* which can be translated as "word." All scholarly books that speak of myth contrast it to another Greek term, *logos,* which is also rendered as "word." The latter is well known to us, as it is visible in the names of such inquiries as "geology" or "theology." The word of *logos* is not the same as that of *myth*. *Logos* usually points to a concept, whereas *myth* normally refers to a *story* perhaps concerning gods and goddesses, and events that are beyond the events in our normal experience.[10]

When as historians of religions we say "myths," we do not mean what popular parlance has in mind. We do not mean "a pack of lies." We mean words, stories, expositions, formulas—all utterings that carry religious tradition from person to person, from generation to generation, and that are an integral part of every religion. If rightly understood in the religio-historical sense, myths do indeed occur everywhere, and not only in a dim past or in distant regions of the earth. Myths are not only things that "others" adhere to, but they are constitutive of human beings in their symbolizing capacity. This is how I think we can understand the American scholar Morris Jastrow, who wrote in 1901, in his introduction to the study of religion, "A myth-making faculty is the common possession of humanity."[11]

Myths, these special stories and usages of words, are crucial in the transmissions between this world and the other, this ordinary human place and the "ultimate" purpose of life. They also underlie all truly serious contacts between people, even if the people come from different religious traditions. This final point is tremendously important. All people belong to some tradition, even if their analytical ability wants to deny that. Hence, when something important is at stake, they fall back on what is *indubitably right* in their own orientation.

In general, we have no difficulty accepting the fact that certain places are sacred to certain people, and even under certain historical circumstances to ourselves. Likewise, we may have no great difficulty accepting the importance some traditions attach to certain things that should be done, and we may not even object to calling those things by the religious term *rituals*. In general, we can recognize that things present in places or cultically enacted can be channels of "the sacred." But words?

Even if we are not skeptics by conviction, in the "modern industrial West" we live in a civilization where we are used to the treacherousness of words. Lawyers, rabbis, and priests all find out in their training that the right use of words is difficult. All of us know that modern advertising techniques are able to pervert speech. Our experiences cause our difficulty in thinking of myths as purveying "real reality." Nevertheless, this term used by Eliade is quite useful at this point. In fact the world of myths in the true sense of the word is much closer to us than we think. The "real reality" of myths is not what we can readily define, but there is very much in human existence that is undefinable and whose reality we would never doubt. The "real reality" of myths is not characterized by lofty or solemn things, such as "eternity." It is no denial of our reason; it does not argue that there is an absolute lack of change in history as we experience it. It is true that, for instance, in the biblical texts God is often compared to a rock—precisely because a rock suggests unchangeability and eternity. But the image of everlasting protection, a shelter sturdier than any other refuge, should not be confused with a timeless law of physics. Myths (and other symbols likewise) change without loss in their dependability. A line in the Dutch national anthem (composed in the sixteenth century) is built on biblical imagery and says, "Thou, God, art my shield and my trust."

It is an interesting question whether human speech is at all possible without "overtones"—vibrations that are not reducible to mere information and are yet essential to speech. In order to live at all, we not only need the curious inflections and ambiguities of speech, but even more mystifying, we need an entire world whose existence we *assume* and to which all we say to each other refers and from which all we say to each other derives its significance. To present *that entire world* it is not necessary to sink into abstract reasonings. Myths are clearer and far more concrete. They provide the evidence that we are touching on the real situation we find ourselves in *qua* human beings.

Myth is not to be measured by comparison to the densely written pages of history, which are pages of war, written by the victors. Neither is it to be measured with the products of our glorious scientific and technical achievements. Myth leans toward the other side of our human knowledge— the side that is more often referred to as "wisdom." And this more-than-mere-rational need that comes with the human nature of religious symbolizing always contains humor. Humor is of course known among scientists, but it is not part of science. But while humor may not be known to all students of religion, it is part of religion.

If myths are expressive of *religion,* how can they be humorous? Actually, humor is not the senseless hilarity served up on television for tired and well-fed audiences. It is not to be found in the "practical joke" that is popular among us, whereby someone becomes the ridiculed victim. Humor does not necessarily make us burst with laughter, but humor is what produces "the smile that liberates." And it always has to do with a breaking out of the confinement of all-too-real facts. It leads not to an escape, but to an altogether new view of things. So many truly good jokes are about religion and religious things, and this is not by chance. We have glimpsed earlier that the rabbinical stories can display a humor that is irresistible. Real humor always understands the subject it is humorous about. It is serious. Insipid jokes are insipid because they lack such understanding.

The following really happened. A medical professor urged his students by all means to abstain from one thing: never tell a patient he is going to die. "If you tell a patient he's gonna die," the professor said, "that patient is gonna piss on your grave." The unexpected rough edge of this remark made the whole room laugh hard. The roughness is not the roughness of the language; it is the subject: the relation between life and death that cannot be sized up in a solid scientific way. The remark carries a subtlety that does not force itself on us. It is something subtle that is assumed and vibrates along in the string of words. It is the very nature of death surrounded on all sides by the painful ignorance in which even our most assured scientific knowledge resides. Our knowledge is set in its proper place. And seeing this clearly, though just for a moment, has a peculiar liberating effect.[12]

Each myth undergoes its own re-mythologizing. Traditions, whether written or oral, change. And even if the same text is handed down for a long time, its interpretation fluctuates. Each generation asks its own questions and answers them as well as it can. In our time, for example in the case of the biblical creation story, questions of a modern scientific nature are imposed on us, and we have to come to terms with them — and in their context we can indeed be led to see more clearly the point of the text.

Let us turn to that biblical text at the root of our great Western religions: the creation story at the very beginning of the Hebrew Bible (the Old Testament). For many years, I have asked college students in introductory courses to do a one-page assignment: First, write down a summary of Genesis 1:1–2,4, draw a line under that part, and then use the rest of the page to name the items in the story that are of importance not to you but to the narrator. No student ever objected. On the contrary, most thought the assignment too simple. After all, the biblical story is barely more than a page to read, and on top of that, most of the students thought they already knew it.

It is true that they did know, as does everyone, that the story narrates "the creation of the world," including the light, night and day, all "natural" elements we are familiar with, sky, earth, heavenly bodies, and all the vegetation and living creatures. But beyond these elements to which we collectively attribute significance, there was on the whole very little that they noticed in the brief account before their eyes. They rarely noticed truly important things that were not, however, important *to them*. Surprisingly few ever noticed the special importance given to the sabbath, the final day of the first week, except for the fact that then God rested — whereby they always assumed that he was fatigued (although the text says nothing of the sort). Creating the *week,* with a climax in the sabbath, at the very origin of the world had to be of special importance to the narrator. The narrator does not fail to tell us explicitly: that day was "made holy."

Three more striking features bypass almost all readers. One is the creation of light on the first day, whereas God makes the sun and moon, together with the other heavenly bodies, only on the fourth! The statement leaps from the page! When people are shown what they missed, they often react by making comparisons to the "Big Bang" theory and such. They are more comfortable when they can read the story as if it tried to teach us astronomy, or geology, or biology.

But then, certainly, the next two points should set us right. One line that everyone seems to skip is Genesis 1:30. The creation is complete, and God says, "All green plants I give for food to the wild animals." What is one to make of that if one insists on reading the story as if it offered itself as a competitor to the natural sciences? Surely the narrator wanted to startle us. Think also of the fact that the story was first told in the Near East, in a land that knew lions. It was common knowledge to the first listeners that lions did not eat grass.

And finally, there is the repeated declaration by God that whatever was just brought forth was "good," and in the end even "very good." The very recurrence of the statement makes clear that this "goodness" was significant to the narrator. Why is this point negligible to us? Only because we have difficulty listening. The goodness posited in the story is in flagrant contradiction to human experience. If nothing else, the nonvegetarian habits

of the lion militate against the declaration. Imagine for a moment a professor of astronomy telling you that the Big Bang (or perhaps the Steady State)
was a *good* thing, or a geologist calling this or the other rock formation
very good!

It is necessary to notice where texts say things different from what we
want them to say. The biblical creation story is definitely not a treatise on
astronomy or geology. Its emphatic positing of goodness implies something that is a very critical addition to all ordinary rational and empirical
dealings with the world. It means, philosophically, that the good has priority over the real, ethics over ontology (the branch of philosophy that
deals with the nature of being or reality) and scientific certainties. Thus the
creation story does not allow us to present the question of the good almost
as a peculiar "anomaly," and thus ignore it.

The story's concern with the goodness of creation is so clear as to make
it impossible—if we are attentive readers—to see the account as if it
described the factual, physical constitution of our world. What we have is
a myth that seems to tell rather of paradise. The image of wild animals eating green plants underlines the repeated statement "and God saw that it
was good." Nor does it follow that we have a fairy tale before us. Typically,
the fairy tale starts out, "Once upon a time . . ." And whatever unlikely
events occur, the time in which they unfold is always presented as the time
we know from our own experience. The beginning of the Book of Genesis
is a creation story of the world. Just like all origin stories, it begins with the
words "In the beginning . . ." This beginning is wholly unlike our experienced time. Many such beginnings, taking us to that unimaginable time-
before-time, can be found in any collection of myths. These beginnings,
these origins, possess an altogether different quality: "In the beginning
there was nothing here but mere appearance, nothing really existed . . . ;"
"In the beginning there was no sun, no moon, no stars. All was dark, and
everywhere there was only water"; "Of old, Heaven and Earth were not yet
separated."[13]

A question arose among ancient biblical commentators concerning the
creation of light on the first day and the sun and the moon's creation on
the fourth. They too interpreted this passage in the light of new questions
and concerns, and *re-mythologizing* is the best term to describe this interpretive activity. We should bear in mind that perhaps with authoritative
guidance and teachings as a given in the world, we can never do more
than "re-mythologize." The rabbinical text did not ignore the cardinal
issue of goodness.

On the first day of creation God produced ten things: the heavens and the earth, Tohu and Bohu [often rendered as something like "formlessness" and "void"], light and darkness, wind and water, the duration of the day and the duration of the night.

Though the heavens and the earth consist of entirely different elements, they were yet created as a unit, "like the pot and its cover." The heavens were fashioned of the light of God's garment, and the earth from the snow under the Divine Throne. Tohu is a green band which encompasses the whole world, and dispenses darkness, and Bohu consists of stones in the abyss, the producers of the waters. The light created at the very beginning is not the same as the light emitted by the sun, the moon, and the stars, which appeared only on the fourth day. The light of the first day was of a sort that would have enabled man to see the world at a glance from one end to the other. Anticipating the wickedness of the sinful generations of the deluge and the Tower of Babel, who were unworthy to enjoy the blessing of such light, God concealed it, but in the world to come it will appear to the pious in all its pristine glory.[14]

Myths are part of history. Hence their changes and reinterpretations should not surprise us. Impressions of an absence of change are generally deceptive. For instance, when an anthropologist does a year's fieldwork among a tribal community and writes a book on the myths of the such and such, he may leave the impression that that collection is unchanging. However, another anthropologist, visiting twenty years later, may well collect many other stories. The important thing to realize is that even if certain traditions insist on writing down their myths, these myths continue to change in the process of interpretation. When they do not, a tradition may seem to have become extinct, and even then, the life of myths does not completely vanish. Think of ancient Egypt, and the mountain of written materials it left behind, and think also of students who go on debating the meanings of those texts. Texts that functioned and summed up the most meaningful assertions in human life continue to shed light.

It cannot be repeated often enough that real humor is far subtler than most of the jokes we tell. Humor is a serious subject in the study of literature and art, and myths are also literature. Humor certainly has different forms in different traditions, precisely because different matters are regarded as most important, or even sacred. And it is accurate to state that everywhere real humor touches on what is most important. In our general study of the history of religions, four distinct types of humorous expression stand out. The first dims the contrast between two opposites whose difference is beyond dispute, and it occurs in most myths. Sometimes we are told that in the beginning of time heaven and earth were not yet separated from each other. One myth from Orissa (in India) begins: "Formerly the sky was very near the earth and everyone found it most troublesome."[15] A second way in which humor surfaces brings about an inverse effect; hence something happens that shocks our normal expectations concerning sequences of events. In a famous Hindu myth we are told that gods and demons together churn the milky ocean in order to bring about the world. What comes out before the goal is reached is a horrendous, world-destructive poison. One god, Śiva, drinks it. Since then, his throat has been blue — but the creation is completed. Another example of the same type of humor occurs in the writings of the church father Saint Augustine. One might call it a narrative in a nutshell when he calls the original sin from which the Savior freed the world *felix culpa,* "a felicitous guilt." After all, through the history of salvation in Jesus Christ it led to a happy ending. The third way is "subjective reservedness." It is the manner in which the literary expression of the narrative comes to terms with an inevitable clash, namely between the more-than-human content of the myth and the mere humanity of the narrator. How can any author, any narrator of a divine tale have part in what is told? How can they truly know it? Many myths of creation bypass subjective reservedness by plunging right into the matter, as it were, as does Genesis 1 with its opening statement "In the beginning God created . . ." Buddhist sūtras begin with a clear awareness that presenting the Buddha's teachings is a mystery, and they always say at the outset, "Thus I was told." Many a tribal myth opens with, "They say that . . . ," or "It is said that . . ." In all such cases the impossible becomes expressible. The fourth way is most easily recognizable for most of us today. It is "the grotesque." It is as common in great literature in general as it is in myth. One of my favorite examples occurs in a verse by Wallace Stevens:

The distance between the dark steeple
And cobble ten thousand and three
is more than a seven-foot inchworm
Could measure by moonlight in June.[16]

Measuring with unusual units is as grotesque as the moving of mountains and streams or the fantastic enumerations that occur in myths. Indeed, no myth is free from the grotesque, as we have seen for ourselves in the

Genesis account. And how else could it be? The events as narrated have nothing in common with the criteria we normally work with.

Literature
Jerry Palmer, *Taking Humor Seriously* (London and New York: Routledge, 1994).; Kees W. Bolle, *The Freedom of Man in Myth* (Nashville, Tenn.: Vanderbilt University Press, 1993), pp. 34–72. Mircea Eliade, *The Sacred and the Profane* (New York: Harcourt, 1959; many reprints), chap. 2, "Sacred Time and Myths," pp. 67–113; G. van der Leeuw, "Primordial Time and Final Time," in Joseph Campbell, ed., *Man and Time* (New York: Pantheon, 1957), pp. 324–50.

MYTHICAL ELEMENTS IN MODERN INDUSTRIAL SOCIETY

The Soviet Union was proud of its secularism. It was not as if the Soviet state persecuted members of the Christian church, or Muslims, or Buddhists within its borders. Part of Marxist, "scientific" study of history held that religion would cease to exist. Unpleasant as it may sound to some of us, the secularization of the Soviet Union was not all that different from the secularization processes in Europe and the United States. It just happened without anyone taking the blame or the credit for it. What is striking, however, and what Western reporters never failed to mention with some irony was the *ritual* performances of the first of May celebration, the great day of the workers in all forms of socialism. The conspicuous parades in Moscow had no parallel anywhere else. Was their symbolism not religious just because it was not related to Russia's great Orthodox tradition? We have emphasized the significance of "symbolizing" as the most typical of all human features often enough to make us hesitate to draw such a conclusion.

In this place we cannot analyze in detail another Soviet phenomenon with conspicuous symbolic features. It is the court proceedings in which "traitors" were condemned and usually executed. In many, if not most cases, the accused confessed. They had betrayed Communist lore.[17] *Lore* is a good term here, for that lore was a matter of proper exegesis of the authoritative scriptures, beginning with those of Karl Marx himself. (It is virtually impossible to speak about those matters without using terms with a religious ring to them, such as *lore, scriptures,* and *exegesis*.)

Is it still unacceptable to mention in the same context the trials in the United States under the guidance of Senator Joseph McCarthy, the militant anti-Communist crusader? Of course, McCarthy's campaigns were not identical to the Soviet Union's trials of "traitors." For one thing, the American political system allowed dissent from the "Commie-hunt" ideology, and many called McCarthy an irresponsible witch-hunter. Nevertheless, the zealous persecution of possible dissenters—people merely dissenting in political matters—points up the tendency in the United States as well as in the Soviet Union toward "absolutistic symbolization" that goes against all sense in a proper study of religion and history. It can nevertheless be viewed and interpreted in the history of religions, for without an adequate understanding of myths, rituals, and symbols, such episodes of our supposedly secularized history cannot be understood.

In a context that to many may not seem equally serious, we have in our self-conscious "secularized" world odd amalgams of science, technology, and religious symbolism. The case of flying saucers alone has received wide attention. In science fiction, in which the scientific element seems to be taken more seriously than the fictional side, we are almost invariably taken on trips with a transcendent goal and a life beyond the level on which we exist. Wherever we turn, it does indeed not seem possible for human beings to escape the religious realm.

Something in us rebels against the obvious: the fact that our own "civilized life" is permeated with myths. It is a common impulse to attribute myths to people other than ourselves.[18] Nevertheless, if any one of the three forms of religious expression is predominant in our case, it is precisely myth.

A couple of centuries of colonialism and imperialism have produced an overbearing verbal and conceptual understanding of the world so ingrained in us that overestimating ourselves in comparison with others has become second nature. The derogatory use of the term *myth*, although far from new, has become virtually the only use: *mere* myths, in contrast to the truth we imagine we possess. This habit has no foundation in reality. We too live in accordance with functioning myths.

It is not really difficult to see that myths always speak with authority. "In the beginning God made the heaven and the earth." In whatever translation we read that, we do not hear a topic announced that we are invited to discuss. The same is true for all myths the world over. This is a major difference between fairy tales or legends and myths (in addition to the stylistic introduction of the myth as reporting on a time before all time). The myth speaks authoritatively and does not conceive of contradiction. However, this does not mean that it simply tells us about undeniable facts that we can verify. The myth tells us authoritatively about the most cardinal realities underlying all there is. Interpretation is not excluded—as we have seen in the rabbinical treatment of the creation of the light—but rather assumed. And still, the original authority does not wane. This is how a living myth functions.

Our culture's myths—like all myths—deal with fundamental matters that are problematic at every point. We fight about them, we disagree, but we do not question their authority. When the smallest thing seems to impinge on freedom of the press, there is at once a storm of protest in our midst. If anyone were to ask, "*Why exactly* is that freedom so important, so basic, so holy?" we really have no answer—no matter how many words we might use. And when someone does make some sense on the subject, chances are that he or she falls back on undeniably religious texts that have no clear historical relationship to freedom of public information at all. Think for instance of "where the Spirit . . . is, there is freedom" (New Testament, 2 Corinthians 3:17), or "you were called to freedom, brethren" (New Testament, Galatians 5:13). Such "explanatory" references, however, would in fact be "remythologizings." One does not question the myth but only reaffirms it in elaborating on its authoritativeness. Things that truly function as myths seem to rest on earlier myths.

Regarding our myth of education: of course, every culture of the world hands down knowledge to its young; but our Western ideas of compulsory education and the right to education and the freedom of education are myths in their own right. They are extremely powerful, giving rise to enormous institutions and organizations. The validity of our myth of education is never questioned, even while we go on arguing about its implications. The right to education has been copied literally in the program of UNESCO (the United Nations Educational, Scientific, and Cultural Organization). It seems to mean that everyone should be entitled to learn how to read and write, and to learn a great many additional things, that professors should have the freedom to speak, students the freedom to discuss. Why? The ultimate answer, like the previous one, is almost impossible to present. For what exactly is this freedom? We attach a great deal of value to it. There is very, very much we can say for it. But what we can say, as in the previous case, rests on a myth that is difficult to reconstruct. Yet that does not matter. We are sure it is valid.

Questioning such functioning myths, like that of education and freedom of the press, would not be impossible but is deemed irrelevant. One might refer to other traditions, where knowledge and wisdom are handed down within the family group, the class of priests, or artisans, and which can be destroyed when a blanket insistence on universal education arrives from the West. One might assert the greatness of the Renaissance — for instance the time when Desiderius Erasmus and Thomas More carried on a correspondence with each other. They had to watch very carefully what they published, however, for freedom in that area did not exist. Yet such observations would not make a dent in the certainty of *our* myth.

Earlier, we spoke of the ongoing current discussions on the death penalty and abortion. On these matters opinions are painfully divided, but both sides clearly have their foundation in myths, even when those myths are only dimly perceived or poorly articulated. Another observation we can make about myths is to say that true, functioning myths always address real and serious problems.

The mythological involvement of our own age and culture especially illustrates that myths are not maps for a neatly organized, simple existence. Myths, some scholars have said, are "paradigmatic." A paradigm sets a standard, and people are guided by that standard; but literally conforming oneself to a myth is not really within reach. (This is how paradigms occur in grammar: for example, a verbal conjugation presents a perfect model, yet the language has its peculiarities that do not fit within it.) Even though virtually all civilized modern nations have abolished the death penalty, who would say that in some dreadful circumstances an exception could not ever be discussed?

Literature
The classic work on myths is Raffaele Pettazzoni, *Miti e leggende,* 4 vols., with many bibliographical references to publications in English (Torino: Unione Tipografico–Editrice Torinese, 1948, 1959, 1953, 1963); Barbara Sproul, *Primal Myths: Creating the World* (San Francisco: Harper, 1979); Mircea Eliade, *From Primitives to Zen* (New York: Harper, 1967); Charles Long, *Alpha: The Myths of Creation* (New York: Braziller, 1963); Alan Dundes, *Sacred Narrative: Readings in the Theory of Myth* (Berkeley: University of California Press, 1984).

RELIGION AND OUR PERSONAL WISHES

Let us turn to a most insidious problem of our age under the topic of religion. This problem is not the pietistic distortion (which demands that I must *feel* religion) nor the Freudian one (by which religion is not real but a mere *projection* mechanism). The most widely shared obstacle to understanding is the tenacity of a cheap romanticism: people (especially in well-to-do circles) are loath to depart from the dream of an enduring happiness. And if religion does not provide it, they profess to lose interest in religion.

Why should we imagine that religion must fulfill our desires? Something as obvious as this, that religion is not necessarily nice, ought to go without saying—if it were not for the peculiar habit in our modern age of requiring of religion, any religion, that it *be* nice in the way we think about niceness. At the very highest level, the West thinks that a religion should be "morally just." And consequently, a fairly common verdict is that a religion such as Christianity "has been around for almost two thousand years—and look at what a mess it has made of the world."

The same demand that religion be in accord with our wishes also occurs in elevated scholarly circles. Scholars may not feel tempted simply to pronounce a judgment on the basis of their own individual ideas of morality, but there are other precious opinions they are less willing to give up. The famous Albert Schweitzer is widely known and admired for his self-sacrificing humanitarian aid to people in Africa, in an area that at the time was still the Belgian Congo, where he served as a missionary and had set up a hospital; he was also a scholar of renown. One of his smaller writings is *Christianity and the Religions of the World,* in which he claims Christianity to be superior to all those other religions.[19] In a series of historical comparisons, his decisive argument involves Christian love (although he allows that the hatred of the World War in the Christian West amounted to a setback). Each and every religion fails to measure up when it comes to the question of the right attitude toward the neighbor which he himself derived from the New Testament. Hinduism had learned to do pretty well, yet in Schweitzer's judgment it still amounted to no more than a "religiosity of compromise," as it could not cut itself loose from its surroundings and its own historical background.[20] Schweitzer's position was not an individual peculiarity. He held it in common with many others early in the twentieth century. But the case of Schweitzer and his contemporaries is far from unique. Scholars in our own time have often failed to overcome comparable temptations, given the fashions and mood of their time.

Albert Schweitzer looked at Hinduism and other religions, and saw what for him and his circle was fashionable to see. More recent decades have witnessed a flurry of theories about human beings, literature, art, society, politics, and religion. It has become fashionable among us to pay little or no attention to the data of religions and instead to derive explanations of religion from anywhere among the flurry of theories themselves. Many a fashionable theory today offers itself as a panacea for our difficulties in interpreting any tradition, whatever its documents. Yet such a procedure is truly indecent. The first rule of method is that you should listen to the people whose religion you try to comprehend.

Literature
In spite of the critique implied in this section, a number of authors who explain religion fully (or think they do) on their own terms are fascinating. The most fascinating, indeed, classical writer is Sigmund Freud, particularly in his *Civilization and Its Discontents* (New York: Norton, 1962), *Totem and Tabu,* and *Moses and Monotheism* (New York: Vintage, 1955). Among recent authors, see Catherine Bell, *Ritual Theory, Ritual Practice* (New York: Oxford University Press, 1992); René Girard, *Violence and the Sacred* (Baltimore, Md.: Johns Hopkins University Press, 1977). Discussions are collected in Thomas A. Idinopulos and Edward A. Yonan, eds., *Religion and Reductionism: Essays on Eliade, Segal, and the Challenge of the Social Sciences for the Study of Religion* (Leiden: Brill, 1994).

SOCIAL AND ETHICAL IMPACT

Religious traditions exert influence on the structures of society. One does not need to think only of the influence that some people exert forcefully on a community. We remember that religion is rarely defined by a consciously confessed "faith," and even if it is—as in Christianity and Islam—the religious impact on society is still primarily a natural outgrowth rather than a willful, forceful reshaping by individuals or groups. Almsgiving has been a regular feature of the religions of India since the most ancient days. Help to those in need, *diakonia,* has been part of the Christian church from its beginning; it continued the customs of Israel and Judaism. Frequently, demonstration of anger is frowned upon in India, no doubt as a result of a very long tradition in which meditation techniques analyzed anger as the worst obstacle to perfect freedom. By contrast, all of us in the West are familiar with such a thing as "righteous anger." In a presidential debate in 1988, George Bush Sr. confronted the Democratic candidate, Michael Dukakis, the governor of Massachusetts. Dukakis, an opponent of the death penalty, did his own campaign a great deal of harm by not showing the anger the nation expected from him when asked to imagine what his course of action would be if his own wife were raped. The occasion when Jesus Christ chased the money changers out of the temple has an appeal to all parties in the West. If nothing else, it does seem to show the validity of righteous anger.[21]

The symbolic forms of religion have a priority that radiates into social attitudes. A religious expressiveness in ritual and myth can set a pattern that is visible in minute social habits and in mere gestures. Almost invariably, Westerners who extend a hand to accept something make a grasping motion with hand and fingers; but observe how, for instance, people from Thailand or Indonesia stretch out a hand more gracefully, not grasping but reaching out toward the object offered to them, as if in reverence. A devout Episcopalian may gracefully accept the Communion Host in his hands, right hand crossed over the left, and yet perhaps spend the rest of his week making grabbing gestures. He may have become used to "the separation of church and state." Anyone who has been present at a Buddhist devotional meeting, or attended a Balinese dance, may be struck by seeing the "prototype" of ordinary gestures that are made in worldly contacts in those cultures. One cannot fail to notice a certain cause-and-effect relation between a religious tradition and the forms observed in society.

We should not forget that our very term *society* is an abstraction of fairly recent vintage. It is barely two centuries old. (The underlying Latin word *societas* is not abstract; it means "companionship.") We have begun to imagine only yesterday that "society" is an *object* we can study, and that in some manner we can *see* it. Of course, that is not true. We can observe many things, we can compile statistics, we can talk about "prestige" and "roles" and "income levels" and make a lot of diagrams, yet "society" is as unempirical as "psyche" all the same.

Before we developed the term *society,* there were much more concrete entities and names for things that really counted for communities of people. In the Indo-European languages, we have in most cases clear evidence of three groups that together make up a communal, humanly livable life. In European medieval history "the three estates" are well known: the nobility, the clergy, and "the third estate." This corresponds to what is spelled out in detail in Sanskrit in ancient India. There the three classes, the *kṣatriya, brāhmaṇa,* and *vaiśya,* are surrounded by an elaborate mythology that sees the three as expressive of three forces (defense, spiritual guidance, and prosperity) which must be in harmony in human existence. The

totality of human existence rests on the divine structure of military protection, on spiritual purposefulness, and of course on the large group that
produces the wealth on which the whole can thrive. The mythology speaks
about conflicts among the three. Nevertheless, the conflicts in the myths
seem important primarily in view of the peace that is eventually reached.
Here we are still far away from the considerably more abstract formulations of Karl Marx regarding the doctrine of class struggle (thereby usher-
ing in something that could be called a new mythology).

Most of us in the West have become used to the idea of the equality of all
people. We like to think of that as "rational" and "natural." But ideas with
such far-reaching consequences usually come about along more various
routes and detours. No doubt, the intellectual revolutions of the seventeenth-
and eighteenth-century rationalists had everything to do with the notion
of equality. Nevertheless, it is difficult, in fact impossible, to discard an
additional and more ancient root. It is the thoroughly biblical notion of
the justice of God ruling impartially over all. This notion Christianity, together with Islam, inherited from Judaism, and the source behind all three
is principally the religion of Israel.

The idea of "human equality" cannot really be said to be "natural." Not
only is there little or no evidence in nature of equality, but in addition,
when it comes to the religious traditions in the world, the vast majority of
these are hierarchical rather than egalitarian. In all instances, the hierarchy
is anchored in symbolism — as is also the notion of equality. After all,
equality among people is an idea, a very important idea, but one without
any evidence in "society." In human life, as expressed in our social and cultural habits, neither hierarchy nor equality offers itself as an object to the
natural sciences. No wonder, because religion is at the root of such concep-
tions. Religions themselves are not "natural." Indeed, they are *institutions*.

All people are ethically aware, yet what ethical awareness actually is
seems difficult to identify. On the face of the earth as a whole, the influence
of one ancient religion has been remarkable. It is Zoroastrianism, which
has its origins in the reform movement of one great man, Zoroaster, the
Greek form given to his own original Iranian name, Zarathustra. Ancient
Iran had a religious tradition not very different from that of early Vedic
religion in India. The languages of both were very close. A major element
in the reform Zarathustra brought about was the opposition between an
ultimate good and an ultimate evil force. This religion was part of Iranian
civilization for long periods of time — including the expansion of the great

Persian (i.e., Iranian) empire under the dynasty of Cyrus and Darius. The ancient Greek historian Herodotus knew much about the Persians and about Zoroaster, and his name was not forgotten in the West, even long before the texts of Zoroastrianism were studied. It is certain that some of the best-known ideas in the world of Judaism, Christianity, and Islam owe their origin, certainly a "trigger," to Zoroastrianism. One scholar lists quite explicitly these terms: "Apocalypse, Kingdom of God, Last Judgment, Resurrection, Man and Son of Man, Prince of this World, or Prince of Darkness, and Saviour."[22] All these notions owe their force to the opposition between Good and Evil. The concern with justice remains thoroughly biblical, both in the Old and New Testaments; it remains thoroughly Qur'anic, and hence remains an inalienable part of Islam. The experience of the opposition between just and unjust is felt strongly and in the special way it is in particular civilizations because at the root there is a specific, religious, symbolically expressed reality.

In our self-conscious (or self-delusional) "secularity," we should not forget that the roots that nourish us remain symbolic, religious. They retain their transcendental reality, while functioning in our thoughts and discussions, and last, but not least, in our eagerness to cast judgments in politics, history, the court system, literature, art, and everything else. In the final analysis, our ethical behavior will depend on a proper understanding of our religious heritage.

Literature
Max Weber, *The Sociology of Religion* (Boston: Beacon Press, 1963); Joachim Wach, *Sociology of Religion* (London: Kegan Paul, Trubner, 1947); Georges Dumézil, *Les dieux des Indo-Européens* (Paris: Presse Universitaires, 1952); C. Scott Littleton, *The New Comparative Mythology: An Anthropological Assessment of the Theories of George Dumézil,* 3rd ed. (Berkeley: University of California Press, 1982); Karl Marx and Friedrich Engels, *On Religion,* introd. Reinhold Niebuhr (New York: Schocken, 1964); Louis Dumont, *Homo Hierarchicus: The Caste System and Its Implications* (Chicago: University of Chicago Press, 1970); Louis Dumont, *From Mandeville to Marx: The Genesis and Triumph of Economic Ideology* (Chicago: University of Chicago Press, 1977) (the French original of this work is called *Homo aequalis,* published in Paris by Gallimard, 1977); James Melvin Washington, ed., *A Testament of Hope: The Essential Writings of Martin Luther King, Jr.* (San Francisco: Harper, 1986); Mary Boyce, *Zoroastrians: Their Religious Beliefs and Practices* (London: Routledge, 1987).

POLITICAL IMPACT

In 1958 the philosopher Henry Duméry reintroduced the old word *institution* in a startlingly useful manner. He described the major features of Christianity to what is often referred to as "the Christian world" but which has actually forgotten what Christianity is all about. Thus he came to write his *Phenomenology and Religion: Structures of the Christian Institution.*[23]

We are of course familiar with "the church" as "an institution," but what we need to realize is that as a religious tradition Christianity encompasses far more than some sort of "organization" of which one may choose or refuse to be a member. Our religious tradition is not a chance circumstance from which we can extricate ourselves if we feel like it. In fact, we cannot speak, or act, or make our judgments on possessions, rights, or anything else around us without being affected by the religious tradition within which all those things exist. Do only boys, growing up, think of "free love"? Probably more boys than girls. But if one is young and dreams of free love, none of the adult realities of life have become very clear yet. Adult reality includes having children grow up, and having children occasionally fight about such things as inheritance laws. Such details take you right back to square one, this time without dreaming. You face that strange thing "reality" in which assumptions made in social life show their proportions. There are certain restrictions, prohibitions, authorities.

In the midst of innumerable issues of this sort, Duméry's use of "institution" takes on its significance. It corrects the mistake we commonly make, to quite an extent as a result of the increased popularity of the natural sciences. The authority accorded to the natural sciences has made it seem "natural" to look upon all human beings as in principle the same. That in some way this is indeed the case is undeniable. An appendicitis attack affects people in more or less the same way and the surgery has little variation. The problem is that human beings are never only "natural" creatures. They live in societies, hence observe certain forms; they live in economic systems, hence have certain assumptions about value and price; they govern themselves and are governed, hence experience justice and injustice; they undergo history in their way and remember it accordingly; and they speak their own languages. What holds human existence together and what brings about the formulation of the major conflicts always take us back to *religion*. A religion is indeed never given with nature; this is true not only for the religions that have a founder (such as Islam, Christianity, Judaism, Buddhism, Jainism), but also for those that do not (such as Hinduism, Taoism, and the many traditional or tribal religious traditions). Across the board, a religion can only be understood as an *institution;* it functions as the blueprint of the entire human edifice. Duméry urges us in our inquiries to hold together "the fact of language, the fact of the great collective myths, the fact of the arts and sciences and religions."[24] Religion has indeed a key role, for without it none of the other facts becomes comprehensible.

No one can deny that there are relations between religions and political structures. And nevertheless, our thought habits obscure the religion-politics relationship. We have been led to think of "power" as if it were something like gravity, a natural force. As soon as we are ready to take religion as an institution seriously, much of that customary confusion disappears. After all, the relation between politics and religion owes its difficulty only to our habit of conceiving of power as a force of nature, acting blindly. It is true that politics has a great deal to do with power, but not everything. I am sure that if a large group of people today were asked what the word *politics* is derived from, quite incorrectly many would say *power. Politics,* however, comes from *polis,* the Greek word for "city," and it relates to what a citizen should know and do, as an adult human being who is able to reason. Among human beings, power functions as something that is alive "in discourse."

Power exists in each and every society, but not always in the same manner. It takes on different forms. Shaped in human settings, it shows in all cases the features given to it by religion. In the words of the historian Leopold von Ranke (1795–1886):

> It would be completely wrong to see in the struggles of historic powers solely the operation of brute force and thus to seize only upon the ephemeral element of the phenomenon; for no state has ever subsisted without a spiritual base and a spiritual substance. In power itself there appears a spiritual substance, an original genius, which has a life of its own, fulfills conditions more or less peculiar to itself, and creates for itself its own domain.[25]

What Ranke said can be borne out by knowledge all of us have of the world's religions. We have much more, and more easily available, information on religious traditions at our disposal than anyone had at his time; we know about the Islamic, Hindu, Buddhist, and other civilizations, and their literatures, arts, and cultural achievements. We know—even if we do not reflect enough on the obvious.

Power, political power, is indeed not brute force, for in all cases it exercises and explains itself in contexts and in ways that are prescribed by some existing religious tradition. As in everything that has to do with religion, this still does not mean that what takes on form is necessarily pleasant! But without elaborating on that again, let me name a few simple matters that are within our general grasp of understanding, without an extensive, specialized study.

The difference that separates the exertion of power among human beings from "brute force" remains evident in the legal term *act of God*. The phrase *act of God* clearly rests on religious tradition and points to brute force as manifest in natural disasters, which must be distinguished from the powers that people can manipulate.

The United States has never lost its pride in Article Six of the Constitution (1787), forbidding religious tests "as a qualification to any office or public trust under the United States," and the First Amendment, which stipulates that "Congress shall make no law respecting an establishment of religion or prohibiting the free exercise thereof." These are the basic words of the separation of church and state. They seem straightforward, but like everything else in history and in religion, under scrutiny they are always more complex—not in the last place in ensuing interpretations.[26]

What fascinates me is that at the present time the separation of religion and government is considered as if it were a self-evident, indeed even a natural, matter in human affairs. This results in a great many errors, including errors with real and tragic consequences, as for example when we in the West misjudge and misinterpret Islam. (There is no place in Islam where laws are ever separate from religion; a very large number of Islamic authorities in all of Islamic history have always been lawyers. Many scriptural texts are legal and have bearing on the formation and nature of state power.) In a worldwide perspective, the eighteenth-century American "doctrine" of the separation of church and state is an important *variant* concerning worldly rule in the religion of Israel which never lost its viability; the myth took on new life in Judaism and in Christianity, and upon the Christianization of Europe, it assumed new forms in European history.

The texts of the Old Testament make clear that Israel did not begin with kingship. On the contrary, the covenant between God and the people begins with the giving of the Law; Moses plays a mediating role and receives the Law that he then brings down to the people of Israel. However, he is not a royal ruler; kingship in Israel begins only centuries later. And the first king, according to the Book of Samuel, comes to power in part because of pressure from the people to be like the nations surrounding them. The text leaves no doubt that the desire of the people is at odds with God's will for them. Saul, the first king, ends up doing all the wrong things, and he himself comes to a bad end. Then God appoints David—the perfect king in the records of Israel, Jews, and Christians alike. The New Testament, the scriptures the Christians added to the Hebrew Bible, sees in Jesus Christ the savior born in the line of David.

What is striking about this entire mythical complex is the ongoing opposition between worldly rule on one side and God on the other. The prophets of the Old Testament on more than one occasion speak out against the king—in spite of the fact that the king is anointed with the approval of God. One prophet, Nathan, even condemns the greatest king of all, David himself, in the name of God. (David has desired Bathsheba, another man's wife. He sends Bathsheba's husband, who is one of his commanders, to a battlefield where he will surely perish. After that occurs, David takes Bathsheba. And then Nathan, the prophet, comes to David telling of a certain rich man in the kingdom who wanted the ewe lamb that was the only possession of a certain poor man; the rich man took the ewe lamb and cooked it for his guest. That man must be punished! says David. He deserves to die, and the ewe lamb shall be paid for four times over. And then Nathan pronounces the words to King David: "You are that man!") The prophets judge men on their actions toward other men and address themselves especially to kings for their actions. Those actions are political, of course. One of the reasons the biblical Books of Samuel and Kings are so fascinating is precisely that we recognize the judgments on history that very good history books aim for. It is literature that is part of our culture (which has nothing to do with the question of whether we are practicing Jews and Christians or not). It is more accessible to us than the ancient Greek historians.

In the New Testament the older symbolism of kingship and prophecy seems to come full circle. Jesus Christ is the son of David, hence king, yet he is also prophet. At the same time, his crucifixion as a common criminal is not exactly the sort of thing typifying a royal career but makes him the sacrificial victim of worldly power. The text of the New Testament, however, clarifies in its own way (more accurately, transmythologizes) the contradiction. Jesus Christ is not only the divine ruler, but he is also presented as the one who carries in himself both the righteousness and the grace of God, hence God's dispensation of justice. (*Grace,* like *righteousness,* is a juridical term.) Thus the opposites of kingship and prophecy appear in a new symbolism.

One of the great issues during the Middle Ages was the antagonism between emperor and pope. It is not as if one side were "perfectly spiritual," the other "perfectly power-hungry." No worldly ruler in the conflict was against the church, and no pope was against worldly power. What one can say is that on the scene of political history, the same old mythical theme took on new life. And that is precisely what happened once again when in the United States—in a debate where few, if any, would have denied their Christian adherence—the separation of church and state was established. It was a new variation on the theme of the contrast between worldly and divine power. No wonder that the issue, though seemingly settled in the eighteenth century, continues to excite people. Myths are that way. They demand, as we have seen before, to be reinterpreted. The discourse goes on.

The mythical theme struck in the religion of Israel likewise reverberated in the history of Islam, yet in ways that have no precise equivalent in the West. The first great inner conflicts in the history of Islam concerned the question of where exactly authority should reside. Although Mohammed was not in any manner divine—in fact, this Christian theme was abhorrent to Mohammed himself and to all Muslims after him—his immediate acceptance of God's word (i.e., the Qur'an) was certain. It was never doubted that the rules given by God should guide the Muslim community. But after the glorious beginnings, who could claim to follow truly in the footsteps of the prophet? Who was to carry on the authority and lead the community? That is where the great problem began, which in time led to the first great split: between Sunni and Shiite Islam.[27] This historical split took on new mythical proportions, yet in its various interpretations on both sides we can see the same central concern of Islam: the divine rules do not hover over the world but are meant to be carried out in the concrete world, most especially when governance of the community is the issue.

The birth of Buddhism may serve to illustrate a vastly different theme. When the Buddha himself creates his monastic community (the *sangha*), his friend, King Bimbisara, provides the wherewithal to shelter and provide for the monks. The history of Buddhism is no less complex than the history of other religions, but it is certainly correct to say that Buddhism has few examples of a spiritual leader *confronting* a ruler in as harsh a manner as, for instance, Nathan confronted King David. The Buddhist realization that all sentient creatures are imprisoned in the chain of existence, and that the highest goal is enlightenment, demonstrates the unmistakable similarity between those who by worldly standards have power and those who do not. The important thing is to meditate. There is no other world to meditate in than this one, in which among other things political power exists; why get too excited about that? What we can only touch on here is symbolically expressed in many places in Buddhist texts. I am not suggesting that social and political concerns are absent in Buddhism![28] During the U. S. war in Vietnam there were monks who set themselves afire. Even in this mere thumbnail sketch, however, it is easy to see that Buddhism does not seek occasions where anger may flare up; this is one of the many features that relates it to the world of Hinduism — to which it owes as much as Christianity owes to Judaism.

These few examples should suffice to make us aware of power not as a brute, anonymous, natural force that in some mysterious manner sets things such as religions in motion. Instead, power, being part of human social and political life, is what it is because of the shape a specific religion has given to it in history. Without recognizing its religious impulses, no political system can be understood.

Literature
John Esposito, *The Straight Path* (New York: Oxford University Press, 1988); Michael Polanyi, *Knowing and Being,* ed. Marjorie Grene (Chicago: University of Chicago Press, 1969), chap. 2, "The Message of the Hungarian Revolution," pp. 24–46, the Bible: the books of 2 Samuel and 1 Kings.

RELIGIOUS SYMBOLISM AND SCIENCE

Isn't religion at odds with science? Anyone who asks the question sees heads nodding. Nevertheless, the yea-sayers do not have the facts on their side. The supposed "conflict" between religion and science is a favorite topic in the fairy tale of the blossoming and growth of science, liberating all of us from the superstition of the past. But it is mainly a fabrication of the nineteenth century. Moreover, it is based exclusively on the particular significance of science in the West, and that means mainly physics. The rest of the world is ignored, and other sciences are not seriously considered.

It is true that since Darwin, the sciences of botany and biology (as well as geology) have moved into the limelight. Discussions are always drawn to Darwin's theory of evolution as "of course" opposed to the religious doctrine of creation. What we have said in this chapter regarding the creation myth in Genesis should serve to disabuse us of that assumption. We might consider too something that Darwin wrote in a letter to a friend while on his famous voyage of discovery: "I often conjecture what will become of me; my wishes would certainly make me a country clergyman."[29]

It will be in order now to speak about how the two realms, of science and religion, reveal themselves not as opposites but as complements. Even more, the two reveal themselves as inseparable in a manner that makes destruction of one by the other unthinkable.

In 1972 Alexander Marshack published a book called *The Roots of Civilization*.[30] Marshack, archaeologist and scientist, had become absorbed in that ancient period, long before agriculture was invented, when a good part of the earth was covered with ice sheets and people had begun to live by hunting big game, including bison, mammoth, horse, even rhinoceros, and, of course, reindeer. It was a long period of great human creativity and, in spite of what to us would seem harsh circumstances, a life of plenty. It is tempting to imagine that in later myths images of paradise— a world that was perfect and preceded ours—were prompted in part by lingering memories and tales of that early age of abundance. One should of course not exaggerate such connections, for the religious and literary imagination is not a mere mechanism; we also find the theme of lands of abundance and perfection ("the land of Cockaigne") and spin-offs in fairy tales, where conditions of hunger and famine formed a more likely and more powerful stimulus.[31] Moreover, the great climatic changes associated with the advancing and receding glaciers, which determined the interim periods (more precisely the interglacial periods) of such special importance to human beings, stretched out over such extraordinarily long spans of time that human memory could not very well have retained much of what had prevailed—or for that matter, much of what was accomplished in the creation of tools or in the articulation of language and religion.[32]

Marshack looked long and hard at archaeological finds from those early days (some twenty-five thousand years ago) of people in the Pleistocene: bones of mammoths and other animals, as well as rocks and slates with scratches in them that could not have been made except by human beings. Earlier prehistorians who collected such evidence had not really made a serious effort to interpret what they saw. As in so many instances, scholars had deemed it sufficient to suggest that those scratches probably had something to do with "magic," which is a dignified way of saying: it has no meaning. In his microscopic analysis, Marshack discovered that those scratches showed regularities. They turned out to be, if not exactly "writing," marks of observation of the seasons and of animals in their shedding and mating seasons. The notations indicating time measuring would strike us scientifically oriented people the most. Especially on the smaller, movable objects, such as animal bones, Marshack found clear lunar notations.

What causes our surprise? Is it that those early ancestors of ours were scientifically interested? Yes, they were, and clearly they possessed a religious interest at the same time. We know that lunar myths are attested to all over the world, and they occur in the most ancient written documents we have. The question is not whether we have reason to speak of religion or science. It is obvious that we may speak of both in one breath. Burial practices of a symbolic nature and hunting rituals are evident from the remains even of the earliest Paleolithic cultures.[33] Our notions of science and religion are more restricted than we may have thought; they are clearly two aspects of one and the same human existence according to the earliest indications of human culture. Our own habit of placing religion and science in two different bags, so to speak, is quite recent. We have to bear in mind that the idea of a contrast (or supposed enmity) between the two did not become habitual in our world of learning until the nineteenth century. Another obvious fact to remember is that people orient themselves always and everywhere not merely in space, but also in time. Rituals require specific times, and most certainly could not wait for what we in our present vocabulary decided to mark as "science."

It has been suggested by one of the most fascinating students of China, Joseph Needham, that China failed to develop real science—and by that Needham meant *physics*.[34] What he did not discuss at length was the remarkable birth in China of musicology. In this science, as in all science, regularity needed to be established. It first occurs in China in the measuring of pitch pipes; the Chinese also laid the foundation of acoustics.[35] Why would the Chinese have done work in this area? The answer, as in all questions concerning the origins of sciences, involves the religious tradition: the religious tradition insisted, from the earliest times, on music in ritual proceedings. Not even Confucius, whose *Analects* are no doubt the most readable "sacred work" of all great religious traditions, and who is sometimes portrayed as the "least religious" sage, could ignore music. Whatever was embedded in ancient, pre-Buddhist China and was considered worth preserving, for the sake of community and family and ancestors, was a matter of ritual feasts and hence music.[36] The case is no different with the Paleolithic hunters, who needed a science—namely, a calendar—for their hunting.

Let me also mention yet another science besides physics proper, in the well-known case of Indian civilization. There, more than two thousand years before scientific linguistics developed in the West, a distinct form of linguistics had already made great strides. Why? The preservation of the memorized sacred text (the Vedas), indispensable for the ritual, required that phonetics and grammar be accurately established. Thus linguistics was born out of a need that could not be neglected; the proper tradition depended on it.

It seems rather arbitrary to insist on *our* sciences—on physics, for example—as the only true science. And besides, why exactly did the West develop its inquiries into "nature" and formulate its first answers to questions of physics? There were many causes, but one thing cannot fail to occur to us: the preoccupation with the doctrine of creation, which set many minds in motion, especially by the end of the Middle Ages and during the Renaissance. Here again, religion and science are not at all as distant from each other as we have been led to believe. The two men who introduced calculus to the world, Isaac Newton and Gottfried Wilhelm Leibniz, did not set out to make life easier for physicists (and even less for insurance companies); they established the formulas of calculus because each in his own way was absorbed by the mystery of God's infinitude.

Literature
Alexander Marshack, *The Roots of Civilization* (New York: McGraw-Hill, 1972); William Temple, *Nature, Man and God* (London: Macmillan, 1949), chap. 2, "The Tension Between Philosophy and Religion"; E. J. Dijksterhuis, *The Mechanization of the World Picture* (New York: Oxford University Press, 1969), part 1, "The Legacy of Antiquity," and part 2, "Science in the Middle Ages," pp. 3–95.

NOTES

1. For basic information and bibliographical references on the complex problem of prehistoric data and religious evidence, see Mircea Eliade, *A History of Religious Ideas,* vol. 1 (Chicago: University of Chicago Press, 1978), chap. 1; for Chou-k'ou-tien see especially pp. 4, 9, 14. See also *Encyclopaedia Britannica,* 15th ed. (Chicago: Encyclopaedia Brittanica, 1974), *Macropaedia,* vol. 4, pp. 297–98; on ochre as manmade substance, see vol. 13, p. 888.

2. See John Nance, *The Gentle Tasaday: A Stone Age People in the Philippine Rain Forest* (New York: Harcourt, 1975).

3. Emile Durkheim, *The Elementary Forms of Religious Life,* trans. Joseph Ward Swain (1912; New York: Collier, 1961), p. 52.

4. An illustration is provided, unintentionally, by Karen Armstrong in her book *A History of God* (New York: Knopf, 1993).

5. We owe the clear distinction of the three modes of expression to the Danish historian of religions Edvard Lehmann (1862–1930). See the summary in Eric J. Sharpe, *Comparative Religion: A History* (La Salle, Ill.: Open Court, 1986), pp. 226–27.

6. The great classic work on the subject is Stella Kramrisch, *The Hindu Temple* (University of Calcutta, 1946; reprint, New Delhi: Motilal Banarsidass, 1976), 2 vols.

7. John L. Esposito, *Islam. The Straight Path* (New York: Oxford University Press, 1988), pp. 93–95.

8. Johanna Broda, "Templo Mayor as Ritual Space," in Johanna Broda, Davíd Carrasco, Eduardo Matos Moctezuma, *The Great Temple of Tenochtitlán: Center and Periphery in the Aztec World* (Berkeley: University of California Press, 1987), pp. 63–64.

9. This and the following quotations from the *Symposium* are taken from W. R. M. Lamb, trans., *Plato: Lysis, Symposium, Gorgias,* Loeb Classical Library (Cambridge: Harvard University Press; London: Heinemann, 1961), pp. 173, 175, 177, 179.

10. There are cases where the line separating *myth,* the symbolic word, from *logos,* the conceptual word, cannot be drawn. For instance, in the beginning of the Gospel of John, Jesus Christ is called "the Logos," the Word.

11. Morris Jastrow, Jr., *The Study of Religion* (1901; Chico, Calif.: Scholars Press, 1981), p. 247.

12. I received my first philological training at the University of Leiden. One of the results is my lasting aversion to long footnotes dealing with matters that in fact belong in the body of the text—a practice often indulged in by poor philologists. Please, allow me this one exception, a deviation from the best instruction I received. The "rough" story just told, including its humor, has its parallels in the teachings of all good practical theologians who teach future priests and ministers about the art of ministering to the sick and dying. "The Lord is the real physician," they say. "He has our life in his hands." Setting this instruction side by side with that of the medical professor, we can see why the same practical theologians might refer their students at this point also to the parable of the dishonest steward in Luke 16:1–9. For Buddhists, the story that comes up at once is that of the "skill in means" as told in the *Lotus of the True Law.* A father saves his children by "lying" to them.

13. These lines are from a few of such beginnings of creation stories collected in Mircea Eliade, *From Primitives to Zen: A Thematic Sourcebook of the History of Religions* (New York: Harper and Row, 1967), chap. 2, pp. 83–200.

14. Translation by Louis Ginsberg, *Legends of the Bible* (Philadelphia: Jewish Publication Society, 1956), p. 3.

15. Kees W. Bolle, *The Freedom of Man in Myth* (Nashville: Vanderbilt University Press, 1993), p. 45.

16. Wallace Stevens, "Loneliness in Jersey City," in *Collected Poems* (New York: Knopf, 1961), p. 210.

17. A recent, revealing study on such gruesome "legal" proceedings is Joshua Rubenstein and Vladimir P. Naumov, eds., *Stalin's Secret Pogrom: The Postwar Inquisition of the Jewish Anti-Fascist Committee,* trans. Laura Esther Wolfson (New Haven: Yale University Press, 2001).

18. For many enlightening remarks on this subject, see Wendy Doniger, *Other Peoples' Myths: The Cave of Echoes* (New York: Macmillan, Collier Macmillan, 1988).

19. Albert Schweitzer, *Das Christentum und die Weltreligionen,* 2nd ed. (Munich: C. H. Becksche, 1925). Schweizer wrote a more elaborate treatment of Indian religions in *Indian Thought and Its Development* (Boston: Beacon Press, 1957; first English ed., 1936).

20. Schweitzer, *Das Christentum,* p. 46.

21. Matthew 21; John 2.

22. Jacques Duchesne-Guillemin, *The Hymns of Zarathustra* (London: Murray, 1952), p. 2.

23. Henry Duméry, *Phenomenology and Religion: Structures of the Christian Institution* (Berkeley: University of California Press, 1975); originally *Phénoménologie et religion: Structures de l'institution chrétienne* (Paris: Presses Universitaires de France, 1958).

24. Duméry, p. 110. To be sure, Duméry is concerned only with the structure of Christianity in its derivation from Judaism, but the logic of his term *institution* no doubt allows for a wider application.

25. From a fragment written in the 1930s, quoted in Fritz Stern, ed., *The Varieties of History* (New York: Vintage, 1973), p. 60.

26. For the historical context, see Sydney E. Ahlstrom, *A Religious History of the American People* (New Haven: Yale University Press, 1972), chap. 32, "The Revolutionary Era."

27. For a clear account, see John Esposito, *The Straight Path* (New York: Oxford University Press, 1988), especially pp. 49–50.

28. The most important book on such concerns in Buddhism is Charles D. Orzech, *Politics and Transcendent Wisdom: The Scripture for Humane Kings in the Creation of National Protection Buddhism* (University Park: Pennsylvania State University Press, 1998).

29. Quoted in Steven J. Gould, *Ever Since Darwin* (New York: Norton, 1979), p. 33.

30. Alexander Marshack, *The Roots of Civilization* (New York: McGraw-Hill, 1972).

31. The most effective tool for locating and classifying themes such as "Paradise" or "Cockaigne" is Stith Thompson, *Motif-Index of Folk-Literature,* rev. and enlarged ed., 6 vol. (Bloomington: Indiana University Press, n.d.).

32. See Johannes Maringer, *The Gods of Prehistoric Man* (New York: Knopf, 1960), p. 5.

33. See Maringer, part 1, chap. 2, "Primitive Man and His Dead," and chap. 3, "Hunting Rites."

34. Joseph Needham, *Science and Civilisation in China,* vol. 2 (Cambridge: Cambridge University Press, 1977); see especially pp. 518–83.

35. Ibid., pp. 550–52.

36. See Arthur Waley, *The Book of Songs* (1937; New York: Grove Press, 1960).

Myth and Poetry

Myth, as we have tried to show, is central in our culture. The significance of myth in our civilization should make us cautious when we speak about such things as supposed contrasts between science and religion, or when we are inclined to oppose our own rationality and the supposed irrationality or "primitive thought" of others. Looking upon people as religious creatures, we cannot help but notice that human thought, if it is serious at all, is accessible to everyone. What I wish to suggest in this chapter is that "literature" in our common modern world is full of evidence that myth truly functions among us.

Literature
Claude Lévi-Strauss, *The Savage Mind* (Chicago: University of Chicago Press, 1966); G. van der Leeuw, "Primordial Time and Final Time," in Joseph Campbell, ed., *Man and Time* (Eranos, 1949; New York: Pantheon, 1957), pp. 324–50; Mircea Eliade, *Myth and Reality* (New York: Harper, 1963).

MYTH AND POETRY?

In our high school education, little of the poetry we are officially exposed to seems to "come across." We may end up with the false impression that literature in general, and poetry in particular, has nothing to do with "real life." So let us begin with poetry in recent history.

It is useful to think of the pressures and miseries that were suffered in the former Soviet Union in the twentieth century. There was a world in which all expression was stifled; speaking aloud was risky and not infrequently fatal. How was it possible to speak at all? In that world, even under the regime of Stalin (from 1922 until his death in 1953), sometimes poets found a voice. They functioned as prophets and mystics—speaking out of real, incontrovertible experience, expressing what needed to be said and demanded to be made clear and kept alive. In oppression, poetry could be passed on by word of mouth, or by secretly copying and passing on texts. And people *listened.*

One of the greatest poets during that era was Osip Mandelstam (1891–1938). He fell into disgrace, was arrested, and died in a transit camp in Siberia. His poems are not political oratory. When we know the circumstances under which they were put together, the actual hardship some lines hint at, they can begin to show us what the word of myth is about. In one of his poems (in 1931), Mandelstam speaks, in passing, of himself, saying,

> I—the brother rejected,
> > the human family's worst outcast—[1]

This has nothing to do with an established religious heritage. The reference is not to some "despised and rejected" Christ figure. As a matter of fact, these lines and the entire poetic work of Mandelstam have no official relation to anything called "religious" in popular parlance. He was not a Christian and would not have liked to be mistaken for one. He was a Jew by birth, but his Jewish heritage was something for which he felt no respect.[2] Early on, he shared a good bit of enthusiasm for the revolution that eventually would lead to his demise.

In 1937 he opened a small poem with the following lines, which are not exactly political but which nevertheless anyone in our political world can understand at once:

> Charlie Chaplin
> > Stepped out of the cinema,
> Two soles,
> > A harelip,
> Two peepers
> > Full of ink
> And of fine astonished energy.

Charlie Chaplin—
>   A harelip,
Two soles—
>   A wretched fate.
Something is the matter with the way we all live.
>   Strangers, strangers.[3]

How does a human being, knowing terrible truths, retain life? How can things be said in the bleakest circumstances, seemingly devoid of hope? This is precisely what myths do. In 1937 Mandelstam wrote:

The mounds of human heads disappear into the distance,

. . . .

But in caressing books, in children's games,
I shall rise from the dead to say: the sun![4]

Let me repeat that Mandelstam's poetry was not political oratory, relevant only at that time and only under a regime whose oppression we did not have to suffer. His work was real poetry, precisely in the sense that it announces realities that all of us know in the entire modern world. "Our" secret police may never have been as bad as "theirs," but it has done its work, all the same. And the lives human beings can live in our "free" society are not free from the horrors of anonymity and rejection, loneliness and meaninglessness. "The mounds of human heads disappear into the distance / I dwindle there, no longer noticed" is an image that is not confined to one land; it reaches across an ocean or two.

Mandelstam's widow, years later, wrote about the sensation of fear in those years which never seemed to come to an end. And her words, though not poetry, cover a range of our common human experience:

Akhmatova [a poet and friend of the Mandelstams] and I once confessed to each other that the most powerful sensation we had ever known—stronger than love, jealousy, or any other human feeling—was terror and what goes with it: the horrible and shameful awareness of utter helplessness, of being tied hand and foot.[5]

Mandelstam wrote his poetry in a way that was truly mythical, in the sense that he spoke for all humankind. There is one poem that may well have triggered his condemnation when it was discovered. It was most certainly a poem that could be passed on only in secret. It was recited for the first time by Mandelstam himself in the apartment of a friend (the writer Boris Pasternak) in 1934; it could not be heard without stirring an image of Stalin:

> We live unconscious of the country beneath us,
> Our talk cannot be heard ten paces away,
> And whenever there is enough for half-a-conversation,
> The Kremlin highlander is mentioned.
> His thick fingers are fat like worms,
> His words hit hard like heavy weights,
> His cockroach's huge moustaches laugh,
> And the tops of his boots shine brightly.[6]

Has our own world been so stuffed with satisfaction that poetry cannot reach us? It is true that in a land where people believe they are governing themselves in spite of brainwashing machines on display all around, where something called "market research" decides whether a book should be published, that no word of mouth will give a poet a prominent place, comparable to that of Osip Mandelstam. And yet, even in America, certain circumstances, certain pressing problems, the oppression of certain groups — and, let it be mentioned, the flouting of truth — can lead a voice to speak prophetically and mythically.

All our dictionaries and encyclopedias mention the name of Billy Sunday. My trusty Webster tells me that he lived from 1863 until 1935 and was an American evangelist. The encyclopedias amplify matters. He was a *successful* evangelist. Another important fact: he died *wealthy*. One younger contemporary of Billy Sunday was Carl Sandburg, the Chicago poet, an *enfant terrible* in the view of some, but certainly a man of the extraordinary, stubborn down-to-earth-ness that the Midwest produces from time to time. To say that he did not like Sunday would be an understatement. The publisher who accepted a bundle of poems by Sandburg refused the original text of a poem he wrote about the successful preacher, and Sandburg had to leave out the name of Billy Sunday.[7]

I urge the reader to find and read the entire poem. Sandburg's verse gives Billy Sunday a tremendous whacking. "You come along squirting words at us . . . so fierce the froth of your own spit slobbers over your lips. . . ." At the same time, however, Sandburg shows us a sense of justice of a considerably higher order than that of the wealthy and popular preacher, who uses the name of Jesus constantly, yet has nothing in common with the real acts and teachings of the central figure in Christianity. And, to be sure, in his chastising of Billy Sunday, Sandburg does not exactly use the sort of speech that too many people associate with sweet Christian piety. He uses phrases such as "I've got your number," and " . . . what the hell do you know about Jesus?" and he goes on to describe what Jesus really was like, how he cared for the poor and did not cater to the wealthy, wholly unlike the celebrated pious orator. Close to the end of his poem Sandburg seems to shout from the page that he does not care for "a lot of gab from a bunkshooter in [his] religion."[8]

It is not important for us to discuss how literary critics evaluate Carl Sandburg's work. We want to point out at least something of a similarity between Sandburg and the prophet Amos, whom we read before. We found in Amos that he was not "in tune" with the dominant idea of what religion should amount to. Yet his severe critique of what he saw did not separate him from his tradition. Rather it made him stand out as one of its most potent, living voices, a great prophet of Israel.[9] Real, great voices, the ones speaking in what we see as myth in a tradition—myth in the sense of the true word in which a religion continues to live and change—are the voices of people of the stature of Amos, Mandelstam, and Sandburg, and many, many more.

EMILY DICKINSON

No one today will deny the greatness of Emily Dickinson (1830–86). She was a Christian, but one whose Christianity, as it figures in her verse, is, to put it mildly, not as straight-laced as her Christian surroundings.

> I never felt at Home—Below—
> And in the Handsome Skies
> I shall not feel at Home—I know—
> I don't like Paradise—
>
> Because it's Sunday—all the time—
> And Recess—never comes—
> And Eden'll be so lonesome
> Bright Wednesday Afternoons—

If God could make a visit—
Or ever took a Nap—
So not to see us—but they say
Himself—a Telescope

Perennial beholds us—
Myself would run away
From Him—and Holy Ghost—and All
But there's the "Judgment Day"![10]

This is not her best or most profound poem, but it shows characteristics that occur throughout her work. In addition, it shows us features of myth occurring in the modern world.

At once, on the surface, we notice the peculiar habit of Dickinson to speak "joltingly." Her poems read like telegrams that mention only the most essential things. Secondly, she deals here, as often, with death.

In her handling of death, she is not merely a great poet, but she is more immediately, humanly, and mythically engaged than most poets. She is not "religious" because she is Christian, but she is structurally religious. She is comparable to Basho, or any of the great Zen poets. This of course does not make her "less Christian" or Basho "less Buddhist" in the comparison. Her poetry, like Basho's, is universal in its scope.

One fundamental feature in myths is that the voice that speaks knows it speaks words that lay claim to "absolute truth," and yet—the voice cannot help but make the listener aware that such truth is not of the sort anyone in his right mind can lay claim to personally. This impossibility itself can be expressed in the humor of "subjective reservedness." No one can express really, fully, adequately, for instance the presence of God, and God's justice (or the judgment day), grace, love, or *nirvāna, moksa,* or *sat, cit, ananda.* And when one still does speak about such things, on what ground does it become possible? Really, no ground is conceivable. But that inconceivability has never stopped any human tradition from speaking.

It seems to me that we reach a certain point where we are forced to realize that our entire human existence depends wholly on what philosophers call "transcendence." We discussed earlier the sense of religious symbols precisely by their reference to something "transcendent." This is what makes religious symbols different from mere signs whose referent is within the limits of our senses and reason. Human beings, especially those with a bit of modern education, tend to resist any implication of having to take "transcendence" seriously. (The second part of this book can almost be read as if the struggle for and against any notion of "transcendence" were the essential problem of all our intellectual dealings with religions.)

Could it not be that our cultural hesitancy in giving poetry our full attention is a clear symptom of our problem? Poets of size indeed present us with human reality in all its dimensions—most especially in those where we hurt most. Emily Dickinson's obsession with images of death is not an ornament. Nor is it something we can explain away by analyzing her Christian upbringing. Death is of course "natural," but if that is *all* it is for someone, it is difficult to recognize that someone as a full-grown human being.

The proverb "No prophet is honored in his own land" is found in the New Testament. No poet is honored in her own surroundings—least of all in her "officially religious" surroundings. The image of the poet as in some way "crazy" is not uncommon. For example, Mandelstam must have been crazy for not going with the tide. Personally I can think of nothing more dreadful than having to read the scholarly literature devoted to the one great love affair in Dickinson's life as the explanation for her writings. This type of thing—which we take for granted—is nothing but a way to make the transcendent common, to cut it down to a petty size. People who write such stuff have a lot in common with talk shows on television that cut humanity down to the size of formulaic, asinine problems.

The tendency to bring everything within reach by reducing it to the size of our operating table, by cutting everything to the size of the categories we are familiar with, would make all scientific and scholarly endeavors futile if it went unchecked. Neither the study of literature, nor the history of religions, nor astronomy, nor any other field would ever advance. We have to focus on the features and the problems that show themselves, not on the solutions we have ready-made for all occasions. Our problem with poetry is that it shows us in detail the dependence of human existence on religious symbolization.

Let us return to the poem by Emily Dickinson. It has undeniable similarities to myths.

The last line speaks of something that is mythical by nature: the "Judgment Day." Even if undefinable, it marks the end of life as we know it. And before hearing the word *judgment,* we had already heard the poet say: I don't feel at home where I am, and I won't feel at home in the other world either. If God could make a visit somewhere, or take a nap, then paradise would be less unbearable. "They say" some things about God in Dickinson's poem. "They" associate God with the activity of seeing without pause. God is a telescope that does nothing but "behold us."

Who are "they" who say all this? To answer, her fellow citizens in nineteenth-century Amherst, Massachusetts, is unenlightening. We commonly use the expression "they" to introduce a generally accepted idea ("They say it is better not to cook on a gas stove if your shirt is made of inflammable material"). The expression is in use all over the world for introducing a venerable tradition that is hard to contradict. And readers of myths, including Bible readers, may well recognize the use of "they say" as one of several standard phrases that point to the authority of what follows. Though not as forceful as opening words such as "In the beginning . . . ," the expression does lend strength to the general statement that it introduces. We remember the custom of Buddhist *sutras* that begin with the phrase "Thus I was told." All such phrases exclude contradiction. They imply: This is not just my opinion!

This final point reminds us of the "subjective reservedness" in myths. "They say" and all other such initial turns distract attention from the speaker, who otherwise would seem to "have" the truth at his or her fingertips. This device is a typical form of humor in literature that has no claim to religious authority — or at least not as directly as works such as the Bible or the Qur'an. In few cases does this mean that we burst into laughter. Still, even in later literature — including our lines by Dickinson — this type of humor can be strong. We experience it as "self-irony." We are aware of it well before we perform any solemn analysis.

In fact the words *they say* as used by our poet are at once humorous to the serious reader. The brevity with which Dickinson speaks about the "Judgment" extends that same humor of "personal reservedness." Whose judgment is really the issue? And especially, who is being judged? Me, the human being? That would stand to reason in the tradition. But is it not really Emily Dickinson, the poet — or I, the reader, reading the poem — who does the judging? For it is this person who plays with the idea of running away! The quotation marks are added by Emily Dickinson herself, and I venture to suggest that she put them there on purpose. They might further encourage readers to recognize that *there is no reason to repress our uncertainties;* our uncertainties are real, especially when they are directed toward some of the terms that express most indubitable certainties: judgment, God's judgment, paradise, and also "being at home."

Going back to the beginning of the poem, the words "I never felt at Home — Below" now seem even more jolting than before. *Home* is among the most basic symbolic terms any language has. Hardly a myth is concerned with the birth of the geological world, the world of mathematics or physics; but myths are always concerned with the world of human beings and human life, and that means the place where one's life is lived: home. What it does *not* mean is "real estate." In fact, this topic is crucial in understanding the tragedy of "tribes," "the Indian nations," the original, native inhabitants of places like Australia or New Zealand; it is also the real issue in the tragedy of the wars in the former Yugoslavia; it is also the central issue in the tragedy of the French, and then American, involvement and war in Vietnam. The list can go on. It is the major issue all over Africa and Latin America.

One reason why we have had increasing difficulty reading Genesis 1 and other myths seriously in the last couple of centuries is that "land," places to live, became merely real estate: land as merchandise. Just like the other subjects myths speak of, such as life, death, and food, "home" is an urgent problem—not a quaint remnant of distant and "archaic" traditions. "Home" does not mean "real estate," just as wheat, rice, and fruit do not mean "calories" or "balanced nutrition" or "diet." The care that our industrialized world (the same world that used to colonize other continents) takes of nations with problems is always tragic in the confrontation of well-intentioned abstractions with dreadfully concrete realities. The peasants of Vietnam had resources that the best minds in the Pentagon could not conceive.[11] One's homeland is a very special thing. It is unlike the ideological obsession we know as "patriotism." It is not identical either with the "territorial impulse" of animals—although in its concreteness it seems closer to that than to patriotism.

We all know about the place where we first learned to orient ourselves. The Polish poet Czeslaw Milosz was living in the United States for the many years of the cold war. When he finally could visit his home again, he began one of his reflective poems

You were my beginning and again I am with you, here, where I
learned the four quarters of the globe.[12]

Emily Dickinson's "home" is akin to the basic "dwelling place," where one is born and in which the meaning of one's life is anchored. Yet even the here and now, the "Below," is not where she (perhaps also the reader?) feels at home. Her words about home are not at all lacking in concreteness, but everything seems interiorized. Her problem with feeling at home is intensified because the other place on which those in her surroundings were likely to set their hearts—the other world, Paradise—is equally unsatisfying to her. That place, always Sunday, with never a Recess—and then, to make matters worse, the ever-seeing eye of God. But is it not Home, the mythical Home, the poet desires in this poem? *"Not this, not that,"* but still, Home is sought.

Though museums show us collections of "primitive art," and we are led to think of such art as art on our terms, virtually all these objects have their living environment within the tradition of peoples and their *belonging*. What Professor Garry W. Trompf says about the Melanesians can be said about North American Indians, Siberian tribal peoples, and countless others:

> Museum holdings of Oceanic "primitive art" around the world . . . convey false impressions by isolating individual oddments from their original context—from their eerie corner in the cult house, let us say, or from use as sacral or practicable objects.[13]

Home, as mentioned by Dickinson, and as we in our less fragmented states of mind know it, is at the same time concretely present and something "transcendental," which means related to what is beyond our ordinary everyday ken (the "transcendent").

In the New Testament, in the Letter to the Hebrews (12:18–19, 22–24), we read:

> You have not come to something that can be touched, a blazing fire, and darkness, and gloom, and a tempest, and the sound of a trumpet, and a voice whose words made the hearers beg that not another word be spoken to them. . . . But you have come to Mount Zion and to the city of the living God, the heavenly Jerusalem, and to innumerable angels in festal gathering, and to the assembly of the first-born who are enrolled in heaven, and to God the judge of all, and to the spirit of the righteous made perfect, and to Jesus, the mediator of a new covenant, and to the sprinkled blood that speaks a better word than the blood of Abel.

One of very many images of home, right here (and yet more than merely here), comes from the ancient Chinese *Book of Songs*. It glories in the splendor of a clan feast, saying such things as

Set out your dishes and meat-stands,
Drink wine to your fill;
All your brothers are here together,
Peaceful, happy, and mild.

And it concludes:

Thus you bring good to house and home,
Joy to wife and child.
I have deeply studied, I have pondered,
And truly it is so.[14]

The term *home* is not used in the scriptures of Mahayana Buddhism, for the purpose of existence is of such significance as to make the place of birth dwindle in comparison. Nevertheless, the texts always take us to a very special place. There the great teachings that set people truly free are set forth, usually by the Buddha himself. The place itself is perfect in beauty, and one can truthfully say that it is the place where one *belongs*. The opening lines of the Lotus of the True Law, the most famous of the sūtras, run as follows:

Thus have I heard. Once upon a time the Lord was staying at Rājagṛha, on the Gṛdhrakuta mountain, with a numerous assemblage of monks, all of them Arhats [monks fully accomplished for Enlightenment], stainless, free from depravity, self-controlled, thoroughly emancipated in thought and knowledge, of noble breed, (like unto) great elephants, having done their task, done their duty, acquitted their charge, reached the goal . . .[15]

It is obvious that differences abound in images of home, the place where one belongs, but everywhere the concrete reality of "home" and its "higher" meaning go hand in hand. Precisely that feature indicates the symbolic quality of the true home. The abundant differences in the symbolism illustrate vividly the formation of "symbolic clusters." After all, each symbol is always interwoven with other religious expressions in a given tradition. And each relationship is interwoven with the civilization in which it functions. For example, the presence of the national flag inside American churches is a surprise to foreign visitors. Yet it can be seen as one of the ways in which the symbolic importance of the "home" is underlined—in this case through the stimulus of nationalism.

Everywhere, no matter how it is conditioned in its details, the symbolism of the home is characterized by the inner relation between "here" and "beyond." And this is the point of contact with Emily Dickinson's poem. I suggested earlier that it may not be her most profound poem, but the "light touch" is very pleasing to us. Her meditation about the real, inner significance of things is something we cannot easily run away from. The real reason why it is difficult for us to ignore a text such as this is that the perennial concreteness of a most basic type of symbolism does not leave us alone. The poet expresses what resists expression, and thereby evokes our response, our own memory, our own home, our own uncertainty, our own desolation, our own hope. Good poetry can indeed do what myths do.

VARIATIONS IN CULTURE

We have looked at poets as religious figures. Why might that seem outrageous? Perhaps unconsciously we expect the writer of a religiously identifiable poem to say "I am religious." However, no poet (including the poets of the Vedic hymns sacred to Hinduism, or the Homeric epics) says anything of the sort.

What, nevertheless, is obvious (as we have discussed early in this book) is the givenness of religion in all ages and all places. There is nothing to suggest that "religion" is a later by-product of culture. The evidence shows that even modern poets speak in a way that depends wholly on religious structures that were present long before they were. Religions are the root, the basic assumption, the ground, on which art comes into being.

All poets live in their own era, within their own cultural environment. Then what allows us to compare Sandburg to Amos? Israel had no churches and it had no aisles down which converts would go to accept Jesus Christ as their Lord and Savior. But there is something else that our common sense perceives: the world teems with Billy Sundays who victimize people. The similarity of Sandburg to Amos is that both insist on *justice*. And that insistence is a *religiously determined* stance in the world. Justice is an inalienable part of God's concern in Israel and its descendants, Judaism, Christianity, and Islam.

Again and again, the Christian world — whether consciously Christian or not is irrelevant — shows a preoccupation with justice. The slightly archaic translation from the Hebrew, *righteousness,* is known to all of us. "The Lord loveth righteousness";[16] it is of supreme importance to "understand righteousness and judgement."[17] According to the biblical texts it is God himself, who made a covenant with his people, to whom true justice belongs.[18]

The idea that a sense of justice would be limited to one cultural tradition is of course ludicrous. For example, Hinduism knows the god Dharma, who is justice. And yet, in the religious customs, in the devotion practiced, the paramount image of the supreme God or Goddess that comes up is not one of divine *justice* but of divine *presence*.

No religious tradition is set in stone, and we could never infer from a religious tradition all its cultural creations. Different periods, different regions, all come up with their own interpretations of what is most significant in the tradition. In this chapter on myth and poetry, we are now going to examine one theme in order to show some variations among cultures.

The theme I have in mind is that of love between a man and woman. It occurs everywhere. However, it never seems to be the same. Let us first listen to Archibald MacLeish, to whom we owe a great many poems that radiate modern, unadorned honesty. The theme in the following lines is love, marital love. The poet himself called it a "Poem in Prose."[19]

As before, I urge you to find and read the entire poem for yourself. If lack of rhyme is a mark of modern poetry, MacLeish's poem for his wife is modern. Though certainly an expression of love, there is nothing "touchy-feely" about the poem. When the poem calls his own effort honest, the reader finds that honesty throughout all stanzas. The poet expresses clearly that his wife does not need to be praised any more than a bright summer day. Peace and life itself simply come with her.

> Wherever she is there is sun
> and time and a sweet air.

It makes me feel guilty that in this chapter on poetry and myth I have to draw your attention back to the remarkable changes that occur in our perception and experience of the world we are in, including the very special world of perfect love between man and woman. This poem of love was composed barely over half a century ago. And I am almost quoting literally when I say that the poet relates the perfect ways and the beauty of his beloved wife to the duty that comes with her love, including—and these three words *are* a literal quote—"the well-swept room." There are still more things in the wife's housework the poet names: curtains, flowers, candles, baked bread, a cloth spread, a clean house.

Archibald MacLeish's poem is splendidly straightforward and requires no complex interpretation. I confess that I like it — for I am old enough to have a liking for it. Yet I realize that I personally could never write anything like this, even if I were a poet. I realize vividly that many readers in the present moment will not appreciate this verse at all. The poem was not written in ancient days but in 1948. Cultural conditionings change fast. Nevertheless, fashions and prejudices aside, could anyone claim that this poem is *not* about love? If you cannot see it that way, it would be difficult to quote some lines from the Song of Songs to you. It is essential to realize, even when reading the lines "There are always curtains and flowers" and so forth, that one's ideas and expressions always take their form in the prevailing winds. Love and marriage have been of crucial, sacred importance since the remotest past. But our endeavor here is not to define what true love is but to show how different it sounds in different times and circumstances.

Let it be noticed that love poems for spouses are not all that numerous in Western literature. The exultation of falling in love has stimulated far more poetry. In this respect, the poem by Archibald MacLeish is part of a smaller collection. Another Western poet in this tradition was a contemporary of Shakespeare. He is Joost van den Vondel, the "prince" of Dutch literature. We find these lines in a chorus of a play he wrote:

Where could one find faithfulness truer
Than between husband and wife?
Two souls, aglow, welded together,
Or chained firmly, linked
In grief and in joy.

. . . .

If love happens like this,
Soul with soul,
Heart with heart,
That love is stronger than death.
No love comes closer to God's love,
Nor is so great.

. . . . . .[20]

The line "That love is stronger than death" was no doubt inspired by the Song of Songs: "Love is strong as death, passion fierce as the grave."[21]

The South African poet Breyten Breytenbach (who became known to the outside world as a fighter against *apartheid*) reflects not only biblical religious inspirations but also Buddhist texts. He is a truly modern man, in the sense that he has an acquaintance with all sorts of traditions but recognizes his own world as the place where the entire world demands full attention.

We know that a great many myths deal with the world's totality and origin. One of Breytenbach's poems is titled *"sandhabhasa en bodhicitta."* *Sandhabhasa* (more usually written *sandhyābhaṣyā*) is the Sanskrit term for "intentional language"; it refers to an esoteric use of language that is understandable only to the initiated. *Bodhicitta* is "understanding of enlightenment"; it also refers to a man's semen. The poem speaks of the world and our involvement in it, and the ultimate purpose of "nothing," in the sense of "enlightenment."

Afrikaans is a marvelously flexible language, even more so through the genius of this artist. Of course, each language has its own surprising poetic flexibilities, but the translation of poetry from one tongue into another has its limits. I hope that the few quotations that follow will render something of the way in which "the most spiritual" is interwoven with "the most concretely worldly and sensual" in this poem.

"Sandhabhasa en bodhicitta" begins with the lines

the body is a cosmos
the poem is a body
and this body is nothing

but words remain

Breytenbach calls these remaining words—in fact, all words—"waste parts." They are what you excrete, lose, what falls off you. And precisely this peculiar, rather questionable matter is the offal that constructs verse! (The element of humor we have noticed in myths is clearly present here—considering that words are the only material poets use.) Eating food obviously stands for giving in to craving, and craving the object of our desire is the fundamental human temptation that Buddhist teachings ask us to resist and that stands in the way of our ever reaching enlightenment. We should realize that food, with which the whole process of our common, ordinary, craving, undisciplined life began in the first place, is really nothing.

This simple idea with an unmistakable Buddhist ring is expressed in a manner that perhaps only Afrikaans allows. Of the two syllables of the word *cosmos,* the first, *cos* in Afrikaans, means "food," and the second, *mos,* corresponds more or less to our term "really." And thus, the poet can express two things at once: *food is really nothing,* and *the entire world, the cosmos, is really nothing.*

Without any philosophical jargon, the poem tells us the central Buddhist teaching concerning the need for abandoning our ego, our selves. The idea that we should give up the illusion that we have "a self" is the briefest possible summary of the Buddha's instructions. In Breytenbach's poem, if you abstain from your cravings—by not eating your body— "your self falls off."[22]

Another poem in the same collection, in which one may also recognize Buddhist themes, is a love poem. It begins with the lines

copulation is meditation
and one as well as the other ends up
in surrender to the nothing . . .

The suggestion that copulation is meditation may not sound very attractive to many a decent citizen. The poet offers more equations that may startle readers, including many a Buddhist. Sperm, he says, is the "thought of enlightenment," and the semen that "explodes in silence" enters the universe of his love's "nothing." It is, moreover, an explosion of light "that brings the darkness."[23]

Breytenbach's imageries are adopted from Buddhist texts in what is known as Vajrayāna Buddhism, where the esoteric use of language I mentioned earlier is characteristic. Buddhist (also Hindu) texts of this nature began to be composed from about the third century on. This is not the place to tell the history of this movement, except to say that the concreteness of enlightenment was rendered in terms of sexual rituals, hence in terms of the most intense experiences known to human beings.

One can see Buddhism in these lines. However, the "nothing" that is like a secret reference to *nirvāṇa,* enlightenment, is grasped in words that are firmly embedded in bodily existence, which would also—probably reasonably—make us think of Christian symbolism in the background. After all, the Old Testament has always been read carefully in the Calvinist churches, also in South Africa, and in those texts life is always embodied life. There is no soul apart from the body, and certainly no idea at all about a heavenly life of incorporeal "spirits" as a goal to be pursued in the present life. In any event, the love imagery is quite concrete.

In expressions of marital love, India's wealth seems inexhaustible. While in Western literature, love outside marriage has played a major role, true love in India as a rule is portrayed as the perfect *marital* relationship. And it may be good to conclude with an example of such a splendid bond. Though perfect, its perfection is unlike Vondel's, precisely because the religious symbolism on which it rests is different. In Hinduism, each supreme god, and each supreme goddess has a steady and supreme consort. Likewise, a supreme, legendary-mythical divine ruler, such as Rāma (who is an embodiment of the supreme god Viṣṇu), has next to him the supreme wife, Sītā. The *Rāmāyaṇa* is an epic that for many hundreds of years has been recited by Hindus. This work in turn has inspired much poetry. One of the most famous poets in the Sanskrit language, Kālidāsa ("the Indian Shakespeare"), wrote a long narrative poem about the ancestors of Rāma. One of these ancestors, also glorified as a perfect king, was Dilipa. Kālidāsa, after enumerating Dilipa's virtues, introduces Sudakṣiṇā, his wife, in the following words:

> His wife was born in the royal house of Magadha. Her name was Sudakṣiṇā.
> This name was properly given to her because of her formal attentiveness in giving gifts, comparable to the formal gifts [*dakṣiṇā*] presented to priests at the end of a sacrifice.
> Although he had women and there was a large harem,
> The king really thought of himself only together with her, this wise lady, his Lakṣmī [= Prosperity, but Lakṣmī is also the name of Viṣṇu's consort].[24]

Such is a perfect marital relation in Indian classical literature. Perfection is not in the feeling of happiness, not in "satisfaction" or "self-fulfillment" at all. The perfect queen is glorified for her perfection in doing what in her high position should be done. Her actions are such as to conjure up associations with the duty a sacrificer has in rewarding the priest in the age-old ritual tradition. We cannot enjoy more than a little taste here, but elsewhere the poem elaborates that for the king, in his function, it is essential to have an heir, and Sudakṣiṇā is the perfect vessel for that purpose. The whole poem is imbued with religious symbolism that one could hardly imagine in the Christianity-affected or modern world we live in.

At the very least the religious symbolism we find in classical Indian texts teaches us not to project the wishes and biases of our own world onto the world that surrounds us. Beyond that, the point is that the poetry of our own tradition and our own modernity is as laden with religious symbolism as any poetry anywhere in the world, and it is certainly possible to overcome habitual biases that blind us to the presence of religion even when it stares us in the face.

NOTES

1. Osip Mandelstam, *A Necklace of Bees: Selected Poems,* trans. Maria Enzensberger (London: Menard Press, 1992), p. 27.

2. See his own descriptions in Clarence Brown, trans., *The Prose of Osip Mandelstam* (Princeton: Princeton University Press, 1967), in "The Bookcase" (pp. 80–85), and in "The Judaic Chaos," (pp. 88–94).

3. Mandelstam, *A Necklace,* p. 39.

4. Osip Mandelstam, *Selected Poems,* trans. James Greene (London: Penguin, 1989), p. 74.

5. Nadezhda Mandelstam, *Hope Abandoned: A Memoir,* trans. Max Hayward (Harmondsworth, England: Penguin, 1976), p. 203.

6. Quoted by Clarence Brown in a critical essay accompanying his translation, *The Prose of Osip Mandelstam,* pp. 3–4.

7. See the introductory essay by George and Willene Hendrick in their edition of Carl Sandburg, *Billy Sunday and Other Poems* (New York: Harcourt, 1993), p. xii.

8. Ibid., pp. 3, 5–6.

9. See chapter 2 of this book.

10. Thomas H. Johnson, ed., *The Complete Poems of Emily Dickinson* (Boston: Little, Brown, 1960), p. 197. (This poem was written circa 1862).

11. The best work on Vietnam with respect to the importance of what I call "home" is still Gerald Cannon Hickey, *Villlage in Vietnam* (New Haven: Yale University Press, 1967). One of its great merits is that it deals soberly and factually with the practical function of religion in the village communities. Insights into the inner conflicts of American soldiers can be gained from Bernard Edelman, ed., *Dear America: Letters Home from Vietnam* (New York: Pocket Books: 1985). One of the most gruesome examples of the "abstractions" of American higher-ups was the "body count." The destruction of Vietnamese

fighters (as well as noncombatants) was translated into numbers meant to show the "successes" scored. It disgusted American soldiers intensely. See chap. 3, "Beyond the Body Count," pp. 103–38.

12. Czeslaw Milosz, trans. by the author and Robert Hass, *Facing the River, New Poems* (Hopewell, N. J.: Echo Press, 1995), p. 64.

13. G. W. Trompf, *Melanesian Religion* (New York: Cambridge University Press, 1991), p. 26.

14. Arthur Waley, trans., *The Book of Songs* (New York: Grove Press, 1960), pp. 203–4.

15. H. Kern, trans., *Saddharmapuṇḍarīka, or The Lotus of the True Law* (New York: Dover, 1963), p. 1.

16. Psalms 11:7, 33:5.

17. Proverbs 2:9.

18. Among scholarly descriptions of "righteousness" in the biblical texts, the classical one is by Johannes Pedersen, *Israel, Its Life and Culture* (London/Copenhagen: Oxford University Press–Branner, 1926), "Righteousness and Truth," pp. 336–77.

19. Archibald MacLeish, *Collected Poems 1917–1982* (Boston: Houghton Mifflin, 1985), pp. 373–74.

20. Joost van den Vondel, *Gijsbrecht van Aemstel.*

21. Song of Solomon 8:6.

22. Breyten Breytenbach, *Met andere woorden* (Amsterdam: Meulenhoff, 1977), p. 111. Translated by the author.

23. Ibid.

24. Kālidāsa, *Raghuvamsa* 1.31–32.

Beginning to Understand Religions

"The Religions of the World"

Academic positions for teaching the history of religions were not established until the last quarter of the nineteenth century. Nevertheless, as soon as the field was officially introduced in institutions of higher learning, efforts were made to present "the religions of the world" to the reading public. Terms like "religions of the world" and the name of the discipline, "history of religions," were not really transparent at the beginning.

Those beginnings themselves—as we shall see in the second part of this book—were turbulent. They could hardly be otherwise, for until the establishment of chairs in European universities, the subject of religion had been left to the discipline of theology. The religions of the world had never been drawn into any formal curriculum. The question of truth in matters concerning religion—until then left to theologians—took on a different aspect. Those novices, teaching the history of religions, had to spend virtually all their time gathering historical information. Their way of working was, at least in principle, empirical. That means they had to look at whatever evidence was available.

From the last quarter of the nineteenth century into our own time, scholars have tried to write handbooks on the religions of the world, and special large encyclopedias of religion can be found in our libraries. Of course, some of these collections are better than others, but the point I want to make is that we have collectively come to take for granted that the knowledge of religious facts is of great significance. "The religions of the world" is not a strange or frightening term for anyone any longer.

Literature

C. P. Tiele, *Geschiedenis van den godsdienst in de oudheid tot op Alexander den Groote,* 2 vols. (Amsterdam: Van Kampen, 1902); Christel Matthias Schrö-der, ed., *Die Religionen der Menschheit,* 37 vols. (Stuttgart: Kohlhammer, 1950–1);. C. Jouco Bleeker and Geo Widengren, eds., *Historia Religionum,* 2 vols. (Leiden: Brill, 1971); G. F. Moore, *History of Religions,* 2. vols. (1914; Edinburgh: Clark, 1971); Helmer Ringgren and Åke V. Ström, *Religions of Mankind, Today and Yesterday* trans. Niels L. Jensen (Philadelphia: Fortress, 1967); G. van der Leeuw, ed., *De godsdiensten der wereld,* 2 vols. (Amster-dam: Meulenhoff, 1940); Henri-Charles Puech, ed., *Histoire des religions,* 3 vols. (Paris: Gallimard, "Encyclopédie de la Pléiade," 1970); James Has-tings, ed., *Encyclopaedia of Religion and Ethics,* 12 vols. (Edinburgh: Clark, 1908–21); Hermann Gunkel, eds., *Die Religion in Geschichte und Gegenwart,* 6 vols., 2nd ed. (Tübingen: Siebeck, 1927); Mircea Eliade, ed., *Encyclopedia of Religion,* 16 vols. (New York: Macmillan, 1987).

KNOWLEDGE

In recent times the term *cognition* has attained popularity in college circles. Technically, it refers to the way in which we perceive or get to know some-thing through our mental functions and the system of our nerves. The process of "getting to know" is an important topic of study for experts in philosophy and psychology. The more general use of the term *cognition,* no doubt attractive because of its learned ring, is not always enlightening when used outside the circles of experts; all by itself it does not bring about a greater understanding of anyone's subject. Nevertheless, students of literature, of society, of art, and of many others fields now use the word *cognition.* It is turning into a solemn substitute for the common word *knowl-edge.* Why do some prefer it to the more accessible terms *knowledge* and *knowing?* I am afraid that they have taken a liking to the more unusual word because *knowledge* carries with it the assumption—perhaps to them the threat—that one should make an effort to get to know the particulars and details of the object of one's discipline. But it is not enough to speak about the process of knowing (cognizing) in general. We have a responsibility toward our subject matter. And in most cases that means hard work. For example, in literature, in sociology, in history, and in the study of religions, our responsibility always involves at least the knowledge of languages. Moreover, interpreting religious matters cannot be done without interpreting *people*. Hence we bear also a *moral* responsibility. This distinguishes our studies from the admittedly important analysis of our brain functions and nervous system in cognition processes. Wielding a scalpel properly is essential in medicine. Anatomy aims to understand the human body; yet, in order to understand it, more than the scalpel is needed.

The important surveys of the religions of the world, and the encyclopedic reference works on religion, are the work of scholars who *know what needs to be known* in order to give us an idea of *what it means to understand.*

We should keep reminding ourselves of the fact that the documents of religion demand most of our time in our field of study. We would do well to remember Heraclitus, who not only said, "Much learning does not teach understanding," but also, "Men who love wisdom should acquaint themselves with a great many particulars." And we should remember of Confucius that he said not only that "to learn without thinking is stultifying," but also that "to think without learning is dangerous."[1] We do not need information only, but we do need information, properly assembled and digested.

What is the study of the history of religions aiming for? *Understanding,* of course. To approach that goal, we need facts, even though we know that not all the facts are within our grasp. Of course, we are not in a dream world in which understanding materializes spontaneously or through free association. Nevertheless, understanding on the basis of whatever facts are available is no strange magic but happens in our everyday world. We get to *know* a person not because we have access to all the "facts" of that person's life. We do not need to wait for a psychoanalytical report or a sociological survey in which that person fits. The facts at our fingertips are never complete, and yet we do arrive at an understanding. What is going on in the understanding of a religion is no different. We can make mistakes in "sizing up" a human being, of course. We can make mistakes in interpreting religious documents. Understanding simply is an activity in which we need training, much like an athlete whose fitness for a match can never be so factually or completely assessed that the race becomes predictable. The athlete simply knows and understands what is ahead.

Most survey books of religions do not say a great deal about the problem of understanding but try to present all the facts. At the same time, whether explicitly or implicitly, they also present something else. They all assume that the facts chosen for presentation are important to know. They assume that the evidence they choose is important and will lead to understanding. Here we can begin to see how certain problems come up in presentations of religions.

PROPHETIC OR HISTORICAL RELIGIONS

That some religions seem to have a certain pattern in common, different from others, has struck the majority of historians. Certain religions show a historical coherence, obvious to all. In this book we have made note more than once of the family relationship of Israel—the historical root— and its offspring in Judaism, Christianity, and Islam. Historically they belong together, and the people and their texts in all three refer to Abraham as their ancestor. No matter how each of the three embroidered upon the figure of Abraham, his symbolic significance becomes clear through his place in the history of Israel; this place considerably precedes the historical formation of the three religions, yet each one establishes its orientation with reference to Abraham. In his line Judah, the patriarch of Judaism, is born; Ishmael, in whose line Mohammed belongs, is one of Abraham's sons; and according to the New Testament, through his family line Jesus Christ is "son of David, son of Abraham" (Matthew 1:1).

As long as we know that we speak about shared historical patterns and a certain common vocabulary, it is certainly possible to speak of a "type" of religion. There is the danger, however, of jumping to conclusions—in this case imagining that we have understood more than we really have. Some scholars like to stress the common element by emphasizing the beginning of "monotheism," the worship of one God, in Israel. But we must ask, in what manner is "monotheism" a religious symbol? It is not a symbol at all and does not function religiously. "Monotheism" is a concept; it contrasts with "polytheism," the worship of many gods. Both terms are labels attached by outsiders, by the coolness of the mind thinking about religion. Neither in the Hebrew Bible (the "Old Testament") nor in the Greek New Testament does the term *monotheism* occur. It is true that by the time Islam came into being, philosophical-theological discussions made it possible to speak about "monotheism"; yet the Arabic term, used in the Qur'an, *tawhid,* is a verbal noun—it does not refer to an idea as much as it refers to an *act:* to declare the unity of God. That oneness of

God is also his ultimate reality, to which nothing can be compared. *Tawhid* is close to the first lines of the Ten Commandments in the Bible: "I am the Lord your God who brought you out of Egypt, out of the land of slavery. You shall have no other god [or gods] to set against me" (Exodus 20:2–3).

Religious symbols, we remember, are not "ideas." Neither a Muslim, nor a Christian, nor a Jew would ever use the term *monotheism* in a prayer. God surely is not interested in the devotee's abstract concepts. And no supplicant will find it necessary to remind God of the fact that he or she is a "monotheist." And apart from the nature of religious facts, we share a sense of language that would tell us that none of the people such as the ancient Greeks or the ancient Indians or Aztecs would ever describe themselves as "polytheists." The very suggestion is ridiculous.[2]

If one wants to speak of types, not too emphatically, one can certainly make a case for the religions deriving from Israel as a "type." In the past this type has often been referred to as "historical" and "prophetic." In this type, God himself is portrayed and experienced as the supreme one who has a hand in what happens in history. He guides his people. He makes and fulfills his promises. He judges. His voice is heard by special people who are called and appointed to speak his word; these are the "prophets." It has also been said, in a word, that in this type of religion God is characterized by the great, central importance of his will. Human beings are servants to his will.

Let me repeat that such characterizations of religions in types may well serve a general purpose of ordering the many, many materials a little bit. But it is worth remembering that each of the three, Judaism, Christianity, and Islam, followed different paths, developed different ways of interpreting the same materials, and has not infrequently been in conflict with the others. And since the reality of religious symbols is a historical reality — the only reality in which people have experience, including religious experience — it is of the greatest importance to realize that even such typologies of a certain preliminary value are no more than a first step, made for the convenience of our mental orientation. They merely touch on Judaism, Christianity, and Islam.

Finally, there are some very serious drawbacks to such preliminary typologies. For instance, even the "prophetic" voices heard in the traditions deriving from the Bible do not occur only in Judaism, Christianity, and Islam. In several of the regions won over by Islam, traditions deriving from early Iranian Zoroastrianism flourished as well. And in some cases, certain "mixed forms" of religion came into being. Such forms were of special importance in the Iranian highlands.[3] In other words, "prophecy" is not exclusive to the historically more or less coherent "historical and prophetic" tradition of the three that are so designated. To make matters even more complicated, could we deny the term *prophetic* to a description of, say, the Buddhist monks who protested against the devastation of Vietnam only a few decades ago?

ANOTHER TYPE: NATURAL RELIGIONS

It has been common to distinguish the "prophetic" or "historical" religions from "natural" religions. The choice of the term *natural* as opposed to *prophetic* seems difficult to justify, yet the intention in using the term is not hard to understand. The study of ancient and distant religious traditions came about in an academic environment that was familiar with Christianity, to some extent with Judaism, and—though to a much lesser extent—with Islam. Whatever did not seem to relate to a revealed concern of God with history fell outside the sphere of familiar knowledge. Everything that presented itself as religion in that outside world seemed easiest to bundle together by ascribing it to "nature." What was meant by *nature* is again to be understood in the Western, Christianity-influenced intellectual tradition. *Nature,* as used in theological discussions ever since the early Middle Ages, leaned on the pre-Christian, classical teachings of a philosophical school known as the Stoa. The name *stoa* (a colonnade with a roof over it) was also the name given to the place in Athens preferred by the philosopher Zeno, whose followers are known as the Stoics; there he liked to hold forth. Perhaps no other philosophy has been so enduring in the history of the West as his. "Nature" in this tradition is not simply nature as an object for physicists and naturalists, but rather a much broader idea of all that is given in the world as the environment in which human beings should search for virtue.

It is useful to remember also that the term *natural religion* has its place in Christian theological history, and that the historians of religions who began to do their work in the latter part of the nineteenth century were as "culturally conditioned" as other people in their surroundings. To put it briefly, the rest of the world of religion outside the Christian world did not seem to possess adequate notions of revelation, and hence could be called "natural." This expression was often used to refer to the Indian religions, the religions of China and Japan, and, very frequently indeed, the tribal religions encountered in the colonies of Portugal, the Netherlands, England, France, and other Western nations.

The term *natural* tells us absolutely nothing about the content of any of the religions thus designated. Furthermore, when *natural* began to be used in deliberate contrast to *prophetic,* its usefulness became even more questionable. No matter how subtly wielded, the terms *prophetic* or *historical* and *natural* cannot hide a devaluation of the religions outside the already "known" ones, particularly Christianity.

Literature
J. M. Rist, *Stoic Philosophy* (Cambridge: Cambridge University Press, 1969).

The Major Difficulty with Typologies

Speaking of the term *natural* as used for "tribal religions," we can see why formulating types of religion is of very limited valued or is even misleading, although none of the terms that we would now instinctively reject was introduced maliciously. We shall see in the second part of this book how important the serious interpretation of communities in colonized parts of the world has been for our study. Words came to be used to group all those communities together: Papuas in New Guinea, Bantu and Mbutu in Africa, Tungus and other communities in Siberia, Eskimos in the far north, North and South American native peoples, and so on. Of course, the term *tribal* to describe all those peoples is a great improvement over terms such as *savages* or *primitives* which were once used widely. The problem with many words is that even if they were not intended to be denigrating, they can easily acquire a tone that makes them precisely that. Obviously, *savage* and *primitive* imply that the peoples thus designated are not on our level. These terms could hardly inspire us to listen attentively to what people have to say. *Tribal* is probably also better than the adjective *archaic,* which has gained a certain currency. *Archaic* might be useful if it did not carry with it the suggestion of "not modern like ourselves." *Tribal,* at least for the moment, seems to be the best word we have, for the simple reason that it can be taken to refer "neutrally" (if such a thing ever occurs) to peoples in small communities. It means that we purposely take refuge in the most external label and imply nothing about understanding. The use of such a term, with its humble, unpretentious air, may also make clear that we have given up any typology. Nothing is left to tell us what the content, the "lived experience," the meaning of religious symbols, rituals, and myths, really is.

Is that a loss? No. Rather, it enlivens our necessary efforts to reach an understanding of the characteristic elements that make up each religion: its symbols, rituals, and myths. As we have understood before, we do not have to mystify these elements at all. They are not hard to perceive, and they are always central to a religious tradition. Even though each religion has its high and esoteric forms, religious symbolization is not necessarily present only in concealed or very elevated places. Its three forms of expression are also the ordinary reality of a tradition. They are given and documented, and they are open to commonsensical historical investigation. They should be studied. Most typologies, however, are like other external generalizations, wholly dependent on our own culturally conditioned assumptions.

Literature
Joachim Wach, *Types of Religious Experience* (Chicago: University of Chicago Press, 1951), chap. 2, "Universals in Religion," pp. 30–47; G. van der Leeuw, *Religion in Essence and Manifestation* (New York: Harper, 1963), vol. 2, part 5, "Forms," pp. 591–649; Raffaele Pettazzoni, *Essays in the History of Religions* (Leiden: Brill, 1954), "East and West," pp. 193–201; Sam D. Gill, *Beyond the Primitive: The Religions of Nonliterate Peoples* (Englewood Cliffs, N.J.: Prentice-Hall, 1982).

EMPIRICISM AND COMMON SENSE

The preceding section should not be read as if it were a condemnation of all our conceptualizing. Concepts, ideas, types, and categories are the tools our intellect uses. It is, however, important to keep in mind this obvious dictum: a method is proper only if it is appropriate for the object of our inquiry. This means that with respect to religious data we have to observe the same rule that any intellectual inquiry or science demands. Admittedly, however, the subject of religion is more controversial (and more tempting for people to voice flimsy opinions about) than most other subjects. Many a problem has resulted from an uncritical obsession with origins. Not all of biology is exhausted in the quest for the origin of life. Even if in the end the question were adequately answered, it still would not be the center of that science. Of course, we in the history of religions might be pleased if we had an adequate answer to the question: what and where is the origin of religion? There is good reason to doubt that that question will ever be answered — no matter how many pens it has set in motion. The obsession with the ultimate cause of something is but one of the conceptual emaciations that can occur in scholarship. Just like all other historians, we should focus on the data we have, and not spend too much time on speculations as to what might have preceded those data. Conceptual discipline is an ongoing duty. Superimposing our own ideas on religious material is easy, and yet we must resist it. Let me offer some examples of specific religious data.

Several hundred years before our era, an Indian text commented at length on a certain ritual, a sacrifice to be performed at the time of the new moon and the full moon. Brahmins, the class of people who according to the socio-religious symbolism in Brahmanism formed the spiritual and priestly leadership of the community, were expected to perform it. We can only guess how long this ritual of half-monthly sacrifices had been observed by people by the time the text (the *Śatapathabrāhmaṇa*) was composed. The custom was considered valid and proper. The text of the commentary did not present one individual's ideas but was comparable to a textbook used in instruction and discussions with pupils who went through their priestly training. The entire ritual took most of two consecutive days, and is still performed. Ceremonially, fire is taken from the householder's fire (the hearth) and used to light two more fires prescribed in the rites. As in all rites of Brahmanism, the sacrificer must take a vow at the very beginning of the proceedings, touch water, and invoke Agni (whose name means fire, especially the sacrificial fire). The ancient commentary says:

> He who is about to enter on the vow, touches water, whilst standing between the Āhavanīya and Gārhapatya (= householder's) fires, with his face turned towards east. The reason why he touches water is, that man is (sacrificially) impure on account of his speaking untruth; and because by that act an internal purification (is effected), — for water is indeed (sacrificially) pure. "After becoming sacrificially pure, I will enter on the vow," thus (he thinks); for water is indeed purifying. "Having thus become purified through the purifying one, I will enter on the vow," thus (he thinks), and this is the reason why he touches water.

Looking towards the (Āhavanīya) fire, he enters on the vow, with the text . . . , "O Agni, Lord of Vows! I will keep the vow! may I be equal to it, may I succeed in it!" For Agni is Lord of Vows to the gods, and it is to him therefore that he addresses these words. In the words, "I will observe the vow; may I be equal to it; may I succeed in it," there is nothing that requires explanation.

After the completion (of the sacrifice) he divests himself (of the vow), with the text . . . , "O Agni, Lord of Vows! I have kept the vow; I have been equal to it; I have succeeded in it;" for he who has attained the completion of the sacrifice, has indeed been equal to it; and he who has attained the completion of the sacrifice, has succeeded in it. It is in this way that most (sacrificers) will probably enter on the vow; but one may also enter it in the following way.

Twofold, verily, is this, there is no third, viz. truth and untruth. And verily, the gods are the truth, and man is the untruth. Therefore in saying . . . , "I now enter from untruth into truth," he passes from the men to the gods.

Let him then only speak what is true; for this vow indeed the gods do keep, that they speak the truth; and for this reason they are glorious; glorious therefore is he who, knowing this, speaks the truth.

After the completion (of the sacrifice) he divests himself (of the vow), with the text . . . : "Now I am he who I really am." For, in entering upon the vow, he becomes, as it were, non-human; and as it would not be becoming for him to say, "I enter from truth into untruth;" and as, in fact, he now again becomes man, let him therefore divest himself (of the vow), with the text: "Now I am he who I really am."[4]

We have seen earlier that in comparison to other traditions, in our own modern religious attitudes and expressions we ourselves are lacking most in ritual behavior. If we have "gone secular," that is the area where we have really beome different from our ancestors a couple of centuries ago. The world of the Middle Ages knew a liturgical order; even if not everyone observed it all the time, it was still part of everyone's experience: "One sound rose ceaselessly above the noises of busy life and lifted all things unto a sphere of order and serenity: the sound of bells."[5] That world is barely imaginable to us today. No wonder a text like the one I have quoted puzzles us. It is so foreign to our inquisitive minds. "Sacrificing to the moon twice a month? Was it still a big surprise to them? And the guy who paid for the sacrifice . . . Isn't that it? He paid for it? He gets changed from human to divine? But then he changes back in the end?"

Our reaction—and I am convinced that all of us can recognize this string of responses—is typical of people who for a long time have set a great deal of store by explaining things rationally. We commonly engage in our custom of analysis-by-ratiocination. (*Ratiocination* does not mean much more than "a frantic moving up and down of the brainwaves.") This custom has entered upon a new boom but has been with us for several centuries, and it has exerted itself on the study of religions for a very long time. The word *cognition* preferred nowadays in scholarly circles is often in tandem with what is basically an obsession, an uncritical refusal to allow anything to exist in its own right. Nothing can be admitted until it is made to conform to what *my* mental cause-and-effect ideas will tolerate. And if such things as rituals in ancient India do not present a reason or purpose to me, and seem senseless to my mind, then for the satisfaction of my "cognition," my mind takes up the right to supply that reason. Thus we have scholarly books in our libraries that explain rituals all over the world by things like anxiety about famine: in order to avert famine, people do their strange things. One would think that the people doing these strange things would have to be mentally underdeveloped, or psychologically out of control. And Freud, who truly is a fascinating person, is on record with the diagnosis that religion is a neurosis.

But the writer of the *Śatapathabrāhmaṇa* gives no sign of mental deficiency. His fault is only that he did not share our idea of an exclusive supremacy of "cognition." When we read that a person moves from untruth into truth for the duration of the ritual, it might be useful for us to think about what happens during our wedding ceremony. However cynical some of us may have become, we also know that what happens in that little remainder of a ritual life even among ourselves cannot be written off. It may not take more than a reminder like this to open our minds to a wider field of searches than we have admitted. It is indeed possible that the most important things (the sacred!) have their center in a place over which we have no absolute control. Such is ritual. And would the ritual really be less likely to reside there than in the little space between our ears?

I am not making a case for irrationality. The text in the *Śatapathabrāhmaṇa* is not irrational. We should try to focus on the reason of the text, on what is real, what finally matters, in the text, rather than dwelling on the value we assign to our system of "cognition." And we need not go off the deep end. For the reality that matters most is right there. It is part of common experience. It is, as we said earlier, "ordinary."

The simple stumbling block between our overly analytical minds and the religious phenomena we want to understand is the *utter practicality* of religion. We have been taught to explain things; we are expected to arrive at the cause of this, that, or the other state of affairs. However, in spite of this habit that we have developed over centuries, even the principal religion of the West, Christianity, did not lose its practical core altogether. Martin Luther was once asked how he could possibly get so much accomplished every day — for the questioner knew that Luther also spent several hours each day praying. And Luther answered more or less like this: "If I did not pray that much, I could not get anything done." We should not draw the conclusion that the point of religion is what we know in business as "efficiency." I would rather draw the conclusion that praying, exactly like meditating in Hinduism and Buddhism, is the practice of getting in touch with what or who matters most. That is why Indian texts speak also of "inner sacrifice." After all, the concentration of our mind on "the highest" is as much a matter of *doing* as is the act of sacrifice.

Buddhism has legends that make the practicality of religion stand out even to the most "secularized" human being. There are legends that speak in an easily accessible way about the profoundest issues of meditation techniques. There is the legend that narrates the origin of Buddhism. We owe its best-known form to the Indian poet Aśvaghoṣa, who wrote the *Buddhacarita* ("The Acts of the Buddha").[6] Before the young Siddhārtha Gautama, the man who was going to be the Buddha, set out on his journey toward enlightenment, he was a prince overly protected by his father. The king, his father, intended that Siddhārtha, the crown prince, would be his successor. And it so happened that before the birth of Siddhārtha, a soothsayer revealed to the king that his son would become either a universal emperor or a Buddha. Needless to say, the king took every possible step to keep any hint of asceticism from entering the young prince's ken. Siddhārtha was always surrounded by pure pleasure. But the inevitable occurred. One day, the young prince escaped from the pleasure gardens of the palace. His charioteer was with him. On the ride into the world, Siddhārtha saw some very ordinary things for the first time: an old man with a cane, a sick man on a bed, and a funeral procession. In each case, he asked the charioteer for an explanation. And in succession, the charioteer said what each thing was: an old man, a sick man, a dead man.

Interestingly, the text also says in each case that the charioteer said the obvious thing as a result of being *moved by the gods* to do so. Thus the real beginning of a search for liberation is depicted. It is a matter of seeing the obvious. The only supremely practical problem is to begin to see the obvious in the right way, as it is—not as self-evident, not as trivial, not as relevant only for others, not as a subject for lofty speculation, not as specialized subjects for experts.

I would like to offer some further examples of the practicality of religion from a tradition that is not among the so-called "great religions"—that of the Ngaju Dayak of southern Kalimantan (Borneo) in Indonesia. I especially like to add these examples because they are part of the loose assembly called "tribal religions" that are too often forgotten. They are not normally thought of when people say "religion," especially when the discussion involves flirtations with the attractive and mysterious East where Taoism, Buddhism, Hinduism, and occasionally the mystical part of Islam (Sufism) attract their intellectual devotees among us.

The "practicality" of this tribal tradition is particularly instructive, for Ngaju Dayak is not a household name in our midst. Among the few scholars who have occupied themselves seriously with the religion of the Dayak, the name of the Swiss Hans Schärer stands out. An ethnologist and missionary, he worked in South Borneo for some ten years. In 1939 he went back to Europe, on leave. The Second World War broke out, and he spent the years of delay working on Ngaju Dayak materials with a renowned socio-anthropologist in Leiden. Back in Borneo, he died suddenly in 1947 at the age of forty-three. The findings he left were not complete, but they are definitely the best we have. Schärer did some of the "obvious" things that may illustrate the points we have been discussing. He learned the local language of the Ngaju Dayak. He learned also the special priestly language used in the myths and rituals. He realized that whatever else religion is, it is a constituent of all life in society, its institutions, its customs, its rules and regulations. He made it his custom to go to the best specialists in the Dayak community in order to understand the total context in which religion, rituals, myths, legal proceedings, and so on functioned.

Not unlike Brahmanism, Ngaju religion relies on oral tradition. This means that a main priest teaches young priests to memorize and repeat the myths. Schärer found that in spite of variations that creep in, all the essentials in the rituals—where myths play a significant role—remained impervious to change.[7] For the general study of the history of religions, one significant fact here is that we cannot ascribe uniqueness to Brahmanism—although the ability of Brahman priests to memorize without error is popularly presented as the one exception in the world to the fallibility of memory. It should be obvious too that this fact by itself is of no significance whatsoever to our understanding of a tradition. A tradition is always far more than the peculiarities that strike outsiders.

Another notable detail concerning the Ngaju Dayak is their use of a special priestly language for religious purposes. It is the *basa helo,* "the speech of earlier times." "Earlier times" refers to the primordial time in which the ancestors and culture heroes were living.[8] Accordingly, the *basa helo* is the speech that in the cultic procedures continues to carry the authority of the myth by its very sound.

Schärer does not fail to point out that in fact the language with that special authority is not all that ancient. It is merely "a cultic use of language in which old elements of speech have been preserved that at present are no longer used."[9] Schärer informs us that in this holy language quite a number of words are borrowed from other Dayak languages and from Malay (Bahasa Indonesia, the language most widely used throughout Indonesia as a *lingua franca).* And he adds that most words of the cultic language are transformations of existing words or words made up with added prefixes and suffixes.[10]

Looked upon soberly, objectively, linguistically, the sacred language is to quite an extent an artificial affair. Does this make it deceitful? An interesting question. Of course, Schärer makes no such suggestion in his elaborate discussion. And of course, the accusation of purposeful deceit would be out of place. If such deceit were practiced here, then quite a number of other "guilty" languages could be enumerated. All of us know that Latin was used in the Western church for a very long time. Only since the Second Vatican Council in the early 1960s have masses celebrated in the vernacular become common practice. The use of the ancient Sanskrit language in India for cultic as well as literary and artistic purposes would have to be called a gigantic deceit, especially if we consider that some of the greatest literary masterworks were written in that language, which virtually no one spoke at home but had to learn! It is interesting to note that just as Sanskrit in Indian tradition was considered "the language of the gods," so the priestly language among the Ngaju Dayak was called the "celestial language."[11] In the ancient Near East, the case of Akkadian and Sumerian should also be mentioned. Akkadian was the everyday language, but the entire written tradition and the tradition of literary and religious imagery was based on the prototype of ancient Sumer, its gods and its language — even though that earliest language of the ancient Near East was completely foreign to the Akkadian scribes, who had to learn how to deal with it. If by "not deceitful" we mean "natural," or "not artificial," then we must say, in a word, that no human tradition is ever "natural." Each tradition uses whatever means it has at its disposal to underline the sacredness of its tradition.

The practical subjects that matter most to the Dayak demand our attention, just as do the most important matters in "the great religions." They matter not because we can equate them with things we know of from elsewhere, but because in spite of all general things we know, they strike us as novel — and such novelty is every time at least as surprising as the light on the first day, the sun and the moon on the fourth, the wild beasts eating green herbs, and the extraordinary significance of the day of rest at the beginning of Genesis. Each novelty that comes to us from the religious traditions we study, moreover, does not necessarily send us into ecstasy but affects us in the ordinary human dimensions in which we exist.

One of the extraordinary facts about the Ngaju Dayak made available to us by Hans Schärer is the way they use their creation myth. It is recited in all its glory most especially at funeral ceremonies.[12] The disposal of the dead is at the center of Ngaju religious attention. When I first became aware of this, the *humor* involved in it struck me the most. After all, what we have in a case such as this is a striking contrast that causes us to smile: the dead are dead, the grave is right there, and what do the Ngaju Dayak do? They listen to the musical recitation of the origin of all life! It only slowly dawned on me that what happened there is something I should have been aware of. In our history classes, we have heard of the shout "The king is dead; long live the king!" But also in undeniably religious customs, the West has similar ways. In an early Reformed liturgy (of 1587), the very last thing that happened at the occasion of burials, following the Lord's Prayer, was the pronouncement of the creed by all those present.[13] And the striking thing, of course, is the utter contradiction of the words to the facts unrolling before one's eyes at the place of burial:

> I believe in God the Father almighty, creator of heaven and earth;
>   And in Jesus Christ, His only Son, our Lord, Who was conceived by the Holy Spirit, born of the Virgin Mary, suffered under Pontius Pilate,

was crucified, dead and buried. He descended to hell, on the third day rose again from the dead, ascended to heaven, sits at the right hand of God the Father almighty, thence he will come to judge the living and the dead;

I believe in the Holy Spirit, the holy catholic Church, the communion of saints, the forgiveness of sins, the resurrection of the body, and the life everlasting.

Amen.[14]

The earliest creeds formulated by the church carry great weight in Christianity. They became known as the church's *symbola,* symbols. The particular one just quoted, known as the Apostles' Creed, was accepted by all of Western Christianity. The moment of its recitation at the gravesite and the resounding words ("resurrection of the body," "life everlasting") are strikingly at odds with each other. Humor (and by this we do not mean "fun" or "hilarity") in all its forms is always characterized by some contrast. No contrast is ever more pronounced than that between life and death. The ritual, or myth, that sounds *life* as its final word—in the sight of the corpse lowered into the pit—is among the strongest expressions imaginable. This contrast is central to the culture of the Ngaju Dayak, and it is powerfully expressed through the ritual recitation of the creation myth. It is not a custom that was observed only for a little while (as in fact the same custom with the Apostle's Creed at the funeral *was* in the early Reformed Church in the sixteenth century). We have no illusion about a "sameness" of the Dayak and the sixteenth-century Reformed churches, and yet, we can recognize one with the help of the other. Through fieldwork, cultural anthropology has discovered that by studying foreign civilizations we can look at our own with a much clearer vision. The history of religions enables us to discover "ultimate realities" in our own—often repressed—religious tradition by a detour to distant and ancient traditions.[15]

Our concluding examples involve the proclamation of life in the face of death. This theme goes well beyond the liturgy of funeral ceremonies. The last word here comes straight from a tradition in our midst. Franz Rosenzweig is a twentieth-century legend. He was philosophically trained and could have looked forward to a comfortable academic career—had it not been for his rediscovery of Judaism. His book *The Star of Redemption* is one of the most astonishing religious phenomena in the modern Western world. To be sure, it is very difficult; it is also mystifying, yet extraordinarily enlightening. The American Christian theologian Reinhold Niebuhr said, "Martin Buber's thought is well known . . . but Rosenzweig . . . had an equal, and possibly larger, share in the religious revolution of modern Judaism."[16] Although the final lines of *The Star* are not in verse, Rosenzweig had them printed in a manner that reminds one of experimental poetry, (and we do not forget that virtually all myths are poetry), in a triangle, pointing down:

. . . . How difficult is every beginning! To do justice and to love mercy—that still looks like a goal. Before any goal, the will can claim to need a little respite first. But to walk humbly with thy God—that is no longer a goal. That is so unconditional, so free of every condition, of every But—first and Tomorrow, so wholly Today and thus wholly eternal as life and the way. And therefore it partakes of the eternal truth as directly as do life and the way.
To walk humbly with thy God—nothing more is demanded
there than a wholly present trust. But trust is a big word.
It is a seed whence grow faith, hope, and love, and the
fruit which ripens out of them. It is the very simplest
and just for that the most difficult. It dares at
every moment to say Truly to the truth. To
walk humbly with thy God—the words are
written over the gate, the gate which
leads out of the mysterious-
miraculous light of the divine
sanctuary in which no man
can remain alive. Whither,
then, do the wings of
the gate open? Thou
knowest it not?
INTO LIFE[17]

Literature
Johan Huizinga, *Homo Ludens: A Study of the Play Element in Culture* (Boston: Beacon, 1955); Jean Bottéro, "Mesopotamian Religion," in *Mythologies,* ed. Yves Bonnefoy and Wendy Doniger (Chicago: University of Chicago Press, 1991), vol. 1, pp. 142–55; Hans Schärer, *Ngaju Religion, The Conception of God Among a South Borneo People,* trans. Rodney Needham (The Hague: Nijhoff, 1963); Kees W. Bolle, *The Freedom of Man in Myth* (Nashville, Tenn.: Vanderbilt University Press, 1993).

TRUTH

In the previous section, I belittled the fashionable overuse of the word *cognition*. I did so in order to curb our uncritical reliance on our own critical ability. The point was of course not to curtail any of our serious attempts to *know*. What we truly want to know we should deal with in the *discipline* of our study. Symbolic expressions may lead to concepts, but they precede concepts, and their primary relation is to experience. And our examples drawn from the world of religions made clear that we do harm to our understanding if we ignore matters that present themselves as matters of experience, in our own tradition as well as others. It is possible to question the sense of saying the Apostles' Creed at the occasion of a burial on the ground that our rational analysis cannot easily articulate what is going on. But if we refuse to recognize anything valuable in this practice, something is amiss with our cognition. Understanding religious data involves proper "cognition," and this always involves proper *recognition* of experience.

As a rule, the question that historians of religions touch on only gingerly is the question of *truth*. It is customary to leave the problem to the philosophers of religion. It is the task of philosophers of religion to examine the validity of religious propositions. We have seen, however, more or less schematically at the beginning of this book, and with more urgency on the basis of the contents of religion in the preceding pages, that it is impossible not to touch on the question of truth.

Myths present themselves with a claim to truth. Certainly they do not express themselves in the same terms as philosophical expositions; but that they assume and posit certain facts as incontrovertible is clear to the listener. Different religions place different things in the center, yet with undiminished authority. If we take seriously the claim to truth inherent in each, how do we deal with this problem?

The lackadaisical idea that all human beings are entitled to their opinion is not very helpful, even if it prevails in the Western, industrial, relatively well-to-do, and always highly individualistic world we live in. The myths of the world are usually not characterized by individualism but more often by strong notions of community.

If we ask, Now that we have taken note of what the Ngaju state in their tradition, and what Hindus, Buddhists, and others say—what *is* true?, we realize that we have no answer readily at hand. We have to remember also that we, "moderns," no matter what we like to think about ourselves, are in fact mythically obsessed.[18]

Of course, we can push the issue further, and ask, But do we not have some sort of modern, philosophical, scientifically based agreement? Whether we like it or not, we cannot say much more than this: Except for some rather mythical circumference within which we do our arguing, we have nothing. We have no clear statements from philosophers that would stimulate us to come out with a formula as to what is true in the manifold world of religions. We do, however, have a number of serious warnings from philosophy against "ultimate" and pretentious statements.

Ludwig Wittgenstein, who taught philosophy at Cambridge, and who has made a lasting impression on many thinkers, spoke not infrequently about matters of religion. Some of his remarks in the course of his lectures are enlightening, especially when they are at the same time exceedingly simple. Some students' notes from his lectures (in 1938) record that during the First World War Wittgenstein "saw consecrated bread being carried in chromium steel. This struck him as ludicrous."[19] The notes are brief and perhaps not altogether accurate. I like to think that Wittgenstein might not have said, "This struck me as ludicrous." He may well have described the sight of the sacred Host in chrome-plated steel and just have smiled. Or instead of "ludicrous" he might well have said "humorous." Would the bread that grants eternal life need such protection against the chance of being struck by shrapnel? Yes and no.

Immediately following this humorous recollection, the notes quote Wittgenstein no doubt rather literally:

> Suppose that someone believed in the Last Judgment, and I don't, does this mean that I believe the opposite to him, just that there won't be such a thing? I would say: "not at all, or not always."
>
> Suppose I say that the body will rot, and another says "No. Particles of you will rejoin in a thousand years, and there will be a Resurrection of you."
>
> If some said: "Wittgenstein, do you believe in this?" I'd say: "No." "Do you contradict the man?" I'd say: "No."[20]

It is often very difficult to abstain from a discussion that cannot go anywhere. Abstaining, or as in Wittgenstein's example, not contradicting, is an act that can be most appropriate if we grant that life itself forms a connecting world between the "wings of the gate" of each tradition.

Karl Jaspers is among the few philosophers in recent times who occupied himself with truly gigantic problems; here are the titles of some of his books: *The Future of Mankind; The Origin and Goal of History; Philosophy of Existence; Socrates, Buddha, Confucius, Jesus; Truth and Symbol; World History of Philosophy.* Jaspers is no more than Wittgenstein inclined to rank himself among religious devotees of any kind. A mere quotation, of course, does not do justice to any thinker of size, but it is worthwhile to read some sentences by Jaspers that touch on the issues of history and transcendence (even though the latter term is not used here) which we have found to be important to our work.

> In fact, one cannot philosophize except in coherency with the history of Philosophy: Not a single human being can begin to think from scratch, although each real thought, one that is thought anew, is also original. Imperceptibly, the thinking that has come down to us elicits one's own thought. Decisive thought comes about only in relationship to that other thought, which it then appropriates or rejects.[21]

Every age has its philosophers. Whatever else they do, they provide inspiration for all who have to use their minds in their work. They articulate better than the rest of us what matters in what we vaguely call "reality." "Reality," after all, we have to take for granted in whatever specialty we make our inquiries. But according to the thinkers I have mentioned, special caution is in order in regard to questions of truth. In the history of religions we realize that the issue of truth is not to be ignored—on condition that it is broached in a way that is itself proper. This way must not be extraneous to the documents we examine. It should be the way of serious interpretation. All religious traditions have their thinkers. They have themselves dealt with the question of how undue simplicities could be avoided. The end of the way of serious interpretation may not soon appear, but precisely for that reason minimalism is better than conceited explanation; the ability to say, "I do not understand this," better than "Let me amend the document so that I can explain it"; the patience to continue listening and to read better than to declare a tradition below one's own level of intelligence.

A way of interpreting, such as this one, is "hermeneutics," the central activity of the historian of religions.[22] This learned word has a long history. It is derived from Hermes, the Greek god who functioned as messenger between the gods and people. Proper and just interpreting is and remains an extraordinary activity for human beings; it is an activity that aims for truthfulness and it can hope to arrive at that only through its own inner consistency. That is why "hermeneutics" has a long career in the study of law, because no law can be interpreted inconsistently from one case to another, and likewise in theology, because an interpretation of scriptural texts demands consistency. Does that mean there is no conflict or argument? Of course there is, but as in the legal profession, an interpretation of one rule cannot be in utter conflict with that of another.

Here we discover the reason why the term *hermeneutics* most precisely indicates the manner used by the historian of religions for breaking through the "wall" separating the descriptive from the systematic disciplines. *Hermeneutics* is short for the serious endeavor to be consistent in our interpretations. It should not be confused with *exegesis,* which is vitally necessary, but is no more than clearing up obscurities in texts. Exegesis answers questions such as, what animal is meant by such and such a word, which must mean some animal? Or: how is this noun related to the use of that verb? Hermeneutics, of course, can never ignore the precision that exegesis may be able to attain. However, there is and remains a wider realm of "discourse" within which the animals, nouns, and verbs make sense. It is a problem of locating the "whole" of the law of a nation, or the totality of an authoritative scripture, or of a religion. This "truth" that one looks for can never be settled by a precise, sufficient definition, or by a simple yes or no. There is a good reason for the divine derivation of the term *hermeneutics!*

Finally, however, we should remember once more that the modesty that modern thinkers have insisted on, in whatever technical way they see fit, is at the core of the entire issue of recognizing the "truth" as it functions in human existence. Hermeneutics is analogous to and inseparable from the very ordinary process of "getting to know someone" in a more than superficial way. It is a matter of being fair and just to people. It is never merely a matter of logic but rather of an entire fabric of mind and heart in which logic should function properly, just as properly as the results of our hard work on the *data.*

NOTES

1. See chapter 1 of this book.
2. See chapter 2 of this book.

3. Marshall G. S. Hodgson, *The Venture of Islam: Conscience and History in a World Civilization*, vol. 1, *The Classical Age of Islam* (Chicago: University of Chicago Press, 1974), p. 128.

4. Śatapathabrāhmaṇa 1.1.1.1–6. *The Satapatha-Brahmana According to the Text of the Madhyandina School*, part 1 trans. Julius Eggeling (1882; Delhi: Motilal Banarsidass, 1972), Sacred Books of the East series, vol. 12, pp. 2–4.

5. J. Huizinga, *The Waning of the Middle Ages* (Garden City, N.Y.: Anchor, 1954), p. 10.

6. Text in Edward Conze, trans., *Buddhist Scriptures* (Harmondsworth: Penguin Books, 1959), pp. 34–66.

7. Hans Schärer, *Der Totenkult der Ngaju Dayak. Mythen zum Totenkult und die Texte zum Tantolak Matei*, part 1, *Mythen zum Totenkult* (The Hague: Nijhoff, 1966), p. 5.

8. Ibid., pp. 7–12.

9. Ibid., p. 8.

10. Ibid.

11. Ibid., p. 9.

12. A good deal about the importance of the creation myth in the funeral ceremonies is available in English through Hans Schärer's *Ngaju Religion: The Conception of God Among a South Borneo People*, trans. Rodney Needham (The Hague: Nijhoff, 1963).

13. G. van der Leeuw, *Liturgiek* (Nijkerk: Callenbach, n.d.), p. 219.

14. The text is presented in all books of church order (such as the Presbyterian *Book of Common Worship*, or the Episcopal *Book of Common Prayer*). The text is printed also in John H. Leith, ed., *Creeds of the Churches*, 3rd ed. (Atlanta, Ga.: John Knox Press, 1983). On the humor of the togetherness of the opposites life and death see Bolle, *The Freedom of Man in Myth* (Nashville, Tenn.: Vanderbilt University Press, 1993), pp. 42–50.

15. Joachim Wach used the term *ultimate reality* in his description of religious experience. See his *Types of Religious Experience* (Chicago: University of Chicago Press, 1951), p. 32. He refers to Paul Tillich, who used the term in his "The Problem of Theological Method," in *Journal of Religion* 27 (1947), p. 23. See also Tillich's use of *ultimate concern*, especially in his *Systematic Theology* (Chicago: University of Chicago Press, 1951), vol. 1, *passim*, and his use of the term *unconditional*, in his *What Is Religion?* (New York: Harper, 1973); in this latter work, see also the very helpful introduction by the translator, James Luther Adams.

16. Quoted on the front cover of Nahum Glatzer, *Franz Rosenzweig, His Life and Thought*, 2nd, rev. ed. (New York: Schocken, 1961).

17. Franz Rosenzweig, *The Star of Redemption*, translated from the 2nd ed.

18. See chapter 2 of this book.

19. Cyril Barrett, ed., *Wittgenstein: Lectures and Conversations on Aesthetics, Psychology and Religious Belief,* compiled from notes taken by Yorick Smythies, Rush Rhees, and James Taylor (Berkeley: University of California Press, n.d.), p. 53.

20. Ibid.

21. Karl Jaspers, *Weltgeschichte der Philosophie. Einleitung,* ed. Hans Saner (Munich and Zurich: Piper, 1982), p. 42.

22. See chapter 1 of this book.

HISTORICAL SURVEY OF WESTERN INTELLECTUAL APPROACHES TO RELIGION

From the Classics to the Renaissance

WHY AN INTELLECTUAL HISTORY?

By the term *intellect* we mean the entire mental apparatus that we carry around with us and bring to bear on whatever we try to understand. It *defines* and *explains* (i.e., expounds the causes of) our object of study; through it we *understand* the people who form the object in our studies. "To understand" refers to our formation of an image of people and their experiences which aims to correspond to what is really the case. As a rule, the work of our intellect *explains* details, but it *understands* larger coherences and relationships. This is as true for the natural sciences as for the social and human studies. In the old image of the French scientist Poincaré, one cannot satisfactorily study an elephant under a microscope. In the subject matter of the history of religions, in myths, symbols, and rituals, coherences and relationships are conspicuous. People pray to their gods, gods create the world and people, rituals are followed and are as a rule communal affairs, traditions are handed down. Details can be explained, but religions being matters of people, they ask for our understanding, and not only explanation.

Looking at some religious phenomena in the first half of this book, we have become thoroughly aware that pointing out simple causes that might come to mind is rarely adequate for what we want to understand. Every discipline of study, if taken seriously, places demands on us that we could hardly have guessed at the beginning. In our discipline of study it is no exaggeration to speak of a necessary *conversion of thought*. That is to say: the idea of thinking and its value are themselves subject to change in the course of time; the practice of thought can be an unending series of "conversions."

We are fortunate to have a great deal of information about the ways people have brought their minds to bear on the multifarious subject of religion. We can learn a great deal from studying efforts that were made in the past.

Is religion only a matter of thought? The first part of this book makes clear that the answer to that question is a firm *no*. We have seen that the three great expressions of religions (myths, rituals, and symbolic places) are primarily related to *experiences*. This does not prevent us from thinking! And of course, no religion ever occurs *without* ideas. On the contrary, each one generates them. All of this challenges the mind and has led our best thinkers to very different philosophical positions. Sometimes the experiences of religion may be exceptional, as in the case of prophets and mystics, but more commonly, the experiences are not separate from the normal events, perceptions, and thoughts in life. Even this ordinariness does not mean that the conversion of thought of which I spoke is superfluous. There is such a thing as a conversion in thought that is needed precisely in order to be just to the ordinariness of religion. And as in the method of all sciences, more than one need for a change in thought is likely.

After these reminders, it is time to give our attention to the problem of ideas about religion and religions. Not only in recent years but in all recorded history, the desire to grasp everything in terms of our own (unexamined) mental habits has never subsided. Our field, the history of religions, is no exception to this rule. Working with our minds, after all, is what all intellectual inquiry is about. At the same time, we realize that working with our minds has its own history, its own vicissitudes. Each culture, each century, each generation, has its own favorite ideas. For the sake of accurate knowledge, we have to be aware of their ups and downs, for our acquisition of knowledge should not be whimsical or uncritical. To discover the concepts, the moods of various periods, or the predominant feelings of a civilization, we have to pay attention to philosophers, and also to others: artists, politicians, missionaries, musicians, and many more. Thereby we come also to see that many of the ideas in our own heads are not original, and in most cases, we can see why they failed to give the great answers people hoped for.

Literature
Ninian Smart, "Religion, Study of," in *Encyclopaedia Britannica, Macropaedia,* 15th ed. (Chicago: Encyclopaedia Britannica, 1974), vol. 15, pp. 613–28; Eric J. Sharpe, *Comparative Religion: A History,* 2nd ed. (La Salle, Ill.: Open Court, 1986); Mircea Eliade, *The Sacred and the Profane* (New York: Harper, 1961; many reprints), pp. 216–32; Jan de Vries, *Perspectives in the History of Religions,* trans. Kees W. Bolle, (Berkeley: University of California Press, 1977).

"Our" Classical World Within the World

We are used to saying "classical" to refer to the civilizations of ancient Greece and Rome. Classical authors raised questions about religion, but we should realize that all human traditions did the same thing, and probably from early times on. We certainly have "classical" writers elsewhere, as in India and China. We cannot deal with them here, for we are limiting ourselves to our immediate ancestors in the development of our thought. But we should not imagine that only our classical cultural ancestors raised significant questions. A couple of illustrations will suffice to make this point.

When we consider the birth of Buddhism in India, around 500 B.C., and its spread from there over large parts of Asia, we should think of this new religion not only as another religion, but also as a crisis for the Indian religious, intellectual, and social situation at the time.[1] The authority in that situation was an early form of Hinduism, known as Brahmanism, which saw itself as based on the absolute foundation of the Vedas—that is, the revealed sacred texts—and which was anchored in the reality of different classes of people (the *varṇas*). The teachings of Siddhārtha Gautama, the Buddha (the "Enlightened One"), the founder of Buddhism, not only questioned but rejected both these principles.

Another serious challenge to the existing tradition in India came from Jainism (founded by Mahāvīra, "the great hero," also called the *Jina,* the spiritual "conqueror"). These passages from a ninth-century (A.D.) text in the Jain tradition may startle us by their seemingly "modern" deconstruction attempts:

> Some foolish men declare that Creator made the world.
> The doctrine that the world was created is ill-advised, and should
>   be rejected.

If God created the world, where was he before creation?
If you say he was transcendent then, and needed no support, where is
    he now?
No single being had the skill to make this world—
For how can an immaterial god create that which is material?
How could God have made the world without any raw material?
If you say he made this first, and then the world, you are faced with
    an endless regression.
If you declare that this raw material arose naturally you fall into
    another fallacy,
For the whole universe might thus have been its own creator, and have
    arisen equally naturally.
If God created the world by an act of his own will, without any raw
    material,
Then it is just his will and nothing else—and who will believe this
    silly stuff?
If he is ever perfect and complete, how could the will to create have
    arisen in him?

. . . .
. . . the doctrine that the world was created by God
Makes no sense at all.

. . . .
Good men should combat the believer in divine creation, maddened
    by an evil doctrine.
Know that the world is uncreated, as time itself is, without beginning
    and end,
And is based on the principles, life and the rest.
Uncreated and indestructible, it endures under the compulsion of its
    own nature,
Divided into three sections—hell, earth, and heaven.[2]

From the perspective of later Hinduism—when this text was written—
Jainism was not another religion to be welcomed but a total disruption of
the religious order. Jainism had come into being at about the same time as
Buddhism, and questions from both Buddhists and Jains about religion
were not accepted as proper, serious inquiries.

These examples may set the tone of a proper humility when we begin to
look at the roots of our own philosophical tradition. For *our* ways of ques-

tioning religion make up only one of many intellectual strands of questioning in world history.

The Greeks, "our" philosophizing beginnings, of course spoke their own language. The Greek word for "god" is *theos*. However, the use of the term *theos* in Greek is very different from the use of the word *God* in our Western, Christianity-affected tradition. A great modern scholar summarizes the difference concisely: "The Greek word . . . has primarily a predicative force."[3] This simply means that the Greeks could say, for instance, "This heroic act, or such virtue, or this victory *is God*." They would not easily turn this type of phrase around, to say such things as "*God is* such and such." In the words of the same author,

> The Greeks did not, as Christians or Jews do, first assert the existence of God and then proceed to enumerate his attributes, saying "God is good," "God is love," and so forth. Rather, they were so impressed or awed by the things in life or nature remarkable either for joy or fear that they said: "this is a god" or "that is a god."[4]

The Greek way of conceiving of gods and the divine is clear from Aristotle's reflections on the movements of heavenly bodies. He studied them, thought about them, was impressed by their eternal, unchanging courses, and he calls them *theios,* divine. It is like an exclamation of wonderment over something that so clearly goes beyond the sphere of human, limited, fickle motions and abilities.[5]

This simple realization of one difference between the Greeks, our "intellectual forebears," and ourselves will help a great deal in understanding the reasonings among Greek thinkers concerning religion. Few, if any, could feel tempted to reject the tradition in which they carried on their conversations. And all Greeks agreed that Greek was *the* language of civilization.[6]

Thales of Miletus lived around 600 B.C.; his name is mentioned among the very first in any book on the history of Western philosophy. He is remembered as the founder of the "Ionic physical Philosophy." (Ionia was the name of a region which today is western Turkey.) As with so many of the earliest Greek thinkers, we do not have his works but only fragments, words remembered and quoted by others. In those fragments of Thales the word *God* does occur. Plato and Aristotle report that according to Thales "everything is full of gods."[7] Another famous teaching of Thales is contained in the statement that "water is the primordial ground (or permanent entity)" of all things.[8]

To an educated nineteenth-century audience, it seemed correct to see in the birth of Greek philosophy the beginnings of Western civilization and science. And the expression "the Greek miracle" took hold. Until this very day, one still comes across it. What is meant is that Thales and the other Milesian philosophers of nature (*phusis*) somehow anticipated the great theories and discoveries of nature, such as those of Darwin.

Such an interpretation of Thales is quite mistaken. Not a single philosopher in ancient Greece ever conceived of anything like our modern sciences; they had other things in mind. Werner Jaeger, a twentieth-century student of Greece, hit the nail on the head:

> His [Thales'] water is a visible part of the world of experience. But his view of the origin of things brings him very close to the theological creation-myths, or rather leads him to compete with them. For while his theory seems to be purely physical, he evidently thinks of it as also having what we may call a metaphysical character. This fact is revealed by the only one of his utterances that has come down to us in verbal form (if, indeed, it goes back to him): *panta plere theon,* "everything is full of gods." Two hundred years later, at the end of this first period of philosophical thinking, Plato cites this apophthegm with special emphasis, almost as if it were the primal word and the very quintessence of all philosophy.[9]

Not only the creation story in Genesis, but numerous cosmogonic myths in the world speak of primordial waters. Doing so, they do not begin to resemble a theory of biochemistry. In fact, these abundant stories all make use of an obvious item of experience that expresses what much later in philosophy would be called "potentiality." That means the state of possibility to become actual, real, existent. The striking thing about water is not only that it is the most easily available fluid, or even that it is necessary for life, but that it takes on the form of whatever container it is poured into. The language of myth, as we have seen, is always concrete; it does not indulge in abstractions. That Thales, even though he began to philosophize, turned to water as the essential element of the world cannot surprise us. Did he "break" with the world of myth? Hardly. Surely, if he had intended to do anything as revolutionary as that, he would have been remembered for it; some hint would have been registered in the fragments.

In fact, the early Greek thinkers who said anything about clearly recognizable religious subjects did so with great care, not at all in order to break with the past, but because they had something very serious to express. The most striking example among the early philosophers is Xenophanes (sixth century B. C.). One of his fragments that seems quite critical of religion has been quoted frequently:

> Mortals suppose that the gods are born (as they themselves are), and that they wear man's clothing and have human voice and body. But if cattle and lions had hands, so as to paint with their hands and produce works of art as men do, they would paint their gods, and give them bodies in form like their own—horses like horses, cattle like cattle.[10]

These remarks by Xenophanes might appear to resemble a theory of modern psychology. And they may seem a devastating analysis of religion to many a modern. But the fragments make very clear why Xenophanes is critical of human foolishness. He himself has a concern for what in his opinion is truly worthwhile, in contrast to what people think:

> God is one, supreme among gods and men, and not like mortals in body and mind. The whole [of god] sees, the whole perceives, the whole hears. But without effort he sets in motion all things by mind and thought. It [i.e., being] always abides in the same place, not moves at all, nor is it fitting that it should move from one place to another.[11]

We should touch here on a fact that is of some significance, although it generally goes unrecognized. We may all be ready to acknowledge in principle that religion is not merely a subject to be examined in logical investigation. However, we may not be equally ready to admit that it is also a matter of social class. No Greek was ever hesitant in recognizing class distinction. The quotation from Xenophanes bears it out, for Xenophanes is distinguishing between the popular and the elite views of religion. And we should keep in mind that this unapologetic distinction between the worthwhile view of the philosophers and the rude religious ideas of the populace at large plays its role in all the literature we have of the Greeks and the Romans.

We ourselves have become familiar with the idea that all people are equal. In the science of anthropology the equality of all people is assumed. However, in "the intellectual world," it is also "normal" to consider ourselves above many religious practices that people indulge in. Religion is often regarded only as the customs of *others*—the ones not as educated as ourselves. Thus it would seem that, at least in this one respect, we are a little bit comparable to the ancients in our mental habits.

The Greek and Roman higher classes who did all the philosophizing that has come down to us were unanimous in disdaining the religious practices of the crowd. This class habit is reflected throughout Greek and Roman history. Although we do owe to the ancients descriptions of such things as peasant religious customs, we have no ancient authority trying to search systematically for the sense that they might have. Neither a Plato nor an Aristotle, nor anyone of consequence in Rome, like Seneca or Lucretius, had respect for popular religion. However, this should not be mistaken for a general, unqualified, and uninformed intellectual contempt for religion (of the type that is not uncommon in our time).

The early Buddhists, the Jain thinker we quoted, and Thales each assessed critically the religious situation in which they found themselves and each from a different point of view. Obviously we could have included in the list Christianity as well, arising as it did in a critique of the existing tradition in whose midst it arose. The key observation to make here is that all of them began to think on the basis of the religious situation in which they found themselves, even though they thought *in reaction*. Certainly they were all quite serious. The simple image of Xenophanes' god who was *unlike mortals in body and thought* still stands out today. Serious critique always arises out of a serious concern. And that is why it is never only destructive. This, it would seem, is very much like a general law in the history of thought about religion and religions—even if at times it takes a while for the serious concern to become evident.

GREEKS AND ROMANS AND THEIR INFLUENCE

The notion that religion is always something "exclusivistic" has to be discarded when we look at the ideas of classical thinkers and scholars. It is true that for the most part the Greeks had a good deal of self-esteem, and we have already alluded to their custom of regarding outsiders as barbarians—mainly because of their incomprehensible languages. However, the same Greeks never tried to impose their own religious customs on others, not even in the case of the Persians, with whom they were at war for a considerable time. On the contrary, the "father of History," Herodotus (fifth century B.C.), speaks at length about the Egyptians in the first book of his famous *Histories,* and he does not hesitate to identify specific Egyptian deities with the deities he knows from his own Greek tradition. He never doubted for a moment that the Egyptians enjoyed the most ancient civilization and could lay claim to the most ancient rights in religious expression. He never doubted the most ancient rights of the Egyptian heritage. He even attributes the first introduction of names of deities in earliest Greece to Egyptian priests! We have seen that the Greeks considered only their own language truly civilized, but this "superiority" of the Greeks in their own consciousness had nothing to do with a distinct subject termed "religion."

As to Rome, the situation was not all that different, in spite of modern biases regarding Rome that are familiar in our own discussions. Of course, we know that Rome became the conqueror and the occupying force over most of Europe and the entire ancient world. Rome produced influences of every kind, influences that lasted and are visible in the Western world into our own time. Ways of building, the use of Latin terminology, the Italian, Spanish, Portuguese, Romanian, French languages, the Latinization of English, entire areas of legal custom and institutions, all stand as the lasting testament of Rome. In the world of learning, the impact of Latin, the language of the Romans, is most remarkable. Until the end of the eighteenth century, Latin was the language in which most professors taught their students. And Latin continued until very recently to be the language in which the Catholic Church conducted the ceremony of the Eucharist (the Communion celebration).

Nevertheless, in spite of the spread of Roman customs, and even the institution of the *cult* of the Roman emperor—an obvious religious phenomenon—we find no evidence of an imposition of religion on the many nations Rome conquered. The spread of the emperor cult itself amounted primarily to additional temples, alongside those of whatever other cults existed. During its imperial period, from Caesar to the end of the Empire, Rome itself experienced an influx of cults that originated far away from Rome and Italy. The multitude of cults was a fact of life. Intellectually, it was a general custom of Romans to see deities, for instance of the Germanic tribes, as other forms of the deities they themselves knew: Mars, Mercurius, and so on.

The Greeks developed a number of theories that dealt with religion explicitly. We can sum them up rather briefly in three distinct groups: (1) allegorical explanation; (2) rational explanation; and (3) euhemerism. Greek thinkers can be credited with the clear formulation of these three. Their clarity no doubt has been the major cause of their lasting use. All three continued to be employed, with only minor variations, well into the nineteenth century, and to be looked upon as adequate approaches to the complex topic of religion.

Allegory and Allegorization.   Most of us know what allegory is. Poets often use it, describing one thing under the image of something else. There is something behind the words used, pointing to what the speaker really intends. "You break my heart," says the disappointed lover. It is not meant literally, but we know what is indicated.

The Frenchman Jean de la Fontaine (of the seventeenth century) wrote animal fables that most of us have heard at one time or another. A crow sitting on a branch holds a piece of cheese in its beak. A fox on the ground addresses the crow: If your voice is as handsome as you are, please sing, let me see! The crow opens its mouth to sing, and sure enough, the cheese falls and the fox gets it. The moral deals with flattery. That is the allegory, and in case you had missed it, La Fontaine explains it at the end of the poem. The words point to something other than what is visible on the surface.

Allegorization takes place when the process of looking for something else behind the words is made into a central method, and educated Greeks freely used it in explaining myths. Plato and others brought it to bear on Homer's great epic poems. Homer's *Iliad* depicts the war between the Trojans and the Greeks. Even the gods choose sides and participate in the skirmishes. Many, many Greek intellectuals then allegorized: though this is a story of war, what really is meant is the struggle between good and evil. Thus many an offensive act that occurs in the narrative, many an indecency on the part of the gods, can be reconciled.

As a way of explaining myths, allegorizing has an obvious drawback. Fables, such as those told by La Fontaine, invite us to look behind the words for an easily identifiable, real intention, but myths as a rule do not. Of course, there are similes, there are comparisons and images, for most myths are poetry, but even the most consistent allegorization leaves much unaddressed in a myth.

At the same time, allegory has sometimes become *more* than mere allegory. We have seen in the case of the biblical creation story that a rabbinical view interpreted the text by "remythologizing" it in a novel and unexpected way. The original light was not ordinary light, so it goes, but light that needed to be hidden, a light so superb and all-reaching that God would not bring it into the open until the very end of his creation was accomplished. Such an interpretation is more than mere allegory. It is akin to what many a great mystic has realized. Among Christian mystics, Bernard of Clairvaux was one who practised allegorization (one would almost say) with a vengeance. He did so in meditating on the Songs of Songs. That Bible book is an unabashed song of passion between two lovers. Bernard presented a series of no fewer than eighty-six contemplative homilies on the text, explaining that its real meaning was the relation between the soul and God.[12] "The kiss of his mouth" becomes the touch of the Holy Spirit, and what the text calls the bride's breasts, and their perfume, becomes the utter and joyful submission to the Lord—who is the one who in his grace has poured the fragrance. Sober-minded readers of the text may not readily accept such allegorizing interpretations. Nevertheless, the great mystics are by definition those rare human beings who anticipate in their experience the highest goal in their religious tradition. Those goals vary from one religion to another, and even from one period to another in the same tradition, but all religious traditions have their saints whose experiences engendered entire movements by virtue of the fact that they inspired others with their new interpretations, and in many cases these new views can be called "allegorization."

Some allegorization may seem extravagant. Nevertheless, an illustration from the Sufi traditions in Islam may show the extraordinary force of what at first sight seems no more than a superficial metaphorical reference. In this instance, the mere thought of an ordinary object, a knife, is interpreted in a way that fills it with a new symbolic significance. Some people went to visit the Sufi mystic Rabi'a (A. D. 717–801) and found her tearing a piece of meat with her teeth. They asked: "'Have you no knife with which to cut it?' She said, 'From fear of cutting off (separation from God) I have never had a knife in my house, so I have none.'"[13]

We witness not an individual's oddity but an experience embedded in a tradition in which in fact the entire world is transformed into a stage of divine action. In spite of our reservations before allegorizing explanations of texts, we should realize that even the most "dubious" methods in some instances lead to undeniably real religious configurations. The allegorizations that we must be wary of are the ones that in no way deepen anyone's understanding, but rather "explain away" the meaning of texts.

Rational Explanation.   More precisely, we might speak of "rationalistic psychologisms." This term is my attempt to group together a number of Greek efforts to analyze the human psyche in order to explain religion. A significant element in all human beings, so these theories assume, is fear. Thus supposedly people were so frightened at one time by phenomena of nature such as thunder and lightning that they began to imagine divine powers at work.

There is no reason to write off fear as a major human experience. But it is necessary to realize that only a very small segment of religious facts seems to allow any explanation along this line. A twentieth-century philosopher, though barely up to date on ethnological or mythological interpretation, remarked, "What is most essential in man's religious life is not the *fact* of fear, but the *metamorphosis of fear*. . . . in myth man begins to learn a new and strange art: the art of expressing, and that means of organizing, his most deeply rooted instincts, his hopes and fears."[14] If we consider the myths we have listened to, there is so much sheer literary beauty in them that fear alone could not have been the cause. Furthermore, the negative ring the word *fear* has should not lead us astray. It can mean *awe*—a term we still remember, even if we do not use it a great deal. Fear as "dread" or "terror" must not be confused with it. "Fear" can occur as an awe people sense before gods and goddesses. It is not the inclination to run away in panic, but rather a profound respect. In addition, it can be the wonder at a clarity that suddenly breaks through, or at a force, a joy, or many other things that present themselves as beyond ordinary human limits. The Greek myths abound in examples. And on such occasions, as we have seen earlier, the Greeks exclaimed: "Here is a god!"[15]

The idea that the principal function of a myth is to explain natural phenomena has had a long life. In our civilization, the first clear suggestions in this direction come once more from Greece. The technical term for the mythical cause of a feature of nature, whether thunder and lightning, or earthquakes, or a flower (such as the narcissus) is the Greek *etios* (meaning cause), and some stories can be called *etiological* and may indeed pay a good deal of attention to *origins*. However, when it comes to ascribing etiological concerns to myth in general, an uncritical assumption is at work: namely, that everything in human speech and thought turns around the obsession to find the essence of things in *items of information*, whether provable (as in the sciences) or imagined (as in psychology).

Euhemerism.   Euhemerus was a storyteller who lived around 300 B.C. We have none of his words in his own writing—as with so many authors of the ancient world. His influence is clear from the custom of calling a particular way of explaining myths by his name—euhemerism or euhemerization—

and from the many times a certain story he composed is referred to by later writers. The story is called *Hiera anagraphe*, "Account of Sacred Things."

His story did not present itself as a learned theory. It seems to have been composed to entertain rather than to instruct. Euhemerus describes an island where the god Zeus used to rule as a human king. And Zeus had a pillar set up on the island, on which he inscribed the account of his own great and beneficial deeds, as well as those of his father and grandfather, who ruled the island before him (Ouranos and Cronos, best known from the mythical genealogy of the gods by Hesiod). Ouranos, for example, whose name means sky or heaven, was credited as the first astronomer, who served mankind by making possible the creation of a calender. Out of gratitude for the benefits bestowed on them by Zeus, Ouranos, and Cronos, the people raised those royal figures to divine rank.

The theory attributed to Euhemerus is concise: gods and goddesses at one time were people, and their impact on human life was so great that they came to be regarded as divine. For what followed in intellectual history, it is important to keep in mind that Euhemerus never said that gods are *mere* people, nor did he say that deities are mere figments of our imagination. He emphasizes the goodness of those early kings and their extraordinary benefits bestowed on humanity as the cause of their deification. The history that followed modified Euhemerus's basic ideas considerably, as we shall see.

There is no doubt that Euhemerus's story is fiction. We might call it a romance. The protagonist tells the story. He traveled eastward and there landed on a mysterious island, Panchaia by name, and if Diodorus, a later Greek historian from whom we have much of our information, recorded matters correctly, the visitor to Panchaia could see India in the distance from a ridge on the east side of the island. We remember that Euhemerus did not set out to provide us with a theory. A point of some importance that might easily escape us today is that whatever the Greeks said about their gods was transmitted by myths. Myths are in story form. The step from here to Euhemerus's storytelling is not as great as it might seem to us. The problem we have in this respect is mainly due to the influence of Christianity. Our Christianity-affected civilization insists that gods and goddesses are not "given." Even most of the professed "atheists" would instinctively agree with the rest of us that if there is a deity, it must be *one*, and most especially, it must be absolutely transcendent. Such insistences could not have bothered Euhemerus. His playfulness is in concert with the myths of his world.[16]

What accounts for the lasting use of euhemerism as an explanation of religion? The principal answer is that it linked the "puzzle" or "mystery" of divinity to "facts" of our own world — even if those "facts" could never be critically analyzed but were themselves a product of the imagination.

Literature

Jean Bayet, *Histoire politique et psychologique de la religion romaine* (Paris: Payot, 1957); Franz Cumont, *Oriental Religions* (New York: Dover, 1956); Werner Jaeger, *The Theology of the Early Greek Philosophers* (London: Oxford University Press, 1967); George Rawlinson, trans., *The History of Herodotus* (New York: Tudor, 1944); Tacitus, *The Agricola and the Germania,* trans. H. Mattingly, rev. S. A. Handford (London: Penguin, 1970); Frederick W. Norris, "Antioch on-the-Orontes as a Religious Center, I. Paganism before Constantine," in Wolfgang Haase and Hildegard Temporini, eds., *Aufstieg und Niedergang der Römischen Welt* (or *ANRW*) (Berlin–New York: Walter de Gruyter, 1990), part 2, vol. 18.4, pp. 2322–79; Ronald Mellor, "The Goddess Roma," in *ANRW,* part 2. vol. 17.2, pp. 950–1037.

THE WORLD OF THE BIBLE

It is common knowledge that our own civilization is a sprout with two different roots: Hellas (Greece) and Israel. The two belong to altogether different language families, and one certainty on which all modern linguists agree is that language and thought are interwoven, and will forever be inseparable — until some unimaginably nightmarish moment when all human beings express all they have to say in mathematical formulas.

Greek, like Latin, is an Indo-European language, like the vast majority of the tongues of Europe, such as English, French, Dutch, Spanish, and Portuguese, which eventually spread to a large portion of the world, sometimes joining, sometimes replacing existing vernaculars. The history and meeting of languages is too vast a topic to include in this book, but the problem of our religious origin from both Semitic and Indo-European roots cannot be left unmentioned.

Historically, Christianity can only be understood as a Jewish sect. Judaism is the only channel through which the heritage of Israel was handed down. Christianity owes all its crucial terms, symbols, and myths to Judaism/Israel. "Kingdom of God," "righteousness," "grace," "Messiah," are anchored in Hebrew. If we think of these symbol-laden terms alone, it becomes understandable that the mixture of two different types of language is not a superficial affair but something of fundamental importance to our intellect. All of us speak "a mixture."

Our "mixture" is not unique. It has been suggested that in the religious history of India something comparable came about. There, an Indo-European language was brought by invaders; it was Vedic, an early form of Sanskrit. Slowly, this new linguistic tradition exerted its influence over the languages that were already present, at the very least in their vocabulary. It has been said—and the evidence is suggestive—that the Vedic-Sanskritic tradition had as its most striking characteristic that it tended to "systematize" and create some conceptual order in religion and whatever else it met, in contrast to the pre–Indo-European Indian traditions, which may well have stressed religious experience—along the lines we notice in later history as *bhakti* ("devotion") and *yoga* (the practice of disciplining the mind).

What happened in the West's religious transformations certainly shows evidence of what in the Indian situation is no more than a likely hypothesis. When the early Christians, speaking Aramaic, as did Jesus himself, moved into a world where Greek and Latin were the vernaculars, a "systematization" accelerated. In the first few centuries of Christianity questions were raised and answered about the nature of Christ, Christ's precise relationship to God, the human and the divine element in the savior, and the nature of the Holy Spirit. An explicit example of a "Latin reasoning" is visible in the formulation known as the "Trinity"; the lawyer and church father Tertullian (c. A.D. 200) was the first to use the term technically to refer to the relationship within God, thinking of course that it did justice to the spirit of the New Testament, which itself does not name such a concept.

It is not as if the biblical texts themselves did not reflect a great deal of thought. Nevertheless, the analytical, conceptualizing tendency that came especially with the Latin, legal tradition, is not the hallmark of the Hebrew Bible or the New Testament. The biblical notion of the power of God is not formulated as the concept "omnipotence," but the Bible has very many references to the "hand of God." No doubt, in the biblical texts the immediacy of God's involvement in the world and his help are *felt* rather than rationally, systematically *analyzed* and *conceptualized*. Similarly, the notion of God's supremacy over the whole world seems an "afterthought" to the concreteness of his presence. Texts that seem to point to a supreme rule over all nations express primarily praise of God. It is not the idea of a universal, exclusive deity, but rather an exclamation that this God, the God of the temple in Jerusalem, the God of the covenant with Israel, can be none other than the one who will be recognized everywhere. Psalm 86:6–10 says:

> Listen, O Lord, to my prayer
> and hear my pleading,
> In the day of my distress I call on thee;
> for thou wilt answer me.
>
> Among the gods not one is like thee, O Lord,
> no deeds are like thine.
> All the nations thou hast made, O Lord, will come,
> will bow down before thee and honour thy name.[17]

Whatever Western intellectuals, including theologians, have argued about in interpreting the meaning of the Bible, this brief reminder of an almost disarming simplicity is very much in order. Perhaps not always in discussions among theologians, but certainly among less conspicuous and usually anonymous people, similar immediacy, concreteness, and simplicity of religious experience continued. Here too, of course, nothing remained unchanged. The greatest changes, however, are visible in the history that we call intellectual in the strict sense of the word. We are thinking, of course, of the educated explicators of religion in late Antiquity, in the period when Christianity spread along the roads created by the Roman Empire, the period in which slowly but steadily Christianity increased its influence on Europe. It is necessary to emphasize the slowness of this process. Some regions on the Baltic Sea did not turn to the Christian faith until the sixteenth and even seventeenth centuries. By that time, Christianity, and also the power of Rome were not what they formerly had been. The Christianity that reached those outlying provinces was Lutheran.

This concluding remark on the long time needed for religious conversion is more than an interesting item of information. In modern times many a voice has reproached the Christian church for having been around for a couple of millennia without improving the world in the least. Apart from the arbitrary quality of the demand that a religion should change the world (it is perhaps a nice idea, but where does it come from, and does any religion look upon that as its raison d'être?), it is sobering to realize how long it takes a "world religion" to spread.

Early Christianity

The growth and spread of Christianity is and remains the greatest revolution in the intellectual history of the West. It caused disorientations more basic than the visible changes in the habits of thought alone. A brilliant recent study on Neoplatonism opens with the words of an orator, Libanius, who worried a great deal about what he saw happening around him in the fourth century A.D. In an appeal to Emperor Theodosius he says:

> [The Christian monks] are spreading out like torrents over the countryside; and in ruining the temples, they are also ruining the countryside itself at one and the same time. For to snatch from a region the temple which protects it is like tearing out its eye, killing it, annihilating it. The temples are the very life of the countryside; around them are built houses and villages, in their shadow a succession of generations have been born up until the present day. It is in those temples that farmers have placed their hopes for themselves and their wives and children, for their oxen and for the ground they have sown and planted. A country region whose temple has been destroyed in this manner is lost, because the despairing villagers no longer have the will to work. It would be pointless to exert themselves, they think, because they have been deprived of the gods who made their labors prosper.[18]

In the face of such upheavals—repeated for centuries in various parts of Europe—we can only be struck in comparison by how little changed in the course of philosophy, and the intellectual world generally. From that perspective, the shift from the classical world to Christianity was by no means as radical as is generally imagined. The intellectual life, with which we are concerned here, goes on almost unabated. Conversions do not wholly transform one's mental image of the world and even of religion. Synesius of Cyrene, a man of distinction and a confirmed Neoplatonist, when offered a bishopric, early in the fifth century, accepted it on one condition: that he could continue to adhere to his beloved (non-Christian) philosophical dialectics.[19] In this case, one could not speak of "conversion" at all.

One person who knew himself as a convert, and who was central to the growth and thought of the church, must figure in our sketch. It is the church father and bishop of Rome Saint Augustine (354–430). With him, the idea of a supreme God takes on a form that with some reservation can be called "exclusive." The idea of God to the exclusion of the existence of other deities was in fact slow in developing. Contrary to our popular view of them, the biblical texts do not expound such ideas. One of the first texts that turn in this direction is not itself canonical but is accepted in the biblical tradition (among the Apocrypha). It is the *Wisdom of Solomon,* composed in Greek some eighty years before Christ. A few of its lines (14:15–17) speak disapprovingly of a father whose son died and who then proceeded to honor "as a god him who once was a dead man." In addition, the father "handed down to his subjects mysteries and rites." The text calls this "an ungodly practice," which, "strengthened by time, came to be observed as law, and by the order of monarchs carved images were worshipped."[20] The reasoning is clearly euhemeristic—without, however, including anything about great benefits bestowed on the human race, or any reciprocal gratitude.

Saint Augustine did not arrive at what to our time would seem the obvious conclusion, namely, that other deities did not exist. Instead, the pagan gods he considered people who had lived and died and as a result of evil acts became demonic beings. Demons were still very much part of the world of thought in Augustine's time. Tertullian (c. A.D. 200) was one of the first great Latin-writing intellectuals of the church. He too never doubted the existence and reality of demons.[21] His conversion to Christianity in the middle of his life did not change that in any manner. The reality of demons would remain normal for centuries to come. Saint Augustine simply accepted the sort of euhemeristic reasoning that then every educated person knew. Two modifications of euhemerization did not stand out at the time but are apparent in a survey on thought about religion. We have mentioned both: first, according to Saint Augustine, the gods were not originally good, exceptional, and royal individuals, but on the contrary *mere* people; second, they were not elevated because of their good deeds, but on the contrary assigned the function of evil demons because of their heinous acts. Such an explanation is still recognizable euhemerism, yet more precisely the modified theory is an "inverted euhemerism," for it turns the logic of Euhemerus upside down. From this time on, such modified euhemerism as a way of explaining religion (that is, "pagan" religion) became a standard tool in the arsenal of ideas.

Something of great consequence becomes visible at the same time. The new inverse euhemerism implies a division between true (and revealed) religion and a false (and demonic) religion. If there is an intellectual watershed between the pre-Christian and the Christian world, this is what marks it.

We have seen that from Xenophanes on, the classical thinkers had also made a distinction in religion — but their line of demarcation only set the serious, educated, thinking people apart from the "common folks" who held on to senseless ideas and images. In this new, Christianity-affected world the division was not based on a social state of affairs and perceptions depending on levels of education, but was a fundamental, philosophical judgment that neither Plato nor Aristotle could have conceived. The assertion of the truth of the new religion and the discarding of the old ones as heathenism is a novelty in human history. Exemplified in Saint Augustine, it is the one basic contribution of early Christianity to the intellectual tradition of the West in matters regarding religion.

A century before Augustine, the Neoplatonist philosopher Plotinus (third century A.D.), like Plato, had no need to speak of "heathens" or "pagans." His work concludes classical thought. When Christian civilization begins, the difference that concerns people is no longer as much between "high" and "low" as it is between truth and untruth. We wait a long time — in fact until the German idealist philosopher Hegel (c. A.D. 1800) — to see another endeavor to imagine approaches to religions without a pre-judgment on truth and falsehood. No one conceives of considering "the other religions" as participating in the same realm of veracities as "our own." The Greeks had done that as if instinctively, for instance in the case of Herodotus seeing Egyptian deities as identical with the ones he knew back home in Athens. And even the world-conquering Romans had had no trouble seeing the gods of the Germanic tribes as simply having other names for their own.

Literature
Saint Augustine, *The City of God,* trans. Marcus Dods (New York: Hafner, 1948), 2 vols., esp. book viii.26; Arthur Cushman McGiffert, *A History of Christian Thought,* book 1: *Christian Thought Until the Time of Irenaeus* (New York: Scribner, 1949), chap. 2, "The Apostle Paul," pp. 16–29; Henry Duméry, *Phenomenology and Religion: Structures of the Christian Institution* (Berkeley: University of California Press, 1975), appendix, "The Philosophy of Religion and Its Past," pp. 84–110; Werner Jaeger, *Early Christianity and Greek Paideia* (Cambridge: Harvard University Press, 1961); Kees W. Bolle, "In Defense of Euhemerus," in *Myth and Law Among the Indo-Europeans,* ed. Jaan Puhvel (Berkeley: University of California Press, 1970), pp. 19–38.

THE MIDDLE AGES AND THE RENAISSANCE

For the sake of convenience the years A.D. 500 and 1450 are set as the beginning and end of "the Middle Ages." This is what we find in dictionaries. What actually happens, and what begins and ends a more or less identifiable period, is not so easy to say. Saint Augustine lived before 500, and although he carried a great deal of classical civilization along in his work, most especially Platonism, he set a mark on the centuries to come. Moreover, some medieval ideas about religion continued what pre-Christian thinkers had already thought. "Middle" in "Middle Ages" points to what lies between the end of antiquity (we can also say "late antiquity," thereby showing again how difficult it is to draw precise lines) and the beginning of the Renaissance. And when exactly the Renaissance began is something else no one can say. All we can agree on is that gradually a new mood arose; it was characterized among many other things by a conscious rekindling of interest in the works of classical civilization. It was also characterized by the beginnings of what in our vocabulary is known as "real science"—including the study of geography, nature, the universe. The historical documentation of the Middle Ages and the Renaissance makes it impossible to separate the Middle Ages from the Renaissance, as if the two formed an opposition, or as if it were a matter of two opposing parties. It is rather a matter of slow changes, transforming the earlier world into the world of "modern history" in which we have our orientation. Normally, medievalists take the two together as one period.

We take note of the absence of absolute breaks in history, especially the history of thought. Moreover, the movement that we call "Renaissance" can be interpreted in a variety of ways. The term itself has various associations. *Renaissance,* in its literal sense "revival," occurred only in Italy. There the movement involved certainly a revival of classical artistic, architectural, cultural, and religious forms. At the same time, Italy's "rebirth" had important political components as well, in a revival of the classical, imposing, imperial forms of Rome as center of the world. These new inspirations, as a movement in culture and religion which began in Italy in the fourteenth century, later spread abroad over central, western, and northern Europe.

The Renaissance can be seen as the end of the Middle Ages, yet it is at the same time the period that points toward the future, to us, our thoughts, our ways. "Renaissance" is merely a *given* name, not the name of an organization or movement that consciously set out to renew culture, art, and so on. *Renaissance* is not the only word attached to this period.

Another is *humanism,* and there are also *renovatio* and *reformatio.* All these terms largely overlap. The last two functioned in theological discussion for a millennium before *reformatio* finally was used for *the* Reformation, the multifaceted renewal and reorganization effort of the Protestants. *Humanism* is the term that indicates the concern for a new orientation of human beings, inspired by classical ideals. Humanist studies of Latin and Greek within the atmosphere of universities have had a great influence on languages; the large number of Latinized and Hellenized terms in English is one of the many witnesses to the impact of humanism. Among the humanists are also Hebrew scholars such as the German Johann Reuchlin (1455–1522), whose basic work, including an edition of the Old Testament, made critical scholarship possible.

Allegorizing Continues and Reaches New Peaks.   We have referred in passing to a medieval monk, Bernard of Clairvaux, in discussing the allegorizing of religious documents. This practice flourished everywhere. The German Johannes Eckhart (c. 1260–c. 1327) was one of the great mystics of the Western world. He was a priest, and in his sermons one sees him interpret the Gospel story of the birth of Jesus as God's birth in the human soul. Although his theology was suspected of heretical tendencies, his allegorizing in itself most certainly did fit the spirit of the time, for we see the activity of allegorizing in its architecture, plastic arts, painting, and literature. This means that we really are dealing with more than merely a technique among the educated. A medieval morality play such as *Everyman* is in fact an extensive allegory. The central figure in the play is meant to represent every human being, and his struggle between good and evil is like a long sermon on human destiny. Vice, Virtue, and others appear as actors in the play. It is useful to realize that very popular productions such as this one, and the many mystery plays preceding it, show that allegorical interpretation, for instance of Greek myths, in circles of well-read people was very close to what was happening all around. It would seem as if the Middle Ages show a more striking religious homogeneity between higher and lower classes than did classical Greece and Rome.

Euhemerism Flourishes.   We have many great examples that bring out the continued popularity of euhemerizing. Although to many of us euhemerism may seem the least defensible and most speculative of ways to explain myths, some examples may make the power of this method understandable. People of the Middle Ages did not merely delight in storytelling; they used storytelling also as an "intellectual tool" to present history. What we today call "the science of history" had not come into being.

A wonderful example of medieval euhemerizing links traditional, pre-Christian certainties to the new, Christian truths. Snorri Sturluson (1179–1241), a chieftain, scholar, and poet, did his scholarly and poetic work almost two centuries after Christianity had entered his island home of Iceland. He wrote one work, the *Heimskringla,* which presents a history of the Norwegian kings, and another, the so-called *Prose Edda,* which, though short, gives us his imposing view of the pre-Christian Norse religious tradition in its relation to both the Greek history of Troy and the biblical account of early history. One explicit purpose of the *Prose Edda* was to stimulate a revival of ancient poetic techniques. The "history" Snorri gives his readers shows a comprehensive view of the world taken together with its divine component. It is not "scholarly" from our contemporary point of view, but it is the sort of universal understanding that was the undisputed goal of medieval intellectual Europe.

Snorri weaves an elegant tapestry that can still enchant the modern reader. Even skeptics who choose to see only fraudulent history can appreciate the art of the poet in Snorri's composition. Snorri begins, paraphrasing the Bible, "In the beginning Almighty God created heaven and earth and everything that goes with them and, last of all, two human beings, Adam and Eve, from whom have come families."[22] His story proceeds, taking the biblical text not too literally, and he adds to it classical elements of geography and legend whose fame traveled all of Europe. All such lore of a potent civilization had acquired its own authority. It had radiated from the Mediterranean world — from which too Roman political prestige had come, much as American prestige spread in the twentieth century. Thus Snorri tells us in his account that the world consists of three parts: Africa, Europe, and Asia. What we call Turkey, he says, is near the center. There the famous city of Troy was built. A grandson of King Priam of Troy was given the name Trór — who is in fact none other than Thór, one of the main gods of the Norse pantheon. Successively, and in similar fashion, other Norse gods and goddesses derive from Trojan princely ancestry; by slight changes their original names are changed into the names by which "we" know them, according to Snorri's tale. A notable feature of the story is that wherever these beings pass in their travels to the North, the lands about them prosper and marvelous harvests and peace ensue. This is true especially in the case of Odhin and his wife, Frigg. All these people who are in fact more than ordinary people are radiantly beautiful and strong. This is the way, tells the *Prose Edda,* in which Norway, Sweden, Denmark, and Germany received their deities.

It is easy to see that Snorri's narrative rests on euhemerism, but it is especially interesting that this euhemerism is not like the "inverted" form we saw in Saint Augustine. It is rather a true, original euhemerization. The gods are born as very special, royal, and beneficent humans, not just anywhere, but near the "center of the world," in the region celebrated in tellings and retellings of the story of Homer's Troy in the *Iliad.* Moreover, in Snorri's account, they even fit into the entire divine plan begun in Genesis 1.

As a piece of interpretation, Snorri's account is not in all respects exceptional. Euhemerizing as fascinating narration, weaving things together and presenting vivid images, is a striking feature of medieval culture. The Homeric epics echoed in many writings of the Middle Ages, and in all cases classical culture was depicted and dealt with in a world that was Christian. Among the best examples is Dante's *Inferno.* Dante Alighieri wrote his superb poem narrating his voyage into hell—a Christian idea par excellence—while he is guided by the classical, pre-Christian poet Virgil. Many stories about the grail, the supposed receptacle of Christ's blood, as in the great medieval epic of Parzifal, and the cycle of narratives of King Arthur's round table, and many more epics and romances are each collages of "pagan" and Christian elements.

It is especially worthy of note that the euhemerizations are not merely characteristic of the educated, upper classes, but are embedded in a shared religio-cultural tradition. The genius of storytelling, the essence of euhemerism where "pagan," "pre-Christian" elements are woven in, is equally visible in the transmission of thoroughly Christian themes. Everywhere stories are told about the childhood of Jesus, in spite of the fact that the New Testament has extremely little to say on that subject. And there is no European country touched by Christianity that does not have its repertory of stories about the Virgin Mary's miracles, all told in very human terms. One group of those stories involves a woman who marries the devil—but in the end is set free thanks to the intervention of Saint Mary.

Another such theme, hardly more "realistic" yet irresistible, among those inspiring Mary stories occurs in *Beatrys,* a piece of narrative poetry by an anonymous Flemish author. We do not know exactly when it was composed, but we have a manuscript that was written around 1374. This is how the poem begins:

Writing poems hardly pays me.
People tell me to stop doing it,
And not to torture my mind.
But for the sake of the virtue of her
Who remained both mother and virgin
I am telling you a beautiful miracle.
No doubt God let it happen
In honor of Mary who suckled him.
I am going to tell you of a nun . . . [23]

Then the story unfolds. It is throughout as simple and disarming as the opening lines. Any question one might raise about its "truth" becomes irrelevant. The narrator did not make it up; he heard the story from an indubitably devout old man belonging to a holy congregation, who had found it in one of his books. The nun (whose name, Beatrys, is mentioned only once in the entire poem) is a paradigm of dutifulness and piety in her convent, ringing the church bell, taking care of the lights and everything needed in the mass, awakening all in the nunnery each morning. Then it happens: she falls in love. And love "brings about great confusion every-where / Sometimes love leads to shame, suffering, pain or hate / sometimes joy and happiness. Love can drive / reasonable people out of their mind, so that they perish / whether they want to or not."[24] She prays, of course, but in the end flees from the convent, leaving her habit on Mary's altar, and hanging the keys to the sacristy nearby. For a while, Beatrys lives with her lover in joy, but then things begin to go awry. Their money runs out. He deserts her. She is left with two children and ends up in utter distress. Of course, she talks to God as never before. A voice in a dream tells her what to do. She doubts and doubts, then obeys. She entrusts her children to God's care, and, as instructed, returns to the convent. Miraculously, it is open! Her absence has never been noticed. Her place all these years has been taken by Mary herself!

Someone among us will say, "But what about her children?" Of course, we notice that in fact she *abandoned* them. And it seems merely a make-shift solution, an excuse, when modern listeners are told that in the end an old abbot—the same one who gives Beatrys absolution—sees to it that the children are given to a monastery, one of the same order as that of the devout old man, who had found the story in one of his books. I have no answer to such questioners, except to say that the discovery of children as "real" or "complete" people is a latecomer in Western history.

LEARNING AND DISCUSSIONS BETWEEN RELIGIONS

There was, as I said, very much that the unlearned and the learned shared in the Middle Ages. We owe to people like Snorri Sturluson a great deal of our knowledge of traditional lore—and that means matters passed on by word of mouth, or folk wisdom. However, there is no doubt that Snorri was a scholar as well as a poet. His age saw a certain revival of the ancient arts and customs of Iceland. Snorri was involved in this movement, showing a younger generation how poetry in the traditional style should be written. No doubt, his learning was formidable.

There were of course many more medieval scholars whose work dealt with religion. Our survey will mention some examples of scholars who showed a special interest in what nowadays might be called "interreligious dialogue." They by no means limited themselves to the Western, Christian world, for the surprising fact is that they indicate a much more encompassing exchange of ideas. The Middle Ages had its great scholars and intellectual leaders both in Islam and Christendom. These two, though sometimes at war, lay adjacent to each other. In both traditions, scholars, Muslims, Jews, and Christians alike, inquired into problems of religion, culture, and civilization. The flourishing culture of Islam was historically a major reason why such interests developed. Our history textbooks have told us about the Crusades against the Muslims. And we have heard about the Turks marching into Europe, eventually as far as the walls of Vienna. Some of this information may have left us with the mistaken impression that all religions ever do is cause war and enmity. What is intellectually of special significance is the genuine interest in real, or even imagined discussion between religions. In the three examples I want to mention we meet respectively with a Jewish, an Islamic, and a Christian scholar.

Ibn Kammuna (c. 1215–c. 1280), a Jewish physician in Baghdad, was interested in philosophical issues all his life. He wrote a treatise that focused on Islam, Judaism, and Christianity, but it drew into the discussion other traditions as well.[25] As a philosopher, he dealt with arguments and doctrines of course, and only obliquely touched on symbols, myths, and rituals. But even within these strictures, the balance, the tolerance, the calm and breadth of his reflection is striking. Though his work did not please everybody, and even triggered a riot (from which fortunately he escaped),[26] it witnesses to a climate in which peaceful discussions did take place.

One passage that I want to single out deals specifically with the "idolators," that is to say the Indians, Chinese, and many others, who from the point of view of Jews, Christians, and Muslims alike seemed to be farthest away from the revealed truth. This is what Ibn Kammuna says:

> The idolators do not believe idols created heaven and earth; no sensible person does. But they do feel that idol worship brings one closer to God. We are informed by the Koran that they said: this is our way to bring us near to God in intimacy.[27]

Other authors expressed views that nowadays we would call "tolerant" and that we might see as akin to what Ibn Kammuna said.[28] In the West, the most articulate voice belongs to Nicholas of Cusa (or Cusanus, 1401–64), almost two centuries after Ibn Kammuna. Cusanus is one of the great Christian mystics of the Renaissance. He rose to the rank of cardinal and was politically, philosophically, and scientifically equally active. (His name figures prominently in the rise of modern science, especially mathematics and astronomy.) In *De pace fidei,* "About the Peace of Faith," written shortly after the Turks conquered Constantinople (1453), Cusanus describes a vision of harmony among the conflicting religions and sectarian convictions in the world.[29] It is the vision of a dialogue in the forecourts of heaven. The views that are expounded coincide with national division within Christendom at the time, but in addition, altogether different religions also have their say. Thus we find among the participants an Englishman, a Frenchman, a Bohemian (and at the time Johannes Hus, a Bohemian, had caused a rift in the church with untraditional opinions on the sacrament of the Communion), an Italian, and also a Jew, an Arab, a Turk, a Syrian, a Persian, an Indian, a Scythian, a Greek, a Chaldean, and a Tartar. The Apostles Peter and Paul also participate, while the Word (of God) presides over the meeting. The central philosophical-theological theme for Nicholas of Cusa is that no one can be truly in harmony with God unless he is what he truly is in his own tradition. Hence the greatest particularity and the greatest unity are inextricably linked, and in fact coincide. The participants in the dialogue of *De pace fidei* may be "fictional," yet they are more than impersonations of Cusanus's philosophical convictions. They do reveal some real knowledge of distant traditions. Quite reminiscent of what we heard from Ibn Kammuna, the Word itself, in answer to a question from the Indian concerning statues and images, says: "Those images which lead to knowledge of God and which are permitted in the true cult of the One God, these are not condemned," and "The names which are attributed to God are taken from creatures, since in Himself He is ineffable and above everything which can be named."[30]

We cannot end this section without mentioning one more name: Ibn Khaldûn (1332–1406), almost a century before Cusanus. He was a Muslim, born in Tunisia. He traveled widely, led a turbulent life, and possessed remarkable powers of observation and great learning. He has been described as the first historiographer, which means a person not only interested in history, but reflective about the principles that allow us to know history. He was certainly also someone whom today we would describe as a historian of religions and culture, as well as a sociologist and political scientist. By way of example, he was probably the first to gain the insight that "prophecy" could not be regarded exclusively as the property of a revelatory religious tradition, but must be seen, in the words of one of his modern commentators, as something with a "decisive role in the development of culture."[31] In our survey of thought in the Christianity-affected world, we do not propose to elaborate on him. His contribution, however, like that of many other Islamic scholars, is a reminder of the youth of "our" present Western civilization.

Literature

Bernard McGinn, with Frank Tobin and Elvira Borgstadt, eds., *Meister Eckhart, Teacher and Preacher* (New York: Paulist Press, 1986), "The Classics of Western Spirituality"; Jean I. Young, trans., *Snorri Sturluson: The Prose Edda, Tales from Norse Mythology* (Berkeley: University of California Press, 1965); Lee M. Hollander, trans., *Heimskringla, History of the Kings of Norway* (Austin: University of Texas Press, 1964); H. R. Ellis Davidson, *Gods and Myths of Northern Europe* (Baltimore: Penguin, 1968); E. O. G. Turville-Petre, *Myths and Religion of the North: The Religion of Ancient Scandinavia* (New York: Holt, 1964); A. C. Cawley, ed., *Everyman and Medieval Miracle Plays* (London: Everyman, J. M. Dent, 1993); Wolfram von Eschenbach, *Parzival: A Romance of the Middle Ages,* trans. Helen M. Mustard and Charles E. Passage (New York: Vintage, 1961); Roger S. Loomis, ed., *Arthurian Literature in the Middle Ages* (Oxford: Clarendon Press, 1959); Roger S. Loomis, *The Grail, from Celtic Myth to Christian Symbol* (New York: Columbia University Press, 1963); Kees W. Bolle, "Renaissance Mysticism," in Robert S. Kinsman, ed., *The Darker Vision of the Renaissance* (Berkeley: University of California Press, 1974), pp. 119–45; Muhsin Mahdi, *Ibn Khaldûn's Philosophy of History: A Study in the Philosophic Foundation of the Science of Culture* (Chicago: University of Chicago Press,

1957); Ibn Khaldûn, *The Muqaddimah: An Introduction to History*, 2nd ed., trans. Franz Rosenthal (Princeton: Princeton University Press, 1967), 3 vols; Gerhart B. Ladner, *The Idea of Reform: Its Impact on Christian Thought and Action in the Age of the Fathers* (New York: Harper, 1967); Frances A. Yates, *Giordano Bruno and the Hermetic Tradition* (Chicago: University of Chicago Press, 1964).

NOTES

1. See E. Zürcher, *Buddhism: Its Origin and Spread in Words, Maps and Pictures* (Amsterdam: Djambatan, 1962).

2. W. Theodore de Bary, ed., *Sources of Indian Tradition* (New York: Columbia University Press, 1959), pp. 79–81.

3. W. K. C. Guthrie, *The Greek Philosophers, from Thales to Aristotle* (New York: Harper, 1975), p. 10.

4. Ibid.

5. Aristotle, *Metaphysics* XII viii. 1074a15–b21.

6. Our words *barbarian* and *barbarous* have a Greek origin. *Barbaros* was the word the Greeks used for all languages outside Greek. Curiously, the Greek term *barbaros* itself seems borrowed from the Sumerian term *bar*, stranger. To the Greek ear the term imitated ugly and confused sounds.

7. Plato, *The Laws* X 899 B; Aristotle, *On the Soul* 411a7.

8. Aristotle, *Metaphysics* I 3.983b6–30.

9. Werner Jaeger, *The Theology of the Early Greek Philosophers*, the Gifford Lectures 1936 (London: Oxford University Press, 1967), p. 21. See comparable statements by W. K. C. Guthrie, *A History of Greek Philosophy*, vol. 1, *The Earlier Presocratics and the Pythagoreans* (Cambridge: Cambridge University Press, 1978) pp. 70–72.

10. T. V. Smith, ed., *Philosophers Speak for Themselves, from Thales to Plato* (Chicago: University of Chicago Press, 1968), p. 14.

11. Ibid.

12. Bernard of Clairvaux, *On the Song of Songs*, 4 vols., trans. Kilian Walsh (Kalamazoo, Mich.: Cistercian Publications, 1981).

13. Margaret Smith, *Rabi'a the Mystic*, A. D. 717–801, *and Her Fellow Saints in Islam* (San Francisco: The Rainbow Bridge, 1977), p. 21.

14. Ernst Cassirer, *The Myth of the State* (Garden City, N. Y.: Doubleday, 1955), p. 58.

15. See W. K. C. Guthrie, *The Greek Philosophers, from Thales to Aristotle* (New York: Harper, 1975), p. 10; see also Guthrie, *The Greeks and Their Gods* (Boston: Beacon, 1955), pp. 135–36.

16. This extraordinarily important point was made eloquently by Truesdell S. Brown, "Euhemerus and the Historians," in *Harvard Theological Review* 38 (1946), p. 263.

17. See also Amos 9:7–8, where God is said to have led not only Israel but also the Philistines and the Aramaeans.

18. Libanius, *Pro Templis* 30.8, quoted in Gregory Shaw, *Theurgy and the Soul: The Neoplatonism of Iamblichus* (University Park: Pennsylvania State University Press, 1995), p. 1.

19. Jay Bregman, *Synesius of Cyrene, Philosopher-Bishop* (Berkeley: University of California Press, 1982). See especially pp. 155–56.

20. J. M. Powis Smith and Edgar J. Goodspeed, trans., *The Complete Bible* (Chicago: University of Chicago Press, 1948).

21. See Tertullian, "On Idolatry," in F. L. Greenslade, ed., *Early Latin Theology,* "The Library of Christian Classics" (Philadelphia: Westminster Press, 1956), p. 100.

22. Snorri Sturluson, *The Prose Edda,* trans. Jean I. Young (Berkeley: University of California Press, 1965), p. 23.

23. H. Adema, ed., *Beatrys, tekst en vertaling* (Leeuwarden: Taal en Teken, 1988), p. 6.

24. Ibid.

25. Moshe Perlmann, trans. and introd., *Ibn Kammuna's Examination of the Three Faiths* (Berkeley: University of California Press, 1971).

26. Ibid., p. 3

27. Ibid., p. 148.

28. John P. Dolan mentions Minucius Felix (third century), Peter Abelard (twelfth century), Raymund Lull, and Roger Bacon. See Dolan, ed., *Unity and Reform: Selected Writings of Nicholas of Cusa* (Notre Dame, Ind.: University of Notre Dame Press, 1962), p. 185.

29. *De pace fidei,* in Dolan, ed., *Unity and Reform,* pp. 195–237.

30. Ibid., pp. 205, 207.

31. See Muhsin Mahdi, *Ibn Khaldûn's Philosophy of History* (Chicago: University of Chicago Press, 1957), p. 193, and *passim.*

S   E   V   E   N

Toward Modernity

"The Birth of Reason"

"The birth of reason" is a metaphor—one that keeps coming up in the history of philosophy. I know a medievalist who argues that only medievalists are familiar with a time that could lay claim to rationality. With respect to a definition of what constitutes real reason, we all have our defensible assumptions but little agreement. We have dismissed the suggestion that with Thales and his fellow Milesian thinkers "reason" came into being—as if until then no one had thought a serious, reasonable thought. Not only is a "birth of reason" quite out of the question physiologically, but also historically such birth processes do not actually occur. Just the same, the metaphor persists, because for various reasons we are obsessed with the nature, the capabilities, and therefore the origin of our rational faculties. Religio-historically, we recognize in this obsession a *mythical drive* in human beings.

What indeed makes us think in an orderly fashion? Historically, one cannot help but recognize that the Greeks helped a great deal in this. Likewise, the century of Thomas Aquinas. The intellectual revolution of the Renaissance is a "birth" of reason, but so is the period of the eighteenth century that is often called "the age of reason." Finally, the application of reason to facts of religion in the nineteenth century is one more such birth of reason. Is "reason" the same thing in all these instances? No, certainly not, and it is interesting how each of these "reasons" is understandable and "reasonable" in its own way. Some circles in some periods

154

insist solemnly on their own final discovery of real reason—they are the ones that are easy to dismiss as a serious subject for discussion—but one thing that concerns us in the history of religions is the myriad ideas and suggestions that have sent us astray.

One very popular notion that has led to many questionable results is a supposed enmity between "science," posited as the perfect application of reason, and religion. (We have already dealt with this idea in chapter 3.) In the history of the West, we have learned on good grounds that the real beginning of our modern science is found in the end of the Middle Ages—that is, the Renaissance—and is far more complicated than any simplistic opposition between science and religion.[1] The suggestion that that period caused a split to occur between reason and religion is still popular; but it is not actually possible to find clear evidence for such a break. Nicholas of Cusa, whom we met before, is one of the crucial figures from that time of origins of "real reason." However, he was also a Christian mystic. And he was a cardinal. In his own writings on science, nothing points to the sort of "break" popular views of history cling to. On the contrary, his mathematical interests in such problems as "infinity" and "limitation" mesh with his theological exposition of God's revelation, the "incarnation," in which the two, both the human, limited form, and the divine, the infinite, meet. In his major work, *De docta ignorantia* ("About Learned Ignorance") he entitles one chapter "In Understanding the Various Realms of the Divine, Mathematics Is Most Helpful" (book 1, chapter 11). In the following chapters, he explains how the infinite line is fundamental to various rectilinear geometric figures. The perfect infinite line is also the infinitely large circle. It encompasses all that can be construed—even the largest polygon. In analogy, Cusanus speaks of the "Absolute Maximum" as the divine reality that encompasses everything and in which everything exists. In *De docta ignorantia* we read:

> The unity of the maximum is absolutely in itself; the unity of the universe is in the restriction called plurality. The plurality of things in which the universe finds its actual limitation could never contain the highest equality for it would then be no longer in plurality. Things must be distinguished by genus, species and number, or by species and number, or by number simply; that each may repose in its own number, weight and measure. Wherefore are all things separated into degrees, that no two may absolutely coincide.[2]

At the same time, this entire universe of particulars is arranged, according to Cusanus, "so that all things, whether they rise or sink or tend to the centre, may approach God."[3] Cusanus's mathematical examples lead him also to a positive understanding of "pagan" names for the divine. Even the best names are finite; they are like a polygon with a large number of angles; they make sense, yet do not become the infinite circle.

Does this lead to the beginning of the sciences we know today? Yes, indeed, and the thinkers usually noted as opening modern history show us likewise an interest that in spite of its novelty is hardly averse to the Christian theological heritage: the names of René Descartes (1596–1650), Thomas Hobbes (1588–1679), and John Locke (1632–1704) come to mind. We can see all these men, together with Cusanus, as "Renaissance figures." At the same time, there are distances between men such as Cusanus or Martin Luther—who have their feet firmly planted in the "Middle Ages"— and the others, beginning with Descartes, whose words let us recognize them more easily as our forebears.

The birth of the sciences was not only the birth of what we tend to isolate as "the natural sciences"; it led to new views of the religious heritage at the same time. The German Martin Luther lived from 1483 to 1546, the Frenchman John Calvin from 1509 to 1564, and their fellow reformer, the Swiss Ulrich Zwingli, from 1484 to 1531. These three initiated the Reformation. We use the term *Reformation* for the changes brought about in the area of religion in the Western church, and reserve the term *Renaissance* for the wider renewal movement in art, thought, scholarship, and culture. Historically, however, the two are interwoven. The first Protestants were seriously engaged in interpreting the Bible text, both Hebrew and Greek; they used all the scholarly tools that had become available in order to find out about the early church, because they wished to model their own church after it. Thus they followed the new scholarly patterns of the time, especially in philology (study of language and literature). We have already mentioned Desiderius Erasmus (c. 1466–1536), one of the most renowned of the Humanists; he remained faithful to the Roman Catholic Church, polemicized against Luther, and became one of the founders of a proper philological and critical study of the Greek New Testament. His philological know-how enabled him to publish the first scholarly edition of the New Testament in 1516.

The supposed "conflict" between religion and science, on which whole books have been written,[4] is interesting as an "ideological" preoccupation, but it does not rest in historical fact.

The Renaissance was marked among other things by a new pride in national (in fact often no more than regional) vernaculars. Among the earliest and most brilliant Renaissance figures is the poet Dante Alighieri (1265–1321), whose fame rests in part on his use of Italian rather than Latin. William Shakespeare (1564–1616) is a central figure in the celebration of the vernacular in England. However, the prospering interest in language and literature occasionally led down odd paths. The tendency to suspend one's critical abilities when it came to the importance of the language of one's own tradition is very much in evidence. Around 1600, hence at the beginning of the "golden age" of the Netherlands, Simon Stevin made it his business to enrich the Dutch language. He was a marvellously talented man in many fields and an expert mathematician. He created Dutch mathematical terms that have remained standard. His fascination with language, however, led him to posit some very strange things. For instance, according to him, the Dutch word *navel* (English "navel") consisted really of two parts: *na* ("after") and *vel* ("skin"); hence, the accuracy of the Dutch language, for the navel is the skin that is left over after birth.[5] Stevin's fantasies were not as farfetched as what another scholar of language, a physician in a village near Hilvarenbeek, had already "proved" in a book in 1569, namely that Dutch was in fact the primordial language spoken by Adam and Eve in paradise.[6] We may laugh, but such was the time of early scientific questioning. In many details, those who worked at that time were wrong. But scientific questioning had begun, and in principle, from now on evidence was sorted out and corrections could be made, slowly but steadily. With respect to historical linguistics, we wait three centuries until solid evidence appears, tenable theses are proposed, and "language families" discovered. Only then could theories such as those of the enthusiastic village doctor be definitively dismissed. Still, the Renaissance marks the real beginning of science.

Literature
E. J. Dijksterhuis, *The Mechanization of the World Picture* (New York: Oxford University Press, 1969), parts 3 and 4, pp. 223–491.

PHILOSOPHERS

Our own present-day bias that conceives of religion and "real knowledge" as enemies is itself the result of history—but for the most part a more recent history than that of the Renaissance. For the moment, let us return to some of the thinkers we mentioned before, Hobbes, Descartes, and Locke, and a few others.

In doing so, we first have to conjure up an age when severe restrictions on publishing were the rule. Both church and state held reins that could not be ignored by people who thought and wrote, for even their very lives might be at stake. At the same time, many thinkers traveled, met one another, and corresponded. A man like Erasmus, though living in Holland, a country that enjoyed more freedom than most, had to be very careful. He exchanged letters with the author and statesman Sir Thomas More (1478–1535) in England. More held the office of lord chancellor for three years, but he refused to recognize King Henry VIII as head of the Church of England and was executed for that. Thomas Hobbes made it a point in his travels to meet Galileo, whose story is well known, as he was condemned for heresy by the Inquisition for his ideas, and for his use of the telescope to prove the truth of the theory about the universe set forth in *De revolutionibus* by the Pole Nicolas Copernicus (1473–1543). From the vantage point of some of us— assuming we take little note of the reports of Amnesty International— it would almost seem as if our own time no longer requires courage from thinkers, scholars, and scientists. At any rate, our ideas today, for instance about freedom, law, and justice, as well as the nature of scientific inquiry, owe very, very much to thinkers of those days, and should not be taken for granted, as if they were natural human possessions.

René Descartes (or Cartesius, 1596–1650). Descartes must be mentioned first; many an intellectual historian would let "modern history" begin with him. If (with some hesitation) we speak of a "birth of reason," it is principally because of him. While Descartes himself did not deal with "religion" as a universal phenomenon, as we do in modern religio-historical inquiries, his impact on philosophers and on thought in general was so great as to leave hardly anything unaffected. Through him the world of thought changed.

Descartes set out to create a philosophy that would be as certain in its propositions as mathematics. He had been inspired by mathematics in his early education at the Jesuit school at La Flèche. His philosophy was to be in harmony with the new world and its discoveries in the universe and nature. Like Spinoza and other great figures at the time, he did not have an "academic career." He spent most of his life traveling as a professional military man. He died in Stockholm.

Descartes's inspiration by mathematics and by the certainty of mathematics is itself a sign of the new age, the beginning of our modern history. Mathematics was the prime ingredient of astronomy and of physics in general. And a philosophy that presented itself as the very coherency of the new world could not be ignored. It was a revolution.

Descartes's *Discours de la méthode* ("Discourse on Method"), appearing in 1637, can be seen as the manifesto of a new age. Together with the work of John Locke, which spread more slowly, the *Discours* set its stamp on everything for centuries to come. Our own trust in reason today, including our specialized inquiries into *uncertainties,* in principle all go by the correctness of a Cartesian reason. Conspicuous examples are our physicists' studies of chaos, or meteorology and seismology, and we certainly may think of more familiar psychological analyses of mental weaknesses.[7] *The very fact that we trust in some analyzable pattern, something apprehensible,* in any object we turn to in our studies, is the result of the influence of Descartes's school of thought. Though some of Descartes's contemporaries, each in his own way, made a departure from what until then had counted as authority—Aristotle, Plato, scholastic philosophy (the thought of the schoolmen of the Middle Ages)—Descartes's notion of what constituted reason was the most visible revolutionary element. His *Cogito ergo sum,* "I think, therefore I am," has continued to reverberate. These words imply a definition of a human being in terms of his mental process. (The instinctive interpretation many of our contemporaries make of Descartes' remark, that *I* am aware of *myself,* of my own existence, is a spurious echo of what Descartes said.) Our thinking means our reason's orderly work with ideas. And the important thing is that those ideas be clear and distinct. Clarity means that they must be capable of explanation to others. Distinctness means that they must not be confused with other ideas, and above all, that truth should be distinguished from untruth. These simple features alone of the method implied a critique of traditional certainties.

None of this means that Descartes was what in an ordinary present-day conversation we might refer to as "a rationalist." Descartes was a Christian, and his strict ideas of reason and its power were not meant to push Christianity aside. Did he show a lack of consistency? At least one man, shortly afterward, seemed to think so—Spinoza—as we shall see. However, there is no way we can make Descartes skip over a couple of centuries and turn him into an "atheist." He dedicated one of his books to the theological faculty of the University of Paris: *Meditationes de prima philosophia, in quibus Dei existentia, & animae humanae a corpore distinctio demonstratur,*

"Meditations on basic philosophy [metaphysics], proving the existence of God and the distinctness of the human soul from the body." This treatise gave a summary of his *Discourse on Method,* and carefully explained that he did not see his philosophy as a substitute for theology. On the contrary, the statement of dedication at the outset points to philosophy as a discipline supporting theology:

> I have always been of the opinion that two questions, viz. about God and the soul, were the main ones to be solved by the reasonings of philosophy rather than theology. For although it is enough for us, the faithful, to believe by faith that there is a God, and that the human soul does not die with the body, it certainly does not seem possible ever to convince the infidels of [the reality of] any religion, or even any moral virtue, if first natural reason is not used to prove these two things to them . . .[8]

Descartes's reference to "natural reason" is in perfect harmony with the tradition of Thomism, the system of the great medieval theologian Thomas Aquinas. Thus, in spite of the novelty he brought, Descartes confirms the rule (which will not surprise a historian of religions) that it is impossible for human beings to lift themselves out of their historical surroundings. Nevertheless, the *myth* of Descartes is as true as a myth could ever be in the orientation of ourselves, "moderns." As in the case of all functioning myths, interpretations abound. The history of philosophy gives us many different versions of Descartes.

The myth of Descartes is not in the least affected in our own day by the fact that serious (indeed, pious) modern Jews and Christians realize that Descartes is far away from our own century's more receptive, and more critical reading of biblical texts. My own interest in the general history of religions was triggered by the realization that biblical Hebrew had no term for "immortality." I had always thought that "religious people" everywhere were obsessed with immortality. Then, turning to the New Testament, I found that there too "immortality" is never a qualification of the human soul, but only of God. What I "discovered" is common knowledge in biblical scholarship. And one would have to knead the texts in the oddest way to squeeze out anything resembling a discussion on the existence or nonexistence of God. So as to an immortality of souls, as well as the existence or nonexistence of God, rational Descartes was still part of a world of Latinized theological abstractions and removed from the immediate shape of religious phenomena that have been made available to us through modern philology. However, before we indulge in self-congratulations on account of the great contributions of close, critical readings which we owe to modern research, let us return to the seventeenth century.

Baruch (or Benedictus) de Spinoza (1632–77).   With Spinoza we take a cautious step forward, in the sense that here was a great thinker who knew the text of the Bible. He received his early education in and around the Sephardic synagogue in Amsterdam, learned Hebrew very well, and acquired a perfect knowledge of Latin. His reading of Descartes spurred him on. He unabashedly embraced reason, even more confidently than Descartes. His synagogue did not approve of his views and publicly excommunicated him. According to many, the most brilliant work he produced was his *Ethica* ("Ethics"), published after his death by his friends. In this work, Spinoza shows himself not merely inspired by mathematics, as was Descartes, but employing quite directly a mathematical method. Discussing the problem of good and evil—and that is what ethics does—he sees fit to guide the argument from axioms, proceeding step by step to theses and their proofs. When the political situation in which Holland found itself threatened human freedom, Spinoza wrote one of his most famous books, the *Tractatus theologico-politicus* ("Theological-Political Tract," 1670); the principle of human freedom and the sufficiency of reason, also in questions of government, were weighty matters in his thought. His decision to decline a professorship in philosophy offered to him by the University of Heidelberg (in 1673) was made in part because the position might have hampered his own freedom of expression. He made a living grinding lenses. He died of tuberculosis.

Some lines from his *Theological-Political Tract* may show the development of Spinoza's views on religion. The first sentence of the preface sets the tone: "If men were able to exercise complete control over all their circumstances, or if continuous good fortune were always their lot, they would never be prey to superstition."[9] Spinoza, like Descartes, does not turn against religion, yet the difference between him and Descartes is obvious: to Spinoza it seems that religion comes to us principally in the garbled form of "superstitions." Since superstitions are unreasonable, they deserve to be ridiculed. The reality of the divine for Spinoza consists in truth and necessity:

> By God's direction I mean the fixed and immutable order of Nature, or chain of natural events. . . . the universal laws of Nature according to which all things happen and are determined are nothing but God's

eternal decrees, which always involve eternal truth and necessity. So it is the same thing whether we say that all things happen according to Nature's laws or that they are regulated by God's decree and direction.[10]

The equivalence of God and Nature (*Deus sive Natura*) is a key idea. The words I have just quoted make clear what Spinoza has in mind. His reasoning is quite consistent, and he uses Bible passages to illustrate how people as a rule have great difficulty understanding God in the way he, Spinoza, understands him. "I know," he says, "how deeply rooted in the mind are the prejudices embraced under the guise of piety. I know, too, that the masses can no more be freed from their superstition than from their fears."[11]

The endeavor at consistency in Spinoza is breathtaking. His knowledge of the Bible leads him to make what is in fact an implied but extreme allegorization of the text. What God "says," what God is credited with saying, according to Spinoza, is as a rule merely a reflection of what rather unintelligent people were capable of fathoming. And it is easy to understand that many of Spinoza's readers over the course of time have felt offended when reading a passage such as the following:

> So when Scripture, in exhorting the Hebrews to obey the Law, says that God has chosen them for himself above all other nations (Deut. ch. 10 v. 15), "that he is nigh unto them as he is not unto others (Deut. ch. 4 v. 4, 7)," that for them alone he has ordained just laws (same ch. v. 8), that he has made himself known only to them before all others (same ch. v. 32) and so forth, it is speaking merely according to the understanding of those who, as was shown in the previous chapter and as Moses also testifies (Deut. ch. 9 v. 6, 7), knew not true blessedness. For surely they would have been no less blessed if God had called all men equally to salvation, nor would God have been less close to them for being equally close to others, nor would their laws have been less just or they themselves less wise if those laws had been ordained for all men.[12]

Two things are worth noting. In the first place, we can observe the survival among humanists of a strong consciousness of class distinction. Second, we see in Spinoza one among many clear examples of the revival of classical Stoic views. The idea of the importance of *Natura* is very reminiscent of a classical Roman writer such as Seneca, for whom *secundum naturam vivere,* living in accordance with nature, was the highest goal in life. Amplified by Spinoza into the *laws* of nature—as found by the budding natural sciences—it is philosophically also approaching a dogmatic stoicism, almost a fatalism, a view where everything is determined, and the human ideal becomes not to be bothered by that but instead to accept it as "the Divine."

There are indeed very positive ways of embracing this attitude on life. But should it serve as a standpoint from which to judge any religion? Humanistic studies have changed since the seventeenth century. For one thing, we are aware that the Hebrew Bible does not know the term *nature* at all. The notion "creation," which it does have, is not the equivalent of "nature." Whether one likes that or not, it is not something one is free to ignore.

Whatever we may want to think, the stage is set, clearly, for the development of more inimical views of religion, certainly of the biblical religions, than the world had known so far.

Literature
René Descartes, *The Meditations, and Selections from the Principles,* trans. John Veitch (La Salle, Ill.: Open Court, 1952); Descartes, *Discourse on Method and Meditations,* trans. Laurence J. LaFleur (New York: Liberal Arts Press, 1960); Baruch Spinoza, *Tractatus Theologico-Philosophicus,* trans. Samuel Shirley (Leiden: Brill, 1991).

EMPIRICISM

Thomas Hobbes (1588–1679).   Thomas Hobbes's life shows that real study cannot easily separate human existence from facts of nature (although with Hobbes we have not yet reached an age in which one could make the choice to study human beings *only* on the basis of natural data). Hobbes conceived a trilogy, consisting of the treatment of three topics whose lines of departmentalization could be characteristic of a modern educational institution. The first was *De corpore* ("About Body"), the second *De homine* ("About Man"), the third *De cive* ("About the Citizen"). This work, which in brief is called *Leviathan,* published in 1651, is his most widely read work of political philosophy. Its full title makes clear how interrelated "politics" and "religion" are for Hobbes: *Leviathan, or the Matter, Form and Power of a Commonwealth, Ecclesiastical and Civil.* Facts of nature and typically human features are not separated. On the contrary, mental movements and movements observable and calculable in nature form a continuum according to Hobbes. His ideas did not gain universal approval. He was suspected of "atheism." He had reason to be afraid and burned some of his work, but had the good fortune to live to a ripe old age.

The words by Hobbes that are invariably quoted in textbooks are *homo homini lupus*, "man is a wolf to man." But every reader who jumps to the conclusion that Hobbes had an unusually gloomy view of humanity is mistaken. The words express an observation, rather than condemnation or dismay, and are related to Hobbes's views on social and political organization. Though comparable to ants and other creatures that live in groups, human beings develop their own way to live an organized life. They transfer their dangerous power to someone who rules over them, a king and judge. This is the principle of society.

Hobbes's views by implication (rather than by outright incisive criticism) affected general ideas concerning religion. Unlike the notion of "nature" in Spinoza (which was philosophically defined and in the end identified with God), in Hobbes the notion of nature begins to reflect the new, scientific, mathematical, and empirical study of nature. In this respect, another renowned English philosopher, Francis Bacon (1561–1626), had already prepared the way. In his old age, Hobbes became more interested in proving things after the model of geometry and physics. Human behavior, he thought, should be able to be described as a system. Although Hobbes may sound a bit like the Spinoza of the *Ethics*, he goes further by announcing the *seculum rationalisticum*, the era of sovereign thought. Hobbes is the first to posit as his goal perfect knowledge, to be reached by the method of arithmetic and measuring. Fewer and fewer people took him seriously. It seemed as if the human individual became invisible under his abstractions. Preoccupation with abstraction is not easily linked with an interest in the concrete expressions that characterize religions. In his later years, Hobbes was no longer widely known in England. His common sense had perhaps faced in too many directions; it might have become too common. Nevertheless, the idea, his idea of the supremacy of reason, triumphed and became part of our Western, shared history.

John Locke (1632–1704).   With Hobbes, Francis Bacon, and especially John Locke, we have the beginning of an entire tradition, particularly evident in Britain, that has been thought of as "common sense. " In spite of the fact that one should avoid ethnic and linguistic generalization, we may observe that many an immigrant to an English-speaking country has found "common sense" to be among the very special expressions that are almost impossible to translate into another language. This line of common sense runs from the Renaissance to the late eighteenth century, in David Hume, and well into the nineteenth and twentieth centuries. Nowhere, however, does this special feature show itself more clearly than in John Locke.

One writer has given us an image of Locke that is so vivid as to make other summary superfluous. George Santayana wrote in 1933:

> A good portrait of Locke would require an elaborate background. He is not a figure to stand statuesquely in a void: the pose might not seem grand enough for bronze or marble. Rather he should be painted in the manner of the Dutch masters, in a sunny interior, scrupulously furnished with all the implements of domestic comfort and philosophical enquiry: the Holy Bible open majestically before him, and besides it that other revelation—the terrestrial globe. His hand might be pointing to a microscope set for examining the internal constitution of a beetle: but for the moment his eye should be seen wandering through the open window, to admire the blessings of thrift and liberty manifest in the people so worthily busy in the market-place, wrong as many a monkish notion might be that still troubled their poor heads. From them his enlarged thoughts would easily pass to the stout carved ships in the river beyond, intrepidly setting sail for the Indies, or for savage America. Yes, he too had travelled, and not only in thought. He knew how many strange nations and false religions lodged in this round earth, itself but a speck in the universe. There were few ingenious authors that he had not perused, or philosophical instruments that he had not, as far as possible, examined and tested; and no man better than he could understand and prize the recent discoveries of "the incomparable Mr. Newton." Nevertheless, a certain uneasiness in that spare frame, a certain knitting of the brows in that aquiline countenance, would suggest that in the midst of their earnest eloquence the philosopher's thoughts might sometimes come to a stand. Indeed, the visible scene did not exhaust the complexity of his problem; for there was also what he called "the scene of ideas," immaterial and private, but often more crowded and pressing than the public scene.[13]

Santayana goes on to suggest that Locke can also be seen as the father of modern psychology (of which Santayana was no admirer, calling it "this airy monster, this half-natural changeling"). However that may be, what is faultless in this image is the thinker who at one and the same time has the

Bible open in front of him and a terrestrial globe and a microscope within reach. Both globe and microscope are creations of science, not of revelation in the traditional sense. But for Locke, the globe is "that other revelation." It does not crowd out the Bible; it is simply there beside it.

The "common sense" tradition of British philosophers avoids extreme views. The practitioner of common sense thinks without losing touch with what we think together, what we notice by using our senses, what is commonly observed; the practitioner of common sense does not easily lose sight of what occurs to every ordinary citizen in ordinary circumstances. Common sense points to what is there, to things that are incontrovertible, matters that do not call for far-flung speculative explanations. With respect to matters of religion as well, these tendencies of "common sense" had their effect. And it is worth noting that in the last couple of centuries, as we shall see, "common sense" has not been the most conspicuous feature of the philosophies of the European continent. Many of the reasonings of the English thinkers we have mentioned turn to what we can observe as constitutive of human life and its organization. This does not involve a denial of the crucial Christian notion of "revelation," or biblical notions like "covenant," for in some measure such notions relate to what is commonly accepted in society. Of course, these English thinkers remain very much part of the philosophical revolution of the Renaissance and the seventeenth century. Nevertheless, even in their radically new orientation—distinct from the explicit authoritativeness of medieval thought—something conservative remains; whatever has been accepted in the past hangs on. Nothing is wholly (as if "on principle") abandoned. If we can speak of "rules," the practice of compromise is the rule of common sense. There is also a stronger "psychological" component here; it is a natural part of the "common sense" approach; it is assumed that normally people follow certain common patterns in their sensations and inner lives. Of course, the commonsense tradition is also a matter of theorizing, as is all philosophy. In comparison, however, much of European Continental philosophy seems almost obsessed with theory. The tradition from Hobbes to Hume is more down-to-earth.

Locke's practical instinct also informed his theory of religion; he saw it to quite an extent as *morality*—the decency expected of people adhering to clear moral rules. Even more encompassing is his insistence on the need to use our eyes. Our mind is a *tabula rasa*—that is, a clean sheet, or an empty room that is only gradually filled by our senses. There are no such things as innate ideas. Locke's empirical interest was no doubt kindled by the widespread enthusiasm for new experiences in those days. Locke lived in the period of discoveries by adventurous navigators and other travelers.

The image of John Locke with Bible and microscope has a great deal to do with "common sense"; it does not go for the either/or. The world is one, and in principle intellectual inquiry is one. We would say: our knowledge should be unified in epistemology, a coherency in our ideas of what it means to know. This idea of knowledge cannot be divided beforehand, not even into what is considered useful and what is not; the practical applications of the intellect to life are rather like "by-products." This is important to register, as it shows that the actual goings-on of science were from the beginning philosophical and theoretical—contrary to our common mental picture of them as being of constant immediate use.

Our enthusiasm for technique—by-product of science—is something that developed in the nineteenth century, and it is easy to see how it was largely responsible for many of today's mistaken notions about knowledge or science. The locomotive had transformed the world by the mid–nineteenth century. Electricity was introduced on a large scale around 1900. All such things made the imagination soar. And this enthusiasm has continued unabated into the twenty-first century. Even the atomic bomb barely made a dent in the eagerness for applied, "manifest" science.

The enthusiasm surrounding science produces ironies. Everyone knows the name of Einstein—even millions of people who are utterly ignorant about physics. In contrast, it is strange to realize that the most important names associated with religion remain unknown, until, in rare instances, they win a Nobel Prize, and even then they rather quickly fade from view—Mother Teresa of Calcutta, for example. Important figures of the past hundred years (Karl Barth comes to mind) are virtually unknown, even in circles where they *should* be known.

We cannot repeat often enough that the period in which scientific observation first enters our world was very different from the present. The "science" that was done eventually became practical in its applications— but that took time. For quite a while science was done with little practical application. It is especially important to remember that for men such as Locke and Descartes, being scientifically engaged did not mean giving up the idea of intellectual inquiry as fundamentally one; it was not divided into "sciences" and "humanities," nor was there a split between "nature" and "religion." Such divisions and conflicts, familiar to us, are slow in developing, and when they develop, they do not always do so on good grounds, as we shall see in greater detail.

The Wider Movement Toward Modernity

It should be obvious that if there had not been a doctrine of creation in theology, our interest in the earth and its place in the universe would not have assumed the importance that it did. In Buddhism too, the world of course plays a role, but from the beginning in Buddhism, the origin or special place of the earth plays no role of significance. We have discussed the relation between myth and science and do not need to reiterate, except for one detail that is significant for our Western history of ideas concerning religion.

That detail is that physics eventually became the "queen of sciences" in the modern university. No law decrees that physics should be first or superior among sciences. The rise of physics did not occur at once, but slowly, until the nineteenth and twentieth centuries made it paramount. This came about simultaneously with Western colonial expansion. The pride in "our" scientific achievements went hand in hand with a haughty attitude toward "the natives" of splendid civilizations such as those of India and China. A scholar of repute wrote in 1974 on the history of science in China (in the fifteenth edition of the *Encyclopaedia Britannica*) that "China failed to become Europe." His assumption was that real science could only be what Europeans did. It is certainly a sign of the longevity of a colonizing mentality. A particular attitude among the intellectual elite assumed that "natives" everywhere were mired in backward religious ideas—a situation from which the evolved West had emerged. Physics served as the chief witness.

One might say sarcastically that the medieval and Renaissance nascent interest in physics is characterized by the wish for domination over dead matter. The remark is unfair, for men such as Hobbes and Locke were inquiring arduously into questions of human life and society. However, as a wise man said, the history of philosophy is the history of misinterpretation. The science of the days of Hobbes and Locke eventually turned into that venerated, eulogized "queen of sciences." Dealing with all matters, including living, human ones, as if they were lifeless things became a real possibility. Even the equation that Spinoza reached in his struggle to make sense out of the world and human existence—that God and "Nature" are the same—could come to be a sort of lifeless mathematical formula that could be applied to any empirical data in the world.

By the end of the seventeenth century, certain tangible results of science were part of daily life and the experience of all. The art of lens grinding, which had enabled scientific observation of the stars, led to the fabrication of eyeglasses. People with inadequate eyesight could now read the many, many things an increasing number of printing presses made available. Our word *optimist* acquired its definite meaning in the first half of the eighteenth century. *Optimus,* a common Latin superlative, means "the very best"; the confidence that everything is for the very best purpose makes the optimist. Optimism does not sum up all there was to the eighteenth century, but is an inseparable part of it.

The widely felt optimism of the first half of the eighteenth century quite naturally stimulated the idea that human reason was a very special, powerful instrument indeed. Eyeglassess and clocks, together with the writings of Descartes and Locke, literally changed the outlook on the world. These things did not put an end to religion—but the stage was set for very new, critical ways of regarding it. The traditional authorities were no longer assumed to have the final say. The freedom of the human mind reached by philosophers in the seventeenth century, and the optimism of the eighteenth century, caused religion itself (that is, Christianity) and the religions in the plural (which new discoveries brought to the attention of people who had been relatively isolated) to become more and more inviting as objects of open and general inquiry.

The "liberation" of the human mind, as felt in ever wider circles by a rapidly growing reading public, also resulted from certain events that had taken place as if by accident, and much earlier. The universities of the Middle Ages had used the word "science," *scientia,* for the study of theology and philosophy. Let us repeat: these were the original sciences, theology and philosophy. In this customary educational system, the Christian world continued what classical culture had created. But, as a result of the great disasters of the bubonic plague in the fourteenth and fifteenth centuries, technical skills that earlier had not enjoyed a great deal of esteem became necessities. Among the *technes* (or in Latin, *artes*) were not only the traditional skills of language, logic, rhetoric, and mathematics, but now the newly added ones of law, and—largely because of the need for help for disease-ridden, suffering populations—medicine. Thus the liberation of human reason, felt so generally in the eighteenth century, had a long birth process.

The discovery of reason, the new technologies, the engagement in scientific inquiry—all these are related to one more feature of modern history, of which the absolute origin is not determinable. It is the birth of "the individual." Individualism may be considered a fact of human nature in many circles of our modern industrialized world, but it is a recent phenomenon, and its growth is a strange hybrid—as are its results. Without it, we would not have had high capitalism, nor Martin Luther King's faith and courage. In the complexity of history, all we can say is that individualism is part and parcel of the same multifarious movement that saw the rise of technology, science, "reason," the great Renaissance mystics, and, yes, also the Reformers.

One aspect of the rise of "the individual" cannot be left unmentioned in a survey of ideas about religion. The great thinkers of the seventeenth century, including Hobbes and Spinoza, and others as well, such as the famous legal scholar Hugo Grotius (1583–1645), were engaged in contemplating the governance of the state. Many minds concerned themselves with the state, the commonwealth, the organization of public life. And all of them agreed that in some measure the proper state paralleled the inner, mental arrangement of the individual.

It is not as if the thinkers of these novel ideas thought of themselves as revolutionaries. They had read their Plato, and, like so many in the Renaissance period, they recognized the relevance of what they read to their own world. Nevertheless, their reading of Plato's *Republic* was not a mere application of old ideas to a new world. A new awareness of people as *individuals* with equal rights gave a new twist to the classical idea of the *res publica*, the Common Good, the republic Plato had in mind. Plato, though one of the few truly classical philosophers in the world's history of thought, was also a child of his time, and he never doubted for a moment the necessity and validity of different classes making up society as a whole.

By contrast, the idea of the individual, together with the idea of the republic (of equals!), was among the seemingly most obvious principles of a nascent rationalism, at the doorsteps of our own modern history. The workings of the human mind can hardly be thought of concretely, functioning in governmental affairs, if the thinker does not think of his own, individual mental equipment. The result was a number of descriptions of the well-arranged state as a projection of the well-functioning human mind, keeping destructive desires in check, and giving the leadership to reason. This practical rationalism, of which we have already caught a glimpse in Thomas Hobbes, became a crucial part of the wider movement toward modernity. Today, few of these ideas would strike us as revolutionary, but we should realize that they could easily come into conflict with ruling views of kingship by the grace of God. The design of the *republic* as a preferable form of administration, if not presented outright, was a plausible suggestion. Political and religious discussions were never separate, and the new ideas found a fertile soil especially among the Congregationalists in America, who brought "democratic" forms into practice in the government of their churches.[14]

In addition to a rational manner of looking at the proper functions of a state through the lens of an individual's intellect, we see also another development, less likely to lead to any optimistic view of "the reason of the state." We have already noted sometimes people who engaged in critical thought were victims of the state's power. Even Grotius, though born in Holland, a country that was comparatively free from tyranny, had a close call. Grotius attained fame as an infant prodigy; he wrote poetry in Latin at the age of eight, and entered the University of Leiden at eleven; and his work is of lasting value in international law. However, he became the leader of the opposition to the government (of Prince Maurice) and was sentenced to life imprisonment. Fortunately he had permission to receive and return books; he hid in a book case and escaped. Such happy endings were rare in the lives of those whose individual convictions contradicted the state. Tragic experiences were far more numerous. There were of course antecedents in religious struggles in the same wide and centuries-long movement that generated our "individualism." A year before Grotius was born, John Calvin wrote a moving letter to comfort five fellow Protestant ministers who had been caught in Lyons, hence in the territory of the French king.[15] Guilty of Protestantism, they were condemned to death. The conscience and conviction of individual people after all are precisely the items that do not necessarily find a copy of themselves in the workings of a state. The greatness and the misery of "the individual" go hand in hand.

THE ENLIGHTENMENT

The Reason of the Philosophes.   In speaking of the Middle Ages and the Renaissance, we warned against artificiality in dividing and characterizing history into sections. Yet it is difficult to deny that some periods are distinctly marked on account of certain prevalent ideas. The Enlightenment is such an age. It occurs roughly in the time span from somewhere in the last half of the seventeenth century to somewhere in the last half of the eighteenth. The "light" of "Enlightenment" is the light of reason, also known simply as Rationalism. It shone first and most brightly in France, which was then still a kingdom—until its revolution put an end to that.

The French nation enjoyed a golden age, and its articulate ideas, intellectual habits, culture, and economic prestige spread over the map of Europe.

The works of John Locke, the English empiricist, and France's own Descartes, the rationalist, were read with fervor. Initially, the former seemed to inspire the French even more than the latter. The Enlightenment thinkers, even when not altogether original, rephrased matters of reason and society with an elegance that the same subjects might not have enjoyed in their original form—not even in the case of Descartes, the master of French clarity and distinctness. The grandest accomplishment of the French Enlightenment was the creation of the *Encyclopédie,* a work to which distinguished men of the time contributed: Diderot, d'Alembert, Rousseau, Montesquieu, and Jaucourt, among many others. Encyclopedias are common enough today, and most of the ones we use have gone through many editions and are taken for granted by professors and students, but that first encyclopedia broke new ground. In 1772 the work was at last finished. It was composed of thirty-eight volumes. For the first time, all the scientific discoveries and all the rational organization in human knowledge had been purposely summed up by a team of writers. Without the newfound trust in the value of human reason, the inspiration that made the *Encyclopédie* possible would not have existed.

There was still a lack of freedom, especially freedom of expression, and yet the life-or-death struggle of the previous centuries is less in evidence. To be sure, the publication of the *Encyclopédie* suffered many a setback, including, for a time, an official ban. In the case of the most outspoken of the "philosophes"—namely, Voltaire—the light touch of his writing style may have helped to protect him. Although some of what he wrote is excessive, it never *seemed* excessive, or else it was phrased with a humor that did not invite attack. In addition, none of the great Enlightenment writers expressed outright revolutionary ideas, even if hindsight may connect them to the great revolution against the monarchy in 1789, when the mental freedom they stood for seemed realized. From the vantage point of our own lives, it is easy to lose sight of an obvious fact: the supporters of the Enlightenment lived in a world where servants were a general feature. Service from people lower in standing was enjoyed by the free spirit Voltaire. Ordinary life was fairly comfortable for the enlightened spirits. Nevertheless, the political situation in France was such as to send Voltaire to the Bastille for some time. He suffered the miseries of exile more than once. Luckily, during his exile to England, he had occasion to enjoy the hospitality of the Scottish philosopher David Hume. Both were men of the Enlightenment, and no doubt they had inspiring conversations. Yet what a difference between those two! Voltaire's wit still sparkles, but for his originality and critical ability Hume has proved to be of more lasting value. Let us begin by speaking of Voltaire.

Voltaire was the assumed name of François-Marie Arouet (1694–1778). His trust in reason is evident on every page he wrote. His presentations can be cutting, yet his humor and his talent for wearing his scholarship lightly easily win readers over. One of his most widely known works is a little novel called *Candide* (1759), a parody on the foibles of human beings, not in the last place his contemporaries, and an optimistic rationalism—not too far removed from his own—is one of his targets. The book gently ridicules the optimism of two German thinkers, Leibniz and Christian Wolff, who were both of the opinion that "everything is for the best in the best of worlds"—which is the world we live in. Voltaire introduces his readers to a philosopher, Pangloss by name, who is truly a caricature of rationalism and optimism. Before a series of fantastic adventures unfolds, the young man Candide partakes with admiration of the "wisdom" of Pangloss, who is the tutor of a baron's son and daughter. The baron's name is Thunder-ten-tronckh and his castle is situated in Westphalia. The reason for Candide's presence in the baron's house is not a matter of public discourse; there is just a hint of suspicion that he might be the illegitimate son of the baron's sister. (The cult of decency in the best of worlds is included in Voltaire's irony.) A specimen of Pangloss's wisdom runs as follows:

> It is demonstrated . . . that things cannot be otherwise; for, since everything was made for a purpose, everything is necessarily for the best purpose. Note that noses were made to wear spectacles; we therefore have spectacles. Legs were clearly devised to wear breaches, and we have breaches.[16]

It follows immediately that stones were made to construct castles, that Baron Thunder-ten-tronckh's castle is most beautiful, as the greatest baron must have the finest, and so on. Voltaire is quick to see the mediocre foolishness of cherished ideas. Pangloss concludes a typical lesson thus: "Therefore, those who have maintained that all is well have been talking nonsense: they should have maintained that all is for the best."[17]

In Voltaire's thought, the archenemy is what we now would call "organized religion." It is unlike "natural religion," which is the paradigm of reason and virtue, but is rather a conglomerate of superstitions, invented by priests and their allies in order that they may profit. In his *Philosophical Dictionary* (1764, first volume) Voltaire wrote the following entry under "Prejudices, Religious":

> If your nurse has told you that Ceres rules over the crops, or that Vistnou and Xaca made themselves men several times, or that Sammonocodon came to cut down a forest, or that Odin awaits you in his hall near Jutland, or that Mohammed or somebody else made a journey into the sky; if, lastly, your tutor comes to drive into your brain what your nurse has imprinted on it, you keep it for life. If your judgment wishes to rise against these prejudices, your neighbors and, above all, your neighbors' wives cry out: "Impious reprobate," and dismay you. Your dervish, fearing to see his income diminished, accuses you to the cadi, and this cadi has you impaled if he can, because he likes ruling over fools, and thinks that fools obey better than those who are not fools. And all this will go on until your neighbors and the dervish and the cadi begin to understand that foolishness is good for nothing, and that persecution is abominable.[18]

Voltaire makes use of a certain code that is easy to decipher. He brings what he knows of the world's religions to bear on the great enemy that surrounds him: the church. As the quote makes clear, he is able to attack without naming his target. Voltaire may perhaps be called the first effective proponent of the idea that religion as it existed all around did not mean anything but was in fact something *to look through*. In wide circles today, this notion is customary and has become a habit. But what exactly is the "reason" of the Enlightenment worth? What does it see of religion when it *looks through* it? How far does it go, for instance, in sizing up evil? Will "reason" be all it takes to cause "your neighbors and the dervish and the cadi" to become wise? We do not get a clear answer.

The "natural religion" that Voltaire envisaged together with many others in his time shows his rationalism as if in full-length portrait. For Voltaire, and many of his anticlerical contemporaries, the idea of God does not disappear, but God's reality is posited as something different from what established religious teachings maintain. The God spoken of by the typical Enlightenment writers is not in need of worship. He is, instead, the architect of the world, who, after having formed that construction, then withdraws. He is, as the favorite comparison had it, like a watchmaker, who is no longer needed when the watch has been made, wound up, and set running. This notion of God, obviously a mechanical affair, is called *deism,* in contrast to *theism.*[19] The latter applies to the religions that know supreme deities of the type we find for instance in Christianity, Islam, and Hinduism; in theism, God is worshipped, God's activity is not restricted to that of a first cause of the universe. One of the strangest things in the world of the *philosophes* from our modern perspective is something that relates to their still very inadequate knowledge of religions. Distant traditions were believed to be *showing* the "natural religion" that the Enlightenment had as a matter of fact thought up. Confucius in particular had an appeal of this sort. His name became the hook on which the philosophes could hang the semblance of reality as far as their natural religion was concerned. This custom was part of a general mystifying of "the Orient" and its art and culture, known — with the light touch of irony known to the best rationalists — as chinoiserie.

That light touch will move further and further into the background, when real knowledge about the religions of the world grows. However, it is worth something. The eighteenth century is full of a sense of humor and self-irony. It is the time of the humorous novel. Books by authors like Henry Fielding, Laurence Sterne, and Jonathan Swift still provide the greatest delight.

But that world, no matter how sharp in its observations, how impelled by common sense, nevertheless is not a world of the greatest profundity, especially with respect to questions concerning religions — and certainly not when, as we have remarked, the actual, historical religious traditions and their data by and large were yet to be discovered. The rationalism of the Enlightenment is somewhat shallow. New information from explorations reached Voltaire and his circle. Members of the Jesuit order had traveled far and wide: some were in North America, and they sent their reports of tribal religions back to Europe; others had gone to China. As we said, it became common during the Age of Reason to regard Confucius as a proponent of the "natural religion" the Enlightenment had dreamed up with its images of the architect of the world, tolerance toward all, a fine morality, a neatly closed system of thought. The creators of the Enlightenment, the philosophes, were children of their time in that they worked only with concepts — exactly like the churchmen they found fault with. They were of course oblivious to such things as myth and ritual. The elements that in fact make up religious traditions were to them mere superstition. For the history of thought about religion, the topic of Voltaire and the Enlightenment is instructive, because the study of religions benefits by our ability to detect superficiality in all its shapes. Voltaire has been depicted as an atheist. His statement "Si Dieu n'existait pas, il faudrait l'inventer" ("If God did not exist, it would be necessary to invent him"), taken by itself, sounds like destructive irony. However, Voltaire wrote the didactic poem in which this statement is made *against* a man whom he opposed for his atheism.

> The place where I live is filled with lizards and rats,
> But there truly is an architect, and whoever denies him,
> Under the guise of a sage, is crazy.
> Ask Zoroaster, and Minos and Solon,
> And the martyr Socrates, and the great Cicero;
> All of them adored a master, a judge, a father.
> This sublime system is necessary for human beings.
> It is the sacred bond of society,
> The very foundation of sacred justice,
> It is what keeps the scoundrels in check, the hope of the just.
> If the heavens, deprived of his august imprint,
> Ever ceased to manifest him,
> If God did not exist, he would have to be invented.
> May the sage announce him and kings fear him.
> Kings, if you oppress me, if your greatness disdains
> The tears of the innocent you force into ruin,
> My avenger is in heaven: learn to tremble.
> This, at least, is the result of a useful belief.[20]

Thus were it not for God (more accurately, the idea of God), the world would fall prey utterly to scoundrels and vicious rulers. Voltaire's teachings keep their charm, and yet, they are far from profound. In fact, they lack all serious consideration of what the world's religious traditions actually say. The tendency to such thinness of thought dominates a good part of the eighteenth century. The celebrated German philosopher Immanuel Kant (1724–1804) is recognizable as a typical man of the Enlightenment. The keystone of his thought system is practical philosophy, that is, ethics; that provides the bridge to the reality of God. Of course, the great achievements of Kant lie outside this detail. The detail merely illustrates once more how the Enlightenment is indeed a period unto itself, whose imprint hardly anyone then living could escape. The importance of *ethics* once more takes us back to the significance of the *individual*. The individual *acts,* and how the individual acts is of supreme importance in the new world of reason we have entered.

The undeniable importance of the Enlightenment with respect to religion remains its opening up of general discussion on matters that had been left to theological experts. Salons came into fashion as meeting places for educated people. The art of discussion was practiced, and there was a growing consciousness that education mattered. Once more, it is the individuals who counted. The eighteenth century discovered that children needed special care in their mental growth. It is in the eighteenth century that the first books designed specifically for the young were written. (When we hear of geniuses from this period who at a very young age learned to read Latin and Greek, we tend to forget that specific writings for children were still in their infancy. People in educated circles, however, had Latin and Greek texts on their bookshelves.)

The Role of Emotion. Even a brief treatment should not fail to mention one more aspect of the Enlightenment. Next to the rational playfulness so abundantly visible, we find as well an emotional element. Even in the ceaselessly rationalizing Voltaire, the concern for justness, no matter how rationally expressed, has something of a "feel" to it. Voltaire's contemporary Jean-Jacques Rousseau (1712–78) is the eighteenth century's great champion of human emotion. Different from Voltaire, who did not think of "uncivilized" human communities as "good," Rousseau made the Renaissance traveler's hope of discovering on earth some glimpse of paradise, some evidence of "the noble savage," into a philosophical image. Unlike Voltaire, he thought that human beings are essentially good, and that evil results only when in civilized life people make use of other people. His obsession with "the good" led him to reiterate in essays and stories how neither man nor God could be accused of having originated evil.[21] Indubitably, Rousseau was unaware that his idea of an evil without originator is widespread in the religious traditions of the world. Many a mythical story sees the origin of evil (and of death) as the outcome of an unintended incident. (The Old Testament itself does not develop a doctrine of a fall; instead, the story in Genesis 2, as narrated in the text, is closer to that more general mythical theme than to John Calvin, or any other Christian theologian.) In *Émile, or on Education* (1762), Rousseau theorizes on the development of a child's soul. What he has to say is anchored in the idea of a "natural" human being, in contrast to the cultural, civilized human being. The first twelve years of a child's life should be totally free, Rousseau avers;

the child until that age should follow his or her instincts. Then only should the child's interest be aroused, with a bit of help from a teacher, for the principles of learning and scholarship. And even that should be accomplished with images, visual things—steering clear of books and abstract notions as much as possible. Not until the age of fifteen should the child be spoken to about God. (That God of course is the God of deism, not of revelation.) All this is in agreement with what is "natural," according to Rousseau. He writes in *Émile:*

> Man has no innate knowledge of virtue; but no sooner is it made known to him by reason than conscience induces him to love and admire it. This is the innate sentiment I mean . . .
> Ah! let us not spoil the man of nature, and he will always be virtuous without constraint, and happy without remorse.[22]

In all Rousseau's works, including his influential *Social Contract,* the theme of the inner, emotional element occurs. The interest in feeling, whether explicitly brought out or not, is never far away in Enlightenment thought. The eighteenth century witnessed pietistic movements—not in the last place the revivals conducted in America by the preacher and theologian Jonathan Edwards (1703–58). Reason and emotion there went clearly hand in hand. And we must always keep in mind that the history of ideas never develops in isolation, as if in a sterile test tube. The famous thinkers of the Enlightenment inhabited the same world in which musicians of much greater and probably more lasting fame were very active. The French boast of Couperin and Rameau, the Italians of Vivaldi, Marcello, and Albinoni, both the Germans and the English of George Frederick Handel, and of course, the entire musical world glorifies Johann Sebastian Bach and Mozart. Musicians know that music is a matter of calculated precision. At the same time, the occasions for music were frequently religious—especially in the case of the great choral works. The *Saint Matthew Passion* of Bach is a monument to the integration of mathematical calculation and religious emotional expressivenes; after Jesus Christ's death, the final chorus (in C minor) sings out (in the words of a poet who is barely remembered): "Wir setzen uns mit Tränen nieder . . ." ("We sit down and weep . . ."). This too is the world in which the Enlightenment had its dwelling place. Rousseau may not be known for his compositions, but even he composed music, in addition to his other activities.

Literature
Voltaire, *Philosophical Letters,* trans. Ernest Dilworth (Indianapolis: Bobbs-Merrill, 1982), in "The Library of Liberal Arts"; Diderot, d'Alembert, and others, *Encyclopedia, Selections,* ed. Thomas Cassirer (Indianapolis: Bobbs-Merrill, 1965), in "The Library of Liberal Arts"; Jonathan Swift, *Gulliver's Travels,* ed. Robert A. Greenberg, with annotated text and critical essays, a Norton Critical Edition (New York: Norton, 1961); Isaac Kramnick, ed., *The Portable Enlightenment Reader* (New York: Penguin, 1995); Leonard M. Marsak, ed., *The Enlightenment* (New York: John Wiley, 1972); Thomas Street Christensen, *Rameau and Musical Thought in the Enlightenment* (New York: Cambridge University Press,1993); Ben Ray Redman, ed., *The Portable Voltaire* (Harmondsworth: Penguin, 1977).

DAVID HUME

David Hume (1711–76) worked on his *Dialogues Concerning Natural Religion* for many years and did not give final form to it until the year of his death in 1776. The Scottish Calvinists he lived among were not more lenient toward free expression of thought than the Catholic Church and the government in France. The first edition of the work did not appear until 1779.[23] It is a dialogue, comparable in form to Plato's dialogues. This impression is strenghthened by the classical names of the speakers: Philo, Cleanthes, Demea. The narrator is given the name Pamphilus. The names are related to a dialogue written by Cicero, on a topic that could be a model for Hume's: *De natura deorum* ("About the nature of the gods").[24] The discussion turns on the nature of religion, and specifically of God.

Hume may have been a friend to Voltaire and Rousseau (the latter, like Voltaire, had to escape France for a while, and was received by Hume), he may even have written and said many things that agreed with the French philosophes, yet if anyone should be credited with the first serious doubts about the naive aspects of Enlightenment thought, it is he. To examine Hume's healthy and serious thought, we will turn to the *Dialogues Concerning Natural Religion.* Let us note, however, that he also wrote a treatise called *The Natural History of Religion* which is interesting as well, as it was the first articulate expression of a developmental pattern of religions in the world (from polytheism to monotheism). Unlike dialogues by Plato, *The Dialogues Concerning Natural Religion* contain no Socrates figure whose voice stands out as the most authoritative. It is rather as if Hume was more fascinated by the process of arguing than by the clarity of the position arrived at in the end. Could it be, also, that presenting himself too bluntly in his own rather skeptical fashion—the attitude most clearly manifest by Philo in the discussion—would have been risky? Nevertheless, Hume remains very much himself in the seriousness and significance overall of the argument, and there is no doubt that through his speakers he arrives at views quite superior to those of the philosophes. In an approximate analogy to Cicero's dialogue, two of the three principal speakers are inclined to skepticism (Philo) and stoicism (Cleanthes). Even in his updated form, the skeptic is clearly related to the classical school. Cleanthes, however, though related to the ancients through the Stoic ethics handed down in the tradition of the churches, is very much an eighteenth-century theological rationalist. Norman Kemp Smith, the editor of Hume's treatise, rightly reminds readers of the distinction Cicero had already made between the question concerning the existence and "that most obscure and difficult question concerning the *nature* of the Gods."[25] Pamphilus, the narrator, introduces the dialogue he is about to present with a few arresting sentences:

> What truth so obvious, so certain, as the *being* of God, which the most ignorant of ages have acknowledged, for which the most refined geniuses have ambitiously striven to produce new proofs and arguments? What truth so important as this, which is the ground of all our hopes, the surest foundation of our morality, the firmest support of society, and the only principle which ought never to be a moment absent from our thoughts and meditations? But in treating of this obvious and important truth; what obscure questions occur, concerning the nature of that divine Being; his attributes, his decrees, his plan of providence? These have been always subjected to the disputations of men: Concerning these, human reason has not reached any certain determination: But these are topics so interesting, that we cannot restrain our restless enquiry with regard to them; though nothing but doubt, uncertainty, and contradiction, have, as yet, been the result of our most accurate researches.[26]

David Hume is skeptical in the sense that he never wants to subscribe to a premature conclusion. With respect to the sufficiency of the human mind, there is plenty of reason for doubt. With respect to the reality of God only one thing is sure, and that one thing is negative: if we speak about that reality seriously, we must realize that we are speaking about something that goes well beyond the restrictions of our reason. Close to the end of the *Dialogues*, Philo (Hume?) says, in a paragraph that Hume added in the final revision,

> If the whole of natural theology, as some people seem to maintain, resolves itself into one simple, though somewhat ambiguous, at least undefined proposition, that the cause or causes of order in the universe probably bear some remote analogy to human intelligence: If this proposition be not capable of extension, variation, or more particular explication: If it afford no inference that affects human life, or can be the source of any action or forbearance: And if the analogy, imperfect as it is, can be carried no farther than to human intelligence; and cannot be transferred, with any appearance of probability, to the other qualities of the mind: If this really be the case, what can the most inquisitive, contemplative, and religious man do more than give a plain, philosophical assent to the proposition, as often as it occurs; and believe that the arguments, on which it is established, exceed the objections which lie against it? Some astonishment indeed will naturally arise from the greatness of the object: Some melancholy from its obscurity: Some contempt of human reason, that it can give no solution more satisfactory with regard to so extraordinary and magnificent a question. But . . . the most natural sentiment, which a well-disposed mind will feel on this occasion, is a longing desire and expectation, that Heaven would feel pleased to dissipate, at least alleviate, this profound ignorance, by affording some more particular revelation to mankind, and making discoveries of the nature, attributes, and operations of the divine object of our Faith. A person, seasoned with a just sense of the imperfections of natural reason, will fly to revealed truth with the greatest avidity; While the haughty dogmatist, persuaded that he can erect a complete system of theology by the mere help of philosophy, disdains any farther aid, and rejects this adventitious instructor. To be a philosophical sceptic is, in a man of letters, the first and most essential step towards being a sound, believing Christian . . .[27]

If we can bring ourselves to read this piece of eighteenth-century prose attentively, we shall find it worth rereading, even though we ourselves might not take the trouble to sculpt our thought to such finesse. A historian of religions will do well to remember that all religions are religions of salvation.

That is crucially related to what Hume is saying here. And it is what put a radical end to ideas of God like an architect or watchmaker — at least in those who listened. The proverbial common sense of British philosophers is clearly in evidence in Hume's exposition. Next to it, the God-as-watchmaker, the god whose only function is to set things in motion, is too far removed from observable facts of religious life to be taken seriously.

Literature

David Hume, *Dialogues Concerning Natural Religion,* ed. and introd. Norman Kemp Smith (Indianapolis: Bobbs-Merrill, 1947), in "The Library of Liberal Arts"; David Hume, *On Religion: The Natural History of Religion, Dialogues Concerning Natural Religion, My Own Life,* ed. and introd. Richard Wollheim (New York: Meridian, 1964).

REASON IN TWO EXCEPTIONAL FIGURES: VICO AND HAMANN

Although the Enlightenment allows for a general characterization more easily than most ages, even there we find figures who do not seem to fit. One of these is the Italian Giambattista Vico (1668–1744), another the German Johann Georg Hamann (1730–88). Some of their contemporaries receive a great deal more attention in the history of literature, art, and culture in general, but for us interested in religion, they are of real significance. Each in his own way reacted strongly to what we have called the "shallowness" of their rational environment.

Vico was a very learned Catholic priest, who knew the classics well, was as informed of the latest events as the best thinkers of the Enlightenment, and, moreover, was well acquainted with the literature that preceded the eighteenth century. He did not admire the intellectual revolution that had begun with Descartes. He was absorbed by questions concerning education, but his ideas about it were strangely at odds with what Rousseau had to say on the subject. In his *Autobiography,* which he wrote not to place himself on a pedestal but in order to aid all who searched for educational examples, he wrote with disdain about the tradition of Descartes as detrimental to the schooling of the young. What he says about himself — all in the third person — is little, yet even that little produces an edifying effect:

He was a boy of high spirits and impatient of rest; but at the age of
seven he fell head first from the top of a ladder to the floor below, and
remained a good five hours without motion or consciousness. The right
side of the cranium was fractured, but the skin was not broken. The
fracture gave rise to a large tumor, and the child suffered much loss
of blood from the many deep lancings. The surgeon, indeed, observing
the broken cranium and considering the long period of unconscious-
ness, predicted that he would either die of it or grow up an idiot. However by God's grace neither part of his prediction came true . . .[28]

What Vico deplores in the method of Descartes is not that reason is
put to use, but that in the spreading fashion of the rationalists education
is debased by abstractions, at the expense of sciences that foster the
imagination.

With reason the ancients considered the study of geometry suitable for
children and judged it to be a logic appropriate to that tender age whose
difficulty in comprehending the genera of things is proportional to its
facility in apprehending the particulars and how to dispose them in
sequence. Aristotle himself, though he had abstracted the syllogistic art
from the method employed in geometry, agrees with this when he says
that children should be taught languages, histories and geometry as
subjects suitable for exercising memory, imagination and perception.
Hence we can easily understand how much undoing, what sort of culture, youth derives from two pernicious practices in use today.
    The first is in introducing philosophy to children barely out of gram-
mar school with the so-called logic "of Arnauld," full of rigorous judgments concerning recondite matters of the higher sciences, remote from
vulgar common sense. The result is a blasting of those youthful mental
gifts which should be regulated and developed each by a separate art, as
for example memory by the study of languages, imagination by the reading of poets, historians and orators, perception by plane geometry . . .
    The other practice consists in teaching youth the elements of the sci-
ence of magnitudes by the algebraic method. For this numbs all that is
most exuberant in youthful natures: it obscures their imagination, en-
feebles their memory, renders their perception sluggish, and slackens
their understanding. And these four things are all most necessary for
the culture of the best humanity.[29]

No one among us would argue that life does not require imagination, and yet we need only look at any of our college or university curricula to realize that in the turn that history took, Descartes emerged the victor, Vico lost. Could we declare that Vico was wrong? Hardly. During the years I have spent writing this book, history departments have been victims of "downsizing"—the fashionable business term for causing layoffs. Frankly, universities always manage to see to it that the imaginative quality in education is diminished first. Even under the best of circumstances, religion is shunted off to a corner of the division of humanities, far away from even such sciences as medicine, where fostering imagination toward human existence and miseries would seem crucial. Imagination is a prerequisite for the practice of human understanding. Vico cannot be dismissed.

He called his principal work *Scienza nuova,* and the science he created was indeed new. It comes closest to what we know as the comparative historical study of religions and cultures, a discipline that in our academic setting is divided between the history of religions and cultural anthropology, located in two different academic divisions. Vico was so original, literally so far ahead of his time, that he has supported all sorts of interpretation in various countries and circles. Defenders of the eighteenth century's favorite ideal of progress, Romantics, rationalists, Hegelians, and Marxists all had their own way of seeing their convictions foreshadowed in him; Marxists were naturally taken by Vico's stress on cultural and social patterns and the unimportance of individuals.[30] In fact, however, for centuries after his death, the number of people who took Vico's works in hand and read them was small indeed.

It is no exaggeration to say that Vico was the first scholar who made it his task to investigate the data of religions and cultures. The first sentence in the second book of the *New Science,* which deals with "Poetic Wisdom," begins by repeating one of the axioms he had established earlier: "All the histories of the gentile nations have had fabulous beginnings."[31] And he spells out the myths of origin of Greece, Rome, and other cultures. Many of his findings could be called "obvious," but we should not forget that precisely these obvious matters continue to be disregarded in our Cartesian world. Vico makes a conspicuously obvious point early on:

> We observe that all nations, barbarous as well as civilized, though separately founded because remote from each other in space and time, keep these three human customs: all have some religion, all contract solemn marriages, all bury their dead. And in no nation, however sav-

age and crude, are any human actions performed with more elaborate ceremonies and more sacred solemnity than the rites of religion, marriage, and burial. For, by the axiom that "uniform ideas, born among peoples unknown to each other, must have a common ground of truth," it must have been dictated to all nations that from these three institutions humanity began among them all . . . For this reason we have taken these three eternal and universal customs as three principles of this Science.[32]

What we discussed about religious symbolization in the first half of this book was clearly anticipated by Vico. The most important general principle of Vico is his insistence on perceiving the given facts of religious traditions. It would be misleading to conclude that Vico literally said what only slowly dawned on our own century. While opposing Cartesian rationality, Vico's idea of truth maintained firm roots in medieval traditions with which we would have difficulty.

It is Vico's thesis that *verum* equals *factum*, "what is true is what is made."[33] This thesis was crucial in Vico's offense against the threatening abstractions of Cartesianism. According to Vico *only God can be a perfect astronomer*, as he had *made* the world of nature. *Men, by contrast, can truly know only "the world of nations, or civil world,"* as they are responsible for having *made* that world.[34] For *us*, with respect to the world of nations, which according to Vico we have made, a problem of knowledge arises: Vico makes it seem as if God's guidance of the world could be read from what we observe in history. He speaks freely of divine providence and of the object of his new science in the conviction that somehow these two converge. As for ourselves, the twentieth century may not have made all of us skeptics, but it has given us much occasion to feel humble in broaching the subject of true knowledge.

It is precisely with a view to this problem that the other exceptional eighteenth-century figure demands our attention. Johann Georg Hamann led a different life, later in the century, on the eve of a new movement — the Romantic movement — in different circumstances, under very different influences, not in the Catholic Mediterranean world, but in Luther's Germany. If Vico's genius was primarily his grasp of all that was valuable in the past, Hamann's genius was the grasp of mental and spiritual problems that were yet to grow to their full extent. Almost everything about Hamann was unusual, including things that at first sight might not seem extraordinary. He had a conversion experience as a young man while on a business trip to London—he was sent probably more for his health's sake than for the importance of the business. The conversion was triggered by his Bible readings at his London lodgings. He fell in love with a young woman but failed to win her hand. He lived as a governor-teacher, and in that capacity spent some time in well-to-do households in the Baltic countries. Later, he moved back into his ailing father's home, and stayed on after his father's death. He lived with his father's housekeeper in a common-law relation; she bore him four children. The highest office he held was that of chief of a Prussian customhouse. All his spare time was devoted to study. The family under his roof at home was remarkable for its warmth and he was noted for his fatherly devotion, as letters from his children later document. He had an intense dislike for the king, Frederick II (Frederick the Great, ruling 1740–86), the same whose friendship Voltaire cultivated for some time; he doted on his army and enjoyed raising tax revenues to lavish upon it while cutting expenses for everything else. Hamann was born and lived in the same city, Königsberg, where Immanuel Kant taught. He knew Kant, talked with him, and criticized him harshly. This last fact, in all its ordinariness, is quite unusual, for serious critics of Kant were not then, nor have they ever been since, very many. He was a Lutheran, but close to the end of his life, he moved west at the invitation of an admirer (who knew him through his writing) to Münster, where he died in a Catholic environment. He was buried in the garden of the Princess von Gallitzin; the clergy had granted its permission, on one condition: that it be recorded that this did not happen because of intolerance on the part of the Catholic authorities.[35] Hamann did a great deal of criticizing during his lifetime. He did not mind sending a letter to Frederick the Great, on one of the occasions when the king once more curtailed the income of his citizens. No one among his colleagues had the courage to sign that letter with him. But the permanent target of his condemnation was the "natural religion," the deism, that was so dear to the great philosophes, whose ideas had become common throughout Europe. The decency that the French Enlightenment advocated had become in its popularization more and more a petty bourgeois morality; in this light even the ordinary fact of Hamann's "living in sin" in a small town takes on significance.

The most indisputably unusual characteristic of Hamann was his writing style. He wove together his knowledge of Arab civilization, classical literature, the Bible, and, by no means least, every bit of news that happened to be current at the moment he wrote. All these things together make his writing obscure for a modern reader. If he had written constantly during his entire life, reading all of his output would be well-nigh impossible. It is perhaps fortunate that he wrote only in spurts, and for long stretches of time wrote not at all—except for letters. (The eighteenth century had made elaborate correspondence a common habit of educated people; the custom continued unabated in the nineteenth century. If one could not visit, one wrote, and one wrote about things of importance.)

The freedom Hamann shows in his criticisms and his ironies resulted no doubt from the conversion he had experienced, because it is exactly from that moment that his life changed. He did not *take* the freedom he displayed; rather, he *found* it. His freedom in offering critique was never a form of self-righteousness. Among the many verdicts Hamann passed on "natural religion," one, made in a letter to the young Romantic writer Herder, is brief and to the point: "Unbelief is the oldest, strongest, and, next to superstition, the only natural religion."[36] These are words with a theological edge which Vico would not have spoken. Hamann was wholly aware of *salvation* as the one overriding topic in religion. For this reason, some decades later, the Danish thinker Kierkegaard became one of Hamann's most ardent readers. The remarkable thing in Hamann, as later in Kierkegaard, is that his clinging to Christian faith never turns into rational possession. Hence his interest in religions other than Christianity is never condescending. God's grace can come through any channel. In spite of their differences, both Hamann and Vico deal with similar problems if we look at them from a religio-historical perspective: they adhere to their Christian tradition, yet are fully conscious of the worldwide range of human and religious forms. Perhaps unlike Vico, Hamann saw the danger in prematurely relating a rational proposition to divine Providence.

One Hamann interpreter presented his findings under the title "Nature and Grace."[37] This pair of terms sums up well the character of human existence in Hamann's thought. The realm of nature comprises all that is open to our mind's inquiries. There is, however, the additional realm of human history. (For the mature Hamann, this latter realm is not opposed to the former; the two are complementary.)[38] Human beings have their existence only in history—which, in Hamann's view, cannot be seriously inquired into without some measure of realization that its purpose is in the hands of God. Vico was of the opinion that we could truly understand history, but on this point Hamann could not have agreed. Of course, according to Hamann human beings do bear responsibility in history. However, the fundamental questions of history and its goal do not come within the purview of our reason's inquiry. It is difficult to imagine that on this point

Hamann would have agreed with Vico's views. Hamann, being the committed Christian he was, could hardly have conceived seriously of the purpose of history otherwise than as a matter of God's decision. Hence he gives his full attention to the problem of the reality of such concepts as salvation in religion.[39]

As historians of religions we realize that by their very nature all religions are religions of salvation. Did Hamann solve the problem of such multiplicity? No, but he saw it clearly and struggled with it. In one of his bursts of writing, he translated Hume's *Dialogues on Natural Religion*. Since another translation was about to appear, he did not execute his plan to publish his translation, together with a postscript. However, we know that, in spite of his admiration for Hume, his postscript would have expressed his dissatisfaction with one of Hume's principal statements, that "the cause or causes of order in the universe probably bear some remote analogy to human intelligence." Such words were too meager for Hamann, and fell short of founding a basis for any real religion.[40] The *salus,* the salvation, the highest well-being a religion leads to cannot have its foundation in the feebleness of human reason. What seems fascinating to me in this view of Hamann's is that it is not a Christian, dogmatic view, to be imposed on one and all. Rather, it is a sensible roadmap for serious people of whatever tradition who are serious in their endeavors to understand people who are fundamentally different from themselves.

Hamann was a man in a specific religion, Christianity, and, provoked by the intellectual upheavals of his age, he created a variation on Heraclitus's theme, "Men who love wisdom should acquaint themselves with a great many particulars." One must cross the line separating the two, and it is not the obliteration of the problem, but the significance of the endeavor that counts. Declaring one of the two, either wisdom or particulars, "absolutely true," is humanly (or, as it would seem, even under divine authority) not permissible. In all the progress we make, our conclusions — as in all sciences — remain provisional, not yet definite, not yet final.

Literature

The Autobiography of Giambattista Vico, trans. Max Harold Fisch and Thomas Goddard Bergin (Ithaca: Cornell University Press, 1963); *The New Science of Giambattista Vico,* trans. Thomas Goddard Bergin and Max Harold Fisch (Ithaca: Cornell University Press, 1976); Mark Lilla, *G. B. Vico: The Making of an Anti-Modern* (Cambridge: Harvard University Press, 1993); Stephen N. Dunning, *The Tongues of Men: Hegel and Hamann on Religious*

Language and History (Ann Arbor, Mich.: Edwards Brothers, 1979), which contains a translation of one of Hamann's writings, "Golgotha and Scheblimini" (pp. 209–28).

EIGHTEENTH-CENTURY HISTORIANS OF RELIGIONS

If truth be told, the *ideas* the eighteenth century gave us are of far more interest than most of the concrete dealings with religious facts by several eighteenth-century scholars who concentrated on the religious facts their age presented them with. In essence, this is a reminder of the importance of ideas. We shall see that in most cases people find only those facts that their ideas have caused them to look for.

One rather noteworthy scholar of religion is Bernard le Bovier Fontenelle (1657–1757). His *Discours sur l'origine des fables* deals with myths (for that is what "fables" referred to) and the question of what gave rise to them. The striking thing about the work from our present perspective is the certainty its author shared with most of his learned colleagues that the biblical texts (specifically about the dispersion of nations after the flood) must point to the real origin and spread of religion; no distinction is made between "revelation" and "historical fact," or rather, the question does not arise. Thus the native population of North America owes its myths to that same absolute origin, except that distortions have crept in. The essential reason for the distortions found here, there, and everywhere in the world, was, according to this eighteenth-century scholar, simply that the natives were unable to understand the true tradition. This attitude has not yet become the disdain for "natives" that the next century will develop, for this lack of intelligence Fontenelle ascribes to all civilizations equally. Moreover, he holds that there is a sameness in human spiritual receptivity. For him this explains the similarity of mythical themes among nations distant from each other in place and time. Historically, it is certainly no accident that this particular theme is struck in eighteenth-century France, for through its revolution equality became one of the great French contributions to the world. Next to Fontenelle, whose clear language is still pleasant to read, Abbé Antoine Banier (1673–1741), Charles de Brosses (1709–77), and Nicolas Sylvestre Bergier (1718–90) may be mentioned. Striking in all these scholars is their attempt to account for religious traditions throughout the entire world in a single way that is intellectually acceptable. That much of their work would not be admissible for us, certainly in the manner in which it is presented, is not as significant as the attempt itself to classify and compare on a worldwide scale. De Brosses arrived at the notion of "fetishism" as an explanatory tool, and displayed a power of observation in details that escaped the conceptualization of the philosophes, such as the fact "that the name God or Spirit among the savages does not at all mean what it does among us."[41] Bergier introduced a notion of "animism" that, greatly changed and elaborated, would return a century later. Euhemerism is mentioned by all these scholars from time to time, though no longer as a special art of storytelling but as a theory to explain religion in its historical development. The unquestioned assumption that all religion is a matter of theoretical concepts, of doctrines, would remain unchallenged for an astonishingly long time (and would hold sway well into the twentieth century). Some first steps are made in the direction of what in the nineteenth century would become full-blown theories of evolution. Still, with all respect for these scholars, the ideas of evolution in religion intimated by Hume, in his *Natural History of Religion,* although not backed up by all that many facts, are clearer, and in the history of scholarship probably more influential than the long treatises by the early French "historians of religions."

One conclusion in particular is worth keeping in mind for our purposes: The eighteenth-century Enlightenment, for all its weak points that are obvious today, is the true watershed in the study of religions. For the first time since the rise of Christianity, the absolute and universal validity of one religion is seriously questioned. The avenue toward a new world of inquiries opens up.

NOTES

1. A beautiful book that sheds light on this complexity is Frances A. Yates, *Giordano Bruno and the Hermetic Tradition* (Chicago: University of Chicago Press, 1964).

2. J. P. Dolan, ed., *Unity and Reform: Selected Writings of Nicholas of Cusa* (Notre Dame, Ind.: University of Notre Dame Press, 1962), pp. 57–58.

3. Ibid., p. 59.

4. A voluminous and frequently reprinted example is Andrew Dickson White, *A History of Warfare of Science with Theology* (New York: Appleton, 1907), 2 vols. As evidence of a shift in "tone," one may turn to a more recent work: Lynn White, *Medieval Religion and Theology: Collected Essays* (Berkeley: University of California Press, 1978).

5. See Jan W. de Vries, *Het verhaal van een taal: Negen eeuwen Nederlands* (Amsterdam: Prometheus, 1993), p. 62.

6. This village physician in the south of the Netherlands was named Joannes Goropius Becanus. His work itself, like all scholarship at the time, was written in Latin. See De Vries, p. 63.

7. A work that has placed studies of seemingly erratic and random facts in the limelight is James Gleick, *Chaos: Making a New Science* (New York: Penguin, 1987).

8. René Descartes, *Méditations* (Paris: Larousse, 1950), p. 15.

9. Baruch Spinoza, *Tractatus Theologico-Politicus*, trans. Samuel Shirley (Leiden: Brill, 1991), p. 49.

10. Ibid., p. 89.

11. Ibid., p. 56.

12. Ibid., p. 88.

13. George Santayana, *Some Turns of Thought in Modern Philosophy* (New York: Scribner, 1933), pp. 1–2.

14. See James Luther Adams's cogent remarks in his *Prophethood of All Believers*, ed. George K. Beach (Boston: Beacon Press, 1986), chap. 13, "The Enduring Validity of Congregational Polity," pp. 127–35.

15. See Albert-Marie Schmidt, *Calvin and the Calvinistic Tradition* (New York: Harper, 1960), pp. 110–14.

16. Voltaire, *Candide*, trans. Lowell Blair (New York: Bantam, 1984), p. 18.

17. Ibid.

18. Ben Ray Redman, ed., *The Portable Voltaire* (Harmondsworth: Penguin, 1977), p. 182.

19. Both terms, used to pinpoint the contrast, fill a scholarly need. The derivation of the terms is not by itself illuminating; no wonder the two have not always been used as opposites. *Deism* is derived from the Latin *deus*, "god"; *theism* from the Greek *theos*, also "god."

20. Voltaire, "Epître 104, à l'auteur du livre des trois imposteurs" (published 1769). Text in *Oeuvres complètes de Voltaire* (Paris: Garnier, 1877), vol. 10, p. 403.

21. This has been brilliantly studied by Jean Starobinski in his *Jean-Jacques Rousseau: La transparence et l'obstacle* (Paris: Gallimard, 1971). See especially pp. 33–35.

22. Leonard M. Marsak, ed., *The Enlightenment* (New York: John Wiley, 1972), p. 115.

23. See the introduction by Richard Wollheim to *Hume on Religion* (Cleveland: Meridian, 1964), p. 13.

24. See Norman Kemp Smith's introduction to his edition of David Hume, *Dialogues Concerning Natural Religion* (Indianapolis: Bobbs-Merrill, 1947), pp. 60–62.

25. Ibid., pp. 60–61.

26. Ibid., p. 128.

27. Ibid., pp. 227–28.

28. Max Harold Fisch and Thomas Goddard Bergin, trans., *The Autobiography of Giambattista Vico* (Ithaca: Cornell University Press, Great Seal Books, 1963), p. 111.

29. Ibid., pp. 123–24.

30. See chapter 4 in the translators' introduction to Vico's *Autobiography* (pp. 61–107).

31. Thomas Goddard Bergin and Max Harold Fisch, trans., *The New Science of Giambattista Vico* (Ithaca: Cornell University Press, 1976), p. 109.

32. Ibid., p. 97.

33. See Mark Lilla, *Vico: The Making of an Anti-Modern* (Cambridge: Harvard University Press, 1993), pp. 24–37.

34. *The New Science,* sec. 331, pp. 96–97.

35. E. Jansen Schoonhoven, *Natuur en genade bij J. G. Hamann* (Nijkerk: Callenbach, 1945), p. 130.

36. Ibid., p. 203.

37. It is the title of Jansen Schoonhoven's book mentioned in footnote 35.

38. Cf. Schoonhoven, p. 142.

39. On the complexity of this issue in Vico, see Lilla, pp. 121–51.

40. Schoonhoven, p. 202.

41. G. van der Leeuw singles out this striking example in his *Levensvormen* (Amsterdam: Paris, 1948), p. 125.

The Romantic Movement

The onset of the Romantic movement was in some way a generational phenomenon. It is as if Enlightenment ideas became too prevalent; they became like the knowledge of dull textbooks. And in the 1770s, a new feeling of life, reacting against the certainties of the older generation, surprised the world. The very earliest appearances of this "feeling" were limited to Germany, but soon the new beginnings led to a movement that washed over Europe and America. In the new movement, certain words stand out, and they are in clear contrast to terms that were dear to the philosophes. The Enlightenment spoke the word "reason"; adherents of the new age concern themselves with "feeling," "vision," "emotion," "ecstasy"; they talk of *experiences* rather than causal links. In contrast to the division of a topic into sections, there is a search for "totality." And the term *genius,* though old, takes on the meaning that is still in use today—that is, exceptional individuals and their creativity. *Creativity* is also among the words that acquired their special ring in the Romantic age. Bach was and saw himself as a craftsman, but Beethoven was a creative genius and did not mind being considered as such. The mood beginning in the 1770s is radically different from what preceded, and the nineteenth and twentieth centuries are incomprehensible without understanding what happened in this turn against and transformation of pure reason.

The notion of "pantheism" became prominent. One can see it almost in clear opposition to "deism." The latter, we recall, was a mechanical affair, whereas pantheism considers the entirety of the world and nature as divine (*pan,* meaning "all"; *theos,* meaning "god"). In ordinary life as well, the "natural" was rediscovered. Beethoven did not wear a wig; his teacher Haydn had worn one. "Nature," which until recently had been the object of rational inquiry, became the inspiration of creative "emotion." Eugène Delacroix, the painter of genius, was a French exemplar of Romanticism, his canvases evoking history, old battles, faraway places, and contemporary events as well. Delacroix created a portrait of the great Polish romantic composer Chopin; it is painted by the canons of "nature." Many of the best-known composers were Romantics: Felix Mendelssohn-Bartholdy, Franz Schubert, Robert Schumann, Johannes Brahms, and others.

The Enlightenment had seen reason as the key toward "progress," one of its favorite ideas. The nineteenth century would come to delight in the idea of "evolution"—a much less modest idea actually, as its laws were thought to encompass everything in human culture and civilization and the physical world besides. There is about the new age that came into being a solemnity that was far indeed from the lightness of a Voltaire, and which permitted less and less that elegant conversation in salons among ladies and gentlemen who were interested in the most diverse subjects. And of course, in the new spirit of a new age, there were consequences for the study of religion and religions. Since the Romantic movement it has become common to associate religion in the first place with *feeling*. Until then, this association would seldom have been made, least of all in works on philosophy and history. So let us turn to some of the events and individuals in the Romantic movement that affected the study of religion: while discussing them, we should bear in mind the entire wide stream of activities in which their efforts took place.

The "outburst" of the beginning Romantic movement is called by its German name *Sturm und Drang,* "storm and stress," after the title of a stage play written in 1776 by an author known for his lack of inhibition. The play glorified human grandeur, the freedom of individual conscience refusing to bend to authority. A significant writer associated with the *Sturm und Drang* period was the young poet Goethe. Like all new movements, the Romantic movement too had its precursors. Rousseau had already spoken of "nature" with a special "feeling," and his words "back to nature!" have probably been quoted most often in German: "Zurück zur Natur!" Vico was not yet widely known. One Romantic who read him attentively was the Danish philosopher-theologian Søren Kierkegaard, but that was only later, when Romanticism was in full bloom. Hamann, though older than the young firebrands, is recognized in the history of literature as an inspiration, especially on the theologian and essayist Herder.

JOHANN GOTTFRIED HERDER

Herder (1744–1803) has special importance for the history of ideas about religion. In an essay he wrote on language (for which he won a prize) Herder elaborated on the *human* origin of language. The essay begins, "Already as an animal, the human has speech . . . ,"[1] and this idea predictably did not go over well with Hamann, for whom speech could not be addressed meaningfully without reference to the mystery of the word of God. Hamann's spirited critique of Herder's notion did not diminish Herder's respect for Hamann, for indeed, like Hamann, he too was certain that language and all human creativity go beyond the realm of pure reason. Herder was probably closer to the pantheism that now set the mood than he would have liked to admit. For Hamann, with his unique perspective, the new mood no doubt was not radically different from that of the Enlightenment. Both seemed to lead to an escape from the real struggle that the realms of grace and nature, of history and reason, required.

The Herder who has perhaps remained most vivid is the self-obsessed Herder of his diaries. There we find exalted writings on his experience of nature, his voyage by ship from Riga in Latvia to Nantes in France. The sentences often finish in exclamation points.

> On May 25 I put out to sea, in order to go I don't know where. A good deal of our life's events is really nothing but happenstance. That is how I came to Riga, to my spiritual office, how I lost it, how I came to travel. I did not like myself, as a social being, nor in the circle I was in, nor in the exile I had chosen myself. I did not like myself as a schoolteacher; that range was too narrow, too strange, too unfitting, and I was too far away for that environment, too strange, too engaged . . . I was disgusted with everything . . .
>
> O God, who knowest what the human spirit is made of, and hast placed it in the earthen vessel, was it necessary only for the sake of wholeness, or for the well-being of the individual, that there should be souls, who, abashed and bewildered, entered into this world, and who never know what they are doing and what they will do . . . Father of human beings, wouldst thou deign to teach me?
>
> That is how one thinks when one moves from one situation to another, and then imagine what wide a sphere a ship, floating between heaven and sea, brings to one's mind! Here everything gives wings and movement and a wide atmosphere to thought! . . .

> There are a thousand novel and more natural explanations of my-
> thology, or rather a thousand inner sensations of myth's most ancient
> poets, when we read Orpheus, Homer, Pindar . . . aboard a ship.[2]

The "gushiness" one might find here does not permeate all of Herder's
writings, yet it is never far away. And he had a great appeal to many, including Goethe. There were in fact few subjects he did not touch. He was a
poet, critic, linguist, philosopher, theologian, and educator. His sense for
nature — and its mysterious, divine quality — is also the most striking feature of his period. The fact that he expressed it so unabashedly, and related
it to everything he dealt with, explains much of his influence. It may seem
strange to see, as in the lines above, personal feelings, theology, pantheism,
and myth all rolled into one. This strangeness, nevertheless, changed our
world. The central Romantic idea of "nature" became part of our notion of
"vacation." "Vacation" is a recent invention. We have come to regard it as a
thing one is entitled to, a time to regain oneself, preferably in "nature." This
part of our mentality is largely due to the lasting influence of the Romantic
movement. Many Romantics complained about the depressing confine-
ments of their cities. The force and primacy of sheer *ideas* can become clear
to us when we realize that hardly any of the cities the Romantics knew
could not be walked through in less than half an hour. Nature, in the literal sense of the word, was never far away. The novel thing was the *idea* of
nature. It is strange to realize that "premodern" people as a rule did not get
excited about nature at all. The medieval cities of Italy did not plant trees
within their walls. Luther traveled over the Alps, preached everywhere he
went, and made use of imagery and experiences he happened upon, yet
he never hints anywhere at the beauty of the mountains. The urge to feel
nature is a Romantic creation.

Implications for the view of religion are evident in many scholarly and
artistic writings of the period. Herder himself was so impressed by the
vision of "the whole" that the idea of an interrelationship of all religions
seemed as natural to him as nature itself. The very first line he writes in a
paper addressed to preachers says, "God has revealed himself to the
human race at various times and ways . . ."[3] Though to us this may not
seem an altogether novel thought,[4] one could hardly imagine a tractate by
Calvin or Luther opening with such words. Herder, however, is eager to
show that religion is not limited to one tradition, and in this paper especially to show that it is infinitely more than the mere moralism to which
the rationalists often seemed to reduce it:

In reality, God has developed the human race on a large scale just as the strengths of an individual child develop. Faith and obedience, love and hope are . . . the first virtues that must be aroused in a child and that for all its life will lead and bear everything: the wonderful and festive qualities of the narrative pour as much light, radiant color, and as much of the heroic and gigantic as is needed to open the eyes of children. In short, the story of religion, unproven, rough and simplistic as it may seem, will always remain for them the first, favorite, and only textbook, from which later in life so much will develop![5]

The idea of the growth of all religion in the world in analogy to the growth of a child or a child's consciousness, already discussed by Lessing and suggested by other eighteenth-century writers, will become a standard idea in the nineteenth century.

In his often quoted *Ideas About the Philosophy of a History of Mankind* (in four parts: 1784, 1785, 1787, 1791), Herder begins the first book, "If at all worthy of the name, our 'philosophy' of the history of the human race has to begin from heaven."[6] And at once he waxes lyrical about the harmony of the spheres, the planets, and the great magnetic forces in the universe. We might wonder at the present time how Herder could link history and astronomy, but we should bear in mind that the Romantic period was not yet characterized by our artificial division between "sciences" and "humanities." In Herder's view, one cannot doubt the central significance of religion in the entire range of human inquiry. At the end of Book 13 of his *Ideas* he says exactly this, very much in his own way:

Religion is the most exalted mark of man's humanity. No one need be startled by my referring to religion in this manner and placing it in this context. The human understanding is the most exquisite gift of man, its business is to trace the connection between cause and effect, and to divine it where it is not apparent. The human understanding does this in every action, occupation and art, for even where it follows an accepted practice, some understanding must originally have settled the connection between cause and effect, and thus have established it. To be sure, we cannot discern the inner cause of natural phenomena. There is little or nothing that we know about how things operate even within ourselves. In a sense, therefore, all the phenomena around us are but a dream, a conjecture, a name, though we regard it as reality if and when we observe the same effects linked with the same occasioning circumstances, often and constantly enough. This is how philosophy proceeds, and the first and last philosophy has always been religion.[7]

In spite of the overassertive and often swollen style, it is difficult to dismiss Herder out of hand, even today. He was also the first to reject the explanation of religion as a product of fear—an explanation given since antiquity. Still in the same context, he writes,

> To maintain that religion originated in *fear,* that fear invented the gods of most people, is to say very little indeed, and to explain even less. Fear, as such, invents nothing. It merely rouses the mind to seek an understanding of given phenomena, to venture into the unknown by conjecture, by true and false surmises. As soon as man, therefore, learned to apply his mind at the slightest prompting, that is to say, as soon as he looked upon the world differently from an animal, he was bound to believe in more powerful invisible beings that helped or injured him. These he sought to make his friends, or to keep as his friends, and thus religion was born. True or false, right or wrong, it served man as guide and comforter in a life full of perplexity, danger, and sizeable areas of darkness . . .[8]

Finally, the Romantics recovered the old term *symbol*. It served their purposes very well. Speculating—as always without adducing much evidence—Herder adds the following on the early human beings he imagined:

> Whatever was to move man and make him more human had to be capable of being thought and felt in human terms. Thus nations that thought and felt in essentially aesthetic terms exalted the human form to divine beauty; whilst others, more inclined to abstract thought, represented the perfections of the Invisible by means of symbols. Even in those instances where God is said to have revealed Himself to man, His words and actions were interpreted in *human* terms and in accordance with the prevailing temper of the times.[9]

Literature
Burton Feldman and Robert D. Richardson, *The Rise of Modern Mythology* (Bloomington: Indiana University Press, 1972), pp. 224–40.

FRIEDRICH SCHLEIERMACHER

A theologian like Herder, Schleiermacher (1768–1834) was nevertheless a very different figure. In all of nineteenth-century scholarship, and in much of the twentieth century, his influence on the study of religion can easily be seen, even when his name is not mentioned—or, not infrequently, when it is not even known. He became part of what was taken for granted. His ideas were less exuberant than Herder's, especially in his later life, but more solid—even if in the end they too did not escape criticism.

Schleiermacher was a Reformed theologian. He was educated early on by the Moravian Brethren, a sect predating the Reformation, also known as Hernhuters, after their settlement in Hernhut, where after many an exile they found a place to live. Although Schleiermacher was called to the dignified office of professor of theology in Berlin, he claimed that he always remained a Hernhuter—except now a better one. Whatever irony hid in those words—for he had parted with the Hernhuters after bringing in books by young Romantics his elders did not approve of—he was not just someone who developed theories about religion but one who lived it. He preached virtually every Sunday, married, baptized, and buried many a parishioner. He belongs to the same category of exceptional beings as Vico and Hamann.

Schleiermacher wrote unbelievably much. One of his enterprises was a complete, new translation of all of Plato. This is indicative of something more than Schleiermacher's own industriousness. Like the Renaissance, when Pico della Mirandola put other work aside in order to translate Plato, the Romantic revolution of thought called for a new, understandable presentation of what Plato wrote so long ago. Rediscovering Plato is not what some may think. As a rule, students today turn to books *about* Plato. Little do they realize that Plato's fame endured because he himself was clear, a great deal clearer and more exciting than most of his interpreters. Schleiermacher was a scrupulous reader of Plato, and realized that "the idea" is something other than "concept."

The first of Schleiermacher's works was written in a flowery style not far from Herder's. It is *Speeches About Religion, Addressed to the Educated Among Its Despisers* (this is the title's literal translation), published in 1799. The title, a marvelous example of eighteenth-century style, describes the contents accurately. Low church attendance is not just a modern phenomenon. At the time Schleiermacher wrote this book, church membership in the United States was probably not above 10 percent of the population, and the story in Western Europe was pretty much the same. Moreover, church membership in Europe was often no more than a formality. Schleiermacher spoke in particular to "the educated," the people in positions of authority, and who, literally, were ignorant of the subject "religion."

> Might I ask one question? On every subject, however small and un-important, you would most willingly be taught by those who have devoted to it their lives and their powers. In your desire for knowledge you do not avoid the cottages of the peasant or the workshops of the humble artisans. How then does it come about that, in matters of reli-gion alone, you hold everything the more dubious when it comes from those who are experts . . . ?[10]

He aimed the question not merely at those who still thought as rational-ists, but also at his fellow Romantics. The question still awaits an answer, and we, who are the offspring of rationalists and Romantics, turn rather to "objective" explanations in matters of religion. The intervening centuries have produced quite an array of them.

There is a special emphasis in Schleiermacher on the theme that we should learn to see religion in the religions. This is worked out in the fifth *Speech About Religion,* called "The Religions." Regarding facts about the reli-gions of the world, not much of significance was available to him. He had learned from Plato to see that "the idea" goes beyond the mere "concept," and his theme regarding all religions was an important step—but it was no more than an important step *in theory.* The only religion apart from Christianity that he talks about at some length is Judaism, and what he has to say about it is best passed over in silence. Moreover, his theological involvement leads him to offer the idea that the "real religion" to be found in "the religions" actually amounts to: Christianity (for "religion is no-where so fully idealized as in Christianity . . .").[11] This is an idea—or should we call it an *idée fixe?*—which in actual religio-historical research does not make sense. And yet, as we shall see, it too survived and came back a century later in the work of a respected scholar of the comparative study of religions, the Swede Nathan Söderblom.

There is something Schleiermacher did that sums up the revolution he surely did not set in motion, but which became possible through him. His major work is one that before him would certainly have borne the title "Theology" or "Dogmatics." Instead, he called it *Der christliche Glaube,* "The Christian Faith." Manifest in this title is the gradual change that had occurred since Thomas Hobbes and Spinoza began to speak of "individuals." Not only the piety of the Moravian Brethren with which he was imbued in his youth but also the mentality of the Romantic movement is reflected in it. Even though *The Christian Faith* does not make any case for the validity of everyone's individual opinion or feeling, in the history of the nineteenth century the mere title reflects a shift in assumptions concerning religion—and religions in the plural, as well, for once the inner emotion is taken very seriously, is taken even as the point of contact with the divine totality, then in principle that emotion becomes a matter of inquiry everywhere, in the many religions of the world and in all of human history.

The Christian Faith expresses a strong opposition to mere literalism in reading the Bible. For Schleiermacher such slavishness to the text is on a par with all empty rationalizing. This view was in harmony with the entire Romantic movement. The real meaning of whatever "the text" says points to something beyond the mere letter. Herder, as we have mentioned, had much to say about symbolism: the universe, if perceived correctly, reveals the purpose of human existence. For Schleiermacher, the theologian, the "real meaning" of things, in literature, in art, but above all in the biblical texts, requires a well-thought-out art of interpreting. Whereas Herder often left the impression that a deepening of our feelings would do all that was needed, Schleiermacher realized that in intellectual inquiry, hard, systematic work is required. These concerns made Schleiermacher one of the great names in the history of hermeneutics.[12]

What set the study of religions going in the nineteenth century is not merely the discovery of new materials. The motivation was primarily a new set of ideas, brought to the fore directly or indirectly by the Romantics, and scholarly curiosity went in new directions, all over the world, outside established Christianity. On the other hand, the search for the meanings of the many religions was and to quite an extent remained a Christian reflex, as we have seen in Schleiermacher.

Literature
Friedrich Schleiermacher, *On Religion. Speeches to Its Cultured Despisers,* introd. and trans. Richard Crouter (Cambridge: Cambridge University Press, 1990); an earlier translation, under the same title, by John Oman

(New York: Harper, 1958), has an introduction by Rudolf Otto; Nathan Söderblom, *The Living God. Basal Forms of Personal Religion,* the Gifford Lectures of 1931 (Boston: Beacon Press, 1962).

FRIEDRICH WILHELM JOSEPH SCHELLING

Schelling's name is usually mentioned together with those of Fichte (1762–1814) and Hegel (1770–1831). These three are the great German Romantic, speculative idealists.

Hegel is known to many people who have no interest in philosophy and is no doubt the most influential of the three. Even a sketch of Hegel's ideas presents an all-encompassing thought system. In brief: Hegel conceived of "the absolute spirit" that gives rise to the world, and manifests itself — in an evolution to which it also gave rise — in a dialectical process, in accordance with a logic that can be conceived by human beings, or at least by Hegel. The exalted purpose toward which the world evolves is the self-recognition of the absolute spirit. Hegel set many minds in motion, and those of us who are not Hegelians find it difficult to give a fair account of his thought. To those among us, it would indeed seem that the only earthly mind to which the evolution of the Spirit became evident was Hegel's. It would seem that Hegel's exposition ignored the question David Hume had addressed to the Enlightenment thinkers: if God (the Absolute) can be thus contained by our reason, what difference does it make what our reason can say about him? We might add that Hegel's philosophy construed a vision of the world's entire historical development, in all its civilizations. This all-encompassing process begins with the rule by Asian tyrants; the Mediterranean, classical civilizations arise; the Germanic nations develop. ("Germanic" for Hegel refers not merely to Germany but to the entire European world of cultures.) In his *Phenomenology of the Spirit,* the seventh chapter is wholly devoted to *"die Religion"*; it tries to present the reality and meaning of all known forms of religion. An interesting thing is that Hegel saw Christianity as one link in the process that would lead to the ultimate self-recognition of the Spirit. As we observed earlier, this is the first time in the West since Plotinus, the great philosopher who concludes the classical tradition, that a thinker concentrates on the world as a whole,[13] and sees Christianity simply as a part of it.

Hegel's dialectic of history provides the mental pattern on which a dubious and destructive creation of the nineteenth century would elaborate: colonialism, together with a cult of "our" superiority over people variously conceived of as "savages," "natives," "tribesmen"—people all over Asia, Africa, America, and Australia. I hasten to add that it would be grossly unfair to suggest that Hegel intended such an application of his thought. Hegel's system in itself has nothing to do with the subjugation of the world to colonial powers. The three-step order of culture evolution that Hegel uses is not a mechanical affair. (Hegel himself never mentions the three steps as a triad of thesis-antithesis-synthesis, although many textbooks speak as though he did.) What Hegel proposes is that people always find themselves in a middle, the *medium*, of what evolves. In all its forms, the evolution he speculates on is to be seen as a growth. The image is organic, not mechanical. Perhaps it has even a certain poetry to it. One prominent Hegel scholar quotes Goethe in his introduction to Hegel's *Phenomenology of the Spirit:*

What is appearance to which there is no essence?
Would there be an essence if it did not appear?[14]

Friedrich Schelling (1775–1854) began his philosophical career as a pupil of the earliest of the three speculative idealists, Fichte. He parted ways with Fichte, and came to oppose Hegel on many points. He became famous, yet by the time Hegel's thought was the topic of all discussion, Schelling had already faded from the limelight; he died almost unknown. Schelling's thought was far less influential on nineteenth-century scholarship than Hegel's, but it is more interesting for the history of ideas about religion. In the present time there is a renewed attentiveness to his ideas,[15] particularly as they are expressed in his last great work, the *Philosophy of Mythology.*[16] Schelling worked on this book for at least the last twenty-five years of his life.

Though he was critical of other idealistic systems, Schelling himself aimed for the completion of a system. What distinguishes him nevertheless from Hegel is his respect for myths as revelatory in the sense that they present true novelty and a true freedom that our minds could not conceive without them. One scholar, discussing Schelling's unique place in the triad of German idealists, describes him as follows: "More than anything else, Schelling is an artist, who rethinks nature intuitively-aesthetically, in his own creative power; and he does not only rethink it, but imagines it anew; he himself creates it."[17] Schelling is difficult reading for very sober minds. This realization reminds us of Schelling as a Romantic.

Schelling is quite sensitive to certain problems that seem to have lost nothing of their relevance. In the seventh lecture in the *Philosophy of Mythology* he contrasts purely empirical work with what he does himself. "Pure empiricism," he argues, does not exist.

> Until now, we have looked upon mythology in general as our object of empirical-historical research, whereby philosophy could play no more than the role one has to assign to it in every, even purely empirical inquiry. So it was natural that the very title "Philosophy of Mythology" would cause irritation. In archeology, just as in natural science, we have so-called pure empiricists, in the sense of people who preclude all philosophy. The generally held image of the empiricist — and the empiricist is the first one to affirm it — is that of a person who admits only facts. What this amounts to in the natural sciences is clear from the innumerable hypotheses in all sorts of empirical researches, in particular from what is known as theories of nature. These theories rest for the most part on presuppositions that are altogether undemonstrable *from an empirical point of view*, as in the case of the so-called molecules. At present, even in Germany, these molecules are made to serve in explaining phenomena of the light of the intellect as well as stoichiometric facts of chemistry.[18]

Schelling is not inveighing against the natural sciences. Of course, he could not have foreseen the great achievements of modern physics. But that is not the point here. He is provoked by a lack of critical thought. In what follows, his ire hits students of religious "facts," through whom precisely what the facts exhibit is ignored in favor of unproven theories. In this context, he blazes out against his contemporary Gottfried Hermann (1772–1848), who, like several other textual scholars at the time, wove theories about conveyors of wisdom in some early, unrecorded time and used the theories to explain the images and symbols in myths.

> The first requirement of every explanation is that it be just to what is to be explained, that it does not repress it, make it mean less than it says, belittle it, or mutilate it in order to make it easier to grasp. It is not called for to ask what view we may win from the phenomenon, so that it becomes conveniently explicable in accordance with whatever philosophy we happen to hold, but the reverse; it is called for to ask what

the philosophy is we need, that is good enough for the object, that can reach its height . . . in what direction do *our* thoughts have to expand in order to relate to the phenomenon.[19]

Schelling also said this:

A theory that explains mythological images merely by studying them individually, separate from each other, and only by approximation, without showing their coherence that is as profound as it is vast, and without rendering them in their exactitude—such a theory shows by what it does that it is neither truly historical, nor truly scientific. What is truly historical agrees completely with what is truly scientific. With respect to their objects, such as the one we focus on, a conflict between history and philosophy is wholly inadmissible.[20]

Schelling's reverence for the "height" of the religious phenomena is no guarantee of the correctness of his understanding in each and every instance. That would have been impossible at his time, and is no doubt impossible at any time. Just the same, reading Schelling, one is truly impressed by his learning. Not only did he know classical literature well, but he was also well informed of the work done by the then very young discipline of Indic studies, as well as of the discoveries in Egypt and the theories built on them. He was neither an archaeologist nor a historian of religions, but a philosopher. He did not propose that we see in myths any full-blown philosophy, nor did he agree with endeavors to view myths as expressions that had not yet reached the lofty heights of philosophy. He tried to uncover the importance of myths for all worthwhile thought. It seemed to him that myths revealed things that we cannot ignore except at our peril. His concern with myths was identical with a concern for the basis of all human inquiry.

The issues that occupied Schelling certainly were embedded in Romanticism, and "Romantic" is hardly an epithet that appeals to most of us today, least of all in our intellectual endeavors. Nevertheless, the issues of reason and its limits, and of a transcendency, by whatever name it is called ("symbols," "myth," "leap," "the infinite"), from which human thought receives its impetus—all this and more comes up in the twentieth century again, often at the very moments of a hue and cry over the miseries of a world sunk in technique and materiality.

WILLIAM BLAKE, HERMAN MELVILLE,
AND SØREN KIERKEGAARD

William Blake (1757–1827) is often counted among the Romantics. However, Romanticism came later to England, and Blake was born just a bit too early to have been brought up among Romantics. Even if one still chooses to call him a Romantic, the statement must be qualified, for Blake is one of those rare artists who is simply too great to fit into one category. He was a great poet, painter, and engraver; in all he did he was a visionary. I would like to mention him as a man who was of extraordinary importance to discussions on religion. I shall not refer to any poem (not even to "Tyger, tyger, burning bright . . .") but will mention only one page in prose by Blake. It is a page few students of English literature may have given their attention to. Blake presents arguments on "natural religion" and condemns it. An attentive reading of Blake's poetry shows that the subject occupied him often, but here we have six rather academic, carefully worded theses followed by a conclusion. That the whole is at the same time a work of art is clear from the etchings he created in about 1788 to accompany it.

THERE IS NO NATURAL RELIGION
[FIRST SERIES]

The *Argument*. Man has no notion of moral fitness but from Education. Naturally he is only a natural organ subject to Sense.

I. Man cannot naturally Perceive but through his natural or bodily organs.

II. Man by his reasoning power can only compare & judge of what he has already perciev'd.

III. From a perception of only 3 senses or 3 elements none could derive a fourth or fifth.

IV. None could have other than natural or organic thoughts if he had none but organic perceptions.

V. Man's desires are limited by his perceptions, none can desire what he has not perciev'd.

VI. The desires & perceptions of man, untaught by any thing but organs of sense, must be limited to objects of sense.

Conclusion. If it were not for the Poetic or Prophetic character the Philosophic & Experimental would soon be at the ratio of all things,

& stand still, unable to do other than repeat the same dull round over again.[21]

By *nature*, "a human being is only a natural organ subject to sense." As we shall see, not only in the course of the nineteenth century but also in our own time, there has been a strong tendency to ignore this observation, and instead to explain religious phenomena while assuming that human existence is *wholly* "natural." Hence religion becomes an object of study that must be determined by biological causalities and material conditionings. But what about "the poetic or prophetic"? Can we ignore what Blake points out? If one rejects it, and insists on arguing that religion is "natural" in its origin and in the stuff from which it is made, on what else does that argument itself rest but an *idea?* There always exist some ideas that tempt us to accept them without question. And nevertheless, we know from history that exceptional characters, scientists, poets, or seers, have brought us further. Blake, like quite a few other such unusual figures, died without being acclaimed. He was buried in an unmarked grave. Only long after his death did fellow artists begin to recognize his significance.

Herman Melville (1819–91), poet and novelist, is the author of *Moby Dick*. It is a novel about a strange sea captain, his sailors, and his voyage: to hunt down one particular whale. A lone survivor tells the tale. It is fabulous and fantastic. Is human life humanly imaginable without the fantastic? Melville's masterpiece is not a record of an exotic economic trade and its practitioners, but a grand vision of human life. It opens with the narrator's account of his meeting with the "savage" Queequeg, from the Pacific, of all people seemingly the most distant from him, but part of the crew of the *Pequod*. The vision of Melville encompasses the earth and all its inhabitants, in whatever specific image he chooses.

Well before our modern scientific age, Herman Melville told us that the great flood of Noah's days is still with us: the largest part of the earth is still covered by the sea, surrounding and overwhelming man with its dangers and horrors. But "in the soul of man there lies one insular Tahiti, full of peace and joy, but encompassed by all the horrors of the half known life. God keep thee! Push not off from that isle, thou canst never return!"[22]

The ship is on her way, and the reader being addressed is every human being. Should we not have left? We know well that desire, that desire like the desire to remain a fetus, a baby, to stay rather than to be born and grow up. Yet in real life, whales have to be pursued, and the outcome of the chase is invisible to human reason. It is certain, however, that the gigantic struggle of human existence, beginning with the orientations and symbols of all religions in an equally gigantic interplay, goes on forever. It transcends not merely the ordinary divisions between peoples, but the limits of the human mind. Almost every page of Melville's splendid book conveys this lesson in a new way. For all the fantastic features he exhibits, the "pagan" South Sea islander turns out to be more courageous and truly human than most. Melville also spends a lot of time presenting a "non-provincial" Christianity—with a humor that must have struck contemporaries as outrageous (not unlike Kierkegaard, as we shall see in a moment). Early on we meet a most unusual Christian preacher. He climbs into his pulpit and descends from it by way of a rope ladder—the risk of the struggle of preaching is the risk of *truth*. Such "truth" is not the mental achievement of a human being or a nation or a religion. Melville presents this theme again and again when he comes to speak in many chapters of the characteristics of whales.

> But why pester one with all this reasoning on the subject? Speak out! You have seen him spout; then declare what the spout is; can you not tell water from air? My dear sir, in this world it is not so easy to settle these plain things. I have ever found your plain things the knottiest of all. And as for this whale spout, you might almost stand in it, and yet be undecided as to what it is precisely.[23]

And a little further we read:

> How nobly it raises our conceit of the mighty, misty monster, to behold him solemnly sailing through a calm tropical sea; his vast, mild head overhung by a canopy of vapor, engendered by his incommunicable contemplations, and that vapor—as you will sometimes see it—glorified by a rainbow, as if Heaven itself had put its seal upon his thoughts. For, d'ye see, rainbows do not visit the clean air; they only irradiate vapor. And so, through all the thick mists of the dim doubts in my mind, divine intuitions now and then shoot, enkindling my fog with a heavenly ray. And for this I thank God; for all have doubts; many deny; but doubts or denials, few along with them, have intuitions. Doubts of all things earthly, and intuitions of some things heavenly;

this combination makes neither believer nor infidel, but makes a man who regards them both with equal eye.[24]

Whatever statements had been made thus far by the eighteenth and nineteenth centuries on the topics of religion, "savages," or the abilities of the human mind, Melville's art outdoes them all. His vision goes well beyond Rousseau's construct of the "noble savage" and the burgeoning "scientific" view of the uneducated "savage" or "primitive" mind for which the eighteenth century had unwittingly laid the foundation (e.g., in Lessing's work). In singing the praises of whales and whaling, Melville brings in many myths and legends touching on whales. "Perseus, St. George, Hercules, Jonah, and Vishnoo! there's a member-roll for you! What club but the whaleman's can head off like that?"[25] And still, none of this is an esoteric or distant oddity; Melville speaks of nothing but our world, the world of mature human beings. A Romantic, yes. But "a mere Romantic"? Absolutely not.

The Dane Søren Kierkegaard (1813–55) was a philosopher, but also a theologian. As a matter of fact, he was primarily a theologian. What occupied him most can be summed up in one of his thoughts, repeated in ever changing, startling ways: Christianity is basically the commitment of individuals to "the absolute paradox." How is it that long after his death, Kierkegaard came to be recognized as the forerunner of existential philosophy, one of the most notable intellectual movements of the twentieth century? The secret no doubt originates in the fact that during his life he was not taken seriously by the theological establishment or in the ruling opinions of the day. His arch-opponent was Hegel, in whose philosophy everything fit perfectly; Kierkegaard pokes fun at Hegel's system time and again. A century later, people fastened on these aspects of Kierkegaard and simply ignored his religious, in fact precisely his Christian theological activity as if it did not matter. The best, or best-known, existentialists of the twentieth century, including Karl Jaspers and Jean-Paul Sartre, were far from endorsing the theological side of Kierkegaard. Sartre proclaimed his own atheism in no uncertain terms. And nevertheless, just like Kierkegaard himself, the emphatically "nonreligious" thinkers who were set in motion by him spurned peace with any closed *system,* and there the connection is visible. The issue of approving or disapproving of "religiousness" becomes in fact irrelevant. Next to "atheistic" existentialists, we also have others who made no secret of their religious commitment: Gabriel Marcel and A. E. Loen.

There was nothing wrong with the judgment of moderns who over-looked the obvious Christian qualities in Kierkegaard. They did see some-thing that could enlarge our vision, that could help us out of the constraints our traditional thought had locked us into. Whatever the "existentialists" were, they certainly agreed with Kierkegaard that answers to questions about our existence are more urgent than theories about abstract problems called "being" or "essence." Kierkegaard's writings are marked by an essay-istic style; they sparkle with understatement, irony, humor, sarcasm, and paradox. This characteristic reminds one of Hamann, whom Kierkegaard admired. The major paradox pervading everything for both men was the incomprehensibility of the grace of God, alongside the ceaseless human activity of figuring things out (as in the system of Hegel). The "real religion" for Kierkegaard is given with Christianity. And yet—in analogy to his spawning of an existential philosophy of "atheists"—his essays break through the opposites we glibly set up in our thinking.

When Kierkegaard speaks of "systems" and the "objectivity" of sys-tems, his words, though directed primarily at Hegel, strike at the whole undue seriousness of his age, as well as the misapplication of rationality in any age. In his time many a scholarly discussion turned around the ques-tion of the genuine nature of Bible books, especially the letters of Paul in the New Testament. With regard to this argument, Kierkegaard chooses to meditate thus: "Is it possible to base an eternal happiness upon historical knowledge?"[26] What if, through rational inquiry, one was able to learn that all, some, or none of the books were genuine? Would that affect our eter-nal happiness? The "objective" and "rational" problem is incommensu-rable (one of Kierkegaard's crucial terms) with the quest that is strictly "subjective" and immeasurably more important. No total and objective system, however well thought out and lucid, will ever merge into that quest. Kierkegaard was not at all a proponent of the thoughtless form of Christianity that even today is often mistaken for "orthodoxy," acceptance of a list of strange, supernatural propositions that together form a "sys-tem," a transparently unintelligent system to boot. He speaks explicitly, and with devastating humor, about "childish Christianity."[27] He does not propose to *give up* reason in order to reach "eternal happiness."

Together with the unstoppable search for eternal happiness, there is the question, how? Not by chance, this question is placed in the mouth of Johannes Climacus, the pseudonym Kierkegaard used in publishing his *Concluding Unscientific Postscript* in 1846. "John Climacus" ("John of the Ladder") is not entirely fictitious! He was a Christian ascetic of the seventh century, whose *Ladder of Divine Ascent* "is a systematic, spiritual and psychological analysis of one's road to the direct vision of God."[28] Kierkegaard wrote all his works under pseudonyms, with the notable exceptions of the ones he wrote as a Christian theologian and preacher. The fictitious identities serve as voices that speak about the most important human questions. Johannes Climacus describes himself in the preface of the *Concluding Unscientific Postscript* as "a common ordinary human being" who precisely in that capacity *assumes* "that there awaits me a highest good, an eternal happiness."[29]

How does one get from here, our ordinary reasonings, to there, our eternal happiness? The answer is intimated by a term Kierkegaard brought into fashion—a fashion that continued for the existentialists—the *leap*. Precisely because there is no commensurability, we can only recognize the abyss and leap. Such "leaps" are not acts of despair, nor are they beyond our understanding when Kierkegaard discusses "stages" of human life in general. At a young age, we know the world around us, yet our experience is "aesthetic," it relates to our senses and our enjoyment. Then, we learn, as a rule by some unpleasant happening in which we were at fault, that there is something qualitatively different from our personal sensual awareness; we have made a "leap" into the ethical realm. The next "stage" likewise is not reached by extending our knowledge thus far accumulated. This is religion. However, Kierkegaard calls this "Religion A," which is still separated by an abyss from "Religion B." Religion A we might understand as the "objective" or "systematic" awareness of religion. Religion B requires the major leap that Johannes Climacus suggested in his preface: the leap toward the highest good, eternal happiness. "Religiousness A can exist in paganism, and in Christianity it can be the religiousness of everyone who is not decisively Christian, whether he be baptized or no. That is only natural."[30]

Understandably readers of Kierkegaard do not always agree on what he was really all about. It is easy to point out the "irrationality" in his arguings, and tempting to look in his life for evidence of an aberrant mind, and to find it in his reaction to his father's death and his love for a girl who loved him too, and to whom he proposed and whom he gave up two days later. However, that Kierkegaard thought consistently (though not systematically for reasons that he made quite plain) cannot be denied. Moreover, for our purpose it is significant to observe the terms he introduced: *incommensurability, paradox,* the *leap* (or "leap of faith"), *religiosity A and B.* We speak about him at such length not simply because he is a Christian thinker of great stature, and not because he deliberately set out to develop a theory for the history of religions (he did not), but because he was of significance in creating the space in which we do our work today. His religiosity A links Christianity with "paganism." There is no separation between the two. As to religiosity B, we can hardly reproach a Christian thinker for linking it to Jesus Christ—but we should not forget to note that Kierkegaard does not create a separation between this salvation and the "eternal happiness" normal people everywhere in some manner have a notion of once they reach some measure of maturity. We on our part may remember that the historian of religions G. van der Leeuw spoke of all religions as religions of salvation. And the philosopher Emmanuel Levinas has spoken of the desire for "the infinite" as the most striking feature of human beings.

Literature
Geoffrey Keynes, ed., *Poetry and Prose of William Blake* (London: Nonesuch, 1961); Herman Melville, *Moby Dick* (Norton Critical Edition), ed. Harrison Hayford and Hershel Parker (New York: Norton, 1967); Søren Kierkegaard, *The Present Age* and *Of the Difference Between a Genius and an Apostle,* trans. Alexander Dru, introd. Walter Kaufmann (New York: Harper, 1962); Heinrich Heine, *Concerning the History of Religion and Philosophy in Germany,* trans. Helen Mustard, in Heinrich Heine, Jost Hermand, and Robert C. Holub, eds., *The Romantic School and Other Essays,* vol. 13, *The German Library,* Volkmar Sander, general ed. (New York: Continuum, 1982), pp. 128–244.

New Religious Data

The quantity of data available for the study of religions increased by leaps and bounds at the end of the eighteenth, and especially in the course of the nineteenth, century. These textual data are divisible into three categories that we are familiar with today as textual, archaeological, and anthropological. The textual data were the first to arouse great interest; they were the documents that seemed most significant from the point of view of a tradition that associated religion with holy scriptures, and the search for authoritative texts in other religious traditions seemed natural. Sanskrit, the ancient language of Hinduism, of which the oldest form is Vedic (the language of the Vedas), came to be studied in a disciplined fashion. The birth of historical linguistics has among its principal names Sir William Jones (1746–94). In 1783 Jones went to Calcutta, to take on the position of judge in the Supreme Court there. The trade of the British East India Company had been going on for almost a century and a half, and officially it was the company rather than the British government that ruled. Warren Hastings was the British governor-general, and British power, making use of dissension among various Indian rulers, consolidated itself. Nevertheless, Hastings was a truly enlightened man at the time, with a great deal of sympathy toward Hindu and Muslim culture. Jones was not the first Westerner to learn Sanskrit. Even earlier, the French missionary Father Coeurdoux had observed the kinship between Sanskrit and European languages. Yet it was Sir William Jones who established beyond a doubt, using as well Romano, the language of the Gypsies, that a true family of languages existed, of which Sanskrit, Latin, and Greek are the most prominent among the ancient branches. This pioneering work created the means for the translation of various classical Sanskrit works. Earliest translations included the Bhagavadgītā, and the stage play Śakuntalā, by Kālidāsa, the most famous writer of worldly literature in Sanskrit—he is the Indian equivalent of Shakespeare. These works found an eager audience among the German Romantics. They added "evidence" for the truth of pantheism. They added fuel to the desire to "intuit" the totality of the world's spiritual unity. The discovery of Indian spirituality, channeled through the Romantics, has had a long and lasting effect on the West, in wave after wave. In 1893, in Chicago, the first congress of representatives from the world's religions took place, and India, in the person of Vivekananda, made a great impression. The West of the twentieth century welcomed Indian gurus, spiritual teachers, and established special communities for the cultivation of Indian spirituality. "The Orient" became a standard in neo-Romantic semi-intellectual circles. There followed comparable formations with a Chinese or Japanese (Zen!) imprint.

Around 1800 a sensation almost comparable to that of Indian religion came from Egypt. In 1799 a basalt stone with inscriptions on it was found near the town of Rashid (Rosetta), some thirty miles from Alexandria. The discovery was made in August of that year by a member of Napoleon Bonaparte's expedition—which consisted not only of thirty-five thousand soldiers, but also of a corps of scientists. Political reversals caused the stone to end up in the British Museum. An Englishman, Thomas Young, made the first strides toward deciphering it. In 1821–22, in peacetime, the Frenchman Jean-François Champollion (1790–1832) turned his attention to the Rosetta stone and succeeded in deciphering the whole thing; he became the first scholarly Egyptologist. The West had always shown a mystified fascination with Egyptian monuments and hieroglyphic writing.[31] Although the content of the writings was of no earthshaking importance, now there was for the first time an opening toward understanding the mysteries of Egypt. One of the three texts on the rock is in Greek—the language the Ptolemaeans used—with renderings into hierogyphics and into demotic (a cursive form of the ancient Egyptian script). The inscriptions were made by priests of the temple at Memphis and list benefits bestowed by a Ptolemaic ruler, Ptolemy V Epiphanes (205–180 B.C.).

Egypt and India were not the only ancient and classical civilizations whose literary texts became available for study. The *Avesta,* the text of ancient Zoroastrianism, in its oldest parts linguistically related to the language of the Indian Vedas, began to be studied and deciphered by the middle of the nineteenth century. North India, Sri Lanka, China, Mongolia, Tibet, and Japan began to reveal their Buddhist documents. Many other civilizations, even if vaguely known, attracted students with modern linguistic methods. Last but not least, many textual documents were excavated in the Near East. They were clay tablets that for thousands of years had served as surfaces to write on. In this case the turbulence of history with its wars and fires strangely preserved rather than destroyed documents; as a result, we know more about the price of sheep in ancient Mesopotamia and economics in general there than in any other ancient land. Treasures of thought, myth, and symbolism from the Mesopotamian world gradually also began to be uncovered. Datable civilizations, some thousands of years older than the Bible, yet related to the biblical documents, came to light. In addition to the textual discoveries, the nineteenth century also saw the beginning of researches into *prehistory,* the exceedingly long period of human life on earth before writing. The research into these very ancient traces of human civilization is the major work of archaeology. The excavation not only of temple foundations, hence obvious religious material, but also of human religious evidence in the ice ages, usually indicated in its dates by geological timetables—all this begins in the nineteenth century. Personally, I like to think of one event that sums up the intellectual revolution in this deluge of new discoveries. It illustrates what I like to think of as the critically applied and constructive imagination required by all science. The story I have in mind is that of Jacques Boucher de Perthes (1788–1868), director of a customhouse in Abbeville, France. He became the first real prehistorian by rightly identifying some evidence as human and belonging to the Pleistocene—the age that lasted until about ten thousand years ago. "Pleistocene," according to my trusty Webster, designates "the first epoch of the Quaternary period in the Cenozoic Era, characterized by the rise and recession of continental ice sheets and by the appearance of man."[32] Boucher de Perthes bent over one day and picked up some flints of a type that had long been regarded as unusual and had been called by such names as "devil's stones"—but he observed that they could have been shaped as they were only by human beings. He made his discovery near Abbeville, in old sediments of the river Somme, in 1841. The work he began, the new science of prehistory, extended the human imagination considerably further than the earliest historical limit around of 4,000 B.C. Subsequent evidence of prehistoric art, as in the cave paintings of southern France and northern Spain, could not be interpreted except as religious symbolism and would widen the horizon even more.

These discoveries are part of a long series that continued into the twentieth century. The traditions of India that had caused such enthusiasm among the Romantics were found to reach further back into the past than one could have guessed. In 1920–22, under the directorship of Sir John Marshall (1876–1958), the Indian Archaeological Survey excavated remnants of a highly developed civilization along the Indus River, a civilization predating the time of the Veda by at least a thousand years. Though it spawned no new Romantic strain in the West, it did fire the imagination of historians. In this chain of new discoveries, "imagination" is not a quality to be taken lightly, for the rule that people discover only what they are prepared to look for is confirmed time and again. Fragments of the ancient Indus civilization, extending from a large part of present-day Pakistan to parts of India and Afghanistan, had been visible ever since they were destroyed. The imagination seems to come first; the search for evidence follows.

In addition to literary texts and the findings of prehistory, a third type of evidence essential to the empirical study of religions is brought forward in the nineteenth century. It is found in the many, many close descriptions by scholars who later on in the century began to call themselves "anthropologists." Many of them were in fact Christian missionaries, especially in the earlier days, before the field was recognized as an academic discipline. Soon, however, governments of colonizing Western powers saw the importance of knowing the nations they ruled, and invoked the professional help of this altogether new type of study.

All three areas of investigation, textual, archaeological, and anthropological, are characterized by a spirit, a special stimulus, which they took from the Romantic movement of the early nineteenth century. In this connection, we should mention also the many large new dictionaries that the nineteenth century saw compiled of the languages that scholars had only recently become acquainted with. Some of these dictionaries are indispensable to us today. The work on such dictionaries, probably no less than many a risky excavation in an exotic land, or the exhausting researches among tribal peoples without comfort of any kind, often without proper food, and obviously without telephonic communication or security, demanded dedication, demanded the certainty that the undertaking had a worthwhile purpose. In this, the Romantic movement is tangible in the background virtually everywhere.

ROMANTICS WHO STUDIED THE NEW DATA: BENJAMIN CONSTANT, JOSEPH VON GÖRRES, FRIEDRICH CREUZER, KARL OTFRIED MÜLLER, AND FRIEDRICH MAX MÜLLER

The names in the heading are given chronologically. The work of these individuals shows something of the "flow" from the beginning influence of Romantic ideas to a type of work that is inconceivable without Romanticism, yet leads into the spirit typical of the nineteenth century.

Benjamin Constant de Rebecque (1767–1830) was born in Lausanne, Switzerland.[33] He spent time in Germany, and met with Romantics, and when he paid a visit to Weimar in 1794, he spoke with no less than Goethe. Although those two did not like each other, German Romanticism is evident in the Frenchman's life and accomplishments, while he also delights Voltaire-like in depicting the foolishness of many a religious custom. There is little in Constant, however, that is reminiscent of Voltaire's concern for decency in human life. Constant is probably the most flamboyant man to be found in any intellectual history concerning religion. He reaped fame with a novel and wrote thousands of pages on learned subjects. His industriousness foreshadows the tireless productivity of much of the nineteenth century. His active sensual life made him resemble the early rebels against rationalism in the "storm and stress," and his enjoyments did not seem to interfere in the least with his work schedule. For example, he began his major work on religion while visiting a lady friend, and he did so on the backs of a deck of playing cards. Completed, this major work comprised five volumes. It announced its scope with its title: *De la religion, considerée dans sa source, ses formes et ses développements* ("About Religion, in Regard to its Origin, Forms, and Developments"). This unusual man, full of inner conflicts, disdainful of the very Germans whose work he read attentively, had a lifelong obsession with religion, while rejecting its outer forms. He does speak emphatically about the inner emotion, or intuition, of religion, *le sentiment religieux*. Van der Leeuw quotes an entry from Constant's diary, "J'ai prié avec Juliette" ("I prayed with Juliette"), whereupon van der Leeuw remarks, "We may assume, however, that he was more interested in Juliette than in prayer."[34] What exactly Constant meant by "the religious sentiment" is not altogether clear, and he himself was not satisfied with what he wrote on it; it continued to occupy his mind until his death. One would expect that he might have had some help from the work of his contemporary Schleiermacher. Schleiermacher, as we know, had much to say on the subjective experience of religion. He associated it with such things as submissive humility, the feeling of dependence, and intuition. But for Constant such expressions did not say what he thought needed to be said, yet he could not articulate it himself. He considered Schleiermacher one of "those Germans" who were "too solemn" and had their hearts on their sleeve at the same time.[35]

That vague but pressing concern with respect to the "inner sentiment" keeps coming back. Into our own day, the thought recurs, "Isn't there something in the inner life that is the same in all religions?" And each time, the discussion ends in the same haziness. Constant is instructive, despite his intentions, by showing himself most honest in moments when he shows his mood as pessimism—precisely the opposite of the optimism that had characterized the thought of the Enlightenment. In 1808 Constant wrote in a letter to a friend, "Every day I understand less what life is. I am about to throw myself on the ground and ask the earth for its secret. Does everyone have this feeling I have, and does everyone conceal it as do I?" And he ends up speaking of death. What is instructive is that this pessimism is never far away in any of the confused discussions about the value of the supposed "essence" of religion as *felt,* for in all instances, it is simply assumed that at one time, or in some exotic place, that reality is alive and well. However, in the present time, as they say, even nostalgia is not what it used to be. A good part of the problem of *le sentiment religieux*—to which Schleiermacher tried to address himself, though his endeavors might not satisfy us—is the confusion of a metaphysical question and a question about sublime personal feelings.

We can be brief about the Germans Joseph von Görres (1776–1848) and Friedrich Creuzer (1771–1858), who belong to the Heidelberg Symbolists. They are interesting principally because they demonstrate in their work the excessive enthusiasms to which the Romantic movement could lead. Görres and Creuzer were both very much taken with the new information coming from India. Both saw the origin of religion nowhere else than on the banks of the Ganges. A few sentences from Görres, whose thought and language are often more swollen than the worst excesses of Herder, will suffice. They are from his two-volume *Mythengeschichte der asiatischen Welt* ("Mythic History of the Asiatic World," 1810) and describe, in the first chapter, what in his view the Indians experienced in their pure, pristine religion:

> That primordial state . . . containing all races [*Geschlechter*], who were still together in their homeland, was a natural realm and hence a priestly state, a theocracy. Rulership was exerted by the forces of nature, and prophets announced themselves as its regents. . .[36]

> The liturgy was simple. There was no temple, no images. They looked up from the earth, for the true realm of fire was in heaven. There the sun burned without cease; there planets and stars struck like flames through the darkness; there the eternal inextinguishable fires burned that shed their rays on earth. That is how the worship of fire became worship of the stars; the sun and the hosts of heaven, below them the elements that served them, were the great immortal powers, the priests of heaven; the world itself was the reflection of the deity that is self-existent, dependent on nothing; so in this sense the religion was *pantheism.*[37]

Görres's enthusiasm did not require detailed documentation. Rushing to write long before much could really be said about a religion was not rare early in the nineteenth century, when eager readers absorbed much new information that was not yet critically presented. Champollion, who made a beginning with the study of Egyptology, was certainly a much more astute scholar than any of the Heidelberg Symbolists, but even he ventured fairly quickly into a work on Egyptian religion—though we should hasten to add that he did not complete it.

Friedrich Creuzer—to whom Görres dedicated his book—was professor of ancient literature in Heidelberg. His great work, in six volumes, is *Symbolik und Mythologie der alten Völker, besonders der Griechen* ("Symbolism and Mythology of the Ancient Nations, especially the Greeks"). It covers the entire world, but India again takes pride of place. Certainly Creuzer was an excellent classicist, and his style is not as puffed up as that of his fellow Symbolist. In his first volume, Creuzer quotes from the account in Herodotus's *Histories,* book 2, that the earliest inhabitants of Greece, the Pelasgians, worshiped gods but had no names for them. In Herodotus, they receive the names for their deities from Egypt, for even then, Egypt counted as ancient and full of wisdom. The names are passed on to the later Hellenes. Creuzer sees fit to state, with a great deal of erudition and references to obscure texts, that the real origin of Greek religion and of all religion is in India, whose wise spiritual guides gave only symbols to the Pelasgians, as they were not sufficiently developed to use words. There is little one can say about this sort of fantasizing.

It must be noted, however, that Creuzer, in the same work, also occasionally says interesting things concerning the notion of "symbol," the central idea around which the Symbolists gathered. Here is one of his statements, worth quoting not only because it gives us a feel for the force the Romantic movement mustered, but also because it touches on issues that keep arising, even in today's discussions:

> Only matters that are impressive are capable of awakening [people] from the slumber of animal-like dumbness. What, however, is more impressive than an image? The image hits at once upon the truth of a beneficial doctrine that would get lost on the wide road of conceptualization. The spiritual, compressed in the moment of a glance and in the focus of the immediately visible is more inspiring for unrefined minds than the most solid teaching.[38]

Next to the output of other Romantic scholars, Karl (or Carl) Otfried Müller's *Introduction to a Scientific System of Mythology* is delightfully sober, still worth reading today. Its importance was recognized; in 1844 an English translation made it available to a wider public. Müller (1797–1840) rejects the eccentric assumptions of his Heidelberg predecessors about the birth of religion in India and the mediation of mysterious priests conveying profundities to the early inhabitants of Greece. (It is true that his denial of *all* ties between the West and India was an exaggeration, for the historical linguistic tie between the two is beyond doubt; however, linguistics had not yet developed to the extent that Müller could be aware of prehistoric language relationships.) He realized that any proper theory about myths should be based on historically verifiable facts, and at the very least on defensible assumptions. He was the first to understand clearly that the Greek myths were creations by poets who made use of earlier oral traditions. On good grounds, he suggests that even oral traditions are not the origin of a process, but are themselves subject to changes in time and are affected by meeting with other myths, and by altogether new additions or misunderstandings. He hits the bull's-eye in describing the weakness of many Romantic endeavors by repeating that neither genius nor intuition arrives at a correct understanding; what we need is scrupulous and patient work. In other words, he belonged to the Romantics, he criticized them astutely, and was among the most impressive of scholars because he held on to what was truly valuable in the Romantic outlook; he *assumed* that the ultimate goal of this dedication to the work of interpreting was worthwhile. In his writing, he discussed his findings with others who shared his ideas as well as with those who did not. With an authoritative older scholar, Christian Gottlob Heyne (1729–1812), he both agreed and disagreed. He ascribed to Heyne the theses that myth is the child of poverty and necessity,[39] that mythical expression should be seen as the infant language of the race, and that the mythical expression itself became gradually confounded with the thing, whereby "the error crept in, that these narrations contained actual occurrences, and was fostered by the priests in order to excite greater interest."[40] He was critical of such mechanical reasonings, which in his opinion did not do justice to the data at hand. Those also who wanted to identify some archaic religious situation with a state of perfection in politics (as we saw with Görres) did not fare well under his scrutiny. A few sentences from the 1844 translation of his *Introduction* may give us a glimpse of C. O. Müller's work:

> Popular tradition, to which we ascribe a higher antiquity, and . . . a higher authority than to the poetical mythus, does not, of course, comprehend everything that was said by any sort of persons among the people. . . . We have no doubt that, during antiquity, popular stories were frequently derived from books, as has been practised in more recent times . . .[41]

> It is . . . wrong to consider the worship paid by the Romans to Virtus, Felicitas, &c., as allegorical in the strict sense; for then it could be no worship at all. Here we have to deal with a mode of contemplating the world, which is quite foreign to our notions, and in which it is difficult for us to enter. It is not incumbent on the historical investigation of mythology to ascertain the foundations on which it rests. This must be left to the highest of all historical sciences, — one whose internal relations are scarcely yet dreamt of, — the history of the human mind.[42]

One wonders what "science" Müller might have envisaged in this last sentence. It suggests more than what we call "intellectual history" or the "history of ideas," which is almost invariably the history of clearly outlined ideas. The "history of consciousness" certainly was not yet intimated a century and a half ago. That new field, as I understand it, is the history focusing on "meta-ideas," the ideas that are implied below or transcend what we think we think. Without a doubt, Müller had in mind some discipline between history and metaphysics. The very suggestion reminds us again of concerns Vico and Hamann expressed. It is perhaps to Müller's credit that he did not venture into speculation as to what those future inquiries should lead to. The mere suggestion that that undefinable new science would be needed suggests to me a scholarly modesty that is rare indeed; he knew that his own work could not give all the answers.

In the ranks of Romantic scholars, Friedrich Max Müller (1823–1900) came to be regarded as the "father of the history of religions." His contemporary and colleague Cornelis P. Tiele (1830–1902) of the University of Leiden was the first to call him that. He wrote several autobiographical books that alone make his place understandable. He was a German who located himself at Oxford, and, though thought of as an Englishman, he remained international in his reputation. He was a talented historical linguist and thus a member of a highly esteemed discipline, and within that discipline he was devoted to the most reputed branch, ancient Indo-European comparative linguistics, with a specialty in Sanskrit, the language of the admired Indian sacred scriptures. That he belongs among the Romantics is clear from what he writes about his life. He took some pride in being the son of a poet, Wilhelm Müller, whose name and hyper-Romantic poetry are unknown today, except to those who look at program notes when Schubert's "Die schöne Müllerin" is performed: the words are his. In his later years, Max Müller reminisced about his youth, when he was meditating on becoming a musician (a wish that an older and wiser friend helped him set aside), and he recalled great performers and composers who became legends during his life: while still at school in Leipzig, for example, he heard the young Liszt play ("Young, theatrical, and terribly attractive, as ladies, young and old, used to say. His style of playing was then something quite new—now every player lets off the same fireworks").[43] He wrote of meetings with Felix Mendelsson, and Robert Schumann and Schumann's wife, Clara Wieck.

Something that to me seems truly worth mentioning is the absence of solemn formality in nineteenth-century academic life, a "goofiness" even, precisely in places where we would least expect it, as in the Germany where Max Müller began his higher education. As an aspiring orientalist, Müller sought out the best education, and his search led him to Friedrich Rückert, whom he knew as a German poet, but whose position in life had also made him into a professor of Persian. Here is how this transpired. The king of Prussia (Frederick William IV) was doing his best to make Berlin into a real city, and its university into a real university. Rückert had been persuaded to teach there. However, Rückert did not like Berlin, and as a celebrated poet he had some clout, enough to set some conditions. He had his classes scheduled in Arabic, Persian, and other Oriental languages; also, he owned a little country estate at some distance from Berlin which he preferred over the city. He sent a petition for leave to spend summers in the country. The king granted his request. Soon thereafter he asked for a leave of absence during a severe winter. He received permission again, but the minister of education sent him a letter inquiring, "But, my dear Professor, if you are always absent during the summer semester, and now ask for leave of absence during the winter semester also, when do you mean to lecture?"[44] When the young Max Müller saw Rückert, and told him he wished to learn Persian, the professor did not exactly welcome him but instead asked why in the world he wanted to do that. Max explained that he was serious; he had already studied Arabic for a year in Leipzig. It was to no avail. Professor Rückert, eager to move to his villa in Neusess, invoked the classical rule held on to by academic institutions in Germany: *tres faciunt collegium,* one needs three students to justify a course. This student did not give in but managed to round up two more students, and in his memoirs he wrote, "One of them actually did wish to learn Persian."[45] Rückert was defeated; he stayed in Berlin and taught the course. His Persian did seem somewhat rusty, but Max Müller is gracious to note that it came back rapidly, and a good time was had by all.

This story is not only at odds with what most of us think about traditional European academics, it is also a far cry from the California of Ronald Reagan, who during his governorship suggested that professors should teach as many hours as high school teachers; a chorus of voices joined in in this opinion, advising, for example, that universities be run the year round, like factories, so as not to waste the facilities. The enormous productivity of the nineteenth century was due not only to the Romantic stimulus, but also to the embrace of a freedom, indeed, a playfulness, that made for breadth of inquiry and discussion.

What about Max Müller's scholarship? It would be impossible and for our purpose unnecessary to list all his works pertaining to technical textual problems. For the general, comparative study of religions his editorship of a series of fifty volumes by an international group of outstanding scholars is of lasting value: *The Sacred Books of the East,* known to all academicians as *S. B. E.,* to which Müller himself contributed important volumes. They are available in the reference section of all major libraries, and contain translations of major texts from Sanskrit, Pali, Avestan, Pahlavi, Arabic, Chinese, and other languages. Some thirty volumes focus on Indian culture; this demonstrates how Sanskrit and the related Pali texts dominated the origins of modern religio-historical studies. Among the many books Max Müller wrote himself is one well-known general, introductory work, *Introduction to the Science of Religion,* published in 1873. These introductory lectures, no less than other writings by Müller and others,[46] show us the self-confidence as well as the optimistic climate of nineteenth-century evolutionism. Müller does not write for colleagues but for all inquisitive minds. Never hiding behind specialisms and big words accounts for a good part of the charm of nineteenth-century scholarship. The "playfulness" of Müller's early encounters with Rückert in Berlin does not fade. At the same time, though, today we see that many of his ideas are perfectly in tune with a time of unmitigated colonialism. The "natives," whether of British India or of Siberia, are fuel for his theories of religion and of language and culture. There is for him no doubt that religion, language, and nationality are interwined. Max Müller's century was the cradle of nationalism. Few Romantics were not politically involved at one time or another. Müller, the Oxford professor, at one time was imprisoned in Germany for his reputed political views aspiring toward a German national unity[47]—which finally materialized in Bismarck, when Müller had been an English citizen for a long time. The two principal ingredients of his theory on the origin and development of religion come respectively out of his Romantic upbringing and out of the nineteenth-century infatuation with evolution. The Romantic impulse can easily be seen in Müller's theory that the light of early morning is the crucial sight in nature that sparked the earliest truly religious sensation. He finds all this reflected in a number of Vedic hymns. For those who realize that the texts actually have something to say, this theory of personal revelry has become comical. A clearer reading shows that the early morning is praised as a rule because it marks the beginning of a sacrifice or, in the earliest Vedic hymns, of battle. The "evolutionistic" element in Max Müller's thinking can be found in his view of linguistic development. He refers to "the disease of language." The earliest expressions of awe come to be misapplied, he believes, as when the radiance of the sun becomes the radiance of a warrior or a king. And there we have it, the origin for the confusion that earlier, rationalistic investigators (such as Voltaire and Diderot) had already associated with historical religions. What can lead us back to the pristine meanings of things? Here the answer is not precise, but the upshot is a mixture of modern Christianity and the bliss of empire, as in Britain.

Müller's expectations of the science of religion were high; he did not wonder whether an essence of religion existed, nor did he doubt that his science could grasp it. And precisely in this, he shows himself a child of his age. Müller does not use the term *essence of religion,* although his age used it freely. He is interested in what religion really is but likes to speak of it as a human "faculty." In the *Lectures on the Science of Religion* he writes,

> We do not mean the Christian or Jewish religion; we do not mean any special religion, but we mean a mental faculty, that faculty which, independent of, nay in spite of sense and reason, enables man to apprehend the Infinite under different names, and under various disguises.[48]

One would like to hear more about that mental faculty and about its various disguises. Are the religions in which people live and die *merely* disguises? Convinced as we are that linguistic tools are required, can those tools guarantee our grasp of what is really the case behind the "disguises"?

I am far from wishing to ridicule Max Müller. Even in his faults, he was not by any means the worst of his age. Far more harmful, indeed, venomous, writings were produced in an innocence that astounds us now. Rudyard Kipling eulogized the glory of imperialism and colonialism, also in utter innocence. The same Rudyard Kipling wrote the kindliest, most enchanting *Just So Stories,* one of the enduring jewels of narration that an adult can read to a child. Somewhere between honest sentiment and crude exertion of power, between devotion and a dehumanizing stance toward other human beings, Max Müller too did his nineteenth-century work, and he said things that still need to be said. One statement, first made by Goethe, and quoted by Müller, cannot be repeated often enough: "He who knows one language, knows none." Müller extends the truth of this to the subject of religions: he who knows only one, knows none.[49] That holds true. If an English-speaking person learns Russian, he may never acquire the fluency of a native speaker, but his understanding of language is likely to become much more extensive. And similarly, it is certain that a Muslim who makes it his business to study church history will gain a more adequate understanding of Christianity than most Episcopalians or Methodists, no matter how pious they are.

As to the question which of these, the student or the adherent, is closer to knowing the "essence" of religion, the modest conclusion, namely, that the essence is not necessarily within the reach of either, would not, I am sure, have been drawn by Müller. The problems he left led into a new age that searched for a more realistic approach to the many forms of religion. That a new approach would need to be more critical of itself cannot surprise us.

Literature
On Joseph Görres and Friedrich Creuzer, see Burton Feldman and Richard D. Richardson, *The Rise of Modern Mythology* (Bloomington: Indiana University Press, 1972), pp. 381–96; C. O. Müller, *Introduction to a Scientific System of Mythology* (1844; New York: Arno Press, 1978); F. Max Müller, *Introduction to the Science of Religion* (1873; New York: Arno Press, 1978).

NOTES

1. Johann Herder, "Abhandlung über den Ursprung der Sprache," in *Sturm und Drang, kritische Schriften* (Heidelberg: Schneider, 1963), p. 403.

2. Herder, "Journal meiner Reise," in *Sturm und Drang,* pp. 291, 293–94, 302.

3. Herder, "An Prediger," in Walter Flemmer, ed., *Johann Gottfried Herder, Schriften* (Munich: Goldmann, 1960), p. 211.

4. Hebrews 1:1 says something considerably more restricted, when it tells of God speaking "to our forefathers," and of various sorts of speech "through the prophets."

5. Flemmer, p. 211.

6. Flemmer, p. 66.

7. Burton Feldman and Robert D. Richardson, *The Rise of Modern Mythology* (Bloomington: Indiana University Press, 1972), p. 234.

8. Ibid., p. 235 (slightly changed).

9. Ibid., p. 125.

10. Friedrich Schleiermacher, *On Religion, Speeches to Its Cultured Despisers,* trans. John Oman, introd. Rudolf Otto (New York: Harper, 1958), p. 2.

11. Ibid., p. 243.

12. See Joachim Wach, *Das Verstehen. Grundzüge einer Beschichte der hermeneutischen Theorie im 19. Jahrhundert* (Hildesheim: Georg Olms, 1966), vol. 1, *Die groszen Systeme*.

13. See chap. 6 of this book.

14. *Der Schein, was ist er, dem das Wesen fehlt?*
   Das Wesen, wär' es, wenn es nicht erschiene?
Quoted by Johannes Hoffmeister, ed., in G. W. F. Hegel, *Phänomenologie des Geistes* (Hamburg: Meiner, 1952), p. vii.

15. Witness, for instance, the new translation by Peter Heath, with an introduction by Michael Vater, of F.W.J. Schelling, *System of Transcendental Idealism* (1800; Charlottesville: University Press of Virginia, 1993).

16. Reprint: F. W. J. Schelling, *Philosophie der Mythologie* (Darmstadt: Wissenschaftliche Buchgesellschaft, 1966), 2 vols. Vol. 1 bears the subtitle *Einleitung in die Philosophie der Mythologie*. This work will be referred to in these notes as "Schelling." See also F. W. Schelling, *Philosophie de la Mythologie*, trans. Alain Pernet, preface by Marc Richir, postscript by François Genet (Grenoble: Millon, 1994), and the bibliographical note by the translator on p. 88.

17. H. van Oyen, "Het speculatief Idealisme," in H. van Oyen, *Philosophia: Beknopt handboek tot de geschiedenis van het wijsgeerig denken* (Utrecht: de Haan, 1949), vol. 2, p. 212.

18. Schelling, vol. 2, p. 135.

19. Schelling, vol. 2, p. 137.

20. Schelling, vol. 2, p. 138.

21. Geoffrey Keynes, ed., *Poetry and Prose of William Blake* (London: Nonesuch, 1961), p. 147.

22. Kees W. Bolle, "The Romantic Impulse in the History of Religions," in *Cultural Dynamics* 2 (1989), p. 402. The concluding quote is from Herman Melville's *Moby Dick,* in the Norton Critical Edition, edited by Harrison Hayford and Hershel Parker (New York: Norton, 1967), p. 236.

23. *Moby Dick,* pp. 312–13.

24. Ibid., p. 314.

25. Ibid., p. 306.

26. Kierkegaard's *Concluding Unscientific Postscript,* trans. by David F. Swenson, completed by Walter Lowrie (Princeton: Princeton University Press, 1944), p. 18. It is the question Kierkegaard had used as subtitle in his earlier work, *Philosophical Fragments.*

27. Ibid., pp. 520–37.

28. John Meyendorff, *The Byzantine Legacy in the Orthodox Church* (Crestwood, N.Y.: St. Vladimir's Seminary Press, 1982), p. 160.

29. Kierkegaard, *Concluding Unscientific Postscript,* p. 19.

30. Ibid., p. 495.

31. See Erik Iversen, *The Myth of Egypt and Its Hieroglyphics in European Tradition* (Princeton: Princeton University Press, 1993).

32. *Webster's New World Dictionary of the American Language* (Cleveland and New York: World Publishing Co.), 1960.

33. What follows is based on the superb portrait painted by G. van der Leeuw in *Levensvormen* (Amsterdam: Paris, 1948), pp. 126–42.

34. Ibid., p. 130.

35. Ibid., p. 132.

36. J. Görres, *Mythengeschichte der asiatischen Welt* (Heidelberg, 1910; reprint, New York: Arno Press, 1978, collection "Mythology"), vol. 1, p. 16.

37. Ibid., p 18.

38. Friedrich Creuzer, *Symbolik und Mythologie der alten Völker, besonders der Griechen,* 2nd., rev. ed. (Leipzig, 1819; reprint, New York: Arno Press, 1978, collection "Mythology"), vol. 1, p. 7.

39. Which happens to be the case with respect to Eros in a well-known account in Plato's *Symposium.*

40. C. O. Müller, *Introduction to a Scientific System of Mythology,* trans. John Letch (London: Longman, 1844), p. 257.

41. Ibid., p. 47.

42. Ibid., p. 61.

43. F. Max Müller, *Auld Lang Syne* (New York: Scribner, 1898), p. 17.

44. Ibid., p. 80.

45. Ibid., p. 81.

46. See especially his *Chips from a German Workshop,* vol. 2 (New York: Scribner, 1869).

47. *Auld Lang Syne,* p. 63.

48. Ibid., p. 17.

49. F. Max Müller, *Introduction to the Science of Religion* (London: Longman, 1873; reprint, New York: Arno Press, 1978, collection "Mythology"), p. 16.

The Nineteenth Century

The nineteenth century was characterized by an explosion of knowledge. In every area of research, new things came to light, new theories were born. Despite the continuing Romantic tendency to trust in intuition and vision, the dominant characteristic of the new world that was beginning was a self-assurance more akin to the "reason" discovered in the Renaissance or in the French Enlightenment. The word that typifies the nineteenth century represents a very complex idea: *evolution*. The new sensation of having discovered the fundamental law of all that is to be known centers in that term. The lengthened form *evolutionism* refers to an increasingly adamant attitude that everything is determined by a process of evolution from low to high, from simple to complex. Initiated in Romantic philosophy (Hegel), the idea of "evolution" now seems to arise and spread on its own, adjusting itself to any circumstances yet remaining recognizable as the intellectual characteristic of the age. The idea predates the famous theory of evolution of nature and life formulated by Darwin. It comes to be used on materials neither Hegel nor Darwin had in mind in their studies of spirit and of nature respectively. Evolution becomes central in the study of civilization, culture, and religion. It is the growing sense of a scientific principle that can be applied as a law to all of reality, which makes it altogether different from the comparatively playful and harmless notion of progress the Enlightenment was so fond of, and also less defined than the evolution Hegel, Herbert Spencer, or Darwin thought. The Enlightenment had associated progress with the idea of education, and not in the last place the moral improvement of human beings.

Like other periods we have tried to characterize, the "nineteenth century" is not simply a convenient length of time. The century is incomprehensible unless we see its preludes in the French Revolution and the Romantic movement, and let it end a bit later than the year 1900. We should see it go on until at least the First World War, and arguably, in the evolutionisms held on to in scholarship, even longer.

ECONOMIC THINKERS

The nineteenth century presents us with an unlikely cast of characters, who nevertheless in a historical perspective must be seen together. It is a large group, distributed over theology, missions, anthropology, high capitalism, imperialism, colonization, and Marxism. What do all these fields have in common? A peculiar certainty that the entire world was available for them. Let us begin with the economic realm.

The Napoleonic wars (1798–1815) had made trade with the colonies more difficult. When peace returned, national governments stepped in for the first time to safeguard those important sources of wealth. The increase in parliamentary, democratic forms of rule in the same period brought with it an increase in the influence of "liberals"; that term did not have the vague, often critical meaning it has taken on recently in the United States, but meant what it still means in most of the world: the businesspeople in favor of free trade—provided it worked in their favor. Thus, early in the nineteenth century, we see the rise of bourgeois capitalism. Government involvement and military ventures made for productivity in new factories enhanced by the still new steam engine. Ships and railroads were built. All this went hand in hand with the development of a "banking industry"— as it is called nowadays. For we are the inheritors of what happened before us and perhaps also the victims in our new sense of what an "industry" amounts to: so we have a banking industry, a real estate industry, a medical industry, a baseball industry, and an entire Olympic Games industry, with countries and cities vying for the gainful honor of hosting the games. In other words, "industry" no longer means the production of goods, but has become exclusively a matter of focusing on *profits*. This is part of the complex process triggered by what happened barely two centuries ago in London, Paris, Amsterdam, Vienna, and Rome.

The theoretical blueprint for this new world had appeared in 1776. It was the Scotsman Adam Smith's *The Wealth of Nations*. The German poet

Heinrich Heine once referred to the *corpus iuris,* basis of traditional legal studies in Europe, as "the Bible of egoism," and that qualification would apply as well to Smith's book, in the opinion of many. However, Smith was praised by no one less than David Hume. And even its most severe critics will admit that his book is amazingly precise in its observations and analyses of the details we now know as the subject matter of economics. What Marx, soon thereafter, came to call "classes" are already delineated in Adam Smith, who does not mince words when he says,

> What are the common wages of labour, depends everywhere upon the contract usually made between those two parties, whose interests are by no means the same. The workmen desire to get as much, the masters to give as little as possible. The former are disposed to combine in order to raise, the latter in order to lower the wages of labour.[1]

Karl Marx (1818 – 83), in his renowned book *Capital,* finds laws at work in the entire development of human history. Although *Capital* is a work of philosophy, in strong opposition to Hegel (but how different from Kierkegaard's opposition!), it has been largely ignored by philosophers. The reason is not hard to guess. A philosopher's task is to think about all there is. And since Marx narrowed down all-there-is to material, economic reality, the error of reductionism is too obvious to be worth a rebuttal. Marx did not overlook the question but quite consciously turned Hegel, the man of mere ideas, upside down:

> My dialectic method is not only different from the Hegelian, but is its direct opposite. To Hegel, the life-process of the human brain, i.e., the process of thinking, which, under the name of "the Idea," he even transforms into an independent subject, is the demiurge of the real world, and the real world is only the external, phenomenal form of "the Idea." With me, on the contrary, the ideal is nothing else than the material world reflected by the human mind and translated into forms of thought.[2]

Where does the subject of religion enter in? It hardly does, except that for Marx, religion is ideology, an imposed set of ideas that serves the purposes of the ruling class. And in Marxist circles this identification became standardized. The independent importance of religion is dismissed entirely.

Let us note that Marx's vision of a "classless society," brought about by the victory of the proletariat, can be seen as akin to the eschatological visions that fit into the structures of much earlier, religious traditions: Zoroastrianism, Israel and Judaism, and Christianity.[3] However one may view that interpretation, no one who reads Marx can fail to hear the tone of moral involvement that lifts the dry economic arguments to another level. In the chapter "Money, or the Circulation of Commodities," we read,

> It is not money that makes commodities commensurable. Just the con-
> trary. It is because all commodities, as values, are realized human
> labour, and therefore commensurable, that their values can be meas-
> ured by one and the same special commodity, and the latter be con-
> verted into the common measure of their values, i.e., into money.[4]

Followers and opponents of Marx alike often quote him as saying that religion is the opium of the people. The words are indeed his, but the pre-ceding sentence, which is never quoted, reveals that Marx's moral indigna-tion is not so much directed at religion as at the sum total of the injustices of human behavior:

> *Religious* distress is at the same time the expression of real distress and
> the *protest* against real distress. Religion is the sigh of the oppressed
> creature, the heart of a heartless world, just as it is the spirit of a spirit-
> less situation. It is the *opium* of the people.[5]

I am not trying to suggest that Marx is defending religion here, but all of Marx's writings, based on his history and his passion for justice, can be called *prophetic*. Some of the most potent expressions of Marx's "debunk-ing" of religion occur in the same article:

> *Man makes religion*, religion does not make man. In other words, reli-
> gion is the self-consciousness and self-feeling of man who has either
> not yet found himself or has already lost himself again. But *man* is no
> abstract being squatting outside the world. Man is *the world of man*, the
> state, society. This state, this society, produce religion, *a reversed world-
> consciousness*, because they are *a reversed world*. . . . [Religion] is the
> fantastic realization of the human essence because the human essence
> has no true reality.[6]

I do not need to belabor the obvious, namely, that Marx himself was sure he had figured out the "fantastic realization" that made up religion. He was not ignorant of the subject, but spent much time reading up on theology. One theologian he read thoroughly was Ludwig Feuerbach (1804–72), whose writing stirred much debate. The contention arose from *The Essence of Christianity,* where Feuerbach argued that the essence of Christianity is none other than the essence of man. This man-centered view naturally did not find favor with most theologians. Marx, however, disagreed strongly with Feuerbach in spite of the fact that the latter could also be called a materialist. Marx seemed to sense that Feuerbach had hit on something that could be used to explain and justify the adherence of the masses. Although the phrase "escape mechanism" was unknown then, it describes what Marx detected in Feuerbach's writing, and he abhorred it. A term Marx did use was *alienation.* And if Feuerbach was accepted, human beings would be stimulated even more in their alienation from reality. Also, from Marx's point of view (we cannot go through his reasonings here), Feuerbach erroneously attached importance to individual human sensations, as if they could reveal "the essence." The reality, the real essence of human life is, for Marx, the fact that we are products of objective historical processes—the processes that Marx had laid bare.[7]

Perhaps the principal point that matters for us in Marx is the typical nineteenth-century self-assurance. Others, unlike Marx, and supposedly "in favor of" religion, were not less certain of their grasp, as we shall see.

Literature
Adam Smith, *The Wealth of Nations* (Harmondsworth: Penguin, 1974); Reinhold Niebuhr, *Marx and Engels on Religion* (New York: Schocken, 1964).

THEOLOGIANS AND MISSIONARIES

The theology that dominates the nineteenth century is quite different from the heritage of Thomas Aquinas, Luther, or Calvin. Instead, it is a theology that is affected by Romanticism, as much as Calvin's thought of predestination was affected by the ruling thoughts of his day. Schleiermacher and Kierkegaard, no matter how different from each other, each in his own way showed Romantic leanings, the former through his special, personal stress on faith (rather than the objective tradition of the church), the latter by bringing into prominence the individual decision. The unusual materialist theologian Feuerbach, whom we have mentioned, accentuated the individual, personal human element to such a Romantic extent that he provoked Marx, whose vision of the perfect future was no less Romantic! The classical theological ideas had all been predicated on the reality and revelation of God, and his acts in forming his church. Although in this new age no one would deny these ideas, no one was able anymore to talk very long of anything concerning God and holiness without asking about *experience*. This remained a central concern in nineteenth-century theology, even when new emphases were added.

A very influential theologian after Schleiermacher in that period was the German Lutheran Albrecht Ritschl (1822–89). He tied issues of truth to historical certainty. His influence on religio-historical scholarship can hardly be overestimated. This optimistic view of human learning was not limited to one scholar. The conviction that historical inquiry would lead to "the truth" became widely accepted, and the growing science of religion was not immune to this attitude. It certainly was a factor in the enormous labor that led a group of scholars to publish the five-volume *Die Religion in Geschichte und Gegenwart* (or *RGG*), "Religion in History and at the Present Time" (1909–13). Of course, one cannot hold one theologian or a few historians responsible for a prevailing idea, nor can we single out some of the contributors to this work for egregious errors in judgment. The "spirit" of the nineteenth century suggested the illusion to writers and readers alike that history, if properly analyzed, would yield truth. It is part of the certainty about laws governing all there is which characterized the age. The time following the first edition of the *RGG*, beginning with the First World War, saw many uncertainties concerning humanity articulated which the previous generation could not have foreseen. The name assigned to the group that produced the first edition of the *RGG* and many who shared their persuasions is "die religionsgeschichtliche Schule," "the religio-historical school," a name itself that suggested that an ultimate truth could be objectively demonstrated. For the sake of fairness in our judgment, we should add that in English, at about the same time (1908–21), an encyclopedic twelve-volume work of many contributors appeared: *The Encyclopaedia of Religion and Ethics*. It stands out even today in clarity and solidity. It was produced at the initiative and under the editorship of the Scottish minister James Hastings. Both these gigantic works were the result of international cooperation.

The new nineteenth-century perception of the world was responsible for an additional idea, namely, that the so-called savages represented beings at lower stages of evolution who were in need of special attention. This concern appeared first not among the traders of the East India Company but, in a profound manner, among a number of Christians. It is true, of course, that the call "to make disciples of all nations" (Matthew 28:19) was an ancient duty; yet historically, it had never given rise to a popular movement. And now, when a vision of the world as a whole had come into being, this duty was felt not by churches but by individuals, who organized missionary societies. These societies were all Protestant, and actually their activities had commenced by the very end of the eighteenth century, before national governments actively began their colonizing.

These Protestants were not the first to go out and conduct missionary efforts. For more than two hundred years, members of Catholic spiritual congregations, especially the Jesuits, had gone abroad. They not only collected valuable material in nations like India and China, but did extensive work among North American native populations. Much of what they found had been published in the *Relations de la nouvelle France.* This was the material that fascinated the Enlightenment philosophes and set them to speculating about a really existing natural religion, preserved in exotic lands.

The Jesuits, but also other congregations, including the Dominicans, Franciscans, and Augustinians, had begun serious missionary activity around 1600 in Asia, Africa, and North and South America. Pope Gregory XV (1621–23) had a special liking for the Jesuits, and he established an organization to benefit them in particular: the Congregatio de propaganda fide (Congregation for the Propagation of the Faith). He had in mind as possible converts both distant lands, and also nations in Europe that had become Protestant. At this point we should pause and remind ourselves that the world at any given time is more complicated than it would seem from our perspective. Our present inclination to condemn our greedy ancestors is an expression of a global perspective among ourselves. However, universal inclinations have always existed. Their universality is expressed in different contexts from our own. On closer inspection, we may even be amazed at the sacrifices people have made for their universal vision, even if it was not like ours.

The Jesuits do not always enjoy a good reputation. However, the contacts they made, worldwide, the converts they made, and the diplomatic activity they engaged in are astounding—if you think merely of the language barriers of the time, the absence of dictionaries, grammars, and trained translators. Because of their activities, they were involved also with the banking system, such as it was, that came into being at the beginning of the great explorations of the world at the end of the Middle Ages. To ascribe all this activity only to greed, or to a zeal for the papacy (which was officially the cause the Jesuits stood for), is insufficient as an explanation. The reasons they went abroad are comparable rather to the reasons why cosmonauts allow themselves to be shot into space. It is rewarding in some manner that we can easily grasp; and yet, there is also a profound reason in it that is difficult to articulate. Structurally, it is something that we can refer to only as a religious symbolism. The expanse of the universe is *there;* Mount Everest is climbed because it is there; the world opened up to the Jesuits was *there* as the entire world created by God was there. The "it" to be climbed, to be traversed, to be baptized is more than a "thing"; it is the visible part of the religious symbol. And there is no doubt about the reality of the other, the "transcendent" part. All this we may bear in mind when we read in a sober historical account:

> Of 376 Jesuits sent to China between 1581 and 1712, 127 were lost on the voyage through disease or shipwreck. It is amazing that so small a company of men achieved so much.[8]

Such sacrifices and their religious motivations, however, had little bearing on what was decided in places such as Rome. In 1773 (July 21, to be exact), the pope, Clement XIV, promulgated a brief, *Dominus ac Redemptor* (a brief is a papal letter not quite as formal as a bull), dissolving the Society of Jesus (Societas Jesu, the Congregation of the Jesuits) altogether. In addition, this pope, who was not well disposed toward the Jesuits,

> sequestered all its property, and declared that no Pope in the future should ever recall it into being . . .
>
> At that time the Society numbered 22,589 members, of whom 11,293 were priests. As a result of the dissolution at least 3,000 missionaries were withdrawn from their fields. A certain number gave up the name of Jesuit and remained on their posts; the great majority were given no choice — they were put aboard ship like cattle and carried off to their country of origin. They were literally irreplaceable; the Pope had condemned Catholic missions to a temporary eclipse.[9]

There are those who would tend to imagine that Rome, and the Jesuits in conspiracy with Rome, had a plan to conquer the world; yet one clearly sees that nothing of the sort appears in the history that unfolded. Completely provincial European forces were at work. One important consideration was that the Jesuits—in part because of their knowledge of the world at large—were open to Enlightenment ideas. And the pope did not like those ideas, least of all those of Voltaire. Furthermore, there were national governments in Europe, whether sympathetic or antipathetic toward the Enlightenment, which were not in favor of the power of Rome; they saw the Jesuits as the principal political instrument of papal power, and hence they lobbied for their overthrow. The Portuguese government had a special complaint to bring to Rome. The power over Paraguay had moved from Spain to Portugal, but by this time in Paraguay a rebellion was afoot for which the Portuguese held the Jesuits responsible. The Christianization of Paraguay was largely the work of the Jesuits. And furthermore, the Jesuits had made the country into a separate, indigenous, more or less communally organized state that was difficult to govern from outside. In fact, from our perspective today, the Jesuits seem indeed the most sensible party in the dispute at the time. The role of Greed was played by the planters, who wanted to get more than the Paraguayans were willing to give them. The principal European minister in this affair, the Portuguese Pombal, was an "enlightened" man, but he believed his own plans thwarted by the Jesuits. He insisted on the dissolution of the order and the confiscation of its possessions. France followed suit and held the order responsible for the bankruptcy of a commercial enterprise on Martinique, in which one single Jesuit was involved. The parliament in Paris declared the order a danger to the state. To be sure, in spite of the official dissolution, the order did not vanish. In Prussia and in Russia, it continued to exist, though under the cloak of a pseudonym. In the end, the tide turned in favor of the Jesuits, but that was only in 1814, under a different pope, Pius VII, who restored the order.

This prelude to the missionary activities of the nineteenth century is instructive. The new missions too came into being and did their work in the interplay between opposing forces. They were born in honest devotion, and under the influence of a more or less Romantic pietism. But they set to work in areas under the control of the expanding empires of the European nations. Although the great Protestant reformers had never conceived of plans to convert the entire world, now such visions became possible. The influence of American Methodism—with which the name of John Wesley should be mentioned — had a great deal to do with the formation of a pietistic climate in which the first Protestant missionary organizations came into being. They were all voluntary, private efforts; they were not church-sponsored. In general, pietism was the great stimulus, and many of the missionaries called themselves Evangelicals. This name may have had very different sounds in different contexts, but in fact it was used in part because it gave less of an emphasis to specific denominations, and more to the ideal of a universal, God-given task. In 1846 the Evangelical Alliance was established in London; in spite of the multiplicity of churches, it translated what needed to be done into one worldwide effort. The London Missionary Society (1795) was the first of many groups. It was followed by the Baptist Missionary Society (1797), the Dutch Missionary Society (1797), and others in Germany, Switzerland, Denmark, and other nations.

The historial importance of these organizations cannot be overestimated. They are rooted in the Romanticism that ignited men like Schleiermacher, but their own mood was something newer, and infectious. A feeling of superiority had sprung up as if by nature. The technical and organizational achievements of Europeans and Americans seemed to validate the spread of Christianity as the goal, the destiny of the planet. Whether this was seen as the result of a natural evolution or as the plan of God did not matter much in practice; one did not quibble about this difference in emphasis when so much needed to be done. The activism of missionary men and women in the field has had consequences in education, and in the disruption of societies, and in all instances also in the move toward a global development of myriad forms. It is important to observe that missionaries in the nineteenth century shared in the same *problems* that nonmissionaries had. This is true in every age, although the shared spirit is so much more easily detected in a century that is a safe distance away. An example from the twentieth century was the rise of fascist nationalism and its spiritual threat. Hendrik Kraemer, a most dynamic missionary worker in Southeast Asia, was one of the missionaries who saw this danger clearly, before the world was forced to take notice of the threat unleashed by Japan and Germany.

Literature
Stephen Neill, *A History of Christian Missions* (Harmondsworth: Pelican, 1964); Hendrik Kraemer, *The Christian Message in a Non-Christian World* (London: Edinburgh House Press, 1947).

SOCIAL STUDIES

Among the achievements of the nineteenth century is the creation of the fields we are now familiar with as the "social sciences": sociology and anthropology. The accumulation of learning by these disciplines has given us much of what we know about human beings and their societies. The German Max Weber (1864–1920) and the Frenchman Emile Durkheim (1858–1917) are the principal founders of the discipline of sociology. We shall make our remarks mainly about Durkheim, because he is most helpful in regard to questions that engage us in the history of religions.

Max Weber is certainly not a scholar to be ignored, however, especially since he was by training and interest a historian with an incredibly wide range of interest. He was a political economist and is considered the founder of sociology. His fame rests especially on the work he did on the relation of Protestantism to the development of capitalism. His methodological and theoretical formulations influenced every branch of the study of human beings, including the history of religions. To begin with, Weber was thoroughly aware of the difficulty of defining the study of society. He defines sociology as "the science whose object is to interpret the meaning of social action and thereby give causal explanation of the way the action proceeds and the effects it produces."[10] He goes on to discuss the term *meaning* by locating it in its natural place: in the subjective meaning it has for the *agent* in any action; the meaning is the meaning the agent assigns to it. Weber also links such meaningful action to the relation between the person who acts and the behavior of someone else. Though Weber did not himself coin the term *ideal-type,* it is mainly through his work that it became known. What we understand of any human action is never available to us in the immediate way a rock is to a geologist. Instead, an image is formed between our subjective mental operation and the object of our understanding. It is that space in-between where the "ideal-type" functions. This is the bridge our understanding constructs in all interhuman mental operations. Obviously, such elementary matters needed to be discussed. They also make it understandable that sociologists spend a good deal of time on the subject of religion, which is always "relational." No wonder that sociology of religion became a topic of specialized study, in spite of the fact that unspecified, general sociology never bypasses religion.

Émile Durkheim gained extraordinary prestige in France through his studies of problems such as education, suicide, the division of labor, and the relations among law, political power, and society. During his career in the French university system and in the course of his studies, issues of religion grew in importance in his thought. Together with talented collaborators, including Marcel Mauss and Henri Hubert, he established the journal *L'année sociologique,* where the new school first aired its views. Durkheim's most immediately relevant work for historians of religions is *Les formes élémentaires de la religion* ("The Elementary Forms of Religious Life"; 1912). Unlike Weber, Durkheim was primarily interested not in history but in philosophy. Immanuel Kant's ideas particularly, on what constitutes our knowledge, shine through in the clarity with which he poses problems. The same tradition obtains in many French scholars, often splendid specialists on religions, who came out of Durkheim's school or were guided by him: Paul Mus (in his studies of Buddhism and Buddhist art), and the student of classical Chinese culture Marcel Granet. Durkheim's sociological, and at the same time thoughtful, articulate tradition is also noticeable in the works on Indo-European comparative mythology of Georges Dumézil. All these writers are as important to historians of religions as they are to sociologists.

Critics of Durkheim often suggest that he reduced religion to social needs. There may be a grain of truth to this, and a recent translator of *The Elementary Forms* entitles her introduction with a phrase from Durkheim himself: "Religion as an Eminently Social Thing."[11] No doubt he did say that, but a careful reading of his work does not allow us to regard it as a simple definition. The translator and the text make clear how Durkheim went out of his way to state what most scholars had failed to see: *religion is reality.* In Durkheim's words: "When I approach the study of primitive religions, it is with the certainty that they are grounded in and express the real."[12] This idea was at odds with all of the nineteenth century's conviction—shared by ethnologists and, not least, by the Christian missionaries, many of whom were also gatherers of information concerning the "primitives." The idea that all of humanity went through a process of evolution that led from lack of intelligence to a supposed present level of superior intelligence was among the most generally held of assumptions, and had already had its first adherents in the eighteenth century in such men as Lessing. The imperialistic world of the educated West had made it into a self-evident assumption. All the more remarkable, therefore, is Durkheim's claim that religion, even "primitive religion," is rooted in the *real.* He went even further, saying, "Fundamentally, then, there are no religions that are false."[13]

It is not as if Durkheim was completely out of sync with the prevailing ideas of his time. *The Elementary Forms* focused on the world of the culturally most backward Australian tribes—backward in the sense that they did not even know about the skill of pottery-making, or about the bow and arrow. Durkheim did share the general idea that the least advanced tribal peoples in the world are in some sense representative of what earliest humanity was like. Hence, they might be of help in revealing to us human life in its "most elementary forms." And here, social structures became important for him. "Totemism" was common among the Australian native population, and according to information passed on to the West, it seemed to be related exclusively to social and kinship relationships. Later scholarship found that this was not entirely the case—but that is how it seemed at the time to Durkheim and others. And Durkheim made what he found in Australian field reports into a more general verity: "Religious representations are collective representations that express collective realities . . . They, too, must be social things, products of collective thought. At the very least . . . it is legitimate to say that they are rich in social elements."[14]

The extraordinary importance of such insights by Durkheim is not diminished by the fact that the data they were based on were not wholly dependable. Furthermore, prehistorians in more recent times have come to see that the entire notion of "evolution" when applied to the development of human thought is inappropriate. It is appropriate in such sciences as geology and biology, where the spans of time are truly gigantic, and there is evidence of changes over such long periods that are indeed startling. By contrast, our human periods of time on planet earth are trifling, and the fluctuations of human minds and expressiveness are not analogous to evolutionary changes studied by the earth sciences. Still, Durkheim opened the way toward understanding human beings elsewhere without the need to denigrate them. All religious representations are collective. History and anthropology have as their task showing this and pointing to the variables. Durkheim's insights were more than a little different from prevailing theological and philosophical ideas. Since Descartes it had been common to think of human beings primarily as defined by their individuality, and all questions, including questions concerning religion, began with "I." Durkheim saw the social, the collective, as basic. And could we contradict him? Not everything—because we know of ascetics and hermits—but virtually all we know of religious traditions is social in nature. And even with ascetics, we can observe that they became ascetics because they followed the impulse to leave a society, which was their starting point.

It is not wise to stereotype an entire nation — but we may be excused for the remark that a Durkheim would hardly have been conceivable in any country other than France. It had to be a Frenchman who discovered the mystery of human existence, the riddle of religion, in the social element. France, the land of Descartes, more than any other nation, consists in individuals. Individualism equals the freedom one is entitled to — a freedom that Americans have a hard time understanding. Bicycling in Europe, I recall how easy it was to spot Frenchmen; they usually hiked alone. Others, especially Americans, virtually always travel in groups. In 1961 William J. Lederer wrote a book called *A Nation of Sheep,* in which he was critical of what he perceived as the American habit of not taking individual responsibility or standing by one's convictions.[15] I don't propose to enter a debate on whether he was right. It is nevertheless puzzling that so many Americans (and not only Americans), when they express curiosity about religion, posit its explanation not in the social, collective nature of human beings but in the peculiarities of individuals and their psyches. Do people tend to locate the essence of religion in the opposite of what they take for granted? The sociology of Durkheim is worth studying. If nothing else, it may restore a balance.

Among other insights, Durkheim dwelt on a distinction between the *sacred* and the *profane.* In doing so, he did not enter into metaphysical speculation. Durkheim simply saw the distinction as characteristic of all human traditions. He rejected the notion of the "supernatural" or "mystery." These notions are latecomers in history; they came about in such religions as Christianity and are not present among "the primitives."

> To be able to call certain facts supernatural, one must already have an awareness that there is a *natural order of things,* in other words, that the phenomena of the universe are internally linked according to necessary relationships called laws.[16]

> Whether simple or complex, all known religious beliefs display a common feature: They presuppose a classification of the real or ideal things that men conceive into two classes — two opposite genera — that are widely designated by two distinct terms, which the words profane and sacred translate fairly well. The division of the world into two domains, one containing all that is sacred and the other all that is profane-such is the distinctive trait of religious thought.[17]

Durkheim has a special place in the development of ideas about religion. He criticized by implication and directly the naive evolutionism that was rampant, even if he himself could not escape all evolutionistic taints. More than anyone he saved the study of the world's religions from sinking into a morass of intuitionism, in which it threatened to perish. Durkheim came close to ridiculing the Romantic, intuitionist "naturism" of Max Müller, and he had no use for English speculative evolutionists who posed as empiricists—about whom we shall have something to say .

Literature
W. G. Runciman, ed., *Weber: Selections in Translation* (Cambridge: Cambridge University Press, 1978); Émile Durkheim, *The Elementary Forms of Religious Life,* trans. Karen E. Fields (New York: Free Press, 1995).

PHILOSOPHERS AND ANTHROPOLOGISTS

Ideas about religion are usually conditioned by unexamined assumptions more than by religious facts. The idea of evolution as a law in the development of the human mind and of religion, together with the glorification of scientific knowledge, had peculiar consequences—which can be observed in people of very different orientations. Missionaries shared enough of their contemporaries' scientific ideals to regard the spiritual life of tribes in Africa or Asia as filled with illusions. Others, who looked more skeptically at Christianity, could express the opinion that *all* religion was a matter of ignorance. The Frenchman Auguste Comte (1798–1857), the greatest modern rationalist, wrote a work entitled *Cours de philosophie positive* ("Course in Positive Philosophy"). Comte's principal thesis was that only the objects of scientific investigation constitute reality. He also posited a powerful doctrine of evolution that found a responsive chord in people who expected much from the new scientific world. The mental evolution through time, according to Comte, led from images of gods, to ideas about things no one could know, and finally to positive thought—that is, *his* thought—based on what our minds are actually equipped to master. He called these three stages of thought respectively the theological, the metaphysical, and the positive stages. Beside the historical evolution of Hegel, Comte's is refreshingly clear in outline. It does not pompously pretend to have interpreted all of history in all its details. Rather, it proposes schematically the arrival of what we should regard as real knowledge.

Comte was as brilliant as he was industrious. The first volume of his great six-volume work was published in 1830, the final volume in 1842, when he was forty-four. The first volume lays the foundation and explains very clearly what he has in mind:

> I believe that I have discovered a great and fundamental law, to which the mind is subjected by an invariable necessity. . . . This law consists in the fact that each of our principal conceptions, each branch of our knowledge, passes in succession through three different theoretical states: the theological or fictitious state, the metaphysical or abstract state, and the scientific or positive state. . . . The first is the necessary starting point of human intelligence; the third represents its fixed and definitive state; the second is destined to serve only as a transitional method.[18]

> Now that the human mind has founded celestial physics, terrestrial physics (mechanical and chemical), and organic physics (vegetable and animal), it only remains to complete the system of observational sciences by the foundation of social physics.[19]

For students of religions or of literature, it is important to keep in mind that Comte's (as well as Hegel's) ideas of evolution have nothing to do with Darwin's. Not only did they predate *The Origin of Species* (1859) by decades, but a confusion of the philosophical ideas with the scientific ideas, based on observation and analysis, might discredit Darwin wholly undeservedly. Comte's vision was encompassing, and, as the final quotation shows, he expected his system to find its crown in *sociology*. I personally find it difficult not to think back for a moment to Voltaire's famous statement "If God did not exist, he would need to be invented," and apply it to Comte and his scientific optimism: if Comte did not exist, we would have to dream up a figure like him to make the all-encompassing optimistic view of evolution of the nineteenth century come completely alive. But Comte really existed, and he must have been a strange man in many—especially many romantic—ways. He came from a wealthy family of French royalists, became alienated from them, had to provide for his own education, became enthusiastic about the budding sciences, was secretary to Saint-Simon (the "utopian socialist," as Marx would call him), got a good many of his ideas from Saint-Simon, and became alienated from him. He fell in love, married, and became alienated from his wife. Years later he fell madly in love with a woman who quite literally changed his life. She refused to live with him, but her influence made Comte aware of the real power and importance of love. He completed, indeed crowned, his life by establishing the idea of a *culte de l'humanité,* a "cult of humanity." In other words, he realized that there had to be a goal, a purpose to the glorious evolution of human mental-spiritual achievements. His final creation of a cult did not, however, shake his system. To all of us, I cannot help but think, many cracks are apparent in his scheme, but at the same time, it is precisely these that make Auguste Comte more human. The "objective" activities of our senses and our reason seem to insist on coming to terms with a common and human sense.

This point of "the human" is vitally important in intellectual inquiry. It may make us think back to Karl Marx, who turned out a fully "objective" system. We noticed in his writings his compassion for human beings and his zeal for justice which seem of a different order than the describable facts of reality-as-economics. In Marx's old age, one of his daughters passed on to him a questionnaire. Somewhere it asked, Which vice do you consider the worst? Marx wrote down, "Servility."[20] Surely, that answer did not well up from an objective study of objective facts.

The Englishman Herbert Spencer (1820–1903) was a thinker who admired August Comte. Like Comte, he tried to develop a system of thought that would be applicable to society. However, he lacked Comte's imaginative abilities. His conception of evolution is more materialistic, more "objectivistic" and mechanical. No wonder Durkheim, who himself owed much to Comte, found fault with Spencer, as well as with an even more important English scholar, the anthropologist Edward Burnett Tylor (1832–1917). What disturbed Durkheim began with their assumptions about "spiritual beings." This abstraction, worked out in great detail by Tylor, seemed to Durkheim completely off the subject of religion as it really functions in archaic and traditional societies.

Tylor's name is inseparable from his invention: the theory of animism. In the decades before and after 1900, the world seemed more than ever obsessed with theories of origins. To some extent, this is understandable, for Darwin's discoveries in the life sciences had gained in influence over the scientific imagination, and stimulated the idea that the methods of the natural sciences could be applicable everywhere, including in inquiries into human life, society, culture, and, of course, religion. If we care to measure by popularity, then Tylor's theory about the origin of religion was one of the most successful ever put forth.

The principles which underlie a solid system of interpretation are really few and simple. The treatment of similar myths from different regions, by arranging them in large compared groups, makes it possible to trace in mythology the operation of the imaginative processes recurring with the evident regularity of mental law.[21]

Tylor's ideas fit in with the general mood for evolutionism, and his writing is superb. Moreover, he writes in the glorious time of the upswing of the British Empire. During Tylor's lifetime, the sacred duty to look after the many "primitives" distributed throughout the world was immortalized in the poetry of Rudyard Kipling, who wrote in 1903:

Take up the white man's burden—
    Send forth the best ye breed—
Go bind your sons to exile
    To serve your captives' need;
To wait in heavy harness,
    On fluttered folk and wild—
Your new-caught, sullen peoples,
    Half-devil and half-child.[22]

Tylor's theory of "animism" posited as the beginning of human mental life the projection of ghosts, spirits. The idea that "animism," Tylor's idea of a primitive worship of spirits inhabiting the world, is actually a religion and is actually the religion of various groups of people in the world, still persists—the term may occasionally be found, for example, in the *New York Times* when a writer wishes to sum up some local religion for his readers. Of course, "animism" is not a religion at all but rather a stage in an evolutionistic theory presented by a nineteenth-century anthropologist. In reflecting on the period it comes from, we need to remember that all people, including anthropologists and poets, can only do their thinking within the coherence of their own era. For historians, and for historians of religions certainly, it is essential to keep in mind that no human beings make themselves; all of us stand on the shoulders of others, as the most poetic of the twentieth century's philosophical historians, José Ortega y Gasset, liked to say. And the shoulders Tylor and many of his contemporaries stood on were not only those of power-hungry materialists, but also of late-blooming Romantics. I find it helpful to remember that not long before Tylor wrote his major work and promulgated his theory of animism,

Charles Dickens had written one of his most beloved stories, a story that was a hit as soon as it appeared. *A Christmas Carol* told of Ebenezer Scrooge, who was haunted by three unforgettable spirits and the ghost of his former business partner. Many, many people in that period took an interest in paranormal phenomena, among them no less than the American philosopher William James. To William James we owe (after Kierkegaard) the most powerful critique of the idealists, as well as an important work on the philosophy and psychology of religion, *The Varieties of Religious Experience: A Study in Human Nature* (1902).

Tylor's intellectual grasp included every bit of information the world had to offer, not only from distant areas but also from all of history. If Max Müller is given the name "father of the history of religions" (a title historians of religions today would not like to grant him), Tylor certainly deserves to be called "father of anthropology." The theory that is identified with his name—animism—is mistaken, but few ideas have set so many researchers to work on questions of culture in general, and of religion in particular. The second edition of Tylor's work was published in 1873, only two years after the first. The impact of his lively writing is clear from many publications in the following years. A very well known study of certain dances among the North American Indians, written by James Mooney, appeared in 1892–1893; it was called *The Ghost-Dance Religion and the Sioux Outbreak of 1890.* The title is striking, and must have struck many early readers because of the influence of Tylor's idea of "ghosts" (his theory of animism) in the ethnological literature. "Ghost-dance" is indeed a proper translation of the word the Lakota use, but Mooney's book tells us also that all the other tribes had very different names for the same ritual dance.[23] As I mentioned, references to animism as if it referred to a specific religion still occur in writings by missionaries and by many other educated people; from the start, many were so impressed by Tylor's theory as to think of "animism" as a religion people adhered to. I suppose that the mistake could hardly be made if one reads Tylor carefully. Tylor in fact set out to collect evidence of what for many generations theologians had referred to as "natural religion." He saw it as his task

> to bring as clearly as may be into view the fundamental animism of the lower races, and in some slight and broken outline to trace its course into higher regions of civilization. Here let me state once for all two principal conditions under which the present research is carried on. First, as to the religious doctrines and practices examined, these are treated

as belonging to theological systems devised by human reason, without supernatural aid or revelation; in other words, as being developments of Natural Religion. Second, as to the connexion between similar ideas and rites in the religions of the savage and the civilized world.[24]

The "natural religion" referred to is precisely what Thomas Aquinas had defined, except for the fact that Aquinas would not have built his entire theology on it, but saw it only as a complement to the whole. Tylor executes the plan as announced. The notion of spirits, ghosts (*animi* in Latin, hence the term *animism*), developed in the minds of our early ancestors, according to the theory, to explain how we could see in our dreams people who had died, and other phenomena of which the causes could not yet be explained as they are by modern science, like the roar of the sea, or the power of a stream, or lightning. It was simply assumed in Tylor's reasoning that religion, to the extent it is worth considering, is the endeavor to formulate knowledge. This assumption he held in common with many others, including his older contemporary Herbert Spencer, who came up with the thesis that the more science expands, the smaller the area of religion is destined to become.

Literature
Auguste Comte, *Introduction to Positive Philosophy,* ed. and trans. Frederick Ferré (Indianapolis: Bobbs-Merrill, "The Library of Liberal Arts," 1977); Henri Gouhier, *La vie d' Auguste Comte* (Paris: Gallimard, 1931); Sir Edward Burnett Tylor, *The Origins of Culture* (New York: Harper, 1958), 2 vols.; William James, *The Varieties of Religious Experience* (New York: New American Library, 1958); John J. McDermott, ed., *The Writings of William James* (Chicago: University of Chicago Press, 1977); Jacques Barzun, *A Stroll with William James* (New York: Harper, 1983).

NOTES

1. Adam Smith, *The Wealth of Nations* (Harmondsworth: Penguin, 1974), p. 169.

2. Karl Marx, *Capital,* ed. Friedrich Engels, in series "Great Books of the Western World" (Chicago: Encyclopaedia Britannica, 1952), p. 11.

3. See R. C. Zaehner, "A New Buddha and New Tao," in R. C. Zaehner, ed., *The Concise Encyclopaedia of Living Faiths* (London: Hutchinson, 1959), pp. 402–12.

4. Marx, p. 42.

5. Karl Marx, "Contribution to the Critique of Hegel's Philosophy of Right" (1844), "Introduction," in Reinhold Niebuhr, *Marx and Engels on Religion* (New York: Schocken, 1964), p. 42.

6. Ibid., p. 41.

7. Ibid., pp. 69–72.

8. Stephen Neill, *A History of Christian Missions* (Harmondsworth: Pelican, 1964), p. 208.

9. Ibid., p. 206.

10. W. G. Runciman, ed., *Weber: Selections in Translation* (Cambridge: Cambridge University Press, 1978), p. 7.

11. Émile Durkheim, *The Elementary Forms of Religious Life*, trans. Karen E. Fields (New York: Free Press, 1995), p. xvii.

12. Ibid., p. 2.

13. Ibid.

14. Ibid., p. 9.

15. William J. Lederer, *A Nation of Sheep* (New York: Norton, 1961). It was the sequel to an earlier book with an equally unflattering title, *The Ugly American,* coauthored with Eugene Burdick.

16. Durkheim, p. 24.

17. Ibid., p. 34.

18. Auguste Comte, *Introduction to Positive Philosophy,* ed. and trans. Frederick Ferré, (Indianapolis: Bobbs-Merrill, "The Library of Liberal Arts," 1977), pp. 1–2.

19. Comte, p. 13.

20. Owen Chadwick, *The Secularization of the European Mind in the Nineteenth Century* (Cambridge: Cambridge University Press, 1975), p. 58.

21. Edward Burnett Tylor, *Primitive Culture,* 2 vols.; part 1, *The Origins of Culture,* part 2, *Religion in Primitive Culture* (1871; reprint New York: Harper, 1958), vol. 1, p. 282.

22. Rudyard Kipling, "The White Man's Burden," included in many an anthology. I am quoting from the ninth printing of a German textbook anthology of English poetry edited by Ph. Aronstein, *Selections from English Poetry* (Bielefeld: Verhagen, 1931), p. 194.

23. James Mooney, *The Ghost-Dance Religion and the Sioux Outbreak of 1890* (Chicago: University of Chicago Press, 1965), p. 35. Tylor barely touches on dance; see p. 507 of the second volume of *Primitive Culture.*

24. Tylor, vol. 2, p. 11.

The Painful Birth
of Sobriety:
The Twentieth Century

The technical anthropological ideas of the nineteenth century run almost without a ripple into the twentieth. The search for the beginnings of religion, especially the efforts by Tylor, set others in search of origins as well. Robert Ranulph Marett reasoned that if animism was defensible, it would be worthwhile to ask what might have preceded it. And he suggested that before the idea of spirits, a not yet animated power would have satisfied the primitive mind. He thought he found support for his idea in reports from Bishop Codrington, who had been at work in Melanesia, where he found the term *mana*. Codrington observed that mana was a force inherent in gods and other spiritual beings; he also described it as the supernatural; he also called it a "power." "Mana" was the hook on which Marett could hang his theory. Marett's essay "Pre-animistic Religion" was published in 1900, when electricity had just begun to illuminate the world. For Marett, electricity was a ready simile for that supposed impersonal power (glossing over mana's characteristic of belonging to more-than-human beings). The theory caught on almost as well as Tylor's. Scholars invoked it for the next half century, and found evidence of mana in unexpected places, as in the Sanskrit term *brahman* ("the absolute") and the Latin *imperium* ("power"),[1] hence in civilizations that could not by any stretch of the imagination be placed on the same level where Marett had located the "primitives," or had imagined very early human beings.

There has been a stream of candidates, before and since "animism" and "dynamism" (the technical term for the impersonal power theory), trying to name the earliest beginning of religion: fetishism, totemism, and diffusionism (the theory that all religion began in one spot, for instance Egypt or Mesopotamia). "Psychologism" is also worth mentioning in this list, although it is a more complex matter. Its earliest and most important role was in philosophy. It refers to the view that our mental processes (our psychology) must be studied because they form the basis of the decision what is true or false in our knowledge. Discussions on these matters go back to John Locke and are at variance with the classical view that logic and epistemology (the study of knowledge as such) are to decide the issue. New variations in the discussions came about as a result of more recent scientific psychological discussions. Mainly as a result of Freud's work, the explanation of religion as a projection of psychological complexes raised questions for students of religion and religions. In the 1960s serious endeavors were made to explain religion in terms of drug-induced visionary experiences. These theories, and many others, have their interesting points, but—as I hope we have seen in this book—the subject of religion is too multiform, too original and creative, to be explained by any single interesting idea. It might seem attractive to explain an idea of God by a psychological projection of an authoritarian father figure into the sky. The variety of great gods, however is too great (Yahweh, Viṣṇu, Zeus, et al.) to permit such simplicity. Too many aspects of myths, rituals, and symbolic places escape the simplicity of any of the psychological origin theories. Moreover, they ignore the traditions in which the notion of a transcendent fatherlike figure is lacking (as in Jainism or Buddhism). A willingness to deal honestly with all the materials is far more important than simplicity.

The human devastations of the First World War shattered the optimism of the sciences that promised to unveil the final riddles of the world, and the Second World War and its willful slaughter of millions produced self-doubt and frantic self-critiques in the disciplines dealing with the orientation of human beings. But even before the events that would alter the whole intellectual climate, there were signs of a coming change. To show this, I would like to look at three people on the threshold of the twentieth century: the English novelist Conrad, the German thinker and poet Nietzsche, and the French poet and essayist Péguy. The list could be lengthened, but these three will suffice to indicate why and how confidence in the knowledge of the nineteenth century came to an end; these figures are at the same time revealing with respect to attitudes toward religion and religions.

JOSEPH CONRAD, FRIEDRICH NIETZSCHE, AND CHARLES PÉGUY

Joseph Conrad (1857–1924) was a Pole by birth, who shared his father's Romanticism and nationalism at a time when Poland was under the heavy hand of Russia. He became a sailor, traveled widely as an adventurer, finally settled in England, and became a superb novelist, writing in the English language. In a word, he was an ideal-typical nineteenth-century man whose life led him from the trappings of a state and the dreams of Romanticism to a recognition of the real world. The film *Apocalypse Now* took Conrad's novel *The Heart of Darkness* as its model, and the course from a naive view (of patriotic duty in Vietnam) to the shock of a disconcertingly human reality is precisely what Conrad portrayed—except that he did so in a time when such a portrayal could hardly be appreciated by his contemporaries. Conrad's story takes place not in Asia, but in Africa. Conrad's own adventures, his desire to explore unknown parts, had taken him to the Congo, and his experiences there changed his Romantic views drastically. What he discovered, he wrote in one of his essays, was "the vilest scramble for loot that ever disfigured the history of human conscience and geographical explorations."[2] The novel's protagonist, Marlow, is the leader of a macabre expedition to find and save a man named Kurtz. On his steamboat, Marlow finds himself in dire straits, together with others, Europeans and Africans. The Africans know from experience about suffering under this "scramble for loot." In the utmost despair of hunger, Marlow recognizes human beings—at which point we cannot help but remember that until then, his time and Marlow himself had been "programed" to see only "savages" or "primitives."

the only thing to eat—though it did not look eatable in the least—I saw in their possession was a few lumps of some stuff like half-cooked dough, of a dirty lavender colour, they kept wrapped in leaves, and now and then swallowed a piece of, but so small that it seemed done more for the looks of the thing than for any serious purpose of sustenance. Why in the name of all the gnawing devils of hunger they didn't go for us—they were thirty to five—and have a good tuck in for once, amazes me now when I think of it. They were big powerful men, with not much capacity to weigh the consequences, with courage, with strength, even yet, though their skins were no longer glossy and their muscles no longer hard. And I saw that something restraining, one of those human secrets that baffle probability, had come into play there. . . . Yes; I looked at them as you would at any human being, with a curiosity of their impulses, motives, capacities, weaknesses, when brought to the test of an inexorable physical necessity. Restraint! What possible restraint? Was it superstition, disgust, patience, fear — or some kind of primitive honour? No fear can stand up to hunger, no patience can wear it out, disgust simply does not exist where hunger is; and as to superstition, beliefs, and what you may call principles, they are less than chaff in a breeze. Don't you know the devilry of lingering starvation, its exasperating torment, its black thoughts, its sombre and brooding ferocity? Well, I do. It takes a man all his inborn strength to fight hunger properly. It's really easier to face bereavement, dishonour, and the perdition of one's soul—than this kind of prolonged hunger. Sad, but true. And these chaps, too, had no earthly reason for any kind of scruple. Restraint! I would just as soon have expected restraint from a hyena prowling among the corpses of a battlefield. But there was the fact facing me—the fact dazzling, to be seen, like the foam on the depths of the sea, like the ripple on an unfathomable enigma . . .[3]

This fragment of Conrad decimates many theories. But does it take away fear, the sick root of illusions people entertain about other people— the sort of fear that Marlow felt? We know that it cannot. Our world is pervaded by fear. In fact, our own time has seen fit to make revolutionary visions, such as Conrad's, of "other people" into mere theories too. Nevertheless, something new and extraordinarily important becomes visible here—and I believe it has everything to do with the reality of religion that Durkheim spoke about. Skepticism about *mere ideas* appears at the beginning of our age. To me it seems a good omen.

Friedrich Nietzsche (born 1844) died in 1900. He is the archrebel of the late nineteenth century. One of his biographers calls him "the greatest diagnostician of European nihilism."[4] The same Nietzsche suffered from a hopeless insanity for more than the last ten years of his life. He was against Kant—the fountainhead of German idealism. He turned against the composer Wagner (after a period of infatuation with his music). He was against Christianity, most specifically the petty Lutheranism he knew so well from his upbringing. Being a poet as much as a philosopher, he was not taken seriously by philosophers. What this rebel was *for* has been a subject of debate ever since he started writing, although during his life very few bought his books. In this respect, he resembles Kierkegaard. Also like Kierkegaard, he did not seem to belong in the nineteenth century. But there the comparison ends. The German Nazis believed that Nietzsche's work prefigured their cause, particularly because of his invention and praise of the *Übermensch,* the "superman." It is largely due to his domineering younger sister that Nietzsche became a legend. It was she who took care of him after his mother's death, when he lost his mind and spent years in an asylum. She had meddled in his life before, and then saw fit to commit forgeries in his work. A veritable cult came into being around him in Weimar after his death.

How is this man important to our topic? To begin with, there is the curious fact that of the friends the sound-minded Nietzsche had during his life, only one remained a faithful visitor after he lost his mind, and that man was a Christian theologian, Franz Overbeck. Even more curious, Overbeck was a major teacher of another theologian who was certainly the most important of the twentieth century: the Swiss Karl Barth. It should go without saying that especially in the case of a figure as controversial as Nietzsche, we cannot speak of a direct line of influence. Nietzsche surely did not hold to any party line. On the contrary, it seemed as if in his judgment anyone with an idea had to suffer for it. Many a blow by Nietzsche seems to hit everyone ("Nothing is more banal among people than death; second in rank is birth, for some die without ever having come to life; thereafter comes marriage").[5]

Nietzsche gave voice to an uneasiness that in the course of time more and more people became aware of. It was an uneasiness over our uses of our intellect and courage. Where were the empire builders of Germany, England, Belgium, taking us? Who and what were the scholars and scientists so busily at work with their approval? To my knowledge, Nietzsche never expressed compassion with colonized peoples, as did Conrad; his interest and his wrath descended upon intellectuals, their unintelligent optimism and pretense of being scientific, above all their hypocrisy and self-deception. In his elaborate correspondence, the warmest, most intimate letters are addressed to Franz Overbeck, to whom he writes in the summer of 1886: "The best people degenerate in this university air: I continually sense as background and as a last resort, even with characters like R., a damnable general indifference and a complete lack of faith in their object."[6]

Most people are aware of Nietzsche's declaration that God is dead. It seems to me that the frequent references to those words—Nietzsche said that God is dead—rest on a careless reading, or are mere parrot-prattle. This "God-is-dead" mantra has taken on a life of its own, an automatic phrase comparable to *Marx said religion is the opiate of the people.* When I hear "As Nietzsche said . . . ," I look for the exit. The habit is not as innocent as it seems. Ever since some Germans in the 1930s took Nietzsche for a model-Nazi, the custom of making him pull the wagon of any newfangled party has become a mark of the clueless and resentful among us. It is indeed true that Nietzsche spoke several times of the death of God. The principal occasion where he did so is worth looking at. It comes up in *Thus Spoke Zarathustra,* of which the first part was published in 1883. When those who quoted Nietzsche actually got around to reading him, that is where they found what they were looking for. The first thing they should have noticed is the exclamation point that follows his words. What we have before us is not a reasoned philosophical proposition; it is more like a scream. The words on God's death *break in.* Nietzsche has his strange character, Zarathustra, pop up in the first sentence, seemingly out of nowhere: "When Zarathustra was thirty years old he left his home and the lake of his home and went into the mountains."[7] He addresses the sun, whose happiness consists in shining on him, and his cave, and on the others. And Zarathustra decides to "go down," as the sun does when it meets the earth, and spread his wisdom "until the wise among men find joy once again in their folly, and the poor in their riches."[8] Going down, thus having become a man again, according to the story, Zarathustra meets an old sage who recognizes him and asks whether he is not afraid to be punished as an arsonist for his descent back to earth after communing with the sun. Why does he want to embrace human life again? Zarathustra answers, "I love man," and is warned that he will not be accepted.[9] The sage prefers to stay in the forest, making songs and praising God. What does Zarathustra have to offer anyone? Zarathustra does not answer the question and says, "What could I have to give you? But let me go quickly lest I take something from you!"[10] The two laugh like boys, and Zarathustra continues his way down. Alone again, he asks himself, "Could it be possible? This old saint in the forest has not yet heard anything of this, that God *is dead!*"[11] Then Zarathustra begins to teach mankind about the *Übermensch* who is to rise above himself.

This beginning suffices to mystify the reader, in spite of its mythlike quality. I won't venture upon an interpretation of an author who is not known for bringing about agreement among his readers. However, facts on the surface cannot be ignored. The name Zarathustra is remarkable. It has been known in the West since the Greeks, in its hellenized form, Zoroaster, and it comes from the ancient Iranian reformer and prophet, the founder of Zoroastrianism. At the time Nietzsche wrote, serious philological study had just begun, and the first translated texts from the Avesta, the Zoroastrian sacred scriptures, had appeared. The Frenchman James Darmesteter (1849–94), with the collaboration of the Englishman L. H. Mills, prepared the three-volume text in English—a publication success of the first order—for Max Müller's *Sacred Books of the East*. The first text was in print in 1883, and the set was completed in 1887. The year 1883 also saw the publication of the first part of *Thus Spoke Zarathustra*. However, Darmesteter had published major works on Avestan studies before, in French. The Francophile Nietzsche was undoubtedly aware of the texts from which he borrowed the name Zarathustra. References to Zoroaster as a figure vying in antiquity and authority with ancient Egyptian texts were part of scholarly and speculative tradition. In the Enlightenment, Voltaire and his spiritual kin invoked the name of Zoroaster to stir up many a mind, setting him side by side with Confucius as a model of "natural religion." Nietzsche, working with his own poetic talents, made use of philological scholarship, which was by now well established, to challenge the world around him with his Zarathustra—more vehemently than anyone before him. In terms of religion, this vehemence becomes all the more apparent if we know something about the context of the final decades of the nineteenth century. During that time the first university chairs were created for the study of the history of religions. This did not happen without a great deal of opposition, from governments and from Christian theologians. The opposition was strongest in those institutions where the chairs were established in the theological faculties, as in Geneva in 1873, and in each of the four public universities in Holland in 1876. In the following years, Germany acquired its chairs in various universities, also in theological faculties (with the exception of Leipzig, where it was established in the division of history and literary studies). Afterward, suspicions on the part of theologians never faded.

Persistent misgivings with respect to the "scientific study of religion" were of course not fanned merely by an outsider's imaginative use of Zarathustra. The work of Nietzsche as a whole, however, was to many a danger sign, threatening the central Christian theological position. The achievements of historical-critical scholarship, especially in its concentration on the biblical texts, had already touched that bulwark.[12] But the turning toward all religious traditions of the world amounted to a shake-up worse than anything that had come before. The scholarship of men like Tylor, taking place outside the strict boundaries of theological schools, had not been a comparable threat. It was even less threatening in that it meant the beginning of anthropology, separate in organization from the precinct of theology. The comparative historical study, by contrast, dealing with the great religions of the past and present, religions with articulate, sometimes doctrinal, claims to universal validity, was sensed as an unconcealed attack undermining biblical revelation.

The beginning of *Thus Spoke Zarathustra,* to which we must limit ourselves here, is symptomatic of the chaotic turning of events, the skepticism, and the fears of skepticism, that take us into our own time. Nietzsche's condemnation of Christianity is no doubt more open to our understanding today than it was before the turn of the twentieth century. If we consider even the few lines of Nietzsche we have quoted, we cannot fail to see him otherwise than as a great poet who would be incomprehensible without his conditioning by Christianity. Of course, he criticized it severely, as much as the Germans of whom he was nevertheless one himself. The "going down" of Zarathustra into the human world is not an altogether new image. It is an overhaul of the cardinal Christian symbolism of the incarnation. In what sense is this a threat? Nietzsche's doings cannot be equated with atheisms of a louder, materialistic, "nihilistic" type. Students much more dispassionate than I have spoken of him as a mystic and a poet, and have given him a special place in a worldwide context.[13] Nietzsche's critique (not only of Christianity, but also of other religions, notably Buddhism) is a great deal stronger than that of the average skeptical atheist. Basic inner contradictions in his many writings, interminable debates he unleashed, do not detract from the passionate skepticism he voiced. Perhaps it is not out of order to think back to the prophet Amos for the sake of comparison. He too despised the religion he saw practiced around him. We remember that no living tradition stays alive without change, without critique.

If the line from Nietzsche, by way of his friend, the theologian Overbeck, to the theologian Karl Barth, has any validity, it is not as a causal nexus. Rather it is in the connection between the self-doubt and mental turmoil of which Nietzsche was the great analyst, and the many, many questions we have now learned to voice without hesitation. Typically, Barth, the Christian theologian, suggested that the Christian notion of "sin" might be in need of some new thought. Whereas the ancient church saw *superbia,* human conceit, as the greatest sin, Barth proposed to consider instead *stupidity* the worst. In fact, Nietzsche, at the beginning of our age, saw a great deal of stupidity, not only in the church, but in the sciences — including history, and not excluding such new disciplines as sociology. In all those instances, he saw the horror of stupidity in the lack of concern for what it truly meant *to know.* Aren't we familiar with the need to keep addressing that question?

Next to Conrad, who does not make his religious adherence explicit, and next to Nietzsche, whose antireligious pronouncements are numerous, we should look for a moment at one of the more unusual Christians who open the twentieth century. Charles Péguy (1873–1914), the French poet and essayist, embraced a Christianity that was itself unusual. Péguy was a socialist, and for socialists to be linked to an official religious tradition was definitely strange at the time. However, he went through a conversion — not one of an emotional, pious sort, yet introspectively, and above all, reflectively. As a result, he was not generally recognized as the Catholic Christian he became, nor by the socialists, who, even if they admired him, were puzzled. Until today, in literary circles he was controversial. François Mauriac, a most distinguished figure in literature, was told that Julian Green, himself well known in literature, was translating some of Péguy's works into English. Mauriac responded: "What a pity that someone doesn't translate him into French!"[14]

The sheer fact of the controversies surrounding Péguy is significant. He was not a person who could fit into any party or system. And in very difficult circumstances he devoted all his energy to issues that mattered. He organized a journal that in the years after his death in 1914 gained more fame than it did in the fifteen years of its publication. Péguy died in the first great battle of the First World War. He had joined the army as a volunteer — another rather unusual thing for a socialist. I want to single out some lines from an essay that illustrate his talent for writing about very common things that not a single "party" or "system" or literary "trope" would be able to do justice to. The word *religion* does not appear, and yet, it is the ordinariness, the givenness of religion in human existence, that to me seems the force in this passage. History herself, the muse Clio, speaks:

Look, she said, at this man of forty. Maybe we know him, Péguy, our man of forty. Maybe we are beginning to know him. Maybe we are beginning to hear speak of him. He is forty, so he *knows.* The knowledge that no teaching can impart, the secret that no method can prematurely entrust, the knowledge that no discipline confers nor is able to confer, the teaching that no school can disseminate, he *knows*. Being forty, he has, in the most natural way in the world, to say the least, received news of the secret that is known to the most people in the world, but which is nonetheless the most hermetically kept. . . . For he knows the great secret, of every creature, the secret that is most universally known but which, nonetheless, has never been leaked, the preeminent secret of State, the secret that is the most universally entrusted, little by little, from one person to another, on chance roadways, and, yet, the secret that is most hermetically secret. The container of secrets that is the most hermetically sealed. The secret that has never been written down. The most widely revealed secret, and that from the people of forty has never passed, beyond the thirty-seventh, beyond the thirty-fifth, beyond the thirty-third year, has never descended to the people below. He knows; and he knows he knows. He knows that one is not happy. He knows that ever since there has been man no man has ever been happy . . . it is surely, the only belief, the only knowledge he values, in which he feels and knows his honor to be engaged, precisely the only one in which there is no understanding, no mask, no connivance. To say it outright, no adherence, no compliance, no *Good will*. No obligingness. No goodness. Now, note the inconsistency. The same man. This man naturally has a son of fourteen. And he has but one thought, that his son should be happy. And he does not tell himself that it would be the first time; that this has yet to be seen. He tells himself nothing at all, which is the sign of the deepest thought. . . . He has an animal thought. Those are the best kind. Those are the only ones. He has only one thought. And it is an animal thought. He wants his son to be happy. He thinks only of this, that his son should be happy. He has another thought . . . a sort of scrupulous and consuming mania. He has only one concern, the judgment that his son, in the secret of his heart, will pass on him. He wants to read the future solely in the eyes of his son. He searches the depths of his eyes. That which has never succeeded, never happened, he is convinced will happen this time. And not only that, but that it will happen as if naturally and smoothly. As a result of some sort of natural law. And history said, I say that nothing is as touching as this perpetual, this eternal, this eternally reborn inconsistency; and that nothing is as disarming before God, and we have here the common miracle of your young Hope. But, she said, suddenly stopping, here we come back to lands you have cleared forever.[15]

Is it such a great discovery that no person is happy? The translator of the passage from which I am taking these lines, Annette Aronowicz, remarks:

> The secret of the man of forty is . . . reminiscent of the famous four visions of the Buddha. The latter, upon seeing a sick man, an old man, a dead man and a monk, realizes that all is suffering. In both cases, there is a head-on collision with our transitory estate, with the fact that time defeats us in our deepest aspirations and will continue to defeat us.[16]

The reminder of the experience of the man who was to become the Buddha seems convincing to me. We may want to economize on our use of the term *religion,* but let us not overdo that. The Enlightenment of the Buddha is not an object of psychology or any other positive science.

Many authors, scholars, and thinkers of the last hundred years have tried to express the "secret" of religion. At the very beginning of this new age of ours, Péguy saw it most clearly, I think. Whether we all are equally impressed by Conrad, Nietzsche, and Péguy, is not important. That all three make a fundamental shift visible with respect to uncritically held assumptions and optimisms should be clear. None of them, it seems to me, came as close to the subject of religion at the very outset of our new age as did Péguy. We could have quoted more from his passage; Clio says about this man, Péguy, who has discovered the secret of life, that it doesn't matter in the least whether he is a philosopher or not, an intellectual or not. The absence of any great revelation, the ordinariness of religion (as we have called it before) is far from being trivial. It is indispensable in human existence. The three great writers we have just looked at did not want to say the word *religion* for the most important thing they wanted to express. The issue of religion, even if we shun the name, even if it is "the lands you have cleared forever," keeps coming back. It does not recur merely as an aggregate of materials, objectively given to our analyses and systems, to be kept at a safe distance, but also as what Kierkegaard called "religiosity B," the peculiar something that issues forth as the only purpose of life, around which everything else reveals its meaning. The old word, we remember, is *salvation.*

Literature
Joseph Conrad, *The Heart of Darkness* (Harmondsworth: Penguin, 1983); Walter Kaufmann, ed. and trans., *The Portable Nietzsche* (New York: Viking-Penguin, 1982); Walter Kaufmann, ed. and trans., *Basic Writings of Nietzsche* (New York: Modern Library, 1968); Charles Péguy, *Basic Verities, Prose and*

Poetry, trans. Ann and Julian Green (New York: Pantheon, 1943); Charles Péguy, *Men and Saints, Prose and Poetry,* trans. Anne and Julian Green (New York: Pantheon, 1944).

GREAT MODERN THINKERS: WILHELM DILTHEY, EDMUND HUSSERL

The jump from the creative pioneers of around 1900 to the contemporary world is not difficult to make. The various modes of skepticism, anti-religious, a-religious, or religious—in gross terms, the order in which we might place Nietzsche, Conrad, and Péguy—have affected all of us deeply. The clearest sign of our link to them is our caution in using the term *religion.* We could take as an example our contemporary Octavio Paz, anthropologist, poet, literary essayist, and more. Paz has written that the path of poetic writing leads to the abolition of writing, for "at the end of it we are confronted with an inexpressible reality."[17] According to him, the reality revealed by poetry appears *behind* language. It is "the reality visible only through the destruction of language that the poetic act represents." Worst (or could it be best?) of all, this reality "is literally intolerable and maddening."[18] Undeniably, we have grown most reluctant to say "religion." We have come a long way from the Romantics, who would not have hesitated to associate the inexpressible reality with the divine. We have also moved away from the nineteenth-century theorists of religion who thought they had their subject firmly under control.

Before we turn to students of religious documents who did their work in the twentieth century, let us first speak of two thinkers whose lifetimes spanned the opening of the twentieth century and to whom the adjective *great* can be assigned without contradiction. We begin with some words about the German thinker-historian Wilhelm Dilthey (1833–1911), in order to set the scene for Edmund Husserl (1859–1938).

Dilthey was one of the first articulate critics of the prevailing thought of the nineteenth century. He was not conservative, and was certainly not afraid of the ascending natural sciences. He became concerned with Immanuel Kant's philosophy insofar as it catered to the natural sciences more than to other inquiries. Almost as much as in the case of Descartes, mathematics, closely followed by physics, seemed a model for Kantian thought. As students of religious facts, even at present, we can sympathize with Dilthey's concerns. The name of Kant marked the age of *knowledge.*

But what about experience—even experience that does not result in "knowledge"? What about ritual? Or hope? What about (theological) eschatology, rather than (philosophical) teleology?

This one-sidedness was a major cause of uneasiness in some nineteenth-century thinkers and artists—such as Conrad, Nietzsche, and Péguy, whom we have seen. In some, the reaction tended toward pessimism. So it did in many Germans: the philosopher Schopenhauer, the composer Richard Wagner, the historian Jacob Burckhardt; but also in the French originator of racist theories Joseph-Arthur Gobineau (obsessed as he was with the "degeneration" of the human race). The German Max Scheler (1874–1928), who has occasionally been counted among the mighty in the study of religions, was not free from pessimistic views either; in addition to works like *The Eternal in Man,* he produced a sizable book intended to stir up the patriotic passions of his country in the First World War—a prelude to the horrors and suicides of the twentieth century. Even Nietzsche's frequent mention of the horrors of decadence—the opposite of the *Übermensch* ideal—can be counted with the fallout of pessimism. Some reactions to the mental climate of the nineteenth century, however, were of a different, forward-looking bent, as we have already seen, and these included the work of the great American thinkers William James (1842–1910) and Charles Sanders Peirce (1839–1914).

Dilthey, of special significance for historians, has received a wide audience. The Spanish philosopher-historian José Ortega y Gasset (1883–1955), who brought Dilthey's work to the attention of the Spanish-speaking world, called him, "to my mind, the most important thinker of the second half of the nineteenth century."[19] (The first edition of Dilthey's collected works outside Germany appeared in Mexico in eight volumes.) Born in 1833, Dilthey was himself a nineteenth-century man. He, however, faced up to the peculiar chaos that came about in his time. As a historian, he realized fully how the ideas of philosophers are inadequate to arouse people from their mental obliviousness, and the slumber that had now come over them again. What do we really understand of history? The question seems even more relevant to America today than it was to the Germany of Dilthey! And beyond this question, more generally, looms another: how can we deal with human matters at all? Thus Dilthey came to devote himself to what he called the "human sciences" (*die Geisteswissenschaften*). Quite consciously, Dilthey saw his own work in contrast to Kant's. Kant had written his *Critique of Pure Reason.* Dilthey coined the expression "critique of historical reason." Thus we can look upon Dilthey's work as an attempt to present a philosophy for the *humanities,* in analogy and in contrast to what Kant had done for the exact sciences. To quite an extent it is possible to see Dilthey in this light. Dilthey himself makes much of the distinction between understanding (*verstehen*) and explaining (*erklären*). Explaining is what the exact sciences aim for. *Verstehen,* understanding, is what history and the other humane disciplines do. However, Dilthey does not construct this distinction as an absolute opposition. Historians also look for explanatory causes of events that have occurred. And astronomers who observe and calculate celestial phenomena are likely to think about a coherency in the universe that is understandable. At the same time, however, historians, let us say, of the French Revolution, are likely to spend most of their time *understanding* the documents that tell them of human motivation and social and ideological settings in which events occurred. Astronomers do not spend most of their time "understanding" the major forces that move the world. *We speak of understanding primarily when we confront human documents.* This is the activity to which Dilthey's work is devoted. For this reason alone, the logic, the whole procedure of Kant's philosophy would not do as a foundation for the *Geisteswissenschaften.* The striking thing about human beings is that they are always historical beings. This human reality is crucial. Dilthey is also regarded as the initiator of the "philosophy of life" or "vitalism" (*Lebensphilosophie*), as distinct from the abstractions of other philosophies. Dilthey does his best to develop categories in his system of human sciences which can function as well as "time" and "space" in physics. There, predictably, the difficulties begin. Categories such as "pattern" and "meaning" are indispensable for the student of history or literature, but are far more difficult to define, and virtually impossible to calculate in formulas.[20] Dilthey never completed his system. Much was left in draft form. We should realize that as a matter of fact, had it become a "complete system" Dilthey's work might have defeated its own purpose. Ortega y Gasset, admiring Dilthey, and more direct in his writing than Dilthey, sums up the key theme:

> Life only takes on a measure of transparency in the light of *historical reason.*
>
> The most disparate forms of being *happen* to man. To the despair of the intellectualist, *being* is in man mere *happening, happening to him:* it "happens to him to be" a Stoic, a Christian, a rationalist, a vitalist. It happens to him to be the paleolithic female and the Marquise de Pompadour, Jenghiz Khan and Stefan George, Pericles and Charles Chaplin.[21]

After praising what we might learn from Dilthey, we must ask some questions. Do we need two different types of logic, one for historians, the other for physicists? Here Edmund Husserl comes in. Husserl was younger, and in most ways different from Dilthey. At first, it seemed as if the two cherished a common cause, or causes similar enough to bring them together. Dilthey's categories in the human studies were perhaps not perfect, but they were appropriate for their object. And Husserl became famous overnight as a philosopher through his outspoken concern for proper method. He is known first of all for his destruction of "psychologism." "Psychologism," as we have already seen, can be described as an undue, methodologically erroneous concentration on psychology; it is the endeavor to cast the rules of logic in terms of psychological laws. Many a well-known philosopher, such as Stuart Mill, has relied on it. In terms of the scheme for approaching our discipline which we tried to develop at the beginning of this book, the problem with psychologism is that it ignores the distinction between the left- and the right-hand side. A state of affairs or a mechanism in a human psyche cannot be equated with a certainty in logic. In general, a person who wants to establish what is true in his or her field of research can do so only by appealing to principles of thought—not merely your thought or my thought, or the unanimity of minds we have canvassed. (For this reason logic is closely associated with mathematics, another discipline that does not wholly depend on individual minds.) These principles have everything to do with such things as noncontradiction, or the *consistency* we demand in any mental operation.

One would imagine that Dilthey liked Husserl's work. However, unlike Dilthey, Husserl was primarily a mathematician who worked on problems of astronomy and physics. (He had earned his doctorate in Vienna with a dissertation on the calculus of variations.) We should note that out of sheer curiosity Husserl sat in on the classes of Franz Brentano in Vienna. Brentano was an influential thinker but also a former priest. He fell in love and married; one did not do such things at the time. Even the government of Austria got involved, thus compounding his notoriety. However, it was not the gossip surrounding Brentano but Brentano's teaching that held Husserl's interest, and thus he became a philosopher.

Husserl developed his own perspective in philosophy. His scope was more embracing than the problem of finding a systematic, justifiable method for history, as was the case with Dilthey. Dilthey and Husserl did talk to one another, but when Husserl sent Dilthey his essay, published in 1910–11, "Philosophie als strenge Wissenschaft" ("Philosophy as a Rigorous

Science"), Dilthey must have realized Husserl's incompetence with respect to history. Dilthey died without answering Husserl. Quite strikingly, Husserl has virtually nothing to say about religion in his generalizations about civilization. In spite of his critical mind, he was still living in a period when it was common to believe in "the Greek miracle." He speaks about the contributions of the Greeks (especially of course in the development of philosophy), but Israel and Judaism do not figure anywhere in his expositions. In this one respect Husserl was much more a child of his age than were some of his younger contemporaries (such as the philosophers and theologians Franz Rosenzweig, Martin Buber, Karl Barth, K. H. Miskotte, and Reinhold Niebuhr, or the historians of religions Raffaele Pettazzoni and G. van der Leeuw).

What then is Husserl's importance? Very few philosophers would not consider him among the greatest. For us his importance has everything to do with what early in this book we came to refer to as a "scheme" for approaching our studies. Husserl did not say, "Everything is chaos in our mental lives," nor did he say, "If only we follow the methods of the sciences that have proved so successful, everything will be all right." Rather he said what we could phrase as follows: "The academic world we are in is filled with disciplines of study that go every which way. The worst thing that can happen is this: we pick our object of study and then we make our method of dealing with our object look as if it had absolute validity, and as if what we do had no bearing on a common quest." The relevance of these views—which Husserl elaborated in infinite ways—can hardly be overestimated. Husserl, with his interest in the exact sciences, was thoroughly aware of methods that can lead to results and yet be logically in conflict with each other. And obviously, different inquiries in various specializations—the study of law, of religion, of history, of biology—can grow apart so as to make discussion of "the quest for knowledge" seem meaningless. Husserl, often in very complex ways, speaks of the ordinary reality from which all inquiry must begin and to which it must return. This is as true for students of religions as it is for students of genetics.

Husserl called his work "phenomenology." *Phenomenon* is a Greek word that means "something that appears." It is an old term and was used by Hegel. However, to some extent Husserl used *phenomenon* in contrast to *noumenon*, "something that is thought," a term of importance especially in Kant's philosophy. Kant and Kantianism can of course not be summed up in a term any more than can Husserl. However, Kant's inspiration by mathematics and physics (in the tradition of Descartes) had led him to a preoccupation with concepts, mental constructs. Husserl's turn toward *phenomena* rather than *noumena* implies a general change in attitude. In a simple way, we can understand this change as the view that the objects we choose for our inquiry have something to say. For historians certainly this suggestion should not be surprising: all their documents have a voice. On this point, there is and remains a certain agreement between the work of Dilthey and that of Husserl which inspired many scholars who were not professional philosophers. An entire phenomenological movement developed. We should not mistake this movement for a "school." The variety of people touched (*touched* may be a more appropriate term than influenced) by Husserl is astounding. Most generally, one might say that even the most specialized empiricists, trained to focus on their object of study, were stimulated to listen more attentively to the voice of their documents.

In philosophy, many who might not call themselves phenomenologists owe much to Husserl. In a wide context, we may mention the French thinkers Gabriel Marcel (1889–1973), Jean-Paul Sartre (1905–80), Maurice Merleau-Ponty (1908–61), Paul Ricoeur (born 1913), Henry Duméry (born 1920), and Emmanuel Levinas (1905–95); the Spaniard José Ortega y Gasset (1883–1955); and the Germans Martin Heidegger (1889–1976) and Karl Jaspers (1883–1969). Many a work in positive fields of research was inspired by Husserl's thought. In sociology, the founder of phenomenological sociology, Alfred Schütz (1899–1959), wrote *The Phenomenology of the Social World.*[22] Among historians of science, the well-known Frenchman Alexandre Koyré (1892–1964) should be mentioned. In the history of religions, G. van der Leeuw became the founder of a phenomenology of religion. Among psychologists affected by the phenomenological change, the Swiss Carl Gustav Jung is best known. Jung in turn became an inspiration for a popular American writer on religious subjects, Joseph Campbell, and for many others as well. This list could be extended. It is meant to show that the "phenomenological movement" was not a self-contained doctrine, but a change of attitude in scholarship. In terms of influence on academic pursuits, it had a much more direct significance than the voices of the great writers around the turn of the century. It was of tremendous importance to the history of religions.

A footnote might be added. The slow development of the general and comparative religio-historical study in the United States might at least in part be due to the hesitance of American philosophers to come to terms with the phenomenological movement. Granted that nothing seemed more commonsensical than to investigate what the phenomena actually said, phenomenologists often seemed to indulge too much in theory. Whatever the precise reasons, and in spite of many a critical voice since William James directed against philosophical idealism and positivism, positivistic tendencies have remained fairly persistent in North America, even when the term *positivism* was shunned. Not only Husserl but also even Dilthey seem to have gained acceptance with great difficulty.[23] The tendency to look upon religions as simple "objects" to be explained rather than to be understood as realities in the human world has remained strong until the present time.

Literature
José Ortega y Gasset, *History as a System and Other Essays Toward a Philosophy of History* (New York: Norton, 1961); H. P. Rickman, ed. and introd., *Wilhelm Dilthey, Pattern and Meaning in History: Thought on History and Society* (New York: Harper, 1961); Wilhelm Dilthey, *Selected Works,* vol. 1, *Introduction to the Human Sciences* (Princeton: Princeton University Press, 1989); Edmund Husserl, *The Crisis of European Sciences and Transcendental Phenomenology,* trans. David Carr (Evanston, Ill.: Northwestern University Press, 1970).

Ludwig Joseph Johann Wittgenstein and Karl Jaspers

The French poet Charles Péguy was concerned with a theme he referred to as the distinction between *politique* and *mystique*. He complained that the politicians of his day had lost sight of what the republic created by the French Revolution was really about. The political maneuvering, the cheap ideologizing that he witnessed was a mockery of the spirit that had brought about the living community experienced and shared by all a century earlier. The *mystique*—which we might translate as "the prophetic spirit"—seemed to have perished. Péguy sought to bring it back to life. All of us in modern industrialized countries know what Péguy was talking about. The reality that surrounds us is political and spiritual at the same time. Our discussions on politics as a rule are oriented by spiritual impulses, even when we are not sure how to realize them in the realities of politics.

This takes our discussion to Wittgenstein (1889–1951), not a poet but a philosopher who was fascinated with the problem of what we can say correctly, what we cannot say correctly, and what we can say not at all. An Austrian by birth, he taught philosophy at Cambridge, England. His *Tractatus Logico-Philosophicus* established his fame.[24] No one less than Bertrand Russell introduced it to the world when it was first published in 1922. In his own preface, Wittgenstein writes, "The whole sense of the book might be summed up in the following words: what can be said at all can be said clearly, and what we cannot talk about we must pass over in silence."[25]

The introduction by Bertrand Russell adds that the treatise "applies the results of this inquiry to various departments of traditional philosophy."[26] Considering that the entire text comprises barely seventy-five pages, the achievement is breathtaking. Wittgenstein moves from an exposition of the principles of symbolism (in the sense of logical signs) through epistemology, principles of physics, and ethics, to a concluding discussion of what he calls "the mystical." As a Dutchman living in the United States, I can understand how the clarity and brevity of Wittgenstein exerted a greater appeal than the lengthy and repetitive elaborations of Husserl, even though each in his own way dealt with the need for honesty in our thought. Wittgenstein's statements touching on problems in the theory of knowledge are remarkably expressive of modesty—not merely of Wittgenstein himself, but of what human beings are able to say on the subject. It may be true that all Husserl's writing is worth reading, yet on many of Husserl's subjects, Wittgenstein summed up what mattered in one proposition. We know about Husserl's destruction of "psychologism," but Wittgenstein said, "Psychology is no more closely related to philosophy than any other natural science."[27] Observe the modesty in the following: "A proposition is a picture of reality," followed immediately by "A proposition is a model of reality as we imagine it." Philosophical propositions cannot be confused with final truths.

With respect to religious matters, Wittgenstein's notion of "the mystical" of course may exert a special attraction. However, in Wittgenstein's discussion it is more important for an understanding of the limits of our knowledge than for a comprehension of "the sacred." On the very last page of the *Tractatus* we read, "There are, indeed, things that cannot be put into words. They *make themselves manifest*. They are what is mystical."[28] What shows itself cannot be ignored. What shows itself is precisely what others called "a phenomenon," as we have seen. Earlier in his book Wittgenstein had already used the term *manifest* with special emphasis: "A proposition shows its sense" or "makes it manifest."[29] Words are significant, yet by themselves remain limited.

The last sentence in the *Tractatus* has been quoted often: "What we cannot speak about we must pass over in silence."[30] It cannot be construed in such a manner as to mean that we cannot speak about religious matters that make themselves manifest. Wittgenstein himself makes this very clear in a little, almost unknown essay, *Remarks on Frazer's Golden Bough*.[31]

The Scotsman Sir James Frazer (1854–1941) is among the many scholars of repute in the study of religion whom we have not mentioned. Frazer reaped fame with an enormous work, *The Golden Bough: A Study in Magic and Religion,* which upon completion contained twelve volumes (1907–15). In spite of the quantity and diversity of materials collected from classical antiquity and tribal life in the modern world, all these tomes are held together by two ideas. One is that religion originated from magic, and that magic, which is still present among "the primitives," was nothing but an erroneous attempt at rationality or science. The other idea consists of Frazer's preoccupation with "fertility," and it pervades the work on almost every page. Whatever ancient Roman peasants did in ritual circumambulation of their fields, and whatever Indian peasants do today that is comparable in acts of sacrifice, and so forth, is all in the (mistaken) belief that fertility would thus be stimulated. I remember how satisfactory this work used to be to scholars. One of my less pleasant memories is of a professor of ancient religions; whatever he spoke of in the religions of Greece or Egypt, one could predict the conclusion: fertility needed to be stimulated in the fields, the cattle, the women. Many a scholar, ruminating on what conclusions to draw, used to take Frazer off the shelf. For our survey here, Frazer is one more example of those who theorized in an uncritical, evolutionistic fashion. Moreover, he had none of the attractive features that characterized Tylor or Durkheim.

What do we read to our delight in Wittgenstein, who not as a scholar of religions but as a good analytical thinker reads the famous Frazer? It does not merely cut Frazer down to size, but many of us:

> Frazer's account of the magical and religious notions of men is unsatisfactory: it makes these notions appear as *mistakes.*
>
> Was Augustine mistaken, then, when he called on God on every page of his Confessions?
>
> Well—one might say—if he was not mistaken, then the Buddhist holyman, or some other, whose religion expresses quite different notions, surely was. But none of them was making a mistake except where he was putting forward a theory.[32]

If any reader of this book would like to remember anything written in it, I would hope it would be these few lines of Wittgenstein. They would help us to avoid perhaps not all but many of the errors we make.

The general shift in orientation that the twentieth century brought is, it seems to me, a cause for joy. The sobriety that has come over us makes us a great deal more cautious in theorizing. To add to our sobriety, it is not great students of religion but colleagues in other fields, including philosophers such as Wittgenstein, who made the difference.

Karl Jaspers (1883–1969) is counted among the existentialists. Like other existentialists, he owed the emphasis on "existence" to Kierkegaard, but he does not belong to the Christian existentialists. For him, the central importance of human existence does not exclude but requires the use of reason. He wrote a small book on "philosophical faith" (*Der philosophische glaube*), in which his rational analysis observes a distance between his "faith" and the faith Christians speak about. He knows that the limits of existence are met in suffering, death, and in the experience of love and of guilt. Clearly, he purposely discusses matters that do not fit in the frame of traditional abstractions. Without the notion of "transcendence" philosophy would be impossible for Jaspers. It is the task of human beings, as for philosophy, to reach the limits and beyond the limits. The goal is known as "being," but Jaspers does not mind using the term *God,* the most definitely "transcendental" term. Whatever the transcendent really is, it is not available to us except in symbols. Symbols are the forms by which the inner contradictions in which all human thought ends are resolvable. When such recognition occurs, a real human existence, "an authentic existence," is realized.

That connection between the use of symbols and the possibility of "authentic" existence is significant to students of religion. A contemporary of Jaspers, a New Testament scholar, Rudolf Bultmann, was of the opinion that the Gospel, in order to yield its message clearly, needed to be divested of its mythical (or symbolic) garments. The "three storey universe" of earth, heaven, and hell would not do in the modern world. Bultmann hoped that Heidegger, on whose work he had based his own, would respond to his interpretation. Heidegger did not, but Jaspers did. Predictably, Jaspers disagreed with Bultmann's rather wooden reasoning; Bultmann made it seem as if the evolution of our worldview had taken us to some sort of maturity in which symbols were no longer of use. A few of Jaspers's words will suffice to show how strong was the response from this non-Christian thinker:

There is no such thing as a modern worldview; what you call "the scientific features of the modern worldview" is nothing but what has existed for thousands of years in materialist, sensualist, and realistic thinking; the scientific superstition, which is universal today, has scarcely anything to do with modern science, except for the fact that a small part of that science so impresses by its technological results, that the scientific superstition finds in it the strongest support . . . [33]

Jaspers is not suggesting that modern science is superstition, but only that the circumstances we are in easily make it so. He points out that Bultmann's dealings with the biblical texts share such superstitiousness. He, Jaspers himself, would not think of treating the Bible in that way:

Even today, the Bible is the book most often printed, a book with which nearly a hundred generations of our ancestors lived; even men who do not recognize its sacred character agree that it is a work to be revered. . . . I would not leave out even resurrection of the dead, demons, or magic, if I could deal with these myths in such a way that it would occur to none of my listeners that they are empirical realities, and if they illumined something that would remain lost without such images. [34]

This is not exactly a confession of faith, but it makes sense. In our own language, if we decree the irrelevance of mythical expression, we would make all existence less than human. One does not need to be a religious convert to see that. Ordinary, fair reasoning suffices—unless, of course, one can explain a philosophical basis on which another stance becomes defensible.

Literature

Ludwig Wittgenstein, *Remarks on Frazer's Golden Bough,* trans. A. C. Miles, rev. Rush Rhees (Retford, England: Brynmill, 1983); Karl Jaspers, *Socrates, Buddha, Confucius, Jesus: The Paradigmatic Individuals,* ed. Hannah Arendt, trans. Ralph Manheim (New York: Harcourt, 1962); Karl Jaspers, trans. *Philosophy of Existence,* Richard F. Grabau (Philadelphia: University of Pennsylvania Press, 1984); Karl Jaspers, *Truth and Symbol,* trans. Jean T. Wilde, William Kluback, William Kummel, (New York: Twayne, 1959); Karl Jaspers and Rudolph Bultmann, *Myth and Christianity* (New York: Noonday Press, 1958); Karl Jaspers, *Der philosophische glaube* (Munich:

R. Piper, 1948); Karl Jaspers, *The Perennial Scope of Philosophy*, trans. Ralph
Manheim (New York: Philosophical Library, 1949).

"Reductionisms," More Philosophy, the Search for Certainty

"Reductionism" is explanation that belittles (reduces) the size or significance of whatever is explained. In the study of religion and religions it
can be a term of abuse romantically inclined students use for the ideas of
their critics. These critics in turn regard them as dreamers or zealots who
for the sake of their precious topic, religion, refuse to use reason. The
serious questions behind such squabbles are often obscured. Does our
rational ability suffice to explain the religious traditions of the world? Do
our techniques allow us to treat religion as an object we can investigate
fully? We should admit that some of the most impressive work of the nineteenth century came about by regarding people as objects. Anthropologists
and missionaries with good intentions entered territories of Africa that had
been conquered by machine gun; more than anything else, this terrible
new weapon spawned the myth of the superiority of the white man, who
was entitled to objectify the world.[35] What is objectivity, really, when we
speak of people, their lives, their orientation as human beings? Any objectivity can turn into something that is far from harmless. How is religion
"an object"? Doesn't it resemble the edge of the universe, a legitimate topic
of research, and yet, forever receding? Good intentions will never suffice.
What we think, what we say, *matters;* it affects people's lives.

Our present world and the state of education have made "reductionism"
into a habit. Many of us pass belittling judgment on fields remote from our
own in our labyrinthine universities. Though few such opinions appear in
print, their effect on what little interdepartmental discussion may exist is
lethal. Hardly a soul is aware of the division between humanities and sciences as a recent innovation—the result of problems Dilthey and some
others tried to solve. In general, historians of religions and anthropologists, though dealing largely with the same problems, subscribe to different
scholarly journals. The realization that knowledge should remain a unity to
be aimed for, that there is an ordinary reality we all return to and exist in,
does not arise without an effort. Few remember that our tradition of free
rational inquiry had a long and painful birth process. The achievements of

the natural sciences, linguistics, or history would not have materialized without it. There is an urgent need to remain alert in a field like ours that is so closely tied to the question of what it means "to know" in all academic inquiry. Since the first question arose concerning religions, the term *myth* has figured in the discussion. And with it came the paradox that it is truth, and yet can be equated with untruth. The opposition of myth and *logos* is of limited value and does not solve the problem; we remember that the Gospel of John in particular identifies the figure of Jesus Christ with the *logos*. Thus *logos* becomes myth.

Both Wittgenstein and Jaspers are fascinating for their ability to remain alive to the question of the "knowledge ground" on which we stand. Our subject demands that we try to understand as well those thinkers whose investigations seem perhaps more rigidly, exclusively rational, close to a caricature of Descartes, perhaps even of the positivism of Auguste Comte.

I have to muster some courage to mention the name of the German Rudolf Carnap (1891–1970), who, like so many, escaped Europe in the 1930s and came to the United States. He is a central figure in the tradition known as "logical positivism." His background was in mathematics and physics, and he remained a philosopher of science throughout his career, writing on subjects such as the logical structure of probability. He had a wide following among philosophers in his dealings with "language analysis." The subject of language was central also to Wittgenstein, but Carnap lacks Wittgenstein's depth of imagination, and for Carnap language is merely a logically consolidated system. For Carnap metaphysical and religious propositions fell outside the pale of sense.

Next to Carnap, many others could be named who exerted much influence in the twentieth century. Karl R. Popper (1902–94) too was fascinated by the sciences and the philosophy they required. It is fair to say about Carnap, Popper, and others that they summed up attitudes that were widely held, often by people who never read philosophy or science. The humanist who feels inclined to dismiss all "positivists" out of hand for their infatuation with the rigor of the exact sciences should remember that they too have continued their discussions. Neither Carnap nor anyone else said the last word. The philosophy of science may not always be interesting, but it has many more representatives today than even a few decades ago. And they continue to search for clarity in the logic of language in order to reach true propositions.

As we have noticed in our survey, not only have philosophy of religion and the general study of religions lived side by side, but often the transition between one and the other has been difficult to detect. From the days of Voltaire to David Hume, from Schelling to William James, thought about religions and endeavors to interpret the facts of religions were part of the same process. The accumulation of data in the nineteenth century, often requiring the study of difficult languages and literatures, made specialization inevitable. To quite an extent, specialization became customary also in philosophy. In our own day we can find, for instance, historians of religions who are philologically obsessed, and in fact never get around to reflecting on the questions religious data raise. I remember a scholarly meeting where a historian of religions discussed ancient Near Eastern texts and bragged of the up-to-date scientific nature of his work. After all, he explained, he analyzed the texts, made clear what they said, and if there were any questions about religion, he forwarded the materials to a psychoanalyst.[36] On the side of the philosophy of religion, we have the anomaly of scholars who are obsessed with theological propositions about the existence of God, or truth, or justice and evil. To be sure, in certain religions such propositional statements are made, and philosophers are habitually attracted to "propositions." But thinkers dealing with them overlook the fact that such propositions do not form the sum total of any religion, not even of Christianity (which they normally choose for their purposes). The results of the climate created by narrow concentration on questions that distort the religious documents unfortunately have consequences in wide circles. One bestselling book purports to deal with "monotheism."[37] The author locates the origin of "monotheism" in Israel, and its continuations in Christianity and Islam. It is not merely disturbing that monotheistic features elsewhere— as in certain forms of Hinduism—are ignored. What is fundamentally wrong is that the work leaves the impression that "monotheism" is a metaphysical creation of a specific religion. Yet "monotheism" is a mental construct, an abstraction, not a religious phenomenon; no one ever prays to "monotheism." The work confuses a concept with a historical religious experience. Such experiences are indeed historically traceable; the great Italian historian of religions Raffaele Pettazzoni studied the subject thoroughly, but the name of Pettazzoni does not even appear in this work on monotheism. In short, the work, in spite of its intention to present religion, gets mired in a jumble of superficial facts and transcendental hogwash. In sum, the reluctance of philosophers to look at religious data and the reluctance of historians and philologists to pay attention to sound reasoning both lead us astray.

In our era and into our own days, numerous students in the comparative history of religion and religions have struck a "sciencelike" pose, no doubt as a result of the perceived successes of the sciences. "Science" remains a flexible concept, and students who like to be associated with it are rarely versed in mathematics and physics. More often, they rely on what they think they understand of the "sciences in between," the disciplines that are often grouped together in university catalogs as "social sciences." These students are victims of the *de facto* separation of the humanities and the exact sciences. They are as a rule ignorant of Aristotle's significance in the development of physics and biology, hence what we call "the sciences" today. More likely, they are familiar with Aristotle only as a writer on ethics, rhetoric, and poetics, and imagine that "scientific" questions are a recent invention. The cumulative result of such misunderstandings is aggravated by their effect on aspiring science students, as they begin to believe that science is in all respects different from the humanities, and that required courses in the humanities are merely a hurdle, a senseless affliction they have to endure. If we could learn from our logical positivists no more than this one certainty, *that in principle all valid knowledge must be unified,* we would gain a great deal. The educational process would profit from the realization that no valid knowledge can come about in the isolation of each of our fields, least of all in the isolation of adjacent fields. No one can be seriously in favor of ceasing discussion among different disciplines, for in the problem of epistemology we cannot avoid meeting each other.

Literature
Thomas A. Idinopulos and Edward A. Yonan, eds., *Religion & Reductionism: Essays on Eliade, Segal, & the Challenge of the Social Sciences for the Study of Religion* (Leiden: Brill, 1994); Wilhelm Dupré, *Patterns in Meaning: Reflections on Meaning and Truth in Cultural Reality, Religious Traditions, and Dialogical Encounters* (Kampen, Netherlands: Kok Pharos, 1994); Charles H. Long, *Significations: Signs, Symbols, and Images in the Interpretation of Religion* (Philadelphia: Fortress, 1986); Jonathan Z. Smith, *Map Is Not Territory* (Chicago: University of Chicago Press, 1993); Paul Arthur Schilpp, ed., *The Philosophy of Rudolf Carnap* (La Salle, Ill.: Open Court, 1991); Richard Swinburne, *Responsibility and Atonement* (Oxford: Oxford University Press, 1989); Karl Popper, *The Poverty of Historicism* (London: Kegan Paul, 1979).

MANY WAYS OF STUDY

It is impossible in this introductory book to mention all the many excellent endeavors made over the last century in the study of specific religious issues and specific areas of religion in the world; some useful reference works are listed in the bibliography at the end of this section. The figures and issues selected for the present discussion are simply my personal choice.

Scholars are affected in every age by the general philosophical climate. In our own time, the division of labor between historians of religions and anthropologists is almost always visible, yet this division does not amount to a sharp separation in method. All work in the same climate. Even the subject matter they choose does not always reflect a division, although historians of religions have continued to deal with historical problems, while anthropologists, ever since their discipline began with the study of contemporary tribal societies, have continued to deal primarily with the world we are in now. In recent years city culture in Western society has attracted anthropological researches. Perhaps even more significant, a "humanistic anthropology" has begun to develop, whose aim is to break through the artificial barrier between social studies and the humanities.

Technical terms and concepts used by all in the study of religions have been largely of anthropological coinage.[38] Beginning with *animism* and *dynamism,* anthropology and sociology have been inventive in their keywords for the mystery of culture and religion. *Totemism* provided a focal point, preceding and surviving *animism* and *dynamism.* After the Second World War, with the growing influence of Freud, psychoanalytic terms came in here and there in anthropological writings to explain cultural behavior (*repression, projection,* etc.). The influence of the Swiss depth-psychologist C. G. Jung resulted in terms like *archetype* and *collective unconscious* appearing in various works that dealt with religious phenomena. (It should be noted that neither of these terms was originally psychological in meaning; *archetype* is a term in traditional Platonic discussion referring to the original pattern or model followed by all things of the same kind; *collective unconscious* derives from the "collective representations" in Durkheim's school and was passed on by the French philosopher Lucien Lévy-Bruhl [1857–1939], who dealt at length with "primitive thought.") *Functionalism* is yet another concept that was used in an endeavor to explain religion more adequately. Although the term came out of Durkheim's school, it attained its influence, though narrowed down considerably, through Bronislaw

Malinowski (1884–1942). Born in Poland, Malinowski was inspired by reading Sir James Frazer and taught at the University of London, later also in the United States at Cornell and Yale. He did outstanding fieldwork; his *Argonauts of the Western Pacific* is a masterpiece of anthropological description. Among his most famous subjects is the *kula* trade, the custom of natives to travel enormous distances over the Pacific in their canoes, with wares that to no observer can possibly possess commercial value, bringing back equally unmarketable items. The borderline of religion and economic function intrigued Malinowski. In the end, economic reality seems to have the upper hand in his theorizings. Everything "cultural" or "religious" is what it is as it "functions" within the whole of life and society; this makes sense to a good Western economist, yet that "whole" seems to escape our understanding. Though Malinowski is probably the most important founder of "social anthropology," his theories are not as impressive as the accounts of his field research. Of the scholars in the Durkheimian workgroup, Marcel Mauss was less reserved with respect to the problem of "the whole." In a splendid treatise entitled *The Gift,* he presents examples from various civilizations and periods where exchanges occur that do not allow a reduction to an economic function in any serious sense.[39] He does not avoid the term *religion,* but he defines all such facts as "'total' social phenomena" that, in fact like all religious symbols, never seem to disclose their secret completely. Concerns comparable to Malinowski's "functionalism" and Mauss's "function" suggested themselves to other scholars as well. The German sociologist Max Weber and others had argued even earlier in favor of the study of larger functioning wholes.

In general, the major tradition in anthropology has viewed "culture" as the umbrella under which religious phenomena occur and seem interpretable. By and large, historians of religions have held on to the specificity of "religion" and its paramount importance in human creativity. The American anthropologist Robert Redfield (1897–1958) was the first to turn his attention to "the little community," the social coherence that seems in many ways more essential than the larger whole (such as a people, a state, or a civilization) to which seekers of the meaning of culture had been drawn. Redfield's focus has been of great influence in and outside the field of anthropology. Victor Turner (1920–83) published his *Forest of Symbols* in 1967, and (coauthored with Edith Turner) *Image and Pilgrimage in Christian Culture* in 1978; the title of the latter clearly shows an interest beyond the confines of one field of study. Turner introduced the term *liminal* to indicate cultural features that took people (as in initiation ceremonies) into states of being that escape definition in hard, objective terms. The term *structuralism* covers a great many scholarly endeavors; it became widely known through the French anthropologist Claude Lévi-Strauss (born 1908). Lévi-Strauss was one of the most interesting anthropologists of the twentieth century. An excellent and prolific writer, he was also artistically talented, and his work is impossible to sum up under one rubric. He did most of his field-work in South America. There he noticed the order native traditions established in the world around them. Peoples wholly ignorant of "science" nevertheless made sense of the world. Basically, Lévi-Strauss addressed a philosophical problem that was especially intriguing to a Frenchman— just as the Durkheimian question about the mystery of society seemed to arise most clearly within the sphere of Descartes. The problem for Lévi-Strauss was the relation between empirical, manifold reality, and the mind, the function that is constituted to create order. An important principle for him is "binarism," that is, the principle of sets of two, best known to us for its significance in the construction of computers; Lévi-Strauss had borrowed it from linguistics, and saw it as fundamental to the human mind. The enormous importance of this prime ingredient in science gave a special weight to the thesis that it is at work everywhere in human culture. The structure of matter and the structure of human ideas seemed to be the same. Lévi-Strauss is a remarkable twentieth-century figure in the great French rationalist tradition. Moreover, it seemed as if in his analysis of human cultures he had solved the difference between Descartes and the empirically inclined John Locke. Kinship systems, myths, in fact everything in culture seemed open to the problem-solving mind. Whatever critique Lévi-Strauss's many works have been subjected to, more than any other anthropologist he succeeded in bringing anthropological questions out of the protected areas of specialists and into the public forum. The historian Mircea Eliade hardly ever made reference to his work, but I do remember one remark of praise Eliade made in conversation: "Claude Lévi-Strauss has the great virtue that he forces American anthropologists to *think*."

Among structuralists, the school of the Dutch anthropologist J. P. B. de Josselin de Jong (1886–1964) deserves mention. It produced many a fascinating study focusing on the "whole" of a community or set of interlacing symbols, less on the rationality that held it together, more on the life that flourished within it. Another anthropologist, Jan van Baal (1909–93), gained fame through his exhaustive study of communities in eastern Indonesia and New Guinea (West Irian).[40]

It is interesting to note that each and every anthropological study succeeds only in part. Each technical term was introduced as pointing in the right direction: *animism,* and all the others. Each one ended up creating more questions than it answered. But later in the twentieth century, important scholars themselves have been thoroughly aware of this. One value of their researches lies in the realization that the final answer to social, cultural, and religious existence is not within our reach. Interdisciplinary discussions, and more teamwork by scholars who are aware of the need for different perspectives, even if these are opposed to each other, are no doubt the most promising way. We shall arrive at the same conclusion by reviewing a few of the leading scholars who are close to or squarely planted in "the humanities."

Literature

Bronislaw Malinowski, *Magic, Science and Religion and Other Essays,* introd. Robert Redfield (New York: Doubleday, 1948); Bronislaw Malinowski, *Argonauts of the Western Pacific* (1922; New York: Dutton, 1961); Marcel Mauss, *The Gift: Forms and Functions of Exchange in Archaic Societies,* trans. Ian Cunnison (New York: Norton, 1967); Claude Lévi-Strauss, *Tristes Tropiques: An Anthropological Study of Primitive Societies in Brazil,* trans. John Russell (New York: Atheneum, 1964); Claude Lévi-Strauss, *The Scope of Anthropology,* trans. Sherry Ortner and Robert A. Paul (London: Jonathan Cape, 1974); Claude Lévi-Strauss, *The Savage Mind* (Chicago: University of Chicago Press, 1968); Octavio Paz, *Claude Lévi-Strauss, an Introduction,* trans. J. S. Bernstein and Maxine Bernstein (New York: Delta, 1967); Robert Redfield, *The Little Community and Peasant Society and Culture* (Chicago: University of Chicago Press, 1960); Jan van Baal, *Symbols for Communication: An Introduction to the Anthropological Study of Religion* (Assen, Netherlands: Van Gorcum, 1971); Rodney Needham, ed., *Right and Left: Essays on Dual Symbolic Classifications* (Chicago: University of Chicago Press, 1973). Anthologies and surveys of anthropological work: William A. Lessa and Evon Z. Vogt, eds., *Reader in Comparative Religion* (New York: Harper, 1979); Adam Kuper, *Anthropology and Anthropologists: The Modern British School,* rev. ed. (London: Routledge & Kegan Paul, 1993); Adam Kuper, *The Invention of Primitive Society: Transformations of an Illusion* (London: Routledge, 1988); Godfrey Lienhardt, *Social Anthropology* (London: Oxford University Press, 1966); T. K. Penniman, *A Hundred Years of Anthropology* (New York: Morrow, 1974); V. F. Calverton, ed., *The Making of Man: An Outline of Anthro-*

pology (New York: Modern Library, 1931); George W. Stocking, Jr., *Victorian Anthropology* (New York: Free Press, 1991).

TWENTIETH-CENTURY HISTORIANS OF RELIGIONS

The work of the German Rudolf Otto (1869–1937) affected many scholars who followed him. One book, first published in 1917, established his fame. It was *Das Heilige* ("The Sacred"), known in the English-speaking world as *The Idea of the Holy*.[41] It has been reprinted again and again. The central theme of the work is the uniqueness of the religious experience. It has often been pointed out that Rudolf Otto was a Lutheran and a Christian theologian and that his profession must have determined his interpretation to some extent. That is not impossible, but in explaining someone's theoretical view of religion, such an observation is not really helpful. Would we need to rely on the anticlerical views of David Hume in order to assess his philosophical views on religion? Considering the continual swings from more subjective to more objective methods and back again, one might almost look upon Otto's publication in the second decade of the twentieth century as a "natural" change under the dominating outlook of evolutionists and Marxists, who all thought they had a firm grip on the subject of religion; the time had come for someone to say something about the religious experience. Rudolf Otto, not by coincidence, found his point of departure in two figures who, although they were not central, had nonetheless never lost their prestige: Immanuel Kant and Schleiermacher. And certainly the latter of these two, as we have seen, made a case for the experience of religion. Schleiermacher spoke about the "feeling of dependence." Early in his book, Otto takes up the same subject but gives it a more exalted form. Schleiermacher meant no more than the human feeling of being merely a creature. To Otto, Schleiermacher's "feeling of dependence" seemed only to be a self-consciousness. Otto wanted to show that what is most typical of religion is the absolute feeling that refers to something utterly outside ourselves. That "something" Otto calls "the numinous." The term comes from the Latin *numen,* which means "a god" or "something divine." Otto was an excellent linguist, and he draws on a variety of texts with eloquent evidence for his thesis: Moses at the burning bush, awe-struck before the voice of God which orders him to do things that seem impossible; the Indian hero Arjuna imploring Krishna to reveal himself in his real, divine form, but when God fulfills his wish, Arjuna begs him to return to the familiar, less frightening (iconic) form. Otto completes his endeavor with a thesis that complements Kant's philosophical stance. Kant had spoken of two *a prioris*; the human mind has a predisposition to recognize what is true, and what is good. Otto proposes a third *a priori*: one that equips human beings with a sense for "the holy." Otto warns his readers not to confuse "the holy" with "the good." Neither the experience of Moses nor of Arjuna nor any such experience ever suggests a moral component to the sacred. The experience of the holy is something all by itself. Otto stresses the paradoxical nature of the numinous: it fills us with the utmost fear (the *tremendum*), and it fascinates and attracts us (the *fascinosum*). The most problematic pages in Otto are those where he tries to argue that in some way the holy, the absolutely other, is nevertheless relevant to the whole of human existence, including our social behavior. There he becomes a great deal less convincing. Was he too much of a theologian after all?

In Germany, the Scandinavian countries, Holland, and the United States, Otto's influence remained powerful for decades. It is no exaggeration to say that for many historians of religions he played the role that Tylor played for anthropology. Special circumstances in those nations accounted for Otto's acceptance; in those lands, traditionally the history of religions was taught in divinity schools—if it was taught at all. (In more recent times, with the growth of the social studies and especially the growth of state universities in the United States, the situation has changed.) It is striking that both in France and in Italy Otto's influence was much more limited from the beginning. Even if he was read, there were forces that counteracted his stress on the experience of the holy. The school of Durkheim was rather dominant in France; its interest in social facts did not mesh well with the experiential interest of Otto. We shall see that in Italy Otto's work was not completely accepted for similar reasons. The growing importance of the "objective" work of Pettazzoni did not create a hospitable climate for inquiries that were closer to "the experiential" and "the theological."

The rise of Raffaele Pettazzoni (1883–1959) was one of the most remarkable phenomena on the religio-historical scene in the twentieth century. He was the principal architect of the history of religions in Italy. This achievement is substantial. Italy was one of the last major countries of Europe to accept the field. Each country had had its own story of obstacles. In Italy, resistance on the part of some members of the clergy certainly played an important part. In the United States, by contrast, where the history of religions became accepted more easily, a benign neglect of the subject of "religion" among the educated, the intellectual's slight feeling of shame associated with it, and the vague sense that religion equals lack of intellectual training, are the main factors that make themselves felt. In Italy, many learned Catholics — the religion of the majority — saw the scientific study of religion as a threat. Nevertheless, the study had gone on there for some time, for instance in Bologna, where Pettazzoni taught from 1914 to 1924. When Pettazzoni had already gained a name internationally, he and his associates saw their efforts crowned with the establishment of a chair at the University of Rome. Pettazzoni held that chair from 1924 until his death. He is the only historian of religions who can be said to have formed a "school." Several names in this school have become well known: Pettazzoni's successor, Angelo Brelich (1913–77), who did his work on a wide variety of subjects, including the Greek heroes, polytheism, and the origin of myths; Ugo Bianchi (1922–95); and Cristiano Grottanelli. The secret of Pettazzoni's talent was his vision for *all* facets of life that related to any topic at hand, as well as the gigantic scope of subjects he dealt with. He wrote a book on the mystery religions, and some volumes on the confession of sins (as a worldwide phenomenon). Together with colleagues he produced the most embracing collection of myths of all the continents. The subject of monotheism kept him occupied a good part of his life — again, not as the creation or discovery of one culture, but as a phenomenon in the world. Part of his motivation in spending so much time on the subject of one supreme god was the need to correct certain views that had been spread by the German ethnologist Father Wilhelm Schmidt (1868–1954).

Schmidt was a priest and a member of the Societas Verbi Divini (Society of the Divine Word), a spiritual order devoted to missionary work. As a scholar, Schmidt possessed at the same time the evolutionistic ideas of the age and the Aristotelian-Thomistic views of a prime mover, hence an idea of God as the primordial cause of the world. His theorizings, always based on the latest findings, would always seem also strangely in harmony with the older notions of a paradisial revelation that left its imprint in the most "primitive" nations. In 1906 Schmidt founded *Anthropos*, a journal devoted especially to the study of ethnology and linguistics. The journal has set a standard ever since, especially by the high level of its book reviews — an absolute must if a serious level of discussion is truly considered important. Schmidt taught in an Austrian seminary, later at the University of Vienna. When Austria was made part of Germany in 1938, Schmidt resettled the institute he had created in Switzerland. He trained missionaries who were sent out especially to parts of the world most remote from the ancient centers of civilization, and where evidence of a "primal monotheism" was expected. Of all the inner contradictions that abound in the history of inspiring intellectual ventures, those of the school of Father Wilhelm Schmidt seem to me the most wonderful ones! In terms of ideas the school was something of a hodgepodge, but the work its missionaries did is splendid. Father Martin Gusinde, Father Wilhelm Koppers, Father Paul Schebesta, and others found evidence of a primordial creator, who in many instances withdrew upon completing the world. The work of Schmidt and his school is far too important for its linguistic and cultural discoveries to be dismissed because they seem to center around one vulnerable theory. However, for our survey of ideas here, and for our understanding of Pettazzoni's reaction, that aspect of it stands out. Both scholars had a lifelong fascination with the same materials.

Pettazzoni worked in his own precise and wide-ranging comparative historical fashion on high god images and myths. Schmidt's great work on the subject was entitled *Der Ursprung der Gottesidee* ("The Origin of the Idea of God"); the final volume, volume 12, appeared the year after his death. The thesis that the earliest hunting-and-gathering peoples of the earth were monotheists had to suffer for its lack of substance under Pettazzoni's onslaught. He convincingly demonstrated that what we can begin to identify as "monotheism" always originates in the supremacy one god attains in an assembly of gods. Historically, such is the beginning of Yahweh and of Allah; early intimations include the rise of Marduk in Mesopotamia. It is not difficult to see that religio-historically, Pettazzoni was right. Schmidt certainly confused theological convictions with historical developments. In our own words, we may be entitled to add that Pettazzoni, on his part, did not feel inclined to soften his verdict on Schmidt by considering that in whatever we can glean from the culture of primitive hunters we have to make room for the obvious point that they too, as in all religious traditions thereafter, had an interest in *salvation*. That Schmidt, who ran a school for missionaries, erred in confusing "origins" with ideas about Genesis 1 and 2 seems clear. Nevertheless, as we have seen often in this book, such an "error" is easy to commit. Moreover, even if the mistake does not become less impermissible, it contributed to goodwill and high expectations among the missionaries of Schmidt's school which must be noted as well. Koppers, Gusinde, and the others found people—still called "primitives" then— in distant places who trusted them, and were willing to tell them myths that until then had not been given proper attention, or had not been recorded at all. Those missionary-anthropologists expected to receive *truth*. Can such expectations between human beings be dismissed? A perfect error-free objectivity is not necessarily a guarantee of perfect trust, and without trust worthwhile information is not easy to acquire.

Literature
Raffaele Pettazzoni, *Essays on the History of Religions,* trans. H.J. Rose (Leiden: Brill, 1954); Raffaele Pettazzoni, *The All-Knowing God: Researches into Early Religion and Culture* (London: Methuen, 1956); Joseph Henninger, "Schmidt, Wilhelm," in *The Encyclopedia of Religion,* ed. Mircea Eliade (New York: Macmillan, 1987), vol. 13, pp. 113–15; Angelo Brelich, "Prolégomènes" in *Histoire des religions,* ed. Henri-Charles Puech (Paris: Gallimard, Encyclopédie de la Pléiade, 1970), vol. 1, pp. 3–59.

TWENTIETH-CENTURY HISTORIANS OF RELIGIONS (CONTINUED)

The Dutchman G. van der Leeuw (1890–1950) was the founder of the "phenomenology of religion." The work that he devoted to it, *Religion in Essence and Manifestation,* which established his fame, was first published in German (1933); it was soon followed by editions in French, English, and other languages. Another book is his *Wegen en grenzen* ("Ways and Boundaries"), translated into English under the title *Sacred and Profane Beauty.*[42] Van der Leeuw taught in the theological faculty of the University of Groningen. He and Pettazzoni were friends, yet Pettazzoni made no secret of his critique of van der Leeuw. Like Rudolf Otto, van der Leeuw was a Christian theologian — reason enough for suspicion to Pettazzoni, who in his own country had carried the standard for the history of religions for so long against a Christian establishment.

What van der Leeuw meant by his "phenomenology of religion" was in the first place a practical way of sorting out religio-historical data. His own teacher, the Dutchman P.D. Chantepie de la Saussaye (1848–1920), had inititiated it. Chantepie had done so in the first edition of a textbook of the history of religions which was regarded as authoritative for decades.[43] A section of more than a hundred pages he calls the "phenomenological part" of his book. It is a descriptive enumeration of empirical forms that occur in religion all over the world: objects of veneration, idols (images or symbols of deities), gods, sacrifice and prayer, sacred places, sacred times, religious communities, sacred scriptures, myths. Chantepie was certainly a *historian* of religions (and the specific histories of specific religions fill most of his work), but his teaching assignment, first in Amsterdam, later in Leiden, included philosophy as well. His phenomenological sketch of religious forms may be seen as an echo of an earlier attempt by Hegel, but in the history of our field of study precisely its empirical form is worth noting. Chantepie did not abstain from philosophical judgments, but did insist on beginning with what was given. Van der Leeuw owes his inspiration first to Chantepie's impulse.

The second influence on van der Leeuw is the work of Dilthey. (One feels odd, however, singling out influences on a man who seemed to read everything under the sun.) In spite of his use of the name "phenomenology," van der Leeuw barely mentions Husserl. Dilthey is cited far more frequently in the footnotes to *Religion in Essence and Manifestation*. A sense of the *givenness* of religion is the most conspicuous feature of the book. The *givenness* of religion is also probably the feature most consistently overlooked by students of religion eager to find "the essence" as they search through documents and sort through theories. This givenness is really the same thing we have tried to describe as the "ordinariness" of religion. It is visible all the time, even when we peer at the horizon. In terms of the sobriety of thought in our time, van der Leeuw is never far away from Husserl's attempt to make scientific views maintain their relation to the everyday world. But while Husserl had great difficulty expressing his version of "ordinariness," van der Leeuw had a poetic ability to hit on the right images.

Like others, van der Leeuw used the term *structure*, but he makes perfectly clear what it means:

> If I place a beer-mug, a long pipe, a book, and a pot of tobacco on a table, there is first no more than a collection of objects. I can try to understand them as a whole by relating them to a common purpose, e.g., to fulfill the wishes of an old-fashioned student. Then, I understand what is there by means of a structure. If a painter decides to create a still life out of them, he too conceives of the objects as a whole; then, however, not their practical purpose, but proportions of lines, colors, and light. If his painting turns into a work of art, this structure is at once clear to the beholder. In one case as well as in the other, each object has meaning only as part of a whole, in the first case utilitarian, in the second, aesthetic.

In other words, structures can be recognized by the sense they make: that is their meaning. It is the sense we make out of reality. They make sense and we make sense. Between object and subject we have a third factor: this is the sense, the meaning, which is both subjective and objective.[44]

In speaking of Dilthey, we discussed the distinction between explaining and understanding, different from each other yet complementary. The same issue arises in the "phenomenological method" proposed by van der Leeuw. This method, he says,

can be arranged in the following order of stages (which must of course not be understood sequentially, one following the other, but rather as ways that come together time and again):

1) *Empathy* [*inleving, Einfühlung*] in the phenomenon, as if "feeling one's own life into it"; it is the opposite of an analysis that kills. Rather it is an understanding from within. It is not a matter of measuring or counting, but a matter of letting the entire thing have its effect on us, of becoming united with it. [William] James used the image of the stream that one does not get to know by taking countless buckets out of it, but by jumping into it. He also used the image of the melody that one never learns by dividing it into notes, but by singing or playing it. And nevertheless, even in our empathy a certain analysis occurs: for we seek the "understandable relation" between the whole and the parts. Or [with the terms of another author], "A true description means putting everything in its right place; you take things in and your mind gives a new life to what is already there before you; you find the right point of view, which shows you your object appropriately, in the way it should be seen in order to be understood in its own life and spirit, so that you can separate from it whatever merely in your own feeling belongs or does not belong to it."[45] However, we should keep in mind that such analysis is not construed, but lived. With this realization we enter the stage of

2) *Arranging*. Here we are to find the "understandable connections" that make the melody into one organic totality. Doing that we become able to formulate

3) *ideal types* and *ideal-typical cohesions*. These coherencies, cohesions, have no value for what is "really out there," but they do form the necessary material for an "echo-experience." This "double" of the original, an echo of what we try to understand, sets the standard for our knowing of

the original, the primary object of our inquiry which in itself cannot be reduplicated. Here we enter the realm of meaning. Ibsen's hero, Brand, seeks death in the wilderness of ice. The real Brand, Ibsen himself, stayed alive. Goethe's Werther shoots himself. His model, Jerusalem, did the same. But his more important model, Goethe, reached a ripe old age. And nevertheless, we can understand neither Goethe nor Ibsen without the construction of an ideal type. Another example: The Reformation is a revolution in religion. Hence, ideal-typically, it is the opposite of the Church of Rome. In reality and in many instances, it rather resembles a German or a Genevan or Dutch Rome. And yet we can understand it only as *Reformation.* The only possible criterion is the criterion of *evidence,* not in a logical, but in an eidetic sense. It can be compared with what is evident for the painter or the composer who is forced by what is evident to divide light and dark in this way and none other.

How can we avoid the very real possibility that this going by evidence will degenerate into utter whimsicality? How can we lead it toward the real goal of true understanding? Or, in other words, how can we reach the goal of the phenomenological method? Only by

4) *an understanding of structures that is as complete as possible,* which demands that one more essential condition be met, and that is the *epoche.* Negatively, this rule of method is nothing but reservedness on our part, a conscious hesitance in passing judgment [*Einklammerung*]. The inquirer envisions and understands his object, while holding back with respect to what reality is, whether ontically or metaphysically. We recognize the structure, the "lived construction" (Max Scheler); we do not pretend to have understood reality itself by means of our construction. On the contrary, we deem this reality as it really is to be in principle ungraspable and nonunderstandable. Understanding is a bridge constructed between one's own reality and the reality that is to be understood. *Epoche* means that this bridgelike character of all understanding is fully realized. One enters reality only and exclusively from one's own reality. There is no other way.[46]

Van der Leeuw was never a mere theoretician of religion. He remained involved in all basic questions of knowledge. During the German occupation of Holland, he joined the resistance movement. Though many of the people we have touched on here lived lives that were far more interesting (and troubled) than I can recount, biographical details can be so much more revealing than intellectual profiles that I cannot resist saying a bit about van der Leeuw's life. After the war, he was minister of education and culture in the first cabinet under the prime minstership of the celebrated socialist—also a resistance fighter—Willem Drees. Van der Leeuw's stimulus to the arts and support of artists in the Netherlands was truly outstanding. As we have mentioned, historians of religions do not as a rule create schools. This is true also in van der Leeuw's case, and yet it would seem that his career was capable of reconciling opposites in the scholarly world. One remarkable and gifted pupil of his, Fokke Sierksma, on the surface seemed the opposite of his master. He had a disdain for theology and theologians, and preferred applying psychoanalytic methods in his work. Nevertheless, his admiration for van der Leeuw was unsurpassed. After van der Leeuw's death, Fokke Sierksma—perhaps not by coincidence also a fervent resistance fighter during the war—wrote a book that he, antitheologian par excellence, entitled *Professor Dr. G. van der Leeuw, Servant of God and Professor in Groningen.*[47] He commemorated van der Leeuw, saying, "In him, Europe lost one of the few Europeans remaining."[48] He quoted with relish what he called van der Leeuw's "majestic words": "That man cannot live by bread alone is *also* a law of economics."[49] Van der Leeuw was able to carry on meaningful discussions with all parties who were seriously engaged in learning, science, politics, the arts. What, indeed, is a specialization all by itself? No wonder he could get along with his critic Pettazzoni and enjoyed his admiration.

Mircea Eliade (1907–86), at present better known in the United States than van der Leeuw, was among his admirers as well. Eliade was a very different person from van der Leeuw in his life and his historical circumstances. The conclusion of the war found him in Lisbon, where he was cultural attaché of his native Romania. In a teaching position in Paris, he gave a course that became the basis of one of his best-known works, *Traité d'histoire des religions,* which the English translator called *Patterns of Comparative Religion.*[50] In Paris Eliade was surprised that van der Leeuw's phenomenology of religion was much less known than he would have expected. Hence he patterned his course after the outline of *Religion in Essence and Manifestation,* presenting the basic elements of religion: sacred space, sacred time, symbols, myths, and so on. Eliade, however, in spite of his all-embracing cultural interests and his impressive talent as a novelist, was much less philosophically inclined than van der Leeuw. He preferred the term *morphology* over *phenomenology,* and he likened his own endeavors to Linnaeus's classification work in botany. What cannot fail to impress the reader is the exhaustive bibliography accompanying each of his subjects. What is also striking, in comparison to van der Leeuw, is the almost "static" and "aesthetic" views Eliade presents of symbols and myths. Cultic expressions receive little attention, and the fact that in ritual *communities* are involved is wholly missing, even in the set of volumes *A History of Religious Ideas* (which was not completed at the end of his life).[51] These volumes, nevertheless, are among the most enlightening historical works on religious expressions ever produced. The slight attention given to communities and to social life in general goes hand in hand with an absence of interest in issues concerning ethics. (Before condemning this, it is worth reflecting that many a scholar would fall under the same judgment. Notably, as we have mentioned, Otto's popular work *Das Heilige* never yields a hint that it was written and published during the horrors of the First World War.) Although the University of Chicago had already been a prominent place for the study of religion, Eliade's appointment there in 1957 gradually made Chicago the paramount center for the history of religions in the United States. Some historians of religions of my generation who were in Chicago before Eliade arrived have occasionally thought aloud that Swift Hall on the University of Chicago campus would have been like Socratic Athens and the library of Alexandria if only Joachim Wach, Eliade's predecessor, had been granted a longer life. The philosophical, hermeneutical talent of Wach, together with the knowledge of religious facts of Eliade, would have constituted intellectual bliss.

Literature
G. van der Leeuw, *Religion in Essence and Manifestation,* trans. J. E. Turner (New York: Harper, 1963); G. van der Leeuw, *Sacred and Profane Beauty: The Holy in Art,* trans. David E. Green (Nashville, Tenn.: Abingdon, 1963); Mircea Eliade, *Patterns of Comparative Religions,* trans. Rosemary Sheed (London: Sheed and Ward, 1958); Mircea Eliade, *A History of Religious Ideas,* trans. Willard R. Trask (Chicago: University of Chicago Press, 1978, 1982, 1985), 3 vols.; Seymour Cain, *Gabriel Marcel's Theory of Religious Experience* (New York: Lang, 1995).

THE HISTORY OF RELIGIONS IN THE UNITED STATES

A mistaken impression one sometimes encounters is that the history of religions is an esoteric craft invented and plied by Europeans. One cannot hold to this opinion after considering the phenomenon of religion as a universal reality and the equally universal impulse to assess its meaning. (The matter-of-fact international state of affairs of religious practice and study struck me forcefully when an anthropologist who did fieldwork in South America told me about a shaman whose rituals he had carefully observed: a copy of Mircea Eliade's book about shamanism rested on the shaman's bookshelf!)

Intellectual dealings with religion have always crossed borders freely. The modern development of religio-historical studies is no exception; it is characterized by international contacts. The occupants of the first academic chairs in the study of religions followed an established tradition by corresponding with learned colleagues in other countries. In 1887 the universities of Scotland were the beneficiaries of a private bequest that at once enhanced the international nature of the history of religions: the Gifford Lectureship. The Gifford Lectures have been presented since the beginning by significant scholars from various lands. Other lectureships followed; among the best known are the Haskell Lectures (1895). Around 1900 international meetings of historians of religions, anthropologists, sociologists, folklorists—all assemblies whose subject matter overlapped— became the rule. The International Association of the History of Religions (I. A. H. R.) was established in 1900. In the years following the Second World War, its congresses have been held in Europe and the United States, Asia and Australia. Among its national member associations is the American Society for the Study of Religion, which was founded by Mircea Eliade of the University of Chicago and by E. R. Goodenough (1893–1965) of Yale. Goodenough became especially known for his thirteen-volume work on symbolism in Jewish synagogues in late Antiquity (*Jewish Symbols in the Greco-Roman Period*), but he also attained fame as a formidable scholar of problems of method in the historical study of religious phenomena in general—his work in this area is enlightening for all students of religion. The I. A. H. R.'s journal, *Numen: International Review for the History of Religions,* has been published since 1953. Other important journals with a worldwide distribution preceded it by many years. Among the oldest and most admirable is the French *Revue de l'histoire des religions,* founded in 1880. In Chicago Mircea Eliade, together with Joseph Kitagawa and Charles H. Long, established in 1961 *History of Religions: An International Journal for Comparative Historical Studies.* In 1906 Wilhelm Schmidt in Austria founded *Anthropos,* equally important to historians of religions and to linguists and ethnologists; *Anthropos* has always published contributions in a variety of languages. There are many more journals of great relevance to our field, including, of course, journals in history, anthropology, sociology, and philosophy. In addition, we have countless periodicals of specialized concern, on specific regions (e.g., the Near East), periods (e.g., late antiquity), and traditions (e.g., Buddhism).

It is not surprising that increasing communication since the nineteenth century has stimulated scholarly discussions on religion. The importance of the United States on the international scene has grown considerably, and certainly not only because of immigrants from Europe and Asia. Among the many scholars who could be discussed, we will mention just a few whose work is notable for general, comparative investigations. Even this limited list will show the wide array of materials addressed in American scholarship, and give a glimpse of the variety in disciplines, from the most widely anthropological to the most specialized philological.

One of the most original American scholars, who included religious data, and especially mystical experiences in his wide undertakings, we have already met in the philosopher and psychologist William James (1842–1910). His name has remained familiar internationally. In about the same period as James, George Foot Moore (1851–1931), text-oriented, yet with a far-ranging historical interest, taught at Harvard. Moore was instrumental in establishing the *Harvard Theological Review,* which through the years has published many an important study in the history of religions. Though a specialist in the Old Testament, Moore was as well an accomplished scholar of ancient Near Eastern traditions other than those of Israel. It is worth mentioning that Moore was also a serious student of rabbinical literature—an unusual feature among Christian scholars at the time. (Moore was an ordained Presbyterian minister and served in that capacity early in his career.) His two-volume work on the "great" religious traditions of the world (first published in 1914 and 1920) is still among the most readable and reliable textbooks.[52] He was one of Goodenough's teachers during the latter's student years at Harvard.

The United States played a significant role in the study of religion in general through the discipline that became known as "cultural anthropology." In all branches of anthropology, most obviously in connection with the earlier inhabitants of the New World, tremendous work has been done and continues to be done. Every student of religion should be aware of the collections of the Smithsonian Institution. Initiated by the English chemist and mineralogist James Smithson, the Institution was accepted as a private gift to the United States and established in Washington, D. C., in

1846. The Smithsonian is sweeping in its support of scholarly ventures. In particular, its publications on indigenous American cultures and religions are invaluable in the study of American Indian traditions.

In the decades around the turn of the twentieth century, American scholars made significant contributions in philological studies in the classical Asian languages, in linguistics, and in translations of religious texts. William Dwight Whitney (1827–94), professor of Sanskrit and comparative linguistics at Yale University, was one of the superb nineteenth-century scholars who opened the world of Indian religious documents to the West. His *Sanskrit Grammar* (1879) is still an indispensable tool. Charles Rockwell Lanman (1850–1941), also a Sanskritist, who taught at Johns Hopkins University in Baltimore, later at Harvard, served as editor of the Harvard Oriental Series, in which translations of important Indian texts continue to be published. Finally, among American classical scholars dealing with the Indian world, we should mention Henry Clarke Warren, who published *Buddhism in Translations* in 1896, as volume 3 in the Harvard Oriental Series; this work has been printed and reprinted ever since and has served as a gateway to an understanding of (Pali) Buddhism for countless readers. In 1915 E. Washburn Hopkins published *The Religions of India* in the series. The same author must be counted among the first Western scholars of epic literature and its religious importance; in 1915 he also published his *Epic Mythology*, based principally on Indian data. For the study of ancient Near Eastern documents, several American universities are of significance, but the University of Chicago's Oriental Institute, home to many outstanding scholars over many years, must be called paramount.

In our time, academic requirements tend to give the impression that the study of religions is sufficiently taken care of by reading translations of primary documents, but *ways* to study those primary documents must also be available. The basic work necessary for virtually all study in religions has a firm foundation in the United States.

The task of singling out scholars who have unlocked the treasures of the world's religions increases in difficulty as we approach recent times. The few choices that follow are drawn from a very long list.

Even before George Foot Moore's sizable work on the great religions of the world, Morris Jastrow (1861–1921) brought out a general introduction, *The Study of Religion* (1901). It is among the very first considered attempts to provide a general orientation for students, along with a critical assessment of philosophical views and what were then newly developed theories. Jastrow was a distinguished Hebrew scholar and Assyriologist. He taught at the University of Pennsylvania, where he also served as librarian. Inevitably, his *Study of Religion* has become outdated in many respects, but it still compares favorably with most contemporary efforts to introduce the subject. Jastrow made a convincing case for the central and abiding importance of the historical method. He pleaded for the cultivation "of a sympathic attitude toward the manifestations of the religious spirit."[53] This openness to all phenomena seems to anticipate the phenomenological method of van der Leeuw.

The University of Chicago, of more recent origin than Harvard, Yale, and the University of Pennsylvania, not only developed imposing programs and attracted notable scholars in area studies (South Asia, China, and others), including of course related religious traditions, but acquired a special reputation in the general, comparative study of religions. At Chicago, the (Canadian) American A. Eustace Haydon (1880–1975) paid special attention to religious-social-moral coherencies, thereby sharing a tendency among liberal Protestant scholars that prevailed for decades in the study of religions on both sides of the Atlantic. At the same time, however, he emphasized as one of the most important changes in the study of religion the move from comparativism, as if for its own sake, toward the specifics of historical studies. He was a strong proponent of the designation "history of religions" for our field. For this reason alone, he has been central for the history of religions "school" of Chicago. A work he edited, for which scholars from American institutions collaborated with two scholars from China and one from India, reflects in its title and organization no doubt some of Haydon's own idealism and interest in progress: *Modern Trends in World Religions.* The four parts of the book are respectively called "World-Religions and Modern Scientific Thinking," "World Religions and Modern Social-Economic Problems," "World-Religions and Intercultural Contacts," and "The Task of Modern Religion."

Haydon's successor, the (German) American Joachim Wach (1898–1955), came to the United States as a refugee from Hitler's Germany. Wach was not inclined to arrange religious materials and questions under the influence of personal ideals. He was more a philosopher than most historians of religions, a great yet critical admirer of Rudolf Otto, and was fascinated by the relationship between religion and society. His abiding interest, however, visible in all his work, was the historical and philosophical problem of the crucial process of human *understanding.* It is the subject of his largest, three-volume book, *Das Verstehen, Grundzüge der Hermeneutik im neunzehnten Jahrhundert* ("Understanding. Basic Features of Hermeneutics in the Nineteenth Century"), still untranslated into English. His writing on understanding never became "merely" philosophical—as usually happens with philosophers writing on the subject—but is based on history *and* philosophy. Especially in the discussion of American contributions to the study of religions, it is of significance to point to the affinity Wach shows in his discussions of religious expression with the American philosopher Suzanne K. Langer, who was a pioneer in the interpretation of symbolism, beginning with her book *Philosophy in a New Key: A Study in the Symbolism of Reason, Rite, and Art* (1942). Several of Wach's studies show him to be a very careful reader of texts and interpreter of historical detail. Wach's influence is as difficult to delineate as that of any significant "master" in the field. I would think, however, of several great teachers who worked under him, in particular Seymour Cain, who, like Wach, was marked by a keen philosophical ability. Shortly before his death, Cain published *Gabriel Marcel's Theory of Religious Experience* (1995). Behind the scenes, but very importantly, Cain worked as an editor on the *Encyclopaedia Britannica's* fifteenth edition (1974), of which many contributions on religious topics compare very favorably with Eliade's *Encyclopedia of Religion* (1987). Charles H. Long, though guided by Eliade, is also clearly recognizable as a pupil of Wach, in his writings, and even more so in his teaching (at Chicago, the University of North Carolina, and elsewhere) and in his impassioned lecturing throughout the country, with a fascination for the vitality of religion in society.

Among scholars for whom the universal presence of religion is basic, and who have been strong influences on present-day historians of religions, more names could be mentioned. One Harvard professor figures prominently: Wilfred Cantwell Smith, widely known especially through his book *The Meaning and End of Religion: A New Approach to the Religious Traditions of Mankind* (1963). Smith objects to the idea of "religions" as matters that can be made into an object and defined, toward which the scholar can maintain his distance. In fact, he argues, there is no need for exclusive attention to an entity known as "religion." Rather, there are religious persons who find meaning through the experience of faith. Smith shows himself an original representative of the rather wide international consensus that formed around the primacy of religious experience proposed by Rudolf Otto in *The Idea of the Holy*.

NOTES

1. See the bibliography in Mircea Eliade, *Patterns in Comparative Religion* (London: Sheed and Ward, 1958), pp. 35–37.

2. Quoted in the introduction by Paul O'Prey to Joseph Conrad, *The Heart of Darkness* (Harmondsworth: Penguin, 1983), p. 12.

3. Conrad, pp. 76–77.

4. Ivo Frenzel, *Friedrich Nietzsche: An Illustrated Biography* (New York: Pegasus, 1967), p. 119.

5. Friedrich Nietzsche, *Werke,* ed. Karl Schlechta (Munich: Hanser, 1966), vol. 1, p. 904 (in the second volume of *Menschliches, allzumenschliches*).

6. Nietzsche, vol. 3, p. 1241. "R" refers to Erwin Rohde, the writer of *Psyche,* who owed a great deal for his major insights to Nietzsche.

7. Friedrich Nietzsche, *Thus Spoke Zarathustra,* in *The Portable Nietzsche,* Walter Kaufmann, ed. and trans. (New York: Viking-Penguin, 1982), p. 121.

8. Ibid., p. 122.

9. Ibid., p. 123.

10. Ibid., p. 124.

11. Ibid.

12. See H. H. Rowley, *The Old Testament and Modern Study* (London: Oxford University Press, 1961).

13. See Graham Parkes, ed., *Nietzsche and Asian Thought* (Chicago: University of Chicago Press, 1991). None of the contributors mentions the Avesta or Zoroastrianism, but they do shed light on Nietzsche's interest in Hinduism and Buddhism.

14. See the introduction by Alexander Dru to his translation of *Temporal and Eternal. Charles Péguy* (London: Harvill Press, 1958), p. 7.

15. Translated in Annette Aronowicz, "The Secret of the Man of Forty," *History and Theory* 32 (1993), pp. 117–18.

16. Aronowicz, p. 103.

17. Octavio Paz, *The Monkey Grammarian* (New York: Seaver Books, 1981), p. 132.

18. Ibid., p. 133.

19. José Ortega y Gasset, *History as a System and Other Essays Toward a Philosophy of History* (New York: Norton, 1961), p. 216.

20. For the problem of categories in Dilthey, see H. P. Rickman, ed. and introd., *Wilhelm Dilthey, Pattern and Meaning in History: Thought on History and Society* (New York: Harper, 1961).

21. Ortega y Gasset, p. 214.

22. Alfred Schütz, *The Phenomenology of the Social World,* trans. George Walsh and Frederick Lehnert (Evanston, Ill.: Northwestern University Press, 1967).

23. The major general work on the subject of phenomenology is H. Spiegelberg, *The Phenomenological Movement: A Historical Introduction,* 2nd ed. (The Hague: Nijhoff, 1978), 2 vols. Much of my brief survey is derived from that work.

24. Ludwig Wittgenstein, *Tractatus Logico-Philosophicus,* German text, trans. by D. F. Pears and B. F. McGuinness, introd. Bertrand Russell (1922; reprint, London: Routledge, 1966).

25. Ibid., p. 3.

26. Ibid., p. ix.

27. Ibid., proposition 4.1121, p. 49.

28. Ibid., proposition 6.522, p. 151.

29. Ibid., proposition 4.022, p. 40.

30. Ibid., proposition 7, p. 151.

31. Ludwig Wittgenstein, *Remarks on Frazer's Golden Bough,* trans. A. C. Miles, rev. Rush Rhees (Retford, England: Brynmill, 1983).

32. Ibid., p. 1e.

33. Karl Jaspers and Rudolph Bultmann, *Myth and Christianity* (New York: Noonday Press, 1958), pp. 104–5.

34. Ibid., pp. 103–4.

35. See John Ellis, *The Social History of the Machine Gun* (Baltimore: Johns Hopkins University Press, 1995), chap. 4, "Making the Map Red," pp. 79–109.

36. Another scholar in the discussion remarked that the only rigor the lecturer seemed to endorse was not the rigor of science but *rigor mortis.* I give these examples that sound like anecdotes only reluctantly, but they illustrate the problems under discussion more directly than long theoretical expositions. I assure readers that they are not mere anecdotes. This particular episode occurred at a meeting of the American Society of Religion. Both the speaker and the critic, formidable scholars, have long since passed away.

37. Karen Armstrong, *A History of God* (New York: Ballantine Books, 1994).

38. One of the notable exceptions is the term *Augenblicksgötter,* "momentary deities," a term H. Usener, a German philologist and historian of religions, used to refer to Roman deities whose existence seemed to be indeed only momentary, as they appeared, or rather had their only existence, in the course of a ritual action.

39. Marcel Mauss, *The Gift: Forms and Functions of Exchange in Archaic Societies,* trans. Ian Cunnison (New York: Norton, 1967), p. 76.

40. Jan van Baal, *Dema. Description and Analysis of Marind-anim Culture* (South New Guinea) (The Hague: Nijhoff, 1966).

41. Rudolf Otto, *The Idea of the Holy: An Inquiry into the Non-rational Factor in the Idea of the Divine and Its Relation to the Rational,* 2nd ed., trans. John W. Harvey (London: Oxford University Press, 1971).

42. G. van der Leeuw, *Sacred and Profane Beauty: The Holy in Art,* trans. David E. Green (Nashville, Tenn.: Abingdon, 1963). Unfortunately, this translation

was based not on the splendid Dutch of the author, but on the German translation, and the illustrations were left out.

43. P. D. Chantepie de la Saussaye, *Lehrbuch der Religionsgeschichte* (Freiburg, I. B.: Siebeck, 1887).

44. G. van der Leeuw, *Inleiding tot de Theologie* (Amsterdam: Paris, 1948), p. 69.

45. Van der Leeuw quotes these lines from the Dutch scholar J. H. Gunning, Jr., in his *Overlevering en wetenschap* (The Hague, 1879), p. 90.

46. G. van der Leeuw, *Inleiding,* pp. 72–74. The passage seems to me clearer than any description of van der Leeuw's method in his *Religion in Essence and Manifestation.*

47. Fokke Sierksma, *Professor Dr. G. van der Leeuw, dienaar van God en hoogleraar te Groningen* (Amsterdam: Wereldvenster, 1951).

48. Ibid., p. 11.

49. Ibid., p. 66.

50. Mircea Eliade, *Traité d'histoire des religions* (Paris: Payot, 1953); *Patterns of Comparative Religions,* trans. Rosemary Sheed (London: Sheed and Ward, 1958).

51. Mircea Eliade, *A History of Religious Ideas,* 3 vols., trans. William R. Trask (Chicago: University of Chicago Press, 1978, 1982, 1985).

52. George Foot Moore, *History of Religions,* vol 1, *China, Japan, Egypt, Babylonia, Assyria, India, Persia, Greece, Rome* (Edinburgh: T. & T. Clark, 1914 [latest reprint 1971]); vol 2, *Judaism, Christianity, Mohammedanism* (Edinburgh: T. & T. Clark, 1920; reprinted 1948 and 1965).

53. Morris Jastrow, *The Study of Religion* (London: W. Scott, 1901; reprint, with new preface by William A. Clebsch and Charles H. Long, Chico, Calif.: Scholars Press, 1981), p. 319.

Farewell to
Too Much of a System

CONCLUSIONS AND MORE QUESTIONS

Our account of ideas concerning religion and religions in the course of Western civilization is almost complete. There is no end to the questions we should ask. Many that we face are the legacy of historical and intellectual changes that occurred before our time. No field of study exists only in its own time. The inevitable questions arise from previous questionings; they also result from interdisciplinary concerns we find ourselves in. More than a few of our questions are short-lived, very many are confused and confusing. But these too contribute to the formulation of new questions. If we have the luxury of receiving an education, the confusions of life do not cease but merely take on a new, intellectual face.

The trends and fashions of our time overwhelm us. The time in which one is living is always the most confusing time of all. As a student in Leiden in the Netherlands, I heard the New Testament specialist Professor J. de Zwaan discuss myriad fashions that had dominated his field. He ended by saying, "And nowadays we hear of someone by the name of Bultmann, who wants to demythologize the New Testament. Ladies and gentlemen, this fashion too will pass." Today many a student has never heard of Bultmann. Trends do pass. However, the infatuation with a new, scientific world, which made Bultmann want to "demythologize" the New Testament, has not come to an end but has taken on many new forms. Occasionally, this same sort of infatuation has turned into fear, and many a new way of theorizing turns into frenzy, or into a barrage of frantic refutation. Sartre, the great luminary of Paris in the years immediately following the Second World War, became roundly criticized by later thinkers who were just as rationalistic as he was, beginning with Claude Lévi-Strauss, Michel Foucault (1926–84), and Karl Popper (1902–94). All such details have an influence on the dominating ideas concerning religion and religions.

Philosophical treatises remain relevant to our subject even when they insist religion is a negligible detail, or a self-deception of some people but not the thinker who writes the treatise. The struggles of such thinkers to become clear on matters that are religious by definition are comical to behold. Treatises that avoid recognizing the very existence of religion make for hilarious reading. Let no one misunderstand! I am not suggesting that you can ignore such literature and its ideas. The writers themselves are religious phenomena.

Jean-Paul Sartre was a confirmed atheist. Nevertheless, a Christian theologian, his contemporary, devoted a book to him and entitled it *The Message of Sartre*.[1] Sartre wrote not only philosophical works but also plays for the stage. He meant to be relevant to all. His play *Huis clos* ("No Exit") made the point that all human existence is locked in *facts*. As human beings we nail each other down on our factual reality. Such utter factuality, the Christian theologian argued, excludes all transcendence. Sartre's view is far more challenging than the views of the average humanist or historian who in his reasonings sees religion gradually fading from the world, as if by a law of nature. Like Nietzsche with his "God is dead," Sartre screams out that life is hell. Hell in his play is people arguing with each other forever, reduced to their factuality, without allowing the others the chance of being anything beyond that state.

A man who seemed to some extent like Sartre, and yet was very different in some cardinal points, was Albert Camus. One of his novels, *The Plague,* is a story told by a doctor who describes the devastation by bubonic plague in a place in North Africa. It is, like *No Exit,* a situation from which there is no escape. Close to the end we read,

> Dr. Rieux resolved to compile this chronicle, so that he should not be one of those who hold their peace but should bear witness in favor of those plague-stricken people; so that some memorial of the injustice and outrage done them might endure; and to state quite simply what

we learn in time of pestilence: that there are more things to admire in men than to despise.[2]

There is no "final victory," Camus reminds us a moment later, but still, there are those "who, while unable to be saints but refusing to bow down to pestilences, strive their utmost to be healers."[3]

We have seen that in an infinite variety of ways reasonable people have tried to be "objective" and others, equally reasonable, have tried to give the subjective reality of human life its due. The desire to be "objective" which emerges time after time is a manifestation of an ancient need. We could call it, as others have called it, the problem of the "isms." We have met with many of them: objectivism, rationalism, romanticism, totemism, functionalism, structuralism, determinism. Without effort, we can lengthen the list. One philosopher, Karl Popper, made a plea for not taking "isms" too seriously.[4] It is advice we should be ready to follow. Let it be noted, however, that in the course of a discussion anyone who does not go by a set system does not get away free either. Karl Popper, being determined not to be a determinist of any sort, inevitably became an "indeterminist." Fortunately, he had enough of a sense of humor as well as of the course of philosophy, to accept the denomination for himself, but qualified it by adding "realist" as well. The struggle of words continues, but we should heed Popper's warning against exaggerated and square applications of any philosophy.

Michel Foucault (1926–84) is no longer alive, yet is referred to so often that he still seems to be with us. A Frenchman, he began to write in a nation where first Sartre, then Lévi-Strauss was on everyone's mind, and thereafter Jacques Derrida (born 1930) and Jean-François Lyotard (born 1924); they and others who followed them are quoted often in history and modern language departments when the lecturer is looking for a *bon mot* or a "final say." Foucault's first publications dealt with madness as a phenomenon that changes constantly, depending on the general "feel" of the time. For example, in the period of French rationalism—when Descartes's system dominated—the mentally disabled were seen as a threat to the world as it ought to be, and they were locked up. As a theoretician (dealing with history and everything else), Foucault seemed never to submit to "isms" of any sort; for him human reason stops at nothing, but at the same time it accepts nothing as a "final say." As we draw near the end of our survey, perhaps we can have great sympathy with that attitude. Foucault says "no" to every proposition. Though he seems to do so almost neurotically, we have to add that he voices the neurosis we have all been touched by. If our intellectual history has made us embarrassed with respect to "final" questions, we might also say that Foucault succeeded in making a virtue out of this embarrassment that led us to an inescapable modesty, and into our inability to repeat the words of the past; ours is the time some like to call "postmodern." Foucault accepts involvement in a puzzle that allows no solution. Unlike Carnap, he does not attack metaphysics. He does not mention it; for him it is a nonissue. Likewise, the subject of religion does not seem to exist for him. All we have is an infinite number of ways of looking at things. What he shows us in his *Archaeology of Knowledge* is not relativism; he does not lead us into a darkness where all cats are gray. What he presents is a way, if not a system, of philosophizing that does not aim for a unity. The term *purpose* plays no role. All there is—the traditional subject of all philosophy—is turned into an interminable puzzle. *This is serious philosophy too!* To me it seems like a theory that might have accompanied the practice that Pettazzoni engaged in. Pettazzoni ceaselessly searched for the settings and relations in the religions of the world; he corrected himself; he never accepted any understanding of a religion as conclusive, let alone as the final and valid reality. Foucault is one of the most persuasive writers who make this "never" into the only feasible method for all there is. Derrida, a philosopher and historian of philosophy, makes for absorbing reading, like Foucault, and can be said to turn the activity of tireless reinterpreting into a method whose principal aim is to warn us away from anything that might be seen as "dogmatic."[5] The significance of Derrida for historians of religions is enhanced by his willingness to use terms like *eschatology* and *God,* and the discussion he enters into with a philosopher of religion (specifically Judaism and Christianity), Emmanuel Levinas, to whom the intellectual world is indebted for his own "antidogmatic" efforts.

The inevitable danger of popularizing the thoughts of Foucault and Derrida in brief summaries is that this caters to lazy minds who crave the quick fix in the interpretation of literature, for whom witticisms are the answer, who shun the study of language and any real inquiry. It is too easy for all of us who are less learned and tenacious than Foucault, Derrida, or Levinas to pontificate around our wonderful audacity to say "no" to every suggestion. A cursory reading of these exciting and important writers invites easy distortions, analogous to the ones Nietzsche's thought led to. Should writers be held responsible for misinterpretations that they do not explicitly stave off? Some have held that the thought of Plato and Aristotle gave rise to repressive regimes. One can push things too far in any direction. It seems to me that we owe a debt of gratitude to France for giving us so many thinkers who opened new perspectives, who put into words what we in our time needed to have expressed clearly and distinctly. Some Germans, some Americans, some thinkers from the Spanish-speaking world, and others have done their part too, but in recent times France has given the lion's share.

With respect to philosophical stimuli for religio-historical study, we can nevertheless suggest, even if we do so with some modesty, that the United States has a valuable tradition. Beginning with thinkers like William James, the creator of "pragmatism," who for years was frowned upon by many a European intellectual, the United States has enjoyed an atmosphere of healthy suspicion toward over-theorizing. In our own day, Richard Rorty is one of the most stimulating thinkers whose views of what the mind is capable of cannot fail to benefit students of religious documents. As always, it is irrelevant whether philosophers use the term *religion*, or whether they consider themselves "religious." Also, serious students of the history of religions learn pretty quickly how to detect "dogmatic" tendencies in philosophy. Contrary to some popular belief, dogmatism is not a property only of certain Christians. As a morbid obsession with rational propositions it flourishes in philosophical circles as well. We can thank our lucky stars that the great thinkers in the United States have not impeded but furthered freedom of research.

Literature

Richard Rorty, *Philosophy and the Mirror of Nature* (Princeton: Princeton University Press, 1980); Richard Rorty, *Contingency, Irony, and Solidarity* (Cambridge: Cambridge University Press, 1995); Emmanuel Levinas, *Nine Talmudic Readings,* trans. and introd. by the historian of religions Annette Aronowicz (Bloomington: Indiana University Press, 1990). Very helpful also is Colin Davis, *Levinas: An Introduction* (Notre Dame, Ind.: University of Notre Dame Press, 1996). Levinas's magnum opus, though more difficult reading, remains *Totality and Infinity,* trans. Alphonso Lingis (Pittsburgh: Duquesne University Press, 1969). Michel Foucault, *The Archeology of Knowledge & The Discourse on Language,* trans. A. M. Sheridan Smith (New York: Harper, 1976); Karl Popper, *The Open Society and Its Enemies* (London: Routledge, 1945; 5th, rev. ed., in 2 vols., Princeton: Princeton University Press, 1966); Michael Polanyi, *Knowing and Being: Essays,* ed. Marjorie Grene (Chicago: University of Chicago Press, 1969); Jacques Derrida, *Spurs. Nietzsche's Styles,* trans. Barbara Harlow (Chicago: University of Chicago

Press, 1979); Jean-François Lyotard, *The Postmodern Explained. Correspondence 1982–1985,* trans. Don Barry (Minneapolis: University of Minnesota Press, 1992); Richard J. Bernstein, *Philosophical Profiles* (Philadelphia: University of Pennsylvania Press, 1986).

ORIENTATIONS TODAY IN THE UNITED STATES

Presenting an accurate picture of one's own time is difficult. Moreover, my principal objective in this final section is not completeness. I would like to offer not a full list of names and achievements, but an admittedly personal view of the situation in which novices in the history of religions find themselves today.

One statement can be made with little controversy: the "Chicago school," which has dominated the scene in the United States for well over half a century, shows no signs of waning. Even though at the present this school includes a greater variety in approaches than it did when the seat of the history of religions was occupied by only one person (Haydon, Wach, or Eliade), in this very variety Chicago might claim to be a model as well as a typical example of the situation in the United States and internationally. I will not venture into the question whether genuine wisdom or a series of coincidences led to this situation. I owe the principal part of my education to Chicago, but no bias is required to affirm Chicago's prominence in the history of religions across the nation.

Wilfred Cantwell Smith's successor as professor and director of Harvard's Institute for World Religions is Lawrence E. Sullivan. A pupil of Eliade, Sullivan is definitely a *general* historian of religions, in the sense of not excluding any tradition from his purview. The book that made him known seems "specialized," yet is based on a vast knowledge of South American religious phenomena: *Icanchu's Drum: An Orientation to Meaning in South American Religions* (1988).[6] His predecessor, Smith, had been concerned principally with the "major religions," beginning with Christianity and Islam, not the religions that fascinated the writer of *Icanchu's Drum,* which Smith still would have called "primitive" without much hesitation.

David Carrasco, now teaching at Harvard, is best known for his publications on the religion of the Aztec, including *Quetzalcoatl and the Irony of Empire. Myths and Prophecies in the Aztec Tradition* (1982), and, written together with Johanna Broda and Eduardo Matos Moctezuma, *The Great Temple of Tenochtitlán. Center and Periphery in the Aztec World* (1987).

Carrasco is also a pupil of Mircea Eliade, and even his seemingly most specialized work bespeaks a general historian of religions, teaching us to recognize human issues that show themselves in our struggle to understand religious phenomena. Carrasco has never made a secret of his indebtedness to Eliade. Together with Jane Marie Law he edited an interesting work, *Waiting for the Dawn: Mircea Eliade in Perspective.*[7] Carrasco's prologue expresses his admiration for his teacher eloquently.

Charles H. Long, though guided by Eliade, is also clearly recognizable as a pupil of Wach, in his writings, and even more so in his teaching (at Chicago, the University of North Carolina, and elsewhere), and in his impassioned lecturing throughout the country, with a fascination for the place of religion in society. His personal style notwithstanding, Long reflects Wach's lifelong interest in social realities. In many of his presentations, Long attends to problems Eliade never dealt with. Long has been paying special attention to what happens under colonialism, the suppression of people, transformations of symbolism honed under circumstances that no one could refer to as nice, pure, pleasant, "purely spiritual." The irrepressible question of meaning in human existence in all circumstances is central to Long's work *Significations.*[8] This is not to say that Long became confused and committed the mistake of explaining religion on the basis of politics. It is rather a matter of realizing something that was expressed early on in this book, that by nature religion is not necessarily a pleasant thing—the strangest lesson to learn for educated and well-off people in modern industrial societies.

Was Eliade himself oblivious to matters of politics? It is necessary to raise the question, for many a difference between Eliade and his pupils hinges on it. No one could ever suggest that the differences in question have anything to do with a lack of knowledge on the part of Eliade: everyone who ever met him has always marveled at his ready and seemingly universal knowledge.[9] (It became a game among some students to try to bring up a title Eliade did not know; I have never heard of anyone who succeeded. In the case of newer publications, Eliade often knew not only the reference but the author as well.)

But to persist for a moment on the matter of politics—when the news spread in 1956 that Eliade was expected to come to Chicago, and thereafter take the place of Wach, I read Eliade's book on shamanism.[10] Many regard this as his very best work and consider it to be of lasting significance. I could not help noticing some information on the book jacket. I had my own recollections of the Second World War in German-occupied Holland.

And there, on the back flap, I read that Eliade had served as cultural ambassador of Romania in the Romanian embassy at Lisbon during the war. I knew, as did everyone else who lived in Europe during that war, that Romania's leader, Antonescu, was an ally of Hitler.

Only after his death in 1986 did some voices begin to be heard questioning Eliade's political purity. Controversy concerning celebrated scholars is not rare; hyenas prefer rich booty. Furthermore, a generation in the United States who knew essentially by hearsay of the Nazi era, easily developed suspicions and judgments without awareness of any complexities. I did not raise questions when Eliade, our religio-historical authority, was alive, nor did anyone else. Eliade published extensive autobiographical writings.[11] He could not avoid the topic of politics altogether, but the reader cannot help but notice the extraordinary naïveté in passages that touch on it. In an entry made on April 27, 1968, the subject of the student unrest at Columbia University comes up. Eliade calls the events "pointless to summarize." Then, summarizing nevertheless, he writes,

> As usual, a handful of professional agitators have managed to fire up a few hundred naïve, ambitious, or eccentric people. They occupy one or several buildings. They are presented on television, photographed, interviewed by journalists—and the propaganda picks up another hundred or two hundred students, but also several hundred curious types or onlookers. What do the "students" want? Something which finally is accepted by the university. But they do not yield, because they demand something more, or at least to receive amnesty. (That is what happened in Chicago and elsewhere.) Thus ultimately, "revolution" without risks. And if, at the final limit, the police intervene to evacuate the premises, the students are again televised and they become famous (as victims of police terror). And all that because of a tiny dynamic minority, well trained in civil or guerrilla warfare.
>
> This evening I was at Theodore Gaster's. His wife, an emigrant of German origins, gave me her impressions: "I seemed to be seeing the same film for the second time." From the S. S. to students ravaging in the name of democracy (we were shown the offices of the university after the students were evacuated), there does not seem to have been a gap of twenty five or thirty years. And several million dead.[12]

In the midst of the war in Vietnam, what can one say about this direct comparison of the students to the SS?

Eliade remains a most extraordinary figure. There is, I believe, the one remarkable blind spot in the area of politics, and, were it not for one closely related matter in the study of religion, it could be left unmentioned. That one thing was Eliade's absence of understanding for and interest in *human action*. All his work on religion, no matter how clairvoyant, is always "aesthetic" in nature. He leads you to the religious symbol to "take it in" as a thing of beauty, splendor, something to captivate you. The mystic vision fascinated him. He could sweep along readers (or crowds of listeners). But the focal point of his appeal remained the individual experience. Striking, as soon as you have begun to notice it, is his lack of serious attention to *ritual*. Is there something here that we share with Eliade? Does the commitment, the participation in things done together with fellow human beings cease when those fellow human beings get too close? Since most of us, modern indwellers of the industrialized world, are individualists, attached to our individual *experiences,* the problem may have escaped us for a long time, but it is a central problem, and, I believe, we are touching on it right here. Eliade's world was the world of urban life. The peasants of whom he frequently writes are closer to the world of his dreams. It is a vision with more than a tinge of Romanticism.

Among Eliade's pupils, Bruce Lincoln is no doubt the most prolific. He is now at Chicago, after teaching for a number of years at the University of Minnesota, where he worked side by side with William W. Malandra, the general historian of religions who was educated at Brown University and the University of Pennsylvania, and is best known for his work in Iranian studies (*An Introduction to Ancient Iranian Religion*).[13] Lincoln's work indeed seems to cover all periods and regions. Lincoln reminds one of Pettazzoni in one important respect: his keen attention to the relation of religious forms of expression to social and political realities. And he resembles Pettazzoni in another respect: the breadth of the terrain over which he moves — issues in ancient and classical civilizations, European history, tribal and traditional cultures, and present-day problems in a world that many would mistakenly regard as a religious vacuum. Among his earlier works, *Priests, Warriors, and Cattle: A Study in the Ecology of Religions* takes us to the economic, political, and mythical significance of cattle in early Asian and African civilizations, in sacrifices and intrepid raids.[14] In 1991 he published, in memory of Mircea Eliade, *Death, War, and Sacrifice: Studies in Ideology and Practice,* whose foreword is written by Wendy Doniger, a talented religio-historical essayist, with special interest in Indian materials.[15] Not only is the range of *Death, War, and Sacrifice* breathtaking, from the symbolism of death and funerals, and sacrificial practices, to contemporary polemics, from ancient Indo-Europeans to present-day skirmishes and horrors, but Lincoln shows himself particularly concerned with the moral stake historians of religions have in forming their judgments. (In the same book, he argues that the celebrated French Indo-Europeanist Georges Dumézil was not beyond criticism in his assessment of the contemporary world's monstrous disaster of the Holocaust. In Lincoln's scrutiny of the life and work of Dumézil, modern political ideologies and methods of studying the ancients turn out to be bent toward each other in reprehensible ways.) *Authority: Construction and Corrosion,* perhaps the most solemn of his books, confronts a problem that by its very nature traverses the boundaries between political science, history, sociology, various other disciplines, and, of course, the history of religions.[16] Lincoln can be spoken of as a brilliant practitioner of the necessary ongoing debate in the center of the academic enterprise, taken wholly seriously. He moves in that place we have called "the central arena." It is true that occasionally Lincoln may appear as an utter materialist, but this impression is misleading. It seems to me that the obstinacy of his argumentation results from his concern for the concreteness of all that human life depends on. It is a concern for justice, and in this vein he turns back time and again to the religious materials and the problem of their interpretation. Far more competently than most others he has occupied himself explicitly with the plight of women; he did so in *Emerging from the Chrysalis: Rituals of Women's Initiation.*[17] In his bundle of essays called *Theorizing Myth: Narrative, Ideology, and Scholarship* Lincoln comes close to identifying "myth" and "ideology."[18] Considering the cloud of politics that comes with the term *ideology,* some readers may feel hesitant before Lincoln's arguments. Given the subtleties of those arguments, however, and the many, many examples chosen from myths, one may equally hesitate to reject the closeness of myth and "ideology" altogether. At the very least one should be aware once more of Lincoln's inclination to show the concreteness of things that make a difference to human beings.

Jonathan Z. Smith of Chicago studied at Yale under Erwin R. Goodenough and, like his mentor, has concentrated on the world of late antiquity. However, many of his essays deal with religious problems elsewhere and do not shrink from controversies in the assessment of religion. On the contrary, Smith delights in them. Among his publications are *Map Is Not Territory: Studies in the History of Religions;*[19] *Imagining Religion: From Baby-*

lon to Jonestown;[20] Drudgery Divine: On the Comparison of Early Christianities and the Religions of Late Antiquity.[21] All these, and others as well, are collections of studies, always full of surprises in materials presented, comparisons made, and views on method. Smith challenges the distinction between "the sacred" and "the profane" as made by Eliade and others (see especially his Map Is Not Territory). Smith seems to rejoice in his complete independence, beholden neither to Eliade nor to Wach. More than a few of his pages almost seem to be written in order to irritate Christian theologians—a temptation known to many historians of religions who value what our sources actually say. On the contemporary scene, a sparkling independence like that of Jonathan Z. Smith is not common.

Influences of the established history of religions centers, especially Harvard and Chicago, are always in evidence. In the last few decades, however, important and original contributions have come from other places, including large state universities that opened or expanded in the 1950s and 1960s. Of special significance is the largely philological work begun under the guidance of William Theodore de Bary, chairman and professor of Oriental Studies at Columbia University, who edited three sizable volumes that compile the efforts of a number of American specialists on the civilizations of India, China, and Japan (Sources of Indian Tradition, 3 vols., New York: Columbia University Press, 1st ed. 1958, reprinted and updated, 1988, 2001). Translations of numerous crucial religious documents are included in these volumes.

Devin DeWeese of Indiana University, a specialist in the languages and cultures that met in Central Asia, wrote an astoundingly enlightening work on the manner in which Islam took root in that region: Islamization and Native Religion in the Golden Horde: Baba Tükles and Conversion to Islam in Historical and Epic Tradition.[22] It is a model for historians of religions in the care it gives to mythical and other literary documents, the subtlety of its method, and its historical vision.

Among contemporary historians of religions, we may mention Jess Hollenback, who published his Mysticism: Experience, Response, and Empowerment in 1996.[23] It is a comprehensive study of a crucial religious topic—a topic of enormous scope, to which no one had dared reach out for almost a century. Like Hollenback, Annette Aronowicz received her training in the History Department of the University of California, Los Angeles. Her work reveals a great concern with issues of politics and literary creativity in modern and recent history—not as an exercise in aesthetics only, but as an analysis of the function of religion in the present day. Her most recent book is *Jews and Christians on Time and Eternity: Charles Péguy's Portrait of Bernard-Lazare* (1998).[24]

Let us conclude by mentioning some work by two anthropologists in order to suggest the "family resemblance" within the wider context in which the work of the historian of religions goes on. I am thinking of Clifford Geertz and Jacques Maquet. Clifford Geertz is known as a student of Indonesia. Early on in his career he wrote *The Religion of Java*. I have heard a historian of religions poke fun at Geertz's preparation for his fieldwork. He learned Bahasa Indonesia, the lingua franca of Indonesia, only to find after he settled in the town he had chosen on East Java that the common language spoken there was Javanese. The idea of calling the work "The Religion of Java" on the basis of conversations through a translator became the narrator's climax of hilarity. Nevertheless, whatever solidity may be lacking from the historian of religions' point of view, Geertz certainly told his story of the Javanese town, and he told it well. Perhaps Geertz's best-known book is *The Interpretation of Cultures*.[25] It includes theoretical questions on the interpretation of culture and religion, issues in specific traditions, and specific anthropological views (with a special essay on Claude Lévi-Strauss). Personally, I am most impressed by Geertz's avoidance of solemnity and undue heaviness in his interpretations. He knows more accurately than many a historian of religions about what we have called "the ordinariness of religion." "Religion," "culture," and "human life" do not come in separate boxes for him.

Jacques Maquet is an anthropologist who escapes simple characterization. He is an expert on traditional Africa. He is also an expert on Buddhism and, I cannot refrain from adding, involved in it. (In some manner, on this point there is—no doubt to his own surprise—a similarity between him and the historian of religions Joachim Wach, who was a committed Christian.) He is the creator of "aesthetic anthropology." His major work on aesthetics is *The Aesthetic Experience: An Anthropologist Looks at the Visual Arts*.[26] It is an oversized book with many illustrations. Presentation of visual art from different times and civilizations inevitably includes "religious art." However, this distinction itself, between religious and nonreligious art, does not receive special attention from Maquet. Like Geertz, Maquet frees his work from unnecessary padding. This is not to say that his work is light reading. It requires thought, but it is exciting to discover the meaning of seeing art as part of ordinary life—not as a form of expertise, as it often threatens to become in our industrial societies, but an essential part of life, everywhere and at all times.

FAREWELL TO TOO MUCH OF A SYSTEM

We have learned from Durkheim and others that all religious documents, myths, and teachings present matters that we should recognize as reality. A hundred years ago, "primitives" seemed least worthy of such treatment, yet Durkheim said, "When I approach the study of primitive religions, it is with the certainty that they are grounded in and express the real."[27]

We have to get used to something that our culture, education, and theoretical constructs have tended to hide from us. This something is indeed "the real." Merely saying so is not the end of our journey. Instead, inevitably, it leads us back to philosophy. What can we truthfully say about "the real"? The real for whom? we ask. And then we sink back into the impermissible belittling of people who "believe in . . ." and hence, we are subtly saying, do not know what is "real." A serious discussion, however, can begin once we realize that in studying religion we deal only with *what shows itself as reality.*

What is "reality"? "What most people consider normal" is definitely not the answer. "We," the general citizens of the industrialized West—already excluding those here who are less well-off—might consider a real bed and a large television set normal, part of normal people's reality. However, we would be foolish to think that inhabitants of the world who do not share in this are abnormal. Nevertheless, strangely, reasonings of this sort have shipwrecked many an endeavor at understanding. For a couple of centuries, serious minds have taken themselves and their habits as the "norm." *Normal* as used in popular speech may *seem* to mean what the majority does, but it does not stop meaning a standard set for all.[28] The strange thing then is that so many studies of other peoples do not abandon the assumption that *we think normally.* By contrast, the Mbuti in Africa do not, and the Vedic Indians did not. The ease with which theories rooted in this assumption were accepted and still exert their influence is of a piece with the history of colonialism in all its forms, including the economic forms spanning the turn of the twenty-first century which are called by such names as foreign aid, loans, or trade agreements.

What seems normal for many is an uncritical trust in science, or, should I say, an ideal image of science. The hold of an ideal image of "science" on the popular imagination is close to superstition. No doubt, Stephen W. Hawking is truly a scientist. He showed his love for physics in his fascinating book *A Brief History of Time*. He expects very much from his field, as everyone should from theirs. He is confident that before long physicists will be able to present a grand unified theory that will explain the universe. As a physicist, he is interested in the cause or causes of our world system, in the origin of the whole natural world. We all know about "nature," of course. We are familiar with it largely because of the successes of physics and astronomy. Something curious happens when Professor Hawking's account of the beginning of the universe and time concludes with a reference to God as an entity that is dealt with completely once we complete our ventures in physics:

> If we do discover a complete theory, it should in time be understandable in broad principle by everyone, not just a few scientists. Then we shall all, philosophers, scientists, and just ordinary people, be able to take part in the discussion of the question of why it is that we and the universe exist. If we find the answer to that, it would be the ultimate triumph of human reason—for then we would know the mind of God.[29]

It is unlikely that Professor Hawking wants to boost once more the general superstition about science. Nevertheless, for the physicist "God" apparently is something like the watchmaker of Voltaire. In this respect, even this great physicist shares a popular opinion held by average educated persons in our society. We should invite him to an actual reading of Genesis 1, where the story of creation presents so much else and more about "why it is" than the average educated person notices today (see chapter 3 of this book). The superstition of science turns out to be a hard enemy to fight, in spite of heroic philosophical attempts. In a section just before the passage I quoted, Hawking summarily dismisses all philosophers since Kant, because they are not up to date with the exact sciences. I think it would be reasonable for a physicist to correct generalizations by historians of religions about science. But why should a scientist writing nonsense that relates to the creation story go unchallenged? Let me not bring in the subject of salvation, which is definitely out of the physicist's reach.

Historians of religions also face the temptation to find the perfect theory. Eliade has a great deal to say about the *axis mundi*, the pillar that connects this world with the other. I have no doubt that it is a useful device for understanding many a symbolism. Nevertheless, if one were present at a ritual of an Australian tribe and saw a real totem pole, would it be necessary or sensible to explain to the people that what they had there was an *axis mundi,* and that that sort of thing linked this world to the other world everywhere on earth? It does not require an unimaginable modesty to say nothing of the sort. Our explanations and ideas are worth acquiring, refining, fighting over, but they can become a stand-in-the-way. A Japanese poet said,

> Careful! Even moonlit dewdrops,
> If you're lured to watch,
> Are a wall before the Truth.[30]

The desire to find a complete theory is not what we need in the human sciences. Does that aspiration help us in any way to see what is shown as real in religious documents? Does it illuminate the norms they set? The old thesis stills holds true: a method is good only if it is proper for its object.

What is of central importance to our field, the history of religions? It will forever be important to interpret religions on the basis of their data. When it comes to purposes, we have a special responsibility, and it is one that may contribute to a sounder basis for "knowledge" itself. We take note of crucial notions such as *eschaton, salus, nirvana,* kingdom of God. They differ, but belong all to "the real." And they go beyond any theory of mere cognition that we can design. We have a special duty to bring such matters to the attention of educated despisers of religion today, before we get stranded in a complete theory, a system without a way out, before we collectively end up in the hell Sartre described so well.

Where should we begin? The question keeps occurring. The answer my teacher Joachim Wach used to give is "The best place to begin is where you are."

From that place we can look at any document. And a document of religion should have the last word in this book.

A Gentile once asked Rabbi Yoshua ben Kapara, "Is it true that you say your God sees the future?" "Yes," was the reply. "Then how is it that it is written (Gen. vi.6), 'And it grieved Him at His heart'?" "Hast thou," replied the Rabbi, "ever had a boy born to thee?" "Yes," said the Gentile; "and I rejoiced and made others rejoice with me." "Didst thou not know that he would eventually die?" asked the Rabbi. "Yes," answered the other; "but at the time of joy is joy, and at the time of mourning, mourning." "So it is before the Holy One — blessed be He! — seven days He mourned before the deluge destroyed the world."[31]

NOTES

1. G. C. van Niftrik, *De boodschap van Sartre* (Nijkerk: Callenbach, 1953).

2. Albert Camus *The Plague,* trans. Stuart Gilbert (New York: Vintage, 1972), p. 287.

3. Ibid., p. 287.

4. Karl Popper, *The Open Society and Its Enemies,* 5th, rev. ed. (London: Routledge, 1945; Princeton: Princeton University Press, 1966), 2 vols.

5. It is interesting to see, for instance, how Derrida meditates about Nietzsche's suggestion in *Beyond Good and Evil* that "truth" might be feminine. See Jacques Derrida, *Spurs: Nietzsche's Styles,* trans. Barbara Barlow (Chicago: University of Chicago Press, 1979), p. 55.

6. Lawrence E. Sullivan, *Icanchu's Drum: An Orientation to Meaning in South American Religions* (New York: Macmillan; London: Collier Macmillan, 1988).

7. David Carrasco and Jane Marie Law, eds., *Waiting for the Dawn: Mircea Eliade in Perspective* (Boulder, Colo.: Westview Press, 1985; Niwot: University Press of Colorado, 1991).

8. Charles H. Long, *Significations: Signs, Symbols, and Images in the Interpretation of Religion* (Philadelphia: Fortress Press, 1986).

9. In addition to Eliade's brilliance in seeing connections in religious data, this astounding knowledge of relevant facts cannot fail to impress anyone. One gets an idea by paging through the name and subject indices alone in the end of his *Patterns of Comparative Religion* (London: Sheed and Ward, 1958), or by flipping through the footnotes.

10. Mircea Eliade, *Le chamanisme et les techniques archaïques de l'extase* (Paris: Payot, 1951); Revised and enlarged edition in English translation by Willard R. Trask, *Shamanism: Archaic Techniques of Ecstasy* (New York: Pantheon, 1964).

11. Mac Linscott Ricketts is a pupil of Eliade and has rendered us a great service by learning Romanian and translating Eliade's often quite illuminating autobiographical writings. Except for the volume mentioned in the next footnote, and *Journal III* listed below, all other volumes of Eliade's autobiography were translated by Mac Linscott Ricketts directly from the Romanian: *Mircea Eliade: The Romanian Roots 1907–1945* (Boulder, Colo.: East European Monographs [distributed by Columbia University Press], 1988); *Autobiography,* vol. 1, *1907–1937: Journey East, Journey West* (San Francisco: Harper & Row, n.d.);

Autobiography, 1937–1960: Exile's Odyssey (Chicago: University of Chicago Press, 1988); *Journal I: 1945–1955* (Chicago, 1990); *Journal III: 1970–1978,* trans. from the French by Teresa Lavender Fagan (Chicago, 1989); *Journal IV: 1979–1985* (Chicago, 1990).

12. Mircea Eliade, *No Souvenirs. Journal, 1957–1969,* trans. from the French by Fred. H. Johnson, Jr. (New York: Harper & Row, 1977).

13. W. W. Malandra, *An Introduction to Ancient Iranian Religion* (Minneapolis: University of Minnesota Press, 1983).

14. Bruce Lincoln, *Priests, Warriors, and Cattle: A Study in the Ecology of Religions* (Berkeley: University of California Press, 1981).

15. *Death, War, and Sacrifice: Studies in Ideology and Practice,* foreword by Wendy Doniger (Chicago: University of Chicago Press, 1991).

16. *Authority: Construction and Corrosion* (Chicago: University of Chicago Press, 1994).

17. *Emerging from the Chrysalis: Rituals of Women's Initiation* (New York: Oxford University Press, 1991).

18. *Theorizing Myth: Narrative, Ideology, and Scholarship* (Chicago: University of Chicago Press, 1999).

19. Jonathan Z. Smith, *Map Is not Territory: Studies in the History of Religions* (Chicago: University of Chicago Press, 1978).

20. *Imagining Religion: From Babylon to Jonestown* (Chicago: University of Chicago Press, 1982).

21. *Drudgery Divine: On the Comparison of Early Christianities and the Religions of Late Antiquity* (Chicago: University of Chicago Press, 1990).

22. Devin DeWeese, *Islamization and the Native Religion in the Golden Horde: Baba Tükles and Conversion to Islam in Historical and Epic Tradition* (University Park: Pennsylvania State University Press, 1994).

23. Jess Byron Hollenback, *Mysticism: Experience, Response, and Empowerment* (University Park: Pennsylvania State University Press, 1996).

24. *Jews and Christians on Time and Eternity: Charles Péguy's Portrait of Bernard-Lazare* (Stanford, Calif.: Stanford University Press, 1998). A fascinating earlier work by Annette Aronowicz is *Freedom from Ideology: Secrecy in Modern Expression* (New York: Garland Publishing, 1987).

25. Clifford Geertz, *The Interpretation of Cultures* (New York: Basic Books, 1973). Reprinted repeatedly.

26. Jacques Maquet, *The Aesthetic Experience: An Anthropologist Looks at the Visual Arts* (New Haven: Yale University Press, 1986).

27. See chapter 9 of this book, under "Social Studies." Another anthropologist, who was no fan of Durkheim, on this particular point of the reality of religion would certainly not have disagreed. See W. E. H. Stanner and John Hilary Martin, *People from the Dawn: Religion, Homeland, and Privacy in Australian Aboriginal Culture* (Antioch, Calif.: Solas Press, 2001).

28. The question fascinated Michel Foucault in his study of madness, *Histoire de la folie* (Paris: Plon, 1961), and Karl Jaspers dealt with it in his earlier work on psychopathology.

29. Stephen W. Hawking, *A Brief History of Time: From the Big Bang to Black Holes* (Toronto: Bantam, 1988), p. 175.

30. Haiku of Sogyo (1667–1731), in Lucien Stryk, *Zen Poems of China and Japan: The Crane's Bill* (New York: Anchor, 1973), p. 85.

31. From the Midrashim: *Bereshith Rabbah,* chap. 27, in M. H. Harris, trans., *Hebraic Literature: Translation from the Talmud, Midrashim, and Kabbalah* (New York: Tudor, 1939), pp. 241–42.

I N D E X

abortion, 25, 63
Abraham, 103
Adam, 22
The Aesthetic Experience, 308
aesthetics, 12, 13, 14, 308–9
Africa, 308, 309
  Bantu in, 106
  Mbutu in, 106
Agni, 51, 108–9
Akkadian, 113–14
Albinoni, Tomaso, 178
Alembert, Jean Le Rond d', 172
Allah, 23, 282
allegory, 133–35, 145, 162, 220
American Society for the Study of Religion, 289
Amos, Book of 2:4–16, 30–31, 36, 85, 92, 256
ananda, 86
anatomy, 13
Anglican Church, 49, 66
animism, 190, 244–47, 249, 275, 278
L'année sociologique, 239
anthropology, 14, 26, 131, 212, 215–16, 238,
  275–78, 290–91, 308–9
  vs. history of religions, 271, 275, 276, 277
  See also Tylor, Edward Burnett
Anthropos, 281, 289
Antonescu, Ion, 304
Aphrodite, 52
Apocalypse Now, 251
Apostles' Creed, 114–15, 117
Aquinas, St. Thomas, 6, 154, 160, 232, 246
archaeology, 14, 20, 212, 214–15
Archaeology of Knowledge, 300
archetypes, 275
architecture, 14
Aristotle, 26, 129, 132, 143, 159, 183, 274, 300
Arjuna, 279–80
Aronowicz, Annette, 259, 307–8

art history, 13, 14
Arthur, King, 147
astronomy, 4, 14, 57, 159, 197, 262, 310
Aśvaghoṣa, 111–12
atheism, 209, 254, 256, 298
Augustine, Saint, 6, 59, 141–42, 143, 144,
  147, 268
Australia, original inhabitants of, 89, 240, 311
Authority: Construction and Corrosion, 306
Avesta, 214, 255
Aztecs, 51, 104, 302–3

Bach, Johann Sebastian, 178, 193
Bacon, Francis, 164
Baker, Russell, 6–7
Balinese Hinduism, 22, 66
Banier, Abbé Antoine, 189–90
banking, 229, 235
Bantu, 106
Baptist Missionary Society, 237
Barth, Karl, 5–6, 167, 253, 256–57, 264
Basho, 86
Basil, Saint, 34–35
Bathsheba, 72
Beatrys, 147–48
Beethoven, Ludwig van, 193, 194
Belcampo, 34–35
Bergier, Nicolas Sylvestre, 189–90
Bernard of Clairvaux, 135, 145
Bhagavadgītā, 213
bhakti, 139
Bianchi, Ugo, 281
Bible, Hebrew, 138–40, 145, 156, 163
  Book of Amos 2:4–16, 30–31, 36, 85,
    92, 256
  covenants in, 166
  immortality in, 160
  justice in, 68, 92–93

Bible, Hebrew (*cont.*)
   soul and body in, 96–97
   Ten Commandments, 104
   See also Deuteronomy; Exodus, Book of;
      Genesis; Isaiah, Book of; Job, Book
      of; Kings, Book of; New Testament;
      Psalms; Samuel, Book of; Song of
      Songs; Wisdom of Solomon
binarism, 277
biology, 15, 23, 28, 74–75, 240, 274
Bismarck, Otto von, 223
Blake, William, 206–7
bodhicitta, 95–96
Book of Songs, 90–91
Borneo, 112–15
Boucher de Perthes, Jacques, 214–15
Brahman, 36, 249
Brahmanism/Vedism, 50–51, 67, 108–11,
      112–13, 127, 309
   See also Hinduism
brāhmaṇa, 66–67
Brahms, Johannes, 194
Brelich, Angelo, 281
Brentano, Franz, 263
Breytenbach, Breyten, 95–96
A Brief History of Time, 310
Broda, Johanna, 302
Brosses, Charles de, 189–90
Buber, Martin, 115–16, 264
bubonic plague, 169
Buddhacarita, 111–12
Buddhism, 214, 239, 256, 291, 308
   attitude toward science in, 38
   the Buddha, 111–12, 127, 259
   Christianity compared to, 21, 37, 39,
      59, 66, 69, 88, 96–97, 111, 132,
      168, 250, 268
   enlightenment in, 33–34, 38, 39, 73–74,
      95–97, 112, 259
   gods in, 21
   Hinduism compared to, 66, 69–70, 74,
      96, 127, 128, 250
   illusion of self in, 96
   Judaism compared to, 73, 132, 250
   Lotus of the True Law, 91
   Mahayana Buddhism, 91
   meditation in, 111
   origin of, 111–12, 127, 132, 259
   use of language in, 95, 96
   Vajrayāna Buddhism, 96

and Vietnam War, 74, 105
   Zen, 33–34, 86
Buddhism in Translation, 291
Bultmann, Rudolf, 269–70, 297
Burckhardt, Jacob, 261
Bush, George, 65

Cain, Seymour, 293
calculus, 4, 77
calendar system, 26, 137
Calvin, John, 6, 29, 49, 96–97, 156, 171, 177,
      196, 232
Campbell, Joseph, 265
Camus, Albert, 298–99
Capital, 230
capitalism, 170, 229–31, 238
Carnap, Rudolf, 272, 300
Carrasco, David, 302–3
Champollion, Jean-François, 213–14, 218
Chantepie de la Saussaye, P. D., 283–84
chemistry, 13, 15
children, 177
China, 76, 106, 127, 149–50, 168, 175, 213,
      234, 235, 239, 307
Chopin, Frédéric, 194
Christianity, 85–86, 200, 202, 224, 231,
      300, 302
   Anglican Church, 49
   Apostles' Creed, 114–15, 117
   Brahmanism compared to, 109–10
   Buddhism compared to, 21, 37, 39, 59,
      66, 69, 88, 96–97, 111, 132, 168,
      250, 268
   change in, 29
   churches in, 49
   Congregationalists, 171
   creation myth of Ngaju Dayak compared
      to, 114–15
   the cross in, 23, 24–25
   and death, 114–15
   Episcopal Church, 49
   equality in, 67
   the Eucharist in, 49, 50, 66, 118, 133, 150
   faith in, 37, 65, 232, 269
   God in, 22, 129, 137, 139–40, 141–42,
      145, 150–51, 155–56, 160
   Hinduism compared to, 21, 37, 50, 64, 65,
      66, 69–70, 93, 98, 111, 175, 273
   the Holy Spirit in, 139
   the incarnation in, 37, 155, 256

Islam compared to, 37, 50, 67, 68, 69, 71,
    73, 92, 103–4, 149–51, 175, 273
  Jesus in, 24–25, 37, 59, 66, 72, 85,
    92, 103, 139, 145, 147, 155, 212,
    256, 272
  Judaism compared to, 37, 59, 65, 67, 68,
    69, 71–72, 74, 92, 103–4, 129,
    138–40, 149–51, 273, 308
  justice in, 92–93
  language in, 113
  love of neighbor in, 64
  Methodism, 236–37
  missionaries, 234–37, 239, 242, 271,
    281–83
  origin of, 138–43
  pilgrimages in, 50
  prayer in, 111
  Protestantism, 37, 49, 50, 96–97, 111, 145,
    156, 170, 171, 179, 234, 236–37, 238,
    286, 292
  pure form of, 16
  Reformed Church, 114–15
  relationship to natural religions, 105–6
  relationship to religion of Israel, 65, 67, 71,
    92, 103, 104, 138–39, 231, 273
  revelation in, 12, 105–6, 155, 166, 196,
    198, 233
  Roman Catholicism, 49, 50, 113, 133, 156,
    179, 234–36, 281, 286
  sacraments in, 21, 50, 66, 118, 133, 150
  saints in, 34–35
  salvation in, 37, 59, 72, 92, 212
  sermons in, 37–38
  sin in, 59, 256–57, 281
  Taoism compared to, 37, 69–70
  as tradition, 28–29
  the Trinity in, 139
  Zoroastrianism compared to, 68
A Christmas Carol, 246
churches, Christian, 49, 50
Cicero, Marcus Tullius, 20, 22, 179, 180
cit, 86
classes, social
  Adam Smith on, 230
  in ancient Greece, 131–32, 143, 145, 170
  in ancient India, 66–67, 127
  in ancient Rome, 132, 145
  and humanism, 162
  Marx on, 230–31
  during the Middle Ages, 145, 147, 149

Clement XIV, 235
Codrington, R. H., 249
Coeurdoux, Fr., 213
cognition, 110
  and knowledge, 101–2, 117
collective unconscious, 275
colonialism, 106, 168, 203, 213, 215, 223,
  224, 229, 253, 271, 303, 309
Columbia University, 307
common sense, 164–65, 166, 167, 182
communism, 60–61
communities, 43, 117
Comte, Auguste, 242–44
Confucius, 10, 76, 102, 175, 255
Congregatio de propaganda fide, 234
Congregationalists, 171
Conrad, Joseph, 250–52, 259, 260, 261
  The Heart of Darkness, 251–52
Constant de Rebecque, Benjamin, 216–17
Constitution of the United States
  Article Six, 71
  First Amendment, 71
Copernicus, Nicolas, 158
2 Corinthians 3:17, 62
Couperin, François, 178
Cours de philosophie positive, 242
creation
  in Genesis, 22, 31, 39, 55–58, 59, 62, 74,
    89, 114, 130, 134–35, 146, 147, 163,
    282, 310
  God as creator, 22, 31, 39, 55–58, 62, 74,
    77, 114, 127–28, 134–35, 146, 163,
    174–75, 185, 281–82
  goodness of, 56–58
  myth of Ngaju Dayak, 114–15
  primordial waters, 130
creativity, 193, 195
Creuzer, Friedrich, 217–19
cross, the, 23, 24–25

Dante Alighieri, 147, 157
Darmesteter, James, 255
darśan, 49
Darwin, Charles, 74–75, 130, 228, 243, 244
David, King, 72
death, 44, 55, 177, 217, 253, 269, 270
  burial rites, 46–47, 111–12, 114–15, 117,
    184–85, 305–6
  death penalty, 25, 63, 65–66
  and Emily Dickenson, 85–86, 87

Death, War, and Sacrifice, 305–6
de Bary, William Theodore, 307
deism, 174–75, 178, 182, 186, 187,
    193, 310
Delacroix, Eugène, 194
demons, 142, 270
Derrida, Jacques, 299, 300
Descartes, René, 156, 158–61, 167, 172,
    240, 241
    on clear and distinct ideas, 159
    Discours de la méthode, 159–60
    on God, 160
    and mathematics, 158, 159, 264
    Meditations, 159–60
    and reason, 159–61, 169, 182–83,
        184, 185, 272, 277, 299
    on theology, 160
descriptive disciplines, 12, 13–15,
    17–18, 120
determinism, causal, 163, 299
Deuteronomy
    4:4 and 7, 162
    4:8, 162
    4:32, 162
    9:6 and 7, 162
    10:15, 162
DeWeese, Devin, 307
Dharma, 93
Dickens, Charles, 246
Dickinson, Emily, 85–92
dictionaries, 215–16
Diderot, Denis, 172, 224
diffusionism, 250
Dilthey, Wilhelm, 260–64, 265, 266, 271,
    284, 285
Diodorus, 137
Doniger, Wendy, 305
Drees, Willem, 287
Drudgery Divine, 307
Dukakis, Michael, 65–66
Duméry, Henry, 69–70, 265
Dumézil, Georges, 239, 306
Durkheim, Émile, 48, 51, 238–42, 268, 275,
    277, 280
    Les formes élémentaires de la religion,
        239–40
    on religion, 239–42, 244, 252, 309
    on the sacred and the profane, 241
Dutch language, 157
Dutch Missionary Society, 237
dynamism, 249–50, 275

Eckhart, Johannes, 145
economics, 26
education, 62, 177–78, 182–84, 199–200,
    206, 228
Edwards, Jonathan, 178
egg, the, as symbol, 35–36
Egypt, ancient, 47, 49, 58, 133, 143, 213–14,
    218, 219, 250, 268
Einstein, Albert, 167
Eisenhower, Dwight, 7
Eliade, Mircea, 277, 289, 302, 307
    Encyclopedia of Religion, 293
    and politics, 303–5
    on religious symbolism, 26, 28, 54,
        287–88, 310–11
    *Emerging from the Chrysalis: Rituals of Women's
        Initiation,* 306
emotions, 41–44, 136, 177–78, 193, 194,
    198, 201, 217, 279, 280
empiricism, 100, 107–8, 163–67, 204,
    242, 277
Encyclopedia of Religion, 293
The Encyclopedia of Religion and Ethics, 233
Encyclopédie, 172
enlightenment
    in Buddhism, 33–34, 38, 39, 73–74,
        95–97, 112, 259
    in Hinduism, 38
Enlightenment, the, 217, 236
    attitudes toward religion during, 173–77,
        178, 179–88, 189–90, 234, 243,
        255, 273
    deism during, 174–75, 178, 182, 186,
        187, 193
    ethics during, 176–77
    music during, 178
    role of emotion in, 177–78
    role of progress in, 194, 228
    role of reason in, 171–77, 193, 194,
        202, 224
Epic Mythology, 291
Episcopal Church, 49, 66
epistemology, 167, 250, 260–61, 272, 274
    cognition and knowledge, 101–2, 117
    data vs. theory, 8–12, 101–3, 125–26
    and history of religions, 3–5
    particulars vs. wisdom, 8–12,
        101–3, 188
equality, 67, 131–32, 170, 189
Erasmus, Desiderius, 63, 156, 158
Eros, 52

eschatology, 300
Eskimos, 106
The Essence of Christianity, 232
The Eternal in Man, 261
ethics, 12, 13, 14, 57, 176–77, 288
    religion and justice, 64, 68
Eucharist, the, 49, 50, 66, 118, 133, 150
euhemerism, 133–34, 136–38, 142,
    145–47, 190
Everyman, 145
evil, 177, 273
evolutionism, 16, 223–24, 229, 240, 242,
    244–45, 268, 269–70, 279, 281
    and Darwin, 74–75, 130, 228, 243, 244
    vs. Enlightenment progress, 194, 228
    and non-European peoples, 234, 237, 239
existentialism, 209–10, 211, 269
Exodus, Book of, 20:2–3, 104

fables, 134
faith, 21, 37–38, 40, 48, 65, 211, 232–33,
    269, 293
families, 43
fear, 136, 198, 252, 280
feelings, 41–44, 136, 177–78, 193, 194, 198,
    201, 217, 279, 280
fertility, 268
fetishism, 190, 250
Feuerbach, Ludwig, 232, 233
Fichte, Johann Gottlieb, 202, 203
Fielding, Henry, 175
flood, the, 58
Fontenelle, Bernard le Bovier, 189
Forest of Symbols, 276
Les formes élémentaires de la religion, 239–40
Foucault, Michel, 298, 299–300
France, 89, 236, 280, 301
    the *Encyclopédie* in, 172
    the Enlightenment in, 171–78, 179, 186
    French Revolution, 171, 172, 189, 229,
        262, 266
    individualism in, 241
    music in, 178
    See also Descartes, René; Voltaire
Frazer, Sir James, 268–69, 276
Frederick II, 186
Frederick William IV, 222
freedom of expression, 172
freedom of the press, 62
Freud, Sigmund, 64, 110, 250, 275
functionalism, 275–76, 299

Galatians 5:13, 62
Galileo Galilei, 158
Geertz, Clifford, 308
Genesis
    1:1–2, 31, 39, 55–58, 59, 62, 74, 89, 114,
        130, 134–35, 146, 147, 182, 310
    1:27, 22
    1:30, 56
    2, 177
    6:6, 311–12
geology, 57, 240
geometry, 13, 164, 183
The Ghost Dance Religion and the Sioux Outbreak
    of 1890, 246
Gifford Lectures, 289
Gobineau, Joseph-Arthur, 261
God, 21, 48, 190, 300, 311–12
    attributes of, 129, 139–40, 180–81
    changes in images of, 16
    in Christianity, 22, 129, 137, 139–40,
        141–42, 145, 150–51, 155–56, 160
    as creator, 22, 31, 39, 55–58, 62, 74, 77,
        114, 127–28, 134–35, 146, 163,
        174–75, 185, 281–82
    divine providence, 185, 187
    existence of, 129, 160, 180–81, 273
    God's love, 86
    grace of, 72, 86, 138, 170, 187, 210
    and history, 72, 104–5, 187–88, 233
    infinity of, 4, 77, 155–56
    in Islam, 23, 282
    in Judaism, 31, 129, 139–40
    justice of, 72, 86, 87–88, 92–93
    as nature, 161–63, 164, 168
    as omnipotent, 139
    oneness/unity of, 48, 103–4, 131, 137,
        141–42
    as prime mover, 281
    revelation of, 12, 105–6, 155, 166, 196,
        198, 233
    as transcendent, 137, 269
    as unchangeable/eternal, 54
    as watchmaker/architect, 174–75, 178,
        182, 186, 187, 193, 310
    will of, 104
    Word (*Logos*) of, 39, 195, 272
    worship of, 174–75
    See also gods and goddesses
gods and goddesses, 16, 53, 282
    Agni, 51, 108–9
    allegorical explanations of, 133–35, 145

gods and goddesses (*cont.*)
  in ancient Greece, 47, 52, 104, 129–31,
    132, 133–38, 143, 184, 219–20,
    268, 281
  in ancient Rome, 133, 143, 184, 220
  Aphrodite, 52
  Eros, 52
  euhemerism as explanation of, 133–34,
    136–38, 142, 145–47, 190
  Great Goddess (Devī), 49
  in Hinduism, 49–50, 59, 93, 97, 250,
    279–80
  Krishna, 279–80
  rational explanations of, 133–34,
    135–36
  Śiva, 49, 59
  Vayu, 51
  Viṣṇu, 49–50, 97, 250
  Zeus, 137, 250
  See also God
Goethe, Johann Wolfgang von, 194, 196, 203,
    216, 224, 286
The Golden Bough, 268–69
Goodenough, E. R., 289, 290, 306
goodness
  of creation, 56–58
  as opposed to evil, 67–68
Görres, Joseph von, 217–18, 220
grace of God, 72, 86, 138, 170, 187, 210
grail, the, 147
Granet, Marcel, 239
Grass, Günther, 35–36
Great Goddess (Devī), 49
The Great Temple of Tenochtitlán, 302
Greece, ancient, 127
  gods and goddesses in, 47, 52, 104,
    129–31, 132, 133–38, 143, 184,
    219–20, 268, 281
  influence of, 132–38, 145, 154, 177,
    199, 264, 300
  language of, 129, 132, 133, 139, 145,
    156, 177, 213, 214
  social classes in, 131–32, 143,
    145, 170
Green, Julian, 257
Gregory XV, 234
Grotius, Hugo, 170, 171
Grottanelli, Cristiano, 281
guilt, 269
Gusinde, Fr. Martin, 282–83

hajj, the, 50
Hamann, Johann Georg, 182, 185–88, 194,
    195, 199, 210, 221
Handel, George Frederick, 178
happiness, 258–59
Harvard Oriental Studies, 291
Harvard Theological Review, 290
Harvard University, 290, 291, 292, 302, 307
Haskell Lectures, 289
Hastings, James, 233
Hastings, Warren, 213
Hawaii, 43
Hawking, Stephen W., 310
Haydn, Franz Joseph, 194
Haydon, A. Eustace, 292, 302
The Heart of Darkness, 251
Hebrews, Letter to the, 12:18–19, 22–24, 90
Hegel, G. W. F., 143, 202–3, 209, 210, 228,
    230, 242, 243, 264, 284
Heidegger, Martin, 265
Heidelberg Symbolists, 217–19
Das Heilige, 279–80, 288, 293
Heine, Heinrich, 230
Henry VIII, 158
Heraclitus, 9, 11, 102, 188
Herder, Johann Gottfried, 195–98
  on God and religion, 196–98
  *Ideas About the Philosophy of a History
    of Mankind,* 197–98
  on symbolism, 198, 201
Hermann, Gottfried, 204
hermeneutics, 18, 119–20, 201, 293–94
Herodotus, 22, 47, 68, 132, 143, 219
Heyne, Christian Gottlob, 220
hierarchy, 67
Hinduism, 112, 212–13
  attitude toward science in, 38, 40
  Balinese Hinduism, 22, 66
  Brahman, 36, 249
  Buddhism compared to, 66, 69–70, 74,
    96, 127, 128, 250
  change in, 29
  Christianity compared to, 21, 37, 50, 64,
    65, 66, 69–70, 93, 98, 111, 175, 273
  enlightenment in, 38
  gods and goddesses in, 49–50, 59, 93, 97,
    250, 279–80
  Islam compared to, 69–70, 93, 175, 273
  Jainism compared to, 128
  Judaism compared to, 69–70, 93, 273

justice (Dharma) in, 93
marital love in, 97–98
meditation in, 111
the *Rāmāyana* in, 97
the syllable ŌM in, 23, 24
temples in, 49–50
as tradition, 28–29
Vedas in, 29, 92
See also Brahmanism/Vedism
history, 22–23, 197, 202–3, 257
as comparative, 16
as descriptive field, 14, 15
Dilthey on, 261–62, 265
exact sciences compared to, 261–63,
271–72
relationship to anthropology, 275–78
relationship to God, 72, 104–5,
187–88, 233
sections/breaks in, 144–45, 155, 171
history of religions, 22–23, 100–102,
189–90, 246, 273–74, 279–88
American Society for the Study of
Religion, 289
vs. anthropology, 271, 275, 276, 277
Anthropos, 281, 289
data vs. theory in, 13–16, 273
and epistemology, 3–5
Harvard Theological Review, 290
and hermeneutics, 18, 119–20
*History of Religions: An International
Journal of Comparative Historical
Studies*, 289
International Association of the History of
Religions (I. A. H. R.), 289
purpose of study of, 102–3
Revue de l'histoire des religions, 289
and theology, 100, 255–56, 283
and truth claims, 16, 117–20, 143, 233
in United States, 180–81, 288–93,
302–9
at universities, 100, 255–56, 280–81,
288, 289, 290, 291, 292, 302–3,
306–7
See also Eliade, Mircea; Müller, Friedrich
Max; Pettazzoni, Raffaele; van der
Leeuw, G.
*History of Religions: An International Journal
of Comparative Historical Studies*, 289
A History of Religious Ideas, 288
Hitler, Adolf, 304

Hobbes, Thomas, 156, 158, 163–64,
168, 170
Holland. *See* Netherlands
Holocaust, the, 306
holy, the, 279–80
home, 88–91
Homer, 92, 134, 147
Hopkins, E. Washburn, 291
Hubert, Henri, 239
Huit Clos, 298
human beings
equality of, 67, 131–32, 170, 189
and happiness, 258–59
as rational, 26–27, 38, 40, 67, 81, 110
as religious by nature, 23, 26–28
as seeking profit, 26–27
as social beings, 26, 27–28
as toolmakers (*homo faber*), 26–27
humanism, 145, 156, 162, 163
human sacrifice, 51
Hume, David, 165, 172–73, 179–82, 230,
273, 279
Dialogues Concerning Natural Religion,
179–81, 188
The Natural History of Religion, 179, 190
on reason, 180–81, 202
as skeptic, 180–81
humor, 114, 118, 175, 208
in myths, 54–55, 58–59, 86, 88
subjective reservedness in, 59, 86, 88
types of, 58–59, 88
Hus, Johannes, 150
Husserl, Edmund, 260, 263–65, 266,
267, 284

Ibn Kammuna, 149–50
Ibn Khaldūn, 151
Ibsen, Henrik, 286
Icanchu's Drum, 302
Iceland, 146, 149
The Idea of the Holy, 279–80, 288, 293
ideology, 41, 203, 306
Iliad, 134, 147
*Image and Pilgrimage in Christian
Culture*, 276
*Imagining Religion: From Babylon to
Jonestown*, 306–7
immortality, 160
imperialism, 229, 236, 239, 245
incarnation, the, 155

India, ancient, 104, 139, 149–50, 168, 223, 234, 268, 291, 307
  almsgiving in, 65
  Indus River civilization, 215
  linguistics in, 76–77
  origin of religion in, 47, 212–13, 218–19
  social classes in, 66–67, 127
  See also Brahmanism/Vedism; Hinduism; Jainism
Indiana University, 307
individualism, 43, 117, 169–71, 176–77, 201, 232–33, 240–41, 305
Indonesia, 277, 308
Indra, 51
intellect, 125–26
  See also reason
International Association of the History of Religions (I. A. H. R.), 289
The Interpretation of Cultures, 308
Iran, ancient, 21, 132
  Zoroastrianism in, 67–68, 104–5
Isaiah, Book of, 39
Ishmael, 103
Islam, 21, 302, 307
  Allah in, 23, 282
  Buddhism compared to, 69
  Christianity compared to, 37, 50, 67, 68, 69, 71, 73, 92, 103–4, 149–51, 175, 273
  equality in, 67
  faith in, 37, 65
  the hajj in, 50
  Hinduism compared to, 69–70, 93, 175, 273
  Judaism compared to, 37, 67, 68, 69, 71, 73, 92, 103–4, 149–51, 273
  justice in, 92–93
  the Ka'bah, 50
  Mohammed, 73, 103
  pure form of, 16
  the Qur'an, 23, 24, 68, 73, 103–4, 150
  relationship to laws and politics, 71
  relationship to religion of Israel, 67, 73, 92, 103, 104, 273
  Shiite Islam, 73
  Sufism, 112, 135
  Sunni Islam, 73
  Zoroastrianism compared to, 68
Islamization and Native Religion in the Golden Horde, 307
Israel, kingdom of, 30–31, 71–72

Israel, religion of
  and politics, 71–72
  relationship to Christianity, 65, 67, 71, 92, 103, 104, 138–39, 231, 273
  relationship to Islam, 67, 73, 92, 103, 104, 273
  relationship to Judaism, 65, 67, 71, 92, 103, 104, 138–39, 231
  structure of, 22
Italian language, 157
Italy, 144, 178, 196, 280–81

Jacob, 32
Jaeger, Werner, 130
Jainism, 69, 127–28, 132, 250
James, William, 246, 261, 266, 285, 290, 301
Japan, 106, 213, 307
Jaspers, Karl, 118–19, 209, 265, 269–70, 272
Jastrow, Morris, 53, 291–92
Jaucourt, Louis de, 172
Jesuits, 234–36
Jesus Christ, 66, 85, 103, 139, 145, 147, 272
  as incarnation, 37, 155, 256
  passion of, 23, 24–25, 178
  as savior, 59, 72, 92, 212
Jewish Symbols in the Greco-Roman Period, 289
Jews and Christians on Time and Eternity, 308
Job, Book of, 39
Jones, Sir William, 212–13
Josselin de Jong, J. P. B. de, 277
Judah, 103
Judah, kingdom of, 30–31
Judaism, 21, 115–16, 200, 231, 289, 300
  Buddhism compared to, 59, 73, 132, 250
  Christianity compared to, 37, 59, 65, 67, 68, 69, 71–72, 74, 92, 103–4, 129, 138–40, 149–51, 273, 308
  equality in, 67
  faith in, 37
  God in, 31, 129, 139–40
  Hinduism compared to, 69–70, 93, 273
  Islam compared to, 37, 67, 68, 69, 71, 73, 92, 103–4, 149–51, 273
  justice in, 92–93
  rabbinical literature in, 31, 55, 57–58, 62, 290, 311–12
  relationship to religion of Israel, 65, 67, 71, 92, 103, 104, 138–39, 231
  Zoroastrianism compared to, 68

Judgment Day, 86, 87–88, 118
Jung, Carl Gustav, 265, 275
justice, 120, 138, 177, 273, 306
   of God, 72, 86, 87–88, 92–93

Ka'bah, 50
Kalakaua, King David, 43
Kālidāsa, 97, 213
Kant, Immanuel, 176, 186, 239, 252, 260,
   261–62, 264–65, 279, 280
Khrushchev, Nikita, 40
Kierkegaard, Søren, 32–33, 187, 194, 208,
   209–12, 230, 246, 253, 259
   Concluding Unscientific Postscript, 210–11
   on eternal happiness, 210–11, 212
   and existentialism, 209–10, 211, 269
   on leap of faith, 211, 232–33
King, Martin Luther, Jr., 50, 170
Kings, Book of, 72
Kipling, Rudyard, 224, 245
Kitagawa, Joseph, 289
knowledge and cognition, 101–2, 117
Koppers, Fr. Wilhelm, 282–83
Koran. See Qur'an
Koyré, Alexandre, 265
Kraemer, Hendrik, 237
Krishna, 279–80
kṣatriya, 66–67
kula trade, 276

La Fontaine, Jean de, 134
land, 88–89
Langer, Suzanne K., 293
language
   dictionaries, 215–16
   in education, 183
   Herder on, 195
   study of, 76–77, 213–14, 215–16, 219,
      221, 223–25, 272, 277
   use in Buddhism, 95, 96
   use by Ngaju Dayak, 112, 113–14
   Wittgenstein on, 267–68, 272
language analysis, 118, 266–69, 272
Lanman, Charles Rockwell, 291
Latin, 113, 133, 139, 145, 177, 213, 249
law, 120, 169
Law, Jane Marie, 303
Lederer, William J., 241
Leibniz, Gottfried Wilhelm, 4, 77, 173
Lessing, Gotthold Ephraim, 197, 209, 239
Leviathan, 163–64

Levinas, Emmanuel, 212, 265, 300
Lévi-Strauss, Claude, 11, 277, 298, 299, 308
Lévy-Bruhl, Lucien, 275
Libianus, 141
liminal features in culture, 276–77
Lincoln, Bruce, 305–6
linguistics, 14, 76–77, 219, 221, 224,
   272, 277
   See also language
Liszt, Franz, 221
Locke, John, 156, 159, 164–67, 168, 169, 172,
   250, 277
   and religion, 165–67
Loen, A. E., 209
logic, 12, 23, 169, 250, 263, 272
logical positivism, 272, 274, 300
London Missionary Society, 237
Long, Charles H., 289, 293, 303
Lotus of the True Law, 91
love, 269
   between man and woman, 93–95,
      97–98, 148
   God's love, 86
   of neighbor, 64
Lucretius, 132
Luther, Martin, 6, 37, 49, 111, 156, 185,
   196, 232
Lyotard, Jean-François, 299

MacLeish, Archibald, 93–94
magic, 268, 270
Mahāvīra, 127
Malandra, William W., 305
Malinowski, Bronislaw, 275–76
mana, 249
Mandelstam, Osip, 82–84, 87
Map Is Not Territory: Studies in the History
   of Religions, 306, 307
Maquet, Jacques, 308–9
Marcel, Gabriel, 209, 265, 293
Marcello, Benedetto, 178
Marduk, 282
Marett, Robert Ranulph, 249–50
marriage, 110, 184–85, 253
Marshack, Alexander, 75–76
Marshall, Sir John, 215
Marxism, 184, 229, 279
   in Soviet Union, 60–61
Marx, Karl, 60, 67, 230–32, 233, 243, 244
   on ideology, 41, 230
   on religion, 230, 231, 254

mathematics, 4–5, 23, 24, 155–56, 169, 260,
    263, 264–65, 274
    algebra, 183
    calculus, 4, 77
    and Descartes, 158, 159, 264
    geometry, 13, 164, 183
    and Spinoza, 161
Matthew, Gospel of
    1:1, 103
    28:19, 234
Mauriac, François, 257
Mauss, Marcel, 239, 276
Mbutu, 106
McCarthy, Joseph, 60–61
The Meaning and End of Religion, 293
Mecca, 50
medicine, 169
Melanesia, 90, 249
Melville, Herman, 207–9
Mendelssohn-Bartholdy, Felix, 194, 221
menstrual cycle, 26
Merleau-Ponty, Maurice, 265
Mesopotamia, 47, 214, 250, 282
metaphysics, 12, 14, 43
Methodism, 236–37
Middle Ages, 73, 77, 109, 144–51, 156,
    166, 168
    bubonic plague during, 169
    euhemerism during, 145–48
    reason during, 154, 155
    relationship to Renaissance, 144–45,
        155, 171
    scholastic philosophy during, 159, 169
    social classes during, 145, 147, 149
Midrashim, 31, 55
Mill, John Stuart, 263
Mills, L. H., 255
Milosz, Czeslaw, 89
Miskotte, K. H., 264
missionaries, 234–37, 239, 242, 271,
    281–83
Moby Dick, 207–9
Moctezuma, Eduardo Matos, 302
Modern Trends in World Religions, 292
Mohammed, 73, 103
mokṣa, 38, 86
money, 231
monotheism, 48, 103–4, 179, 273, 281–82
Montesquieu, Charles-Louis de Secondat,
    baron de, 172

Mooney, James, 246
moon, the
    and the calendar system, 26
    and menstrual cycle, 26
    as symbol, 25–26, 28, 76
Moore, George Foot, 290, 291
Moravian Brethren, 199, 201
More, Sir Thomas, 63, 158
Moses, 71
Mozart, Wolfgang Amadeus, 5–6, 178
Müller, Friedrich Max, 221–25, 242,
    246, 255
    The Sacred Books of the East, 223
Müller, Karl Otfried, 219–21
Müller, Wilhelm, 221
music, 5–6, 76, 178, 193, 194, 221
Mus, Paul, 239
mysticism, 126, 135, 145, 150, 155, 170
myths, 48, 53–63, 66, 107, 125, 177, 184,
    250, 269–70, 281, 287–88
    allegorical interpretations of, 133–35, 145
    as authoritative, 61–63, 88
    and community, 117
    as concrete, 54, 130
    and euhemerism, 137
    as explaining natural phenomena, 136
    and fear, 136
    home in, 88–91
    humor in, 54–55, 58–59, 86, 88
    and ideology, 306
    in modern society, 60–63
    Karl Müller on, 219–20
    origin of, 189
    as paradigms, 63
    and poetry, 81–98, 116, 219–20
    relationship to experiences, 126
    remythologizing of, 57–58, 62, 72–73,
        134–35
    Schärer on, 112–13, 114, 115
    Schelling on, 203–5
    and truth, 117, 272
    water in, 130

Napoleonic wars, 229
Nathan, 72
nationalism, 91, 223, 237, 261
A Nation of Sheep, 241
nature
    as divine, 161–63, 164, 168, 193, 195,
        213, 218

relationship to religions, 69–70, 105–6,
    136, 173–75, 186, 206–7, 234,
    246–47, 255
during Romantic movement, 194, 196
Needham, Joseph, 76
Neoplatonism, 141, 143
Netherlands, 157, 158, 280, 286–87, 303–4
New Guinea, 106, 277
New Testament, 64, 68, 103, 139, 142
    Bultmann on, 269–70, 297
    2 Corinthians 3:17, 62
    and Erasmus, 156
    Galatians 5:13, 62
    Hebrews 12:18–19, 22–24, 90
    immortality in, 160
    relationship to Hebrew Bible, 72
    worldviews in, 39
    See also Bible, Hebrew; Matthew, Gospel of
Newton, Isaac, 4, 77, 165
New Zealand, original inhabitants of, 89
Ngaju Dayak, 112–15
Nicholas of Cusa, 150–51, 155, 156
Niebuhr, Reinhold, 115–16, 264
Nietzsche, Friedrich, 250–51, 252–57, 259,
    260, 261, 300
    on God, 254, 298
    Thus Spoke Zarathustra, 254–55
nirvāṇa, 33, 38, 39, 86, 95–97
No Exit, 298
normative disciplines, 12–15, 17–18, 120
North American native peoples, 90, 106, 189,
    234, 246, 291
    medicine men among, 40

old age, 111–12
Old Testament. See Bible, Hebrew
ŌM, 23, 24
optimism, 169, 173, 217, 223
original sin, 59
The Origin of Species, 243
Ortega y Gasset, José, 36–37, 245, 261,
    262, 265
Otto, Rudolf, 279–80, 283, 292, 293
Overbeck, Franz, 253, 256

pantheism, 161–63, 164, 168, 193, 195,
    213, 218
Papuas, 106
Paraguay, 236
Parzifal, 147

Pasternak, Boris, 84
Patterns of Comparative Religion, 287
Paz, Octavio, 260
Péguy, Charles, 17–18, 250–51, 257–59, 260,
    261, 266, 308
Peirce, Charles Sanders, 261
Peking man (Homo pekinensis), 47
pessimism, 261
Pettazzoni, Raffaele, 264, 273, 280–81, 282,
    283, 287, 300
Phaedo, 52
phenomenology, 264–66, 267, 283–86,
    287, 292
Phenomenology of the Spirit, 202–3
Philippines, 47
philology, 4, 14, 156
philosophy
    aesthetics, 12, 13, 14
    and common sense, 164–67, 182
    dogmatism in, 301
    epistemology, 3–5, 8–12, 101–3, 117,
        125–26, 167, 188, 250, 260–61,
        272, 274
    ethics, 12, 13, 14, 57, 176–77
    existentialism, 209–10, 211, 269
    importance in study of religions, 14–15
    language analysis, 118, 266–69, 272
    logic, 12, 23, 169, 250, 263, 272
    metaphysics, 12, 14, 43
    as normative discipline, 12
    ontology, 57
    Péguy on, 17–18
    phenomenology, 264–66, 267, 283–86,
        287, 292
    positivism, 242–43, 266, 272, 274, 300
    relationship to science, 267, 272, 310
    and theology, 12, 14, 169, 272–73
    and truth, 117–20
    See also Aristotle; Descartes, René; Fichte,
        Johann Gottlieb; Hegel, G. W. F.;
        Hobbes, Thomas; Husserl, Edmund;
        James, William; Kierkegaard, Søren;
        Locke, John; Plato; Schelling, Friedrich
        Wilhelm Joseph; Thales; Wittgenstein,
        Ludwig; Xenophanes
Philosophy in a New Key, 293
physics, 15, 74, 76, 77, 159, 164, 168, 204,
    260, 264–65, 274, 310
Pico della Mirandola, 199
pietism, 43, 178, 201, 236, 237

pilgrimages, 21, 50
Pius VII, 236
The Plague, 298–99
Plato, 51–52, 129, 132, 143, 144, 159,
     170, 199, 200, 275, 300
     Phaedo, 52
     Republic, 170
     Symposium, 52
Plotinus, 143
poetry, 81–98, 116, 183, 206–7,
     219–20, 260
Poincaré, Henri, 125
politics, 69–74, 170–71, 220, 266,
     303–4, 305
polytheism, 48, 104, 179
Popper, Karl R., 272, 298, 299
popular psychology, 38, 41–42, 43–44
positivism, 242–43, 266, 272, 274, 300
postmodernism, 300
prayer, 41, 111, 125, 284
Priests, Warriors, and Cattle, 305
prophets and prophesy, 71–72, 104–5,
     126, 151, 206–7
     Amos, 30–31, 36, 85, 92, 256
Prose Edda, 146–48
Protestantism, 50, 96–97, 292
     Calvinism, 179
     and capitalism, 238
     Evangelicals, 237
     Methodism, 236–37
     and missionaries, 234, 236–37
     Reformation, 37, 49, 111, 145, 156, 170,
          171, 286
providence, divine, 185, 187
Psalms, 39
     86:6–10, 140
     104:2, 31
psychoanalysis, 43, 64, 110, 250, 273, 275
psychologism, 135–36, 250, 263, 267
psychology, 14, 101, 131, 136, 159, 165, 265
     popular psychology, 38, 41–42, 43–44
     psychoanalysis, 43, 64, 110, 250, 273, 275

Quetzalcoatl and the Irony of Empire, 302
Qur'an, 23, 24, 68, 73, 103–4, 150

Rabi'a, 135
Rāma, 97
Rameau, Jean-Philippe, 178
Ranke, Leopold von, 70
Reagan, Ronald, 222

reason
     and Descartes, 159–61, 169, 182–83,
          184, 185, 272, 277, 299
     during the Enlightenment, 171–77, 193,
          194, 224, 228
     and Hamann, 182, 187–88, 195
     and Herder, 195
     and Hobbes, 164, 170
     and Hume, 180–81, 202
     and Kierkegaard, 210
     and optimism, 169
     relationship to religion, 133–34, 135–36,
          154, 271
     during the Renaissance, 154–55, 228
     and Romantic movement, 195, 205, 216
     and Spinoza, 161
     and the state, 170–71
     and Vico, 182–83, 184, 185
     and Voltaire, 173, 224
Redfield, Robert, 276
reductionism, 230, 271
Reformed Church, 114–15
Relations de la nouvelle France, 234
religion
     allegorical explanations of, 133–35,
          145, 162
     and animism, 190, 244–47, 249, 275, 278
     biases concerning, 5
     and communism, 60
     doctrines in, 21
     euhemerism as explanation of, 133–34,
          136–38, 142, 145–47, 190
     and evolutionism, 190, 228, 242–43,
          268, 279
     and fear, 136, 198, 280
     and feelings/emotions, 41–44, 136, 194,
          198, 201, 217, 279, 280
     and fertility, 268
     and humor, 54–55, 58–59
     and ideology, 41, 58–59, 230
     individual religions distinguished from,
          20–22, 40, 46, 48, 200, 201, 224,
          225, 272–73, 293
     and language, 113–14
     ordinariness of, 23, 25, 46–47, 107,
          110–11, 126, 259, 284, 308
     origins of, 47, 107–8, 110, 189–90, 198,
          207, 223, 244–47, 249–50, 268,
          281–82
     and phenomenology, 265–66, 283–86,
          287, 292

practicality of, 111–15
relationship to experiences, 117, 126,
    261, 279, 293
relationship to faith, 37–38, 40, 48,
    65, 293
relationship to intellect, 125–26, 233
relationship to justice, 64, 68
relationship to magic, 268
relationship to personal wishes, 63–65
relationship to reason, 133–34, 135–36,
    154, 271
relationship to science, 5, 15–16, 18,
    26–28, 38, 40, 55, 56–57, 64, 69,
    74–77, 81, 136, 155–56, 165–68, 242,
    244–45, 247, 250–51, 255–56,
    260–61, 268, 269–70, 271–72, 273,
    274, 281, 297–98, 309–11
relationship to truth, 117–20, 143, 233
sacred vs. profane distinction, 241, 307
sacrifice in, 50–52
salvation in, 37, 39, 41, 44, 181–82, 187,
    188, 212, 259, 282, 310
the supernatural distinguished from,
    40–41, 310
universality of, 23, 27, 46–47, 92,
    184–85
worldview distinguished from, 38–40
See also religions; religious symbolism
Religion in Essence and Manifestation, 283,
    284, 287
Die Religion in Geschichte und Gegenwart, 233
The Religion of Java, 308
religions
    changes in, 16, 29–37, 55, 85, 93, 104
    comparisons between, 15–16
    critique as component of, 30–33, 85,
        132, 256
    desire for pure forms of, 16
    developmental patterns in, 179
    equality and hierarchy in, 67
    importance of philosophy in study of,
        14–15
    as institutions, 69–70
    as interrelated, 196–97
    mystery religions, 281
    as prophetic/historical, 103–6
    relationship to nature, 69–70, 105–6,
        136, 173–75, 186, 206–7, 234,
        246–47, 255
    relationship to politics, 69–74, 170–71,
        220, 266, 303, 305

relationship to reality, 239, 252,
    309–10, 311
relationship to society, 65–67,
    292–93, 303
religion distinguished from, 20–22,
    40, 46, 48, 200, 201, 224, 225,
    272–73, 293
religious facts/primary documents con-
    cerning, 14, 20, 23, 101–3, 107–16,
    125–26, 189–90, 212–16, 272–73,
    283–84, 311–12
saints in, 135
secondary documents concerning, 14
as social, 240–41
structure in, 22
as syncretic, 16
in traditional/tribal societies, 43–44,
    70, 106–7, 112–15, 175, 239–40,
    241, 242, 244, 246–47, 249–50,
    281–83, 311
as traditions, 16, 28–37, 55, 67, 85, 132,
    135, 175, 240, 255, 256, 282
and truth, 14, 16, 117–20
types of, 103–7
worldviews in, 38–40
See also religion; religious symbolism
The Religions of India, 291
religious symbolism, 4, 23–28, 46, 104, 276
    as absolutist, 60–61
    definition of, 25
    Eliade on, 26, 28, 54, 287–88, 310–11
    in places, 48, 49–50, 53, 107, 125, 126,
        250, 284, 287
    and poetry, 81–98
    relationship to experiences, 126
    in rituals, 48, 49, 50–52, 53–54, 60, 66,
        76, 77, 107, 108–11, 112–13, 114–15,
        117, 118, 125, 126, 133, 150, 175,
        184–85, 250, 261, 284, 288, 305–6
    and secularism, 60–61, 68, 109–10
    signs compared to, 23–24, 86
    and society, 65–67, 68
    transcendent referent in, 28, 48, 86–87,
        90, 91, 235, 269
    and the unconscious, 24
    in words, 48, 53–63, 66, 72–73, 76,
        81–98, 107, 112–14, 117, 125, 126,
        134–35, 136, 175, 177, 184, 203–5,
        219–20, 250, 269–70, 272, 281,
        284, 287
    See also religion; religions

religious tolerance, 132–33, 143, 149–51, 187
Renaissance, 63, 77, 150, 156, 168
    reason during, 154–55, 228
    relationship to Middle Ages, 144–45,
        155, 171
    vernacular languages during, 157
Republic, 170
Reuchlin, Johann, 145
revelation, 12, 105–6, 151, 155, 166, 189,
    196, 198, 233, 247, 259
Revue de l'histoire des religions, 289
Ricoeur, Paul, 265
righteous anger, 65–66
righteousness. *See* justice
Ritschl, Albrecht, 233
rituals, 48, 50–52, 53–54, 60, 76, 77, 107,
    108–11, 175, 250, 261, 284
    in Brahmanism, 50–51, 108–9, 112–13
    as communal, 125, 288, 305
    the Eucharist, 49, 50, 66, 118, 133, 150
    related to burial, 46–47, 111–12, 114–15,
        117, 184–85, 305–6
    relationship to experiences, 126
Roman Catholicism, 49, 50, 113, 133, 156,
    179, 281, 286
    Jesuits, 234–36
Romantic movement, 260, 299, 305
    feeling/emotion in, 193, 194, 201
    intuitionism in, 228, 242
    music in, 194
    nature in, 194, 196
    pantheism in, 193, 195, 213, 218
    and reason, 195, 205, 216
    role of creativity in, 193
    and symbolism, 198, 201, 205
Rome, ancient, 127, 268
    gods and goddesses in, 133, 143, 184, 220
    influence of, 133, 145, 177
    religious tolerance in, 133, 143
    social classes in, 132, 145
Rorty, Richard, 301
Rosenzweig, Franz, 115–16, 264
Rosetta stone, 213–14
Rousseau, Jean-Jacques, 172, 177–78, 179,
    182, 194, 209
Rückert, Friedrich, 222, 223
Russell, Bertrand, 267

sabbath, the, 56
sacraments, 21, 50, 66, 118, 133, 150
The Sacred Books of the East, 223, 255

Sacred and Profane Beauty, 283
sacrifice, 50–52
Saint Matthew Passion, 178
saints, 135
Saint-Simon, Henri de, 243
Śakuntalā, 213
salvation, 39, 41, 44, 181–82, 187, 188, 259,
    282, 310
    in Christianity, 37, 59, 72, 92, 212
Samuel, Book of, 71–72
Sandburg, Carl, 84–85, 92
sandhabhasa/sandhyābhaṣyā, 95–96
Śankara, 9
Sanskrit, 113, 139, 212–13, 221, 223,
    249, 291
Santayana, George, 165
Sartre, Jean-Paul, 209, 265, 298, 299, 311
sat, 86
Śatapathabrāhmaṇa, 108–11
Saul, King, 72
The Savage Mind, 11
Schärer, Hans, 112–13, 114, 115
Schebesta, Fr. Paul, 282
Scheler, Max, 261, 286
Schelling, Friedrich Wilhelm Joseph, 202–5
    Philosophy of Mythology, 203–4
Schleiermacher, Friedrich, 6, 199–202, 217,
    232–33, 237, 279
    on Biblical interpretation, 201
    Der christliche Glaube, 201
    *Speeches About Religion, Addressed to the
        Educated Among Its Despisers*, 199–200
Schmidt, Fr. Wilhelm, 281–82, 289
Schopenhauer, Arthur, 261
Schubert, Franz, 194, 221
Schumann, Clara, 221
Schumann, Robert, 194, 221
Schütz, Alfred, 265
Schweitzer, Albert, 64
science, 257, 264
    empiricism in, 204
    vs. history, 261–63, 271–72, 274
    history of, 26, 265
    vs. humanities, 167, 261–63, 271–72, 274
    origin of, 130, 144, 150, 155–56, 157,
        168, 170
    relationship to philosophy, 267, 272, 310
    relationship to religion, 5, 15–16, 18,
        26–28, 38, 40, 55, 56–57, 64, 69,
        74–77, 81, 136, 155–56, 165–68, 242,
        244–45, 247, 250–51, 255–56,

260–61, 268, 269–70, 271–72, 273, 274, 281, 297–98, 309–11
See also anthropology; archaeology; astronomy; biology; mathematics; physics; sociology; technology
Second Vatican Council, 113
secularism, 38, 60–61, 68, 109–10
self-esteem, 43
Seneca, 132, 162–63
seriousness vs. solemnity, 6–7
sermons, 37–38, 145
Shakespeare, William, 157
shamanism, 289, 303
Siberian tribal peoples, 90, 106, 223
sickness, 111–12
Sierksma, Fokke, 287
Significations, 303
sin
   Barth on, 256–57
   confession of, 281
   original sin, 59
Sītā, 97
Śiva, 49, 59
skepticism, 252, 256
Smith, Adam, 229–30
Smith, Jonathan Z., 306–7
Smith, Normal Kemp, 180
Smith, Wilfred Cantwell, 293, 302
Smithsonian Institution, 290–91
Snorri Sturluson, 146–48, 149
socialism, 243, 257
   See also communism; Marxism; Marx, Karl
society, 65–67, 68
sociology, 14, 23, 27–28, 238–42, 243, 257, 265
Socrates, 52
Söderblom, Nathan, 200
solemnity vs. seriousness, 6–7
soma, 51
Song of Songs, 94, 95, 135
South America, 236, 302
   native peoples of, 106
Soviet Union, 40, 60–61, 82–84
specialization, 7–8, 264, 273, 274, 276, 287
Spencer, Herbert, 228, 244, 247
Spinoza, Baruch de, 158, 159, 170
   on God as nature, 161–63, 164, 168
   and mathematics, 161
   and reason, 161
   and religion, 161–62
Stalin, Joseph, 84

Sterne, Laurence, 175
Stevens, Wallace, 59
Stevenson, Adlai, 7
Stevin, Simon, 157
stoicism, 105, 162–63, 180
structuralism, 277, 299
The Study of Religion, 291–92
Sufism, 112, 135
Sullivan, Lawrence E., 302
Sumerian, 113–14
Sunday, Billy, 84–85, 92
Swift, Jonathan, 175
Symposium, 52
Synesius of Cyrene, 141

Taoism, 112
   Christianity compared to, 37, 69–70
   as tradition, 28
technology, 167, 168–69, 170, 229, 237, 270
   See also science
Teresa, Mother, 167
Tertullian, 139, 142
Thales, 129–30, 132, 154
theology, 229, 232–33, 246–47, 264, 273
   Descartes on, 160
   and hermaneutics, 120
   and history of religions, 100, 255–56, 283
   importance to study of religions, 14–15
   as normative discipline, 12, 14–15
   and philosophy, 12, 14, 169, 272–73
Theophan the Recluse, 41
Theorizing Myth: Narrative, Ideology, and Scholarship, 306
theory vs. data, 8–12, 101–3, 125–26
Thus Spoke Zarathustra, 254–55
Tiele, Cornelis P., 221
The Tin Drum, 36
totemism, 240, 250, 275, 299
Tower of Babel, 58
Tractatus Logico-Philosophicus, 267–68
traditional/tribal societies, 11, 203, 271, 309
   religions in, 43–44, 70, 106–7, 112–15, 175, 239–40, 241, 242, 244, 246–47, 249–50, 281–83, 311
Traité d'histoire des religions, 287
Trompf, Garry W., 90
Troy, 134, 146, 147
truth, 12, 109, 185, 208, 267, 273, 283
   and history of religions, 16, 117–20, 143, 233
   and philosophy, 117–20

truth (*cont.*)
   relationship to myths, 117, 272
   relationship to religion/religions, 14, 16,
      117–20, 143, 233
Tungus, 106
Turner, Victor, 276, 276–77
Tylor, Edward Burnett, 244–47, 249, 256,
   268, 280

uncertainty, 159
understanding, 292–93
   vs. explanation, 125, 262, 285–86
   See also hermeneutics
UNESCO, 62
United States
   Constitution of the, 71
   history of religions in, 280–81, 288–93,
      302–9
   and individualism, 241
   philosophy in, 301
   religions in, 43
   separation of church and state in, 71, 73
University of Chicago, 288, 289, 291, 292,
   302, 306, 307

vacations, 196
vaiśya, 66–67
van Baal, Jan, 277
van der Leeuw, G., 41, 212, 264, 265,
   283–88, 292
   Religion in Essence and Manifestation,
      283, 284
The Varieties of Religious Experience, 246
Vayu, 51
Vedas, 29, 77, 92, 212, 214, 223–24, 309
   Vedism/Brahmanism, 50–51, 67, 108–11,
      112–13, 127
Vico, Giambattista, 182–85, 187–88, 194,
   199, 221
Vietnam War, 74, 89, 105, 251, 304
Virgil, 147
Virgin Mary, 147–48
Viṣṇu, 49–50, 97, 250
Vivaldi, Antonio, 178

Vivekananda, 213
Voltaire, 172–77, 179, 194, 216, 236, 273
   Candide, 173
   on God, 174–76, 243, 310
   on natural religion, 173–75, 186, 255
   on organized religion, 173–74
   Philosophical Dictionary, 174
   and reason, 173, 224
Vondel, Joost van den, 94–95, 97

Wach, Joachim, 288, 292–93, 302, 303,
   308, 311
Wagner, Richard, 252, 261
*Waiting for the Dawn: Mircea Eliade in
   Perspective,* 303
Warren, Henry Clarke, 291
water, 130
The Wealth of Nations, 229–30
Weber, Max, 238, 276
Wesley, John, 236–27
Whitney, William Dwight, 291
Wisdom of Solomon 14:15–17, 142
Wittgenstein, Ludwig, 118, 266–69, 272
   Remarks on Frazer's Golden Bough, 268
   Tractatus Logico-Philosophicus, 267–68
Wolff, Christian, 173
women, 306
World War I, 229, 250, 257, 261
World War II, 250, 286–87, 303–4

Xenophanes, 131, 132, 143

Yahweh, 250, 282
yajamāna, 51
Yale University, 289, 292, 306
yoga, 139
Yugoslavia, 89

Zen Buddhism, 33–34, 86
Zeno, 105
Zeus, 137, 250
Zoroastrianism, 67–68, 104–5, 214, 231, 255
Zwaan, J. de, 297
Zwingli, Ulrich, 49, 156